Assembly Language Programming with the IBM PC AT

Assembly Language Programming with the IBM PC AT

Leo J. Scanlon

Brady Communications Company, Inc.
A Simon&Schuster Publishing Company
New York, NY 10020

Assembly Language Programming with the IBM PC AT

 For information, address Brady Communications, Inc., Simon&Schuster Building, 1230 Avenue of the Americas, New York, New York 10020.

Library of Congress Cataloging in Publication Data
Leo J. Scanlon
Assembly language programming with the IBM PC AT

Includes index.
1. IBM Personal Computer AT—Programming
2. Assembler (Computer programming Language) I. Title.
QA76.8.I2595S29 1986 005.265 85-17428
ISBN 0-89303-484-3

Printed in the United States of America

86 87 88 89 90 91 92 93 94 95 96 1 2 3 4 5 6 7 8 9 10

Contents

Preface

Why Assembly Language?

Many people write all of their computer programs in one of the so-called "high-level languages," particularly BASIC. BASIC is easy to learn, easy to use, and fast enough for most computing tasks. That being the case, why would anyone want to use any other language? One reason is that BASIC, like human languages, is not well-suited to everything. Some tasks are much easier in other languages. Imagine, for example, trying to describe fine cooking without some French words or symphonies without some Italian terms. Similarly, special computing tasks like graphics, music, or word processing are often easier in special languages.

Furthermore, BASIC is quite slow. The term "slow" may surprise the beginner, since short programs seem to run instantaneously. However, problems occur in the following situations:

1. When large amounts of data are involved. You will notice how slow BASIC is when a program must, for example, sort a long list of names and addresses or accounts. Similarly, BASIC will be quite slow when a program must search though a 50-page report or keep inventory records on thousands of items.
2. When graphics is involved. If a program is drawing a picture on the screen, it must work quickly or the delay will be intolerable. If objects in the picture are supposed to move, the program must be fast enough to make the motion look natural. This is particularly difficult when the picture contains many objects (such as space ships, base stations, and alien invaders), all of which are moving in different directions.
3. When a lot of decisions or "thinking" is required. This is often necessary in complex games like checkers or chess. The program has to try many possibilities and decide on a reasonable move. Obviously, the more possibilities there are and the more analysis required, the longer it will take the computer to move.

Why is BASIC slow? In the first place, the computer actually translates each BASIC statement into simple internal commands (so-called machine or assembly language). It does this every time it runs the BASIC program. Thus, much of the computer's time is spent translating the program, not running it.

There are versions of BASIC called *compilers* that perform the translation once and then save the translated version. However, BASIC would still be slow because of its mechanical nature. It is really like an automobile with an automatic transmission; no amount of coaxing can ever get you the performance or fuel economy that a skillful driver can achieve with a manual transmission. The human being is simply a more flexible, more skillful, and smarter operator than is the automatic transmission or the BASIC interpreter or compiler.

Assembly language is the computer equivalent of a manual transmission. It gives the programmer greater control over the computer at the cost of more work, more detail, and less convenience. Like an automatic transmission, BASIC is good enough most of the time for most programmers. But for those who must get maximum performance from their computers, assembly language is essential. You will find that most complex games, graphics programs, and large business programs are written at least partially in assembly language.

Even if assembly language *is* your likely choice, you may be wondering whether you have enough background to learn assembly language programming. You *do* if you have done some programming of *any* kind. If you know BASIC or some other high-level language, that's fine. If you have developed programs in an assembly language, that's even better. For the benefit of former high-level language users, the book has two starting points.

If you have never programmed in assembly language, start with Chapter 0, which gives you a "crash course" in the *binary* and *hexadecimal* numbering systems. Otherwise, if you already know what these terms mean and understand how to use them, proceed directly to Chapter 1.

The Contents of This Book

In Chapter 1 we introduce the 80286 microprocessor—the AT's "brain"—and discuss its role in the system.

Chapter 2 discusses assemblers in general and then describes the IBM *Macro Assembler*. All PC AT-compatible assemblers do the same job: they translate instructions *you* can understand into numeric codes the computer's microprocessor understands. Therefore, most of the principles we describe will apply to any other assembler you might have. Chapter 2 also presents a simple program, and tells you how to enter it into the computer, assemble it, and execute (run) it.

Chapter 3 describes the 80286's instruction set, the assembly language commands you use to communicate with your AT. This book treats the instructions in functional groups, rather than alphabetically. That is, we group add with subtract, multiply with divide, and so on. Through this approach you not only get to *understand* what the instructions do, but you also appreciate how they fit together.

Chapter 4 tells you how to combine instructions to perform extended math operations that the microprocessor's instruction set doesn't provide directly. Chapter 5 covers operations on lists and tables.

The PC AT has a built-in operating program called the Basic I/O System or *BIOS* that regulates the equipment in the system. That is, it does everything necessary for the microprocessor to "talk" to the keyboard, screen, disk drive, printer, and other peripherals. Hence, BIOS serves as the computer's "chief administrator." BIOS contains many useful features that can save you hours of programming time. Chapter 6 tells you how to take advantage of them.

Chapter 7 describes programs that display messages and simple graphics on the screen. Chapter 8 describes how the keyboard works and discusses ways you can use to communicate with it.

Chapter 9 discusses programs that generate sounds (and, eventually, *music!*) through the AT's built-in speaker.

Chapter 10 covers *macros*. A macro is a miniprogram that you insert in a main program simply by mentioning its name. Macros can make assembly language programs nearly as easy to develop as BASIC programs. This chapter also includes a "library" of more than 30 useful macros.

Chapter 11 describes the use of *object libraries*, disk files that contain assembled subroutines. An object library is, in effect, a collection of ready-made tools your program can choose from.

Chapter 12 describes another useful feature of the Macro Assembler: it lets you develop *structured* assembly language programs. By a "structured" program, we mean one that contains high-level statements that are similar to IF-THEN and FOR-NEXT in BASIC. Structuring can both speed up your programming effort and make your programs easier to understand.

Finally, in Chapter 13 we discuss the 80287 Math Coprocessor, an optional chip that can perform complex arithmetic operations.

The "Disk User's Guide" tells you how to use the programs that come on the optional diskette.

Study Exercises

Most chapters conclude with a set of questions and programming exercises. Some of these test your understanding of the material in the chapter;

others are meant to extend your knowledge of the material into additional, related topics.

The Appendices

The book provides five appendices for your convenience. Appendix A has tables that help convert hexadecimal numbers to decimal, or vice versa. Appendix B shows the characters and shapes you can display on the screen. Appendices C and D summarize the 80286's instruction set in alphabetical order, and show how long it takes to execute each instruction, how many bytes each instruction occupies in memory, and which status flags it affects. Appendix E summarizes interrupts (programs within the computer) that are useful for everyday programming work.

What You Need With This Book

To use this book, you need an IBM Personal Computer AT in either the base or enhanced model. You also need two software packages: an *assembler* and IBM's *Disk Operating System (DOS)*.

Supplementary Material

This book is designed to complement the Macro Assembler manual and the manuals that come with the computer, so you probably won't need any other reference books. However, every serious AT user should have a copy of the IBM PC AT *Technical Reference* manual, which is an invaluable source for technical details. Among other things, the Technical Reference contains a complete and fully-documented listing of the computer's built-in operating program, the BIOS.

You might also want to invest in a copy of IBM's *DOS Technical Reference* manual for DOS 3.0. This has detailed information on disk organization, DOS features you can call from assembly language, and other "goodies."

Finally, for the full details on the chips in the system, you may want to get a copy of the *iAPX 286 Programmer's Reference Manual*, including the *iAPX 286 Numeric Reference*. Order it from Intel Corporation, Literature Dept.; 3065 Bowers Ave.; Santa Clara, CA 95051.

Assembly language is a fascinating and efficient programming tool, and I hope you have as much satisfaction using it as I had writing this book.

Leo J. Scanlon
Inverness, FL

Limits of Liability and Disclaimer of Warranty

The author and publisher of this book have used their best efforts in preparing this book and the programs contained in it. These efforts include the development, research, and testing of the theories and programs to determine their effectiveness. The author and publisher make no warranty of any kind, expressed or implied, with regard to these programs or the documentation contained in this book. The author and publisher shall not be liable in any event for incidental or consequential damages in connection with, or arising out of, the furnishing, performance, or use of these programs.

Note to Authors

Have you written a book related to personal computers? Do you have an idea for developing such a project? If so, we would like to hear from you. Brady produces a complete range of books for the personal computer market. We invite you to write to Editorial Department, Brady Communications, Inc., General Reference Group, Simon&Schuster Building, 1230 Avenue of the Americas, New York, New York 10020.

Trademarks

- Apple II and Macintosh are registered trademarks of Apple Computer Inc.
- Intel is a trademark of Intel Corporation.
- IBM Personal Computer, Personal Editor, XT, and AT are trademarks and IBM a registered trademark of International Business Machines Corp.
- WordStar is a trademark of MicroPro International Corp.
- MS is a trademark and Microsoft a registered trademark of Microsoft Corp.
- MultiMate is a trademark of Multimate International Corp.
- Commodore 64 and VIC-20 are trademarks of Commodore Business Machines.
- TRS-80 is a trademark of Tandy Corporation.

About the Author

Leo Scanlon was raised in Pittsburgh, Pennsylvania, and received his B.S. degree in Aeronautical Engineering from St. Louis University. He also studied Electrical Engineering and Computer Science at the University of California at Berkeley.

Leo's experience includes technical writing in the minicomputer and microcomputer industries. He also served as technical publications manager with Computer Automation, Inc. in Irvine, CA and Rockwell International Corp. in Anaheim, CA.

Leo is the author of 14 microcomputer books, including *IBM PC & XT Assembly Language, 8086/88 Assembly Language Programming,* and *MultiMate on the IBM PC,* all published by Brady Communications Company.

A freelance writer in Inverness, Florida, he enjoys listening to jazz and boating with his wife, Pat, and sons Roger and Ryan.

0

Crash Course in Computer Numbering

Unless you are visiting from another planet, you have spent your entire life counting things using decimal numbers. Mathematicians call decimal the *base 10* numbering system, because it has 10 digits, 0 through 9.

Human beings are quite comfortable counting in decimal (probably because we have ten fingers and toes), but computers are not. Instead, they count with the base 2 (or *binary*) numbering system, which has only two digits, 0 and 1. Hence, to communicate with the computer at its own level (as you do when you program in assembly language), you must be familiar with binary numbering. Besides binary, assembly language programmers also use another numbering system—base 16 (or *hexadecimal*)—so you must be familiar with it as well.

This chapter is a "crash course" in computer numbering systems, for readers who have no previous exposure to them. That's why we call it Chapter *0*. If you already understand binary and hexadecimal numbering, feel free to skip this chapter and begin at Chapter 1.

0.1 Binary Numbering

A computer gets all program instructions and data from its *memory*. Memory is comprised of integrated circuits (or "chips") that contain thousands of electrical components. Like light switches, these components have only two possible settings: "On" or "Off." Still, with only these two settings, combinations of memory components can represent numbers of any size. How? Read on.

The On and Off settings of a memory component correspond to the two digits of the *binary numbering system*, the fundamental system for computers. Having only two digits, 1 (On) and 0 (Off), the binary numbering system is a *base 2* system. Again, it differs from the standard decimal numbering system, which has 10 digits (0 through 9).

The switch-like components of memory are called "bits," short for *bi*nary digi*ts*. By convention, a bit that is On has the value 1 and a bit that is Off has the value 0. This appears to be woefully limiting, until you consider that a decimal digit (no, it's not called a "det") can range only from 0 to 9. Just as you can combine decimal digits to form numbers larger than 9, you can combine binary digits to form numbers larger than 1.

As you know, to represent a decimal number larger than 9 requires an additional "tens position" digit. Likewise, to represent a decimal number larger than 99 requires a "hundreds position" digit, and so on. Each decimal digit you add has a *weight* of 10 times the digit to its immediate right.

For example, you can represent the decimal number 324 as

$$(3\times 100)+(2\times 10)+(4\times 1)$$

or as

$$(3\times 10^2)+(2\times 10^1)+(4\times 10^0)$$

Thus, each decimal digit is a power of 10 greater than the preceding digit.

A similar rule applies to the binary numbering system. Here, *each binary digit is a power of two greater than the preceding digit.* The rightmost bit has a weight of 2^0 (decimal 1), the next bit has a weight of 2^1 (decimal 2), and so on. For example, the binary number 101 has a decimal value of 5, because

$$\begin{aligned} 101_2 &= (1\times 2^2)+(0\times 2^1)+(1\times 2^0) \\ &= (1\times 4)+(0\times 2)+(1\times 1) \\ &= 5_{10} \end{aligned}$$

Do you now understand how binary numbers are constructed? To find the value of any given bit position, you double the weight of the preceding bit position. Thus, the binary weights of the first eight bits are 1, 2, 4, 8, 16, 32, 64, and 128, as shown in Figure 0-1.

7	6	5	4	3	2	1	0	BIT POSITION
2^7	2^6	2^5	2^4	2^3	2^2	2^1	2^0	POWER OF TWO
128	64	32	16	8	4	2	1	DECIMAL VALUE

Figure 0-1. Weights of eight binary digits.

To convert a decimal value to binary, you make a series of simple subtractions. Each subtraction produces the value of a single binary digit (bit).

To begin, subtract the largest possible binary weight from the decimal value and enter a 1 in that bit position. Then subtract the next largest possible binary weight from the result and enter a 1 in *that* bit position. Continue until the result is zero. Enter a 0 in any bit position whose weight cannot be subtracted from the current decimal value. For example, to convert decimal 50 to binary:

50	
−32	Bit position 5 = 1
18	
−16	Bit position 4 = 1
2	
− 2	Bit position 1 = 1
0	

Entering a 0 in the other bit positions (Bits 3, 2, and 0) yields a final result of 110010.

To verify that the binary equivalent of decimal 50 is indeed 110010, add the decimal weights of the "1" positions:

32	(Bit 5)
16	(Bit 4)
+ 2	(Bit 1)
50	

Eight Bits Make a Byte

The Apple II, Commodore 64 and VIC-20, Radio Shack TRS-80, and many other popular microcomputers are designed around *8-bit microprocessors.* Eight-bit microprocessors are so named because they process information eight bits at a time. To process more than eight bits, they must perform additional operations.

In computer terminology, an 8-bit unit of information is called a *byte*. With eight bits, a byte can represent decimal values from 0 (binary 00000000) to 255 (binary 11111111).

Because a byte is the fundamental unit of processing, microcomputers are described in terms of the number of bytes (rather than bits) their memories can hold. Microcomputer manufacturers construct memory in blocks of 1,024 bytes. This particular quantity reflects the binary orientation of computers in that it represents 2^{10} bytes.

The value 1,024 has a standard abbreviation: the letter *K*. Hence, a computer that has a "256K memory" contains 256 × 1,024 (or 262,144) bytes.

Adding Binary Numbers

You can add binary numbers the same way you add decimal numbers: by carrying any excess from one column to the next. For example, to add the decimal values 7 and 9, you must carry a 1 into the "tens" column to produce the correct result, 16. Similarly, to add the *binary* values 1 and 1, you must carry a 1 into the "twos" column to produce the correct result, 10.

Adding multi-bit numbers gets slightly more complicated, because you must include a carry from a previous column. For example, this operation involves two carries:

```
  1011
+   11
  ----
  1110
```

The addition of the rightmost column (1+1) produces a result of 0 and a carry of 1 into the second column. With the carry, the addition of the second column (1+1+1) produces a result of 1 and a carry into the third column.

The general rules for binary addition are shown in this table:

Inputs			Results	
Operand #1	**Operand #2**	**Carry**	**Sum**	**Carry**
0	0	0	0	0
0	1	0	1	0
1	0	0	1	0
1	1	0	0	1
0	0	1	1	0
0	1	1	0	1
1	0	1	0	1
1	1	1	1	1

Signed Numbers

Until now, we have been discussing how to represent *unsigned numbers* in binary. As we mentioned earlier, each bit in an unsigned number has a weight that reflects its position. The rightmost (or least-significant) bit has a weight of 1, while each more-significant bit has a weight twice that of its predecessor. Therefore, if all eight bits in a byte are 0, the byte has the value 0; if they are all 1, the byte has the value 255.

However, you often want to operate on positive or negative values; that is, on *signed numbers*. When a byte contains a signed number, only the seven least-significant bits (0 through 6) represent data; the most-significant bit (7) specifies the sign of the number. *The sign bit is 0 if the number is positive or zero and 1 if it is negative.* Figure 0-2 shows the arrangement of signed and unsigned bytes.

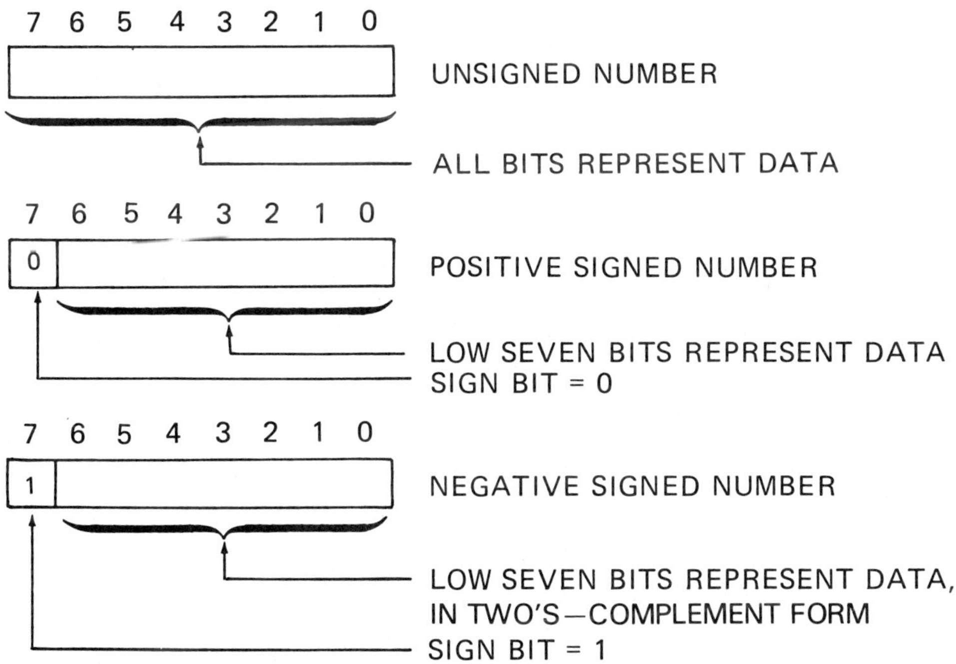

Figure 0-2. Representation of signed and unsigned numbers.

When holding a signed number, a single byte can represent positive values between 0 (binary 00000000) and +127 (binary 01111111) and negative values between -1 (binary 11111111) and -128 (binary 10000000).

Note that -1 in binary is 11111111. Wouldn't it be simpler to make it just 10000001 (that is, 1 with a minus sign bit)? No, that would produce wrong answers. Consider, for example, what happens if you add +1 and -1. The answer should, of course, be 0, but instead you get

$$\begin{array}{lcl} 00000001 & = & +1 \\ \underline{10000001} & = & -1 \\ 10000010 & = & -2 \end{array}$$

Thus, what we need is some way to represent -1 so that when you add it to +1 you get 0. That's why mathematicians came up with 11111111 for -1: it produces the right answer. To test this, let's do our addition again:

```
  00000001   = +1
  11111111   = -1
1 00000000   =  0
```

The extra 1-bit at the beginning is a *carry*, a leftover bit from the addition. We simply ignore it.

Two's-Complement

Like -1, all negative signed numbers are represented in a special form that makes additions produce the right answers. This is called the *two's-complement form.*

To find the binary representation of a negative number (that is, to find its two's-complement form), simply take the positive form of the number and reverse each bit—change each 1 to a 0 and each 0 to a 1—then add 1 to the result. The following example shows how to calculate the two's-complement binary representation of -32:

```
  00100000   +32

  11011111   Reverse every bit
+        1   Add 1
  11100000   -32, in two's-complement form
```

Of course, the two's-complement convention makes negative numbers difficult to decipher. Fortunately, you can use the same procedure we just gave to find the positive form of a (two's-complemented) negative number. For example, to find what value 11010000 has, proceed as follows:

```
  00101111   Reverse every bit
+        1   Add 1
  00110000   = 16 + 32 = +48
```

Assembler programs let you enter numbers in decimal form (signed or unsigned), and automatically do all converting. However, you may want to interpret a negative number that is stored in memory or in a register, so you should know how to make these conversions yourself.

0.2 Hexadecimal Numbering

Although the binary numbering system is an accurate way to represent numbers in memory, strings of only ones and zeros are very difficult to work with. They are also error-prone, because a number like 10110101 is extremely easy to mistype.

Years ago, programmers found that they were generally operating on *groups* of bits, rather than individual bits. The earliest microprocessors were 4-bit devices (they processed information four bits at a time), so the logical alternative to binary was a system that numbered bits in groups of four.

As you know, four bits can represent the binary values 0000 through 1111 (which are equivalent to the decimal values 0 through 15), a total of 16 possible combinations. If a numbering system is to represent those 16 combinations, it must have 16 digits. That is, it must be a *base 16* system.

If base 2 numbers are called "binary" and base 10 numbers are called "decimal," what term is appropriate for a base 16 system? Well, whoever named the base 16 system combined the Greek word "hex" (for six) with the Latin word "decem" (for ten) to form the word hexadecimal. Hence, the base 16 system is called the *hexadecimal numbering system.*

Of the 16 digits in the hexadecimal numbering system, the first ten are labeled 0 through 9 (decimal values 0 through 9) and the last six are labeled A through F (decimal values 10 through 15). Table 0-1 lists the binary and decimal values of each hexadecimal digit.

Table 0-1. Hexadecimal numbering system.

Hexadecimal Digit	Binary Value	Decimal Value	Hexadecimal Digit	Binary Value	Decimal Value
0	0000	0	8	1000	8
1	0001	1	9	1001	9
2	0010	2	A	1010	10
3	0011	3	B	1011	11
4	0100	4	C	1100	12
5	0101	5	D	1101	13
6	0110	6	E	1110	14
7	0111	7	F	1111	15

Like binary and decimal digits, each hexadecimal digit has a weight that is some multiple of its base. Since the hexadecimal numbering system is based on 16, each digit weighs 16 times more than the digit to its immediate right. That is, the rightmost digit has a weight of 16^0, the next has a weight of 16^1, and so on. For example, the hexadecimal value 3AF has a decimal value of 943, because

$$(3 \times 16^2) + (A \times 16^1) + (F \times 16^0)$$

reduces to the decimal form

$$(3 \times 256) + (10 \times 16) + (15 \times 1) = 943$$

Uses of Hexadecimal Numbers

While BASIC and other high-level languages usually display numbers in decimal form, assembly language generally displays them in hexadecimal form. This includes addresses, instruction codes, and the contents of memory locations and registers. Therefore, to get maximum benefit from your programming, try to "think hexadecimal." This is difficult at first, but it becomes easier as you gain more experience.

To help you along, Appendix A provides tables for converting decimal numbers to hexadecimal, and vice versa. And if you don't want to bother with the tables, the optional disk contains a program called HEX2DEC.EXE that converts a hexadecimal number of up to four digits to both signed and unsigned decimal form. To run it, type **hex2dec** and press Return. To leave this program, press Return in response to the prompt.

Study Exercises (answers on page 399)

1. Convert the following decimal values to binary:

   (a) 12 (b) 17 (c) 45 (d) 72

2. Convert the following unsigned binary values to decimal:

   (a) 1000 (b) 10101 (c) 11111

3. How do you represent the three binary numbers in Exercise 2 in hexadecimal?
4. List the decimal equivalent of hexadecimal D8 if:

   (a) D8 represents an unsigned number
   (b) D8 represents a signed number

1

Introduction

1.1 What is Assembly Language?

Like BASIC, assembly language is a set of words that tell the computer what to do. However, the words in the assembly language instruction set refer to computer components directly. It's like the difference between telling someone to walk to the mailbox and telling them precisely how to move their muscles and maneuver past obstacles. Obviously, a simple command is sufficient most of the time; only athletes or mountain climbers need the more detailed instructions.

Assembly language programs give the computer detailed commands, such as "load 32 into the AX register," "transfer the contents of the CL register into the DL register," and "store the number in the DL register into memory location 3,456." As you see, BASIC and assembly language differ in how you instruct the computer. *With BASIC, you speak in generalities; with assembly language, you speak in specifics.*

Although assembly language programs take more time and effort to write than BASIC programs, they also run much faster. The level of detail is the key here. The idea is the same as an athlete who runs faster or jumps farther by watching every step of what he or she does. Precise form is essential to achieving maximum performance.

Because assembly language requires you to operate on the computer's internal components, you must understand the features and capabilities of the integrated circuit (or "chip") that holds these components, the computer's microprocessor. In this book we will study the microprocessor that is inside the IBM PC AT: the *Intel 80286*. But before we delve into the details of this chip, let's take a brief look at how it came into being.

1.2 Evolution of the 80286

The earliest microprocessors were 4-bit devices. This means they transferred only four bits of information at a time. To transfer more than four bits, they performed several separate transfer operations. Of course, this also made them slow.

The Intel 8008, introduced in 1972, was the first commercial *8-bit* microprocessor (it transferred information eight bits at a time), and is still considered the foremost "first-generation" 8-bit microprocessor. Designed with a calculator-like architecture, the 8008 had an accumulator, six scratchpad registers, a stack pointer (a special address register for temporary storage), eight address registers, and special instructions to perform input and output. In 1973, Intel introduced a "second-generation" version of the 8008, named the 8080.

The 8080 is an enhanced 8008; it has more addressing and input/output (I/O) capability, more instructions, and executes instructions faster. The internal organization is better, too, although Intel maintained the overall 8008 architectural philosophy in the 8080. The 8080 is historically the de facto standard in second-generation microprocessors; the one many people still think of first when someone mentions microprocessors.

By 1976, advances in technology allowed Intel to produce an enhanced version of the 8080, called the 8085. Essentially a repackaged 8080, the 8085 added such features as power-on reset (to initialize the microprocessor), vectored interrupts (to service the needs of peripherals), a serial I/O port (to attach printers and other peripherals), and a single, +5-volt power supply (the 8080 requires two supplies).

By the time the 8085 arrived, Intel had heavy competition in the 8-bit microprocessor marketplace. Zilog Corporation's 8080 enhancement, the Z80, was catching on, as were non-8080 designs such as the Motorola 6800 and the MOS Technology (now Commodore) 6502. Rather than continue the struggle on the now-diluted 8-bit front, Intel made a quantum leap forward in 1978 by introducing the 8086, a *16-bit* microprocessor that can process data ten times faster than the 8080.

The 8086 is software-compatible with the 8080 at the assembly language level. This means that with some minimal translation, existing 8080 programs can be reassembled and executed on the 8086. To allow for this, the 8080 registers and instruction set appear as subsets of the 8086 registers and instructions. With this compatibility, Intel could capitalize on its experience with the 8080 to gain acceptance in more sophisticated applications.

In the same vein, realizing that many designers still wanted to use the cheaper 8-bit support and peripheral chips in their 16-bit systems, Intel produced a version of the 8086 with the same 16-bit internal data paths, but with an *8-bit data bus* coming out of the chip. This microprocessor, the 8088, is the one that IBM uses in the Personal Computer (PC), the PC XT, and the Portable Computer.

In 1982, Intel introduced the 80186 (and a companion, 8-bit 80188), which packs the processing power of the 8086 plus the support circuitry of 15 other chips. This "computer on a chip" contains two independent DMA (direct memory access) channels for high-speed peripherals such as disk drives, and a programmable interrupt controller. In terms of software, it provides the 8086 instruction set plus some additional instructions that are valuable to people who are designing high-level language translators or compilers.

The same year, Intel spawned the 80286, the microprocessor that controls the IBM PC AT. The 80286 (or 286 for short) is an enhanced 80186 that provides special features necessary for memory management and protection. These features are important for *multiuser* applications, in which several users share the computer (usually through a local area network, or LAN). They are also important for *multitasking* applications, in which several programs run at the same time. With this introduction in mind, let's take an overview look at the 80286.

1.3 Overview of the 80286 Microprocessor

Operating Modes

The 80286 is actually two microprocessors in one, because it can operate in two modes, called *real address* and *protected virtual address* (or protected, for short).

Real Address Mode

In the *real address mode,* the 80286 operates essentially as a high-performance 8086. Here, it supports all of the 8086 instructions (plus some of its own), but runs programs two to five times faster than an 8086. When you turn the computer's power on, the 80286 starts in the real address mode. It stays in this mode until a program explicitly switches it to protected mode.

Protected Mode

In the *protected mode*, the 80286 provides everything it does in the real address mode plus some sophisticated features for data protection and memory management. The most significant aspect of the protected mode is that it allows the 80286 to access huge amounts of memory using a technique called *virtual addressing.*

Virtual Addressing

With virtual addressing, the 80286 deals with two kinds of memory: a *physical address space* and a *virtual address space*. The physical address space is the amount of memory that the 286 can currently work with, while the virtual address space is the amount that is available to it. There is quite a difference in sizes here. The physical address space can be up to 16 million bytes (or 16 *megabytes*) long; this is 2^{24} bytes. The virtual address space can be up to one billion (2^{30}) bytes long, or one *gigabyte*.

The word "virtual" is used because if a program needs to access memory that is not in its physical address space, an operating system can use the 286's memory management capability to swap in the applicable piece of virtual memory. This memory swapping is invisible to the programmer, so he or she can write programs that freely access locations anywhere in the entire address space, right up to the one-gigabyte limit.

Virtual Disk

In DOS 3, IBM has provided an excellent use for the memory above one megabyte: you can use it as a "virtual disk" (sometimes called a RAM disk). To access that high memory, the computer momentarily switches to the protected mode, performs the data transfer, then shifts back to the normal real address mode. The overall result is that you gain a good size of storage (whatever your computer has) that is extremely fast—much faster than a hard disk can produce. For details on the virtual disk, see the description of the VDISK.SYS program in the DOS manual.

Other than the virtual disk, the protected mode is best left to designers of operating systems. Casual programmers should stay away from it. With this is mind, we will generally concentrate on the real address mode throughout this book.

Internal Registers

Internally, the 80286 holds information in a group of 16-bit boxes called *registers.* It has 14 registers in all: 12 data and address registers, plus an instruction pointer (the program-addressing register) and a status (or "flags") register. We can divide the 12 data and address registers into three groups of four registers, called *data registers, pointer and index registers,* and *segment registers.* The segment registers play a part in the way the 286 requires programs to be divided in memory. This scheme is called *segmentation.*

Segmentation

With many microprocessors, you refer to a memory location by supplying a single number, the location's address. With the 80286 (or the 8088 or 8086), however, each memory reference requires two terms: a *segment number* and an *offset*. The reason for this odd addressing scheme is that the 80286 requires program instructions and data to be in separate parts of memory. These parts or partitions of memory, called *segments,* can be up to 64K bytes long.

Kinds of Segments

The 80286 can work with four different kinds of segments at a time. Each has a unique function, as follows:

- The *code segment* contains the program instructions that the 286 is currently executing.
- The *data segment* contains variables that the program uses.
- The *stack segment* holds a special kind of data structure called a "stack" that acts as a temporary depository for data and addresses. While a subroutine is being executed, the 286 uses the stack to hold a return address—a place marker that gets the processor back to its original place in the program. You can use the stack, too, to preserve the contents of registers that a subroutine alters. We will say more about the stack later.
- The *extra segment* is like a spare data segment. It is primarily used in string operations.

Every program must have at least a code segment and a stack segment (there's an exception for stack segments, which we'll cover later). If you are operating on data, you must have a data segment and/or an extra segment, too.

Each segment has associated with it a register that holds the segment's starting address, or *segment number*. These are the code segment register, the data segment register, the stack segment register, and the extra segment register.

The segment number in a segment register provides one of the terms needed to address a memory location. The other, the *offset,* tells how far the location is from the beginning of the segment. For example, to read the contents of a variable address in the data segment, the 286 needs the address of the beginning of the segment (from the data segment register) and the position of the variable within that segment (its offset).

Addressing a memory location with this two-term approach is similar to locating an item in an encyclopedia. The index tells you the item is in Volume 5 (that's the segment), page 31 (that's the offset).

Fortunately, you generally don't have to bother with segment numbers. Once you tell the computer your segment's name, it automatically supplies the segment number. You provide only the offset (and that is usually a name, too). Hence, you end up working with names, and leave numbering up to the microprocessor.

How the 80286 Forms Addresses

Once the 80286 has obtained the segment number and offset, it combines them to form one large *20-bit address*. It does this by adding the 16-bit offset to the contents of a segment register multiplied by 16. That is:

Physical Address = Offset + (16 × Segment Register)

In reality, the 80286 doesn't actually *multiply* the segment register contents by 16, but instead uses the register as if it had four extra zero bits at the end (see Figure 1-1). Adding zeros to the end is the same as multiplying, however, because each time you displace a binary number one bit position to the left, you double its value. Thus, displacing the segment register value *four* bit positions to the left "multiplies" it by 16, since 2×2×2×2 = 16.

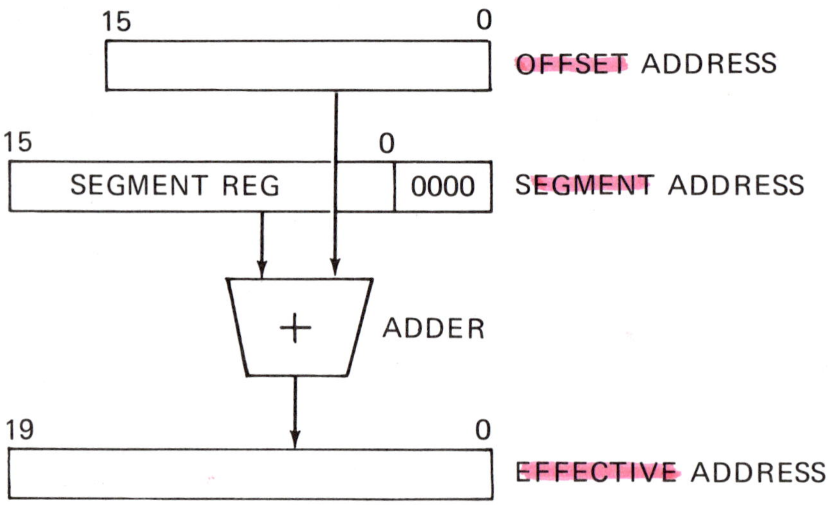

Figure 1-1. How a 20-bit address is generated.

For example, if the offset has the value 10H—where the H suffix means hexadecimal—and the segment register contains 2000H, the 80286 calculates the physical address as follows (operands are shown in binary form):

0000 0000 0001 0000	Offset
+ 0010 0000 0000 0000 0000	Segment number
0010 0000 0000 0001 0000	Physical address

Therefore, the memory location referenced here has the 20-bit address 20010H.

With a 20-bit address at its disposal, the 80286 can access any of 1,048,576 bytes. (We refer to this value as *one megabyte;* think of it as 1024K bytes, if you like.) That's 16 times the addressing range of the 8080!

Software Features

The 80286's software features are impressive by any standard, but they will be especially welcomed by programmers who struggled with the earlier 8-bit microprocessors. The 286 can perform arithmetic operations on signed or unsigned binary numbers of either eight bits or 16 bits, and on decimal numbers stored in either "packed" (two digits per byte) or "unpacked" (one digit per byte) form. It can also operate on character strings such as messages up to 64K bytes long. (Contrast this with IBM's SYSTEM/360, the large mainframe computer, which limits strings to 255 bytes. It makes you really appreciate your PC!)

The 80286 provides more than 100 basic instruction types as well as seven different addressing techniques or *modes* for accessing data. The combination of the instruction types, the addressing modes (each with a variety of operand combinations), and the various data types we just mentioned gives the 286 *thousands* of possible instructions to execute.

Measuring Speed

Like electronic watches, microprocessors are powered by quartz crystals. The crystal sends out pulses at a steady, fixed rate, which determines how fast the microprocessor operates. In the PC AT, the crystal emits six million pulses per second.

Computerists don't refer to pulses per second, however, but to *cycles per second,* or *Hertz.* Pulses per second, cycles per second, and Hertz all mean the same thing, but in this book we will use the term Hertz (abbreviated Hz). Hence, we say that the AT has a six-million Hertz or 6-MHz clock.

At 6 MHz (six million cycles per second), the AT's clock "ticks" every 167 nanoseconds, where a nanosecond (abbreviated ns) is one billionth of a second, or 10^{-9} seconds. We refer to the 167-ns value as the computer's *clock cycle*.

The fastest instructions—for example, one that copies the contents of one register into another—execute in two cycles, or 334 ns. The slowest instruction, a signed 16-bit by 16-bit division, can take up to 25 clock cycles, or about 4 microseconds. (A microsecond, abbreviated μs, is one millionth of a second, or 10^{-6} seconds, or 1000 nanoseconds.) As you can see, even this "slowest" instruction executes in the remarkable time of 0.000004 second!

Input/Output Space

Input/output (I/O) devices such as the display screen, keyboard, speaker, or modem are controlled by integrated circuits, or "chips," somewhere in the computer system. These chips may be inside the computer, on an adapter board, or within the device, depending on the peripheral. In most cases, the 80286 communicates with these chips through one or more "hardware windows" called *ports*, using special input and output instructions. (These instructions are similar to BASIC's INS and OUT.) There are 65,536 (64K) I/O ports available, but the PC AT uses only some of them. IBM has reserved others, the rest are available to developers of add-on hardware.

Memory Allocation

Most of the one-megabyte address space in the real address mode is available for system and user programs, but the 80286 uses some of the highest and lowest locations for special purposes. The highest 16 bytes of memory hold system reset instructions that the 286 executes when you switch the power on. The lowest 1024 hold the addresses of programs the 286 executes when something interrupts it. It's time to discuss interrupts.

Interrupts

The microprocessor in a computer (an IBM or any other) does not simply run programs. As the chief regulator of the system, it gets involved in one way or another with everything that happens. For instance, when you press a key at the keyboard, the microprocessor must find out which key has been pressed and do whatever is appropriate for that particular key. (For example, pressing Ctrl-Break causes something entirely different than pressing T.)

Similarly, when a disk drive is transferring data to or from the computer's memory, it is the microprocessor that is responsible for running the instructions that make that transfer happen. As I just said, the microprocessor has a role in *everything* that involves the computer.

Well, how does a microprocessor get involved with a peripheral device? Certainly, it doesn't have ESP; it can't sit there asking each peripheral whether it needs something. If the microprocessor polled peripherals all day, it wouldn't get anything else done—it would never have time to run programs. This is like having a telephone with no bell. You have to pick up the receiver every so often just to find out whether anyone is on the line!

In fact, microprocessors and peripherals communicate in a very efficient fashion. What happens is this. The microprocessor continues to run a program (say, DOS or BASIC or a word processor) until a peripheral device such as the keyboard, disk, or display screen says, "Excuse me, micro, but I need your help in getting something done. Would you please stop what you're doing long enough to do my job?" Of course, peripherals don't actually talk to the microprocessor; they send it a special "help me" signal called an *interrupt*.

How Interrupts Operate

Interrupts take different forms in different microprocessors, but in the 80286 (and 8088 and 8086), here is what happens. When a peripheral device sends an interrupt signal, it also sends an identification number called a *type code* that tells the 286 which device is requesting service. The keyboard has one type code, the floppy disk drive another, the hard disk yet another, and so forth. The 286 can recognize 256 different type codes in all.

So here is a device, type code in hand, ringing the processor's doorbell. Sometimes the processor is doing something so important that it can't stop to service the interrupt request. In that case, the 286 simply says, "Let the bell keep ringing. I'll answer when I can."

Otherwise, if the processor is doing something that can be interrupted, it makes some notes about the current job (so it knows where to resume later), then opens the door and takes the type code. It then uses this code—a number between 0 and 255—to calculate an address at the beginning of memory. From the calculated address, it reads a second address.

This new address, called an *interrupt vector*, is the address of the program that handles that particular interrupt. For standard peripheral devices in the PC AT, interrupt servicing programs are generally stored in the AT's built-in operating system chip (called its Basic Input/Output System, or *BIOS*) or loaded into memory by DOS.

Now that the processor knows which program to run, it goes off and runs it. When it finishes, it uses the notes it made earlier to get back to the original job.

Sources of Interrupts

So far we have only mentioned external interrupts, those that can be activated by peripheral devices. These account for only some of 256 possible interrupt types in the 286. The remaining interrupt types don't go unused, however. There are two other sources:

- Programs can also use interrupts of their own, by activating them with special interrupt-generating instructions. Having "canned" instruction sequences as interrupt routines in memory lets any program run the sequence by issuing a single instruction. This can make programs shorter and more versatile.
- In certain cases, the 286 can even interrupt itself! This happens, for example, if you try to divide a number by zero.

This ends our overview of interrupts. We'll discuss interrupt-generating instructions in Chapter 3 and BIOS and DOS interrupts in Chapter 6.

Data and Address Buses

The 80286 is a 68-pin integrated circuit, or "chip." Memory addresses and I/O port addresses come out of the chip on a 24-line *address bus*, while data travels in or out on a separate 16-line *data bus*.

1.4 Internal Registers

Since this book is primarily devoted to programming the 80286, the most logical place to begin is by discussing the internal registers at your disposal. Figure 1-2 shows the three groups of data and address registers, the 16-bit Instruction Pointer (IP), and the 16-bit Flags register.

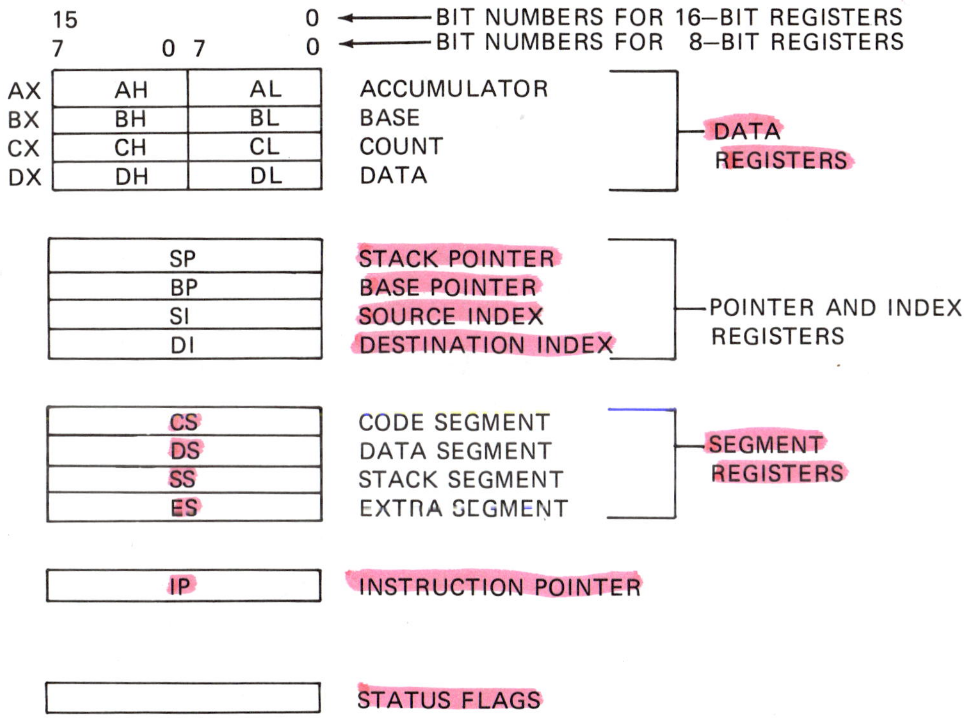

Figure 1-2. Programmable registers within the 80286.

Data Registers

You may treat the data registers as either four 16-bit registers or eight 8-bit registers, depending on whether you are operating on 16-bit words or 8-bit bytes. The 16-bit registers are named AX, BX, CX, and DX. Within these "X" registers are 8-bit registers named AH, AL, BH, BL, CH, CL, DH, and DL; here, L and H identify the high-order and low-order bytes of the 16-bit registers. For example, AH and AL form the high and low bytes of AX. All data registers are available for general programming use, but certain instructions also use them implicitly. Specifically:

- *AX, the Accumulator*, is used in word-size multiplication, division, and I/O operations, and in some string operations. The *AL register* is used in the byte-size counterparts of these same operations, and in translate and decimal arithmetic operations. The *AH register* is also used in byte-size multiplications and divisions.
- *BX, the Base register*, is often used to address data in memory.

- *CX, the Count register*, acts as a repetition counter for loop operations and as an element counter for string operations. The *CL register* holds the shift count for multiple-bit shift and rotate operations.
- *DX, the Data register*, is used in word-size multiplication and division operations. It can also provide the port number in I/O operations.

Former 8080 or 8085 programmers will note that AH is the only data register unique to the 80286; the others are relabeled 8080/8085 registers. In the 8080, AL is called A, while BX, CX, and DX are called HL, BC, and DE, respectively.

The data registers are the only ones you may reference as either 8- or 16-bit. The registers in the remaining groups are exclusively 16-bit registers.

Segment Registers

As we mentioned in Section 1.3, the segment registers hold the starting addresses of the 80286's four segments. Specifically:

- The *code segment (CS) register* points to the segment that holds the program currently being executed. The 286 combines the contents of CS (multiplied by 16) with the contents of the instruction pointer (IP) to calculate the memory address of its next instruction.
- The *stack segment (SS) register* points to the current stack segment.
- The *data segment (DS) register* points to the current data segment, which usually holds variables.
- The *extra segment (ES) register* points to the current "extra" segment, which is used in string operations.

Pointer and Index Registers

Remember that the 80286 calculates the address of an instruction by combining a segment number in CS with an offset in IP. It accesses data in other segments similarly; by combining a segment number in a segment register with an offset in another register. To access the data segment, it gets the segment number from DS and the offset from BX or an *index register (SI or DI)*. To access the stack segment, it gets the segment number from SS and the offset a *pointer register (SP or BP)*. It can also access the extra segment by using a segment number from ES (more about this in Chapter 2).

Internal Units

Many microprocessors execute a program by reading an instruction from memory, decoding it, executing it, then reading the next instruction, and so on. This plodding, one-at-a-time approach naturally slows the processor down, because it must wait until each new instruction has been read and decoded before executing it. The 80286 eliminates much of this delay by assigning these three tasks—reading, decoding, and executing instructions—to separate, special-purpose units within the chip. Intel calls them the Bus Unit, Instruction Unit, Execution Unit, and Address Unit.

Bus Unit (BU)

The Bus Unit (BU) is the 286's mail carrier; its job is to read instructions from memory and pass data between the processor and the "outside world." The BU puts each new instruction in a "code queue," where it is available for access by the chip's Instruction Unit.

Instruction Unit (IU)

The Instruction Unit (IU) grabs instructions from the BU's code queue, decodes them, and places the code in its "instruction queue," or *pipeline*—the electronic equivalent of a vending machine. The pipeline can hold up to three decoded instructions.

Execution Unit (EU)

The Execution Unit (EU) executes instructions under control of its built-in "microcode" ROM (read-only memory). When it nears completion of the current instruction, the ROM signals the EU to take the next one out of the instruction queue.

Note the independent nature of this system. The BU and IU do their jobs while the EU is executing a previously-fetched instruction. Thus, when the EU needs another program instruction, it usually finds the instruction in the pipeline. Figure 1-3 shows the interaction between the Bus, Instruction, and Execution Units.

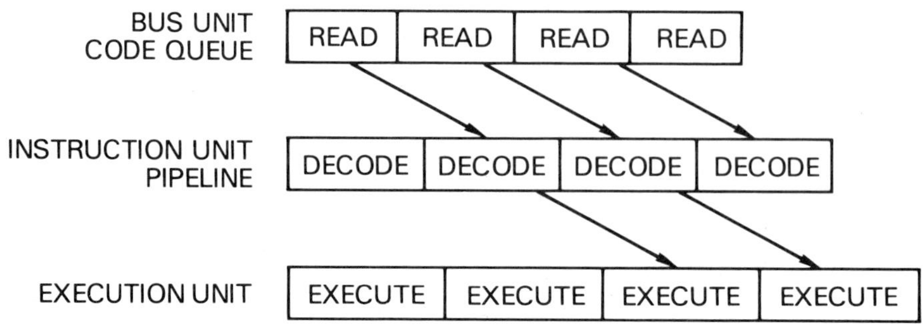

Figure 1-3. Parallel operations in the 80286.

Address Unit (AU)

The Address Unit (AU) performs memory management and protection functions by translating virtual addresses to physical addresses and checking protection rights, all simultaneously.

Instruction Pointer (IP)

Since the BU cannot know the sequence in which the program executes, it always fetches instructions from consecutive memory locations. Therefore, the only time the EU must wait for an instruction to be read from memory is when program execution transfers to a new, non-sequential address. When that happens, the EU must wait for the BU to clear its code queue and fetch the next instruction. Then, and only then, the 80286 waits like many other microprocessors wait for *every* instruction to be read.

Because the 80286 works in this rather unique way, the people at Intel chose to differentiate their "next execution address" register from other manufacturers' "next fetch address" register by calling it an *instruction pointer (IP)* instead of a program counter (PC). The IP always contains the offset of the instruction the 286's EU will execute next. Because the IP has this one dedicated purpose, you cannot perform arithmetic on its contents. However, the 286 has instructions that explicitly change the IP and others that transfer its contents to and from the stack.

Flags

You will often want your program to make a "decision" based on the result of the instruction the 286 just executed. For example, you may want to do one thing if an addition yields zero (perhaps print "Balance is zero!" in an accounting program) and something entirely different otherwise.

The 16-bit *Flags register* reports various status conditions that help your programs make decisions. Six bits hold statuses, three let you control the 80286 from within a program, and two others pertain to the protected mode. Figure 1-4 shows how these 11 "flags" are arranged. (The shaded bit positions are unused. If you ever read the status of the Flags register, these bits will be 0.)

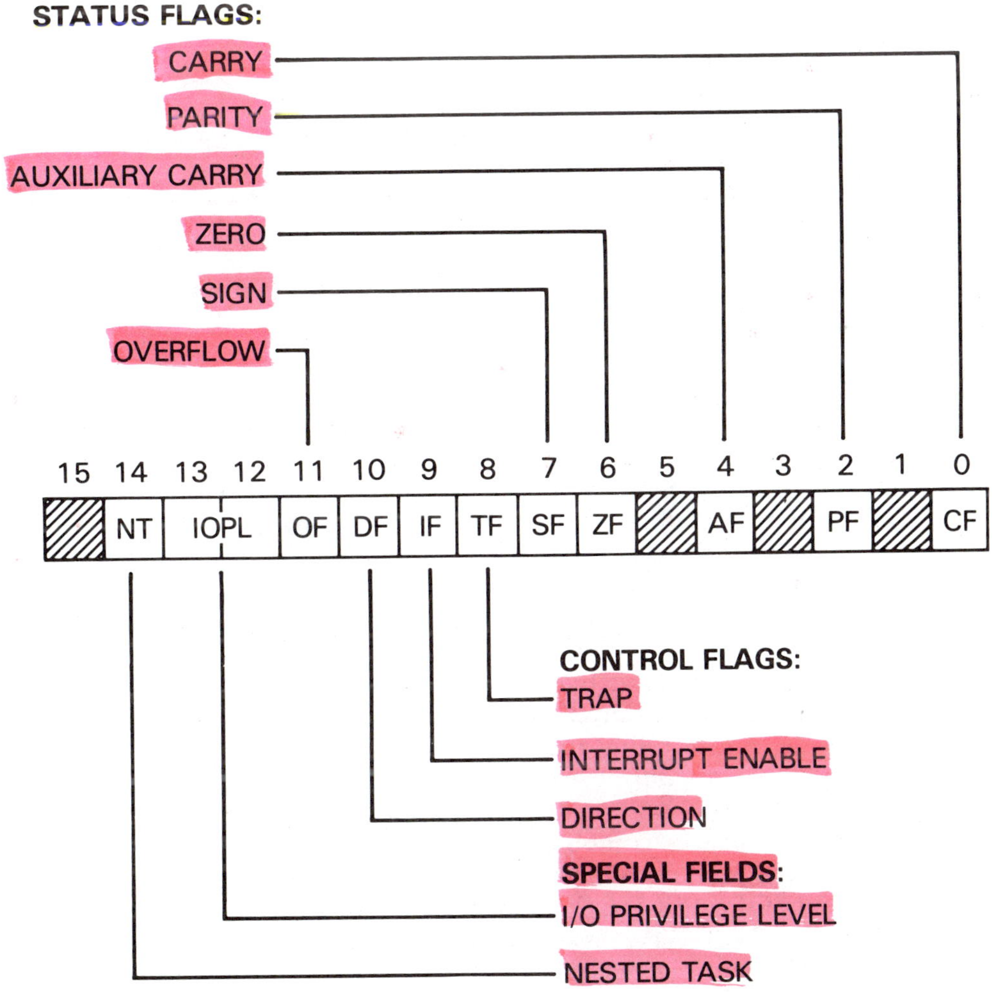

Figure 1-4. Flags register.

Here are details on the flags:

1. *Bit 0, the Carry Flag (CF)*, is 1 if an addition produces a carry or a subtraction produces a borrow; otherwise, it is 0. CF also holds the value of a bit that has been shifted or rotated out of a register or memory location, and reflects the result of a compare operation. Finally, CF also acts as a result indicator for multiplications. See the description of bit 11 (OF) for details.
2. *Bit 2, the Parity Flag (PF)*, is 1 if the result of an operation has an even number of 1 bits; otherwise, it is 0. PF is used primarily in data communications.
3. *Bit 4, the Auxiliary Carry Flag (AF)*, is similar to the CF bit, except AF reflects the presence of a carry or borrow out of bit 3. CF is useful for operating on "packed" decimal numbers.
4. *Bit 6, the Zero Flag (ZF)*, is 1 if the result of an operation is zero; a nonzero result clears ZF to 0.
5. *Bit 7, the Sign Flag (SF)*, is meaningful only during operations on signed numbers. SF is 1 if an arithmetic, logical, shift, or rotate operation produces a negative result; otherwise, it is 0. In other words, SF reflects the most-significant (sign) bit of the result, regardless of whether the result is 8 or 16 bits long.
6. *Bit 8, the Trap Flag (TF)*, makes the 80286 "single-step" through a program for debugging purposes.
7. *Bit 9, the Interrupt Enable Flag (IF)*, allows the 80286 to recognize interrupt requests from external devices in the system. Clearing IF to 0 makes the 286 ignore interrupt requests (until IF becomes 1).
8. *Bit 10, the Direction Flag (DF)*, makes the 80286 decrement (DF=1) or increment (DF=0) the index register(s) after executing a string instruction. If DF is 0, the 286 progresses forward through a string (toward higher addresses, or "left to right"). If DF is 1, it progresses backward (toward lower addresses, or "right to left").
9. *Bit 11, the Overflow Flag (OF)*, is primarily an error indicator during operations on signed numbers.

   OF is 1 if adding two like-signed numbers or subtracting two opposite-signed numbers produces a result that the operand can't hold; otherwise, it is 0. OF is also 1 if the most-significant (sign) bit of the operand changed during an arithmetic shift operation; otherwise, it is 0.

   The OF flag, in combination with the CF flag, also indicates the length of a multiplication result. If the upper half of the product is non-zero, OF and CF are 1; otherwise, both flags are 0.

   Finally, OF is 1 if a divide operation produces a quotient that overflows the result register.
10. *Bits 12 through 14* are used when the 286 is operating in the protected mode.

Don't make the mistake of assuming that the flags are in one state or another at any given time. The 286 has instructions that let you set or reset flags. When in doubt, *use* them!

The 80286 has conditional transfer instructions that test the state of the status flags, and cause program execution to continue in-line or at some other location in memory, depending on the outcome of the test.

Study Exercises (answers on page 399)

1. Why is the 80286 called a *16-bit* microprocessor?
2. How many bytes of memory can the 80286 address when it is operating in the real address mode?
3. What physical address does the 80286 generate when you combine an offset value of 2H with a segment register containing 4000H?
4. What is a nanosecond? A microsecond?
5. Suppose an instruction takes 10 clock cycles to execute on the PC AT. How long is that in real time?
6. If the AX register contains 1A2BH, what does AL contain?
7. What are the four segments an 80286 program can use? How long can each segment be? Which register is normally used to address each of these segments?
8. Which segment register normally accesses variables in your programs?
9. Which bit in the Flags register tells whether a preceding subtract operation produced a negative result?

2

Using an Assembler

2.1 Introduction

Assembly language provides the best of two worlds. That is, it lets you write programs at the level the microprocessor understands, but it doesn't force you to memorize a set of numeric codes. Instead, you write instructions as English-like abbreviations, then run an *assembler* program to convert them to their numeric equivalents.

The program written using abbreviations is called the *source program* and the numeric, microprocessor-compatible form of it is the *object program*. Thus, the assembler's job is to convert source programs you can understand into object programs the microprocessor can understand.

Macro Assembler Packages

Rather than trying to describe every assembler on the market, we will concentrate on the most popular package: IBM's *Macro Assembler.* The features this package provides should be similar to those of any other assembler you might own. In particular, the IBM Macro Assembler is nearly identical to the Microsoft Macro Assembler, because Microsoft developed this product for IBM. Hence, most of what we say in this book will apply to the Microsoft Macro Assembler as well as the one from IBM.

To date, IBM has produced two versions of the Macro Assembler, 1 and 2. For the PC AT, you need Version 2, which accepts instructions for an Intel 80286, the microprocessor the AT uses. (For the Microsoft Macro Assembler, you need Version 3.)

The IBM Macro Assembler disk holds two separate assembler programs, called the *Small Assembler (ASM)* and the *Macro Assembler (MASM).* The Small Assembler is intended for use with PCs that have less than 128K bytes of memory, and provides only a subset of the Macro Assembler's features.

In fact, it doesn't even accept instructions that are unique to the 80286. Therefore, we describe only the Macro Assembler here and disregard the Small Assembler. (The Microsoft Macro Assembler does not include the Small Assembler.)

The Macro Assembler manual provides complete details, so we will not attempt to describe everything. Instead, we cover only the features you will probably use most often, and provide some tables for quick reference.

2.2 Developing an Assembly Language Program

Although assembly language programs look quite different from BASIC programs, you follow the same procedures to develop them. However, in assembly language the *mechanics* are more involved. There are six steps in developing an assembly language program:

1. Define the task and design the program. This often requires drawing a *flowchart,* a "blueprint" of how the program operates.
2. Type the program instructions into the computer using an *editor,* then save the program on disk.
3. Assemble the program using an *assembler.* If the assembler finds errors, correct them with the editor and reassemble the program.
4. Convert the assembler output to an executable "run module" using the *linker.*
5. Execute (run) the program.
6. Check the results. If they differ from what you expected, you must find the errors or "bugs"; that is, you must "debug" the program.

If your program is short and simple, you can perform these steps quickly. However, longer and more complex programs require more time on each step; especially defining the program itself. We suggest an efficient approach for developing programs in the "Top-Down Program Design" subsection at the end of this section.

Editor

Step 2 above refers to an *editor.* This is a program that lets you enter and prepare your program. You can use any popular word processor or editor program that can produce pure "ASCII" text—regular characters without any special control codes or formatting codes. These include *WordStar, Microsoft Word, MultiMate,* and IBM's *Personal Editor.*

If you don't have one of these programs, you can use the *EDLIN* program that comes on the DOS disk. EDLIN is a line editor; that is, its commands operate on numbered lines in your program. You will learn how to use it in Section 2.7.

Assembler

The computer cannot directly execute the program you prepare using an editor. An assembler must convert it into an *object program* the computer can understand.

Linker (LINK)

IBM DOS can store a program at any convenient place in memory; this frees you from having to tell it where to put the program. However, to use this feature you must convert the assembled program to a form that can be moved around (the computer term is *relocatable*). This involves using a program called LINK, which is on the DOS Supplemental Programs disk.

The IBM manuals refer to a disk file that contains an assembled program as an *object module*. Similarly, they refer to a file that contains a relocatable version of the assembled program as a *run module*. Hence, LINK's job is to create a run module from an object module.

Another Job For the Linker

You can also build programs one section at a time, like you would build a model airplane. To do this, you enter one section of the program and assemble it. If the assembler reports errors, you correct them and assemble again. Once this first module assembles without errors, you repeat the process for the second module, then for the third (if any), and so on. Thus, you eventually wind up with several object modules that, in combination, do whatever you designed the program to do.

You can probably guess what the Linker's second job is. It links assembled object modules to form a single run module.

You must run the Linker for every program you write, even those that have only one object module. For programs with one module, the Linker simply makes the module relocatable. For programs with two or more modules, it combines them and makes the *result* relocatable.

A Debugging Program (DEBUG)

You can run your completed program in two ways:

1. You can simply enter its name from DOS.
2. You can run it under control of the DEBUG program.

Generally, you only run a program from DOS when you are sure it has no mistakes. Until then, you run it under DEBUG.

The DEBUG program (on the DOS Supplemental Programs disk) lets you control your program as it runs. Among other things, DEBUG lets you change and display values, stop your program at a particular point, or run it one instruction at a time. DEBUG thus provides tools that help you to identify and correct errors in programs.

Top-Down Program Design

When creating a program on a computer, one's natural inclination is to charge into it just as you would with pencil and paper: to enter the first instruction, then the second, third, and so on, to the end. This "brute force" approach may work for programs that are short or simple, but more often it leads to errors and produces programs that are difficult to understand (and even more difficult to update later). Thanks to the editing capabilities of word processor and editor programs, there is an easier, more reliable, and more efficient way to develop programs. It is called *top-down design*.

Top-down design simply means starting with a plain English outline of the program, then filling in the details gradually. The outline should be a series of lines that tell what steps you want the program to perform. For example, if you want to develop a program that performs one of several tasks based on a choice the user makes from a menu, your outline might look like this:

```
; Display a menu of selections.
; Ask the user to choose.
; Read user's selection.
; Check for an illegal entry.
; If entry is legal, do what the user has asked.
```

The semicolons here indicate that these lines represent comments rather than instructions. They do the same thing as REMs in BASIC.

From here you can use the editor to insert instructions between the comment lines. Because each line defines a simple task, you can complete them individually and test each one before proceeding to the next one. That is, begin by inserting the first group of instructions (the ones that display a menu, in our example), then save the program on disk and perform the rest of the program steps (assemble, link, and execute). Executing this partially-completed program tells you whether it is working correctly so far. If it isn't, debug it and try again. When the first part is working correctly, proceed to the second part, then the third, and so on.

This may seem like a slow way to develop a program, but it has several advantages:

1. It forces you to plan an orderly approach to the program.
2. The comment lines provide a certain amount of top-level documentation to the finished product.
3. It ensures that each step is working correctly before you proceed.

2.3 Source Statements

Now that we have discussed the mechanics of developing programs, we can look at what goes into them. The source program you enter into the computer is a sequence of *statements* designed to perform a specific task. A source statement (a line in the program) can be either an assembly language instruction or a pseudo-operation.

Assembly language instructions are shorthand notations for the 80286 microprocessor's instruction set. Some manuals refer to them as "machine instructions," because they tell the "machine" (the 80286) what to do. By contrast, *pseudo operations*—or "pseudo-ops" for short—tell the *assembler* what to do (with the instructions and data you enter).

Source statements of either kind can also include *operators*, which give the assembler information about an operand, where ambiguities exist. We discuss assembly language instructions, pseudo-ops, and operators in the sections that follow.

Constants in Source Statements

The assembler lets you enter constants in several forms. The most common are:

1. *Binary*—A sequence of 1's and 0's followed by the letter B; for example, 10111010B.
2. *Decimal*—A sequence of the digits 0 through 9, with or without the letter D; for example, 129D or 129.
3. *Hexadecimal*—A sequence of the digits 0 through 9 and the letters A through F, followed by the letter H. The first character must be one of

the digits 0 through 9; for example, 0E23H. (Here, the 0 prefix tells the 80286 that E23H is a number, rather than a symbol or a variable name.)

4. *Character*—A string of letters, numbers, or symbols enclosed in single or double quotes. IBM provides both forms so you can put quotation marks inside message strings, as in "Don't enter a number here!" or "Your reply to the 'Please try again' prompt is illegal."

Negative Numbers

You can also specify negative numbers. If the number is a decimal value, you simply precede it with a minus sign (e.g., -32). If it is a binary or hexadecimal value, you must enter its "two's-complement" form. For example, 11100000B and 0E0H are two's-complement forms of decimal -32.

2.4 Assembly Language Instructions

Each assembly language instruction in a source program can have up to four *fields*, as follows:

```
[Label:]  Mnemonic  [Operand]  [;Comment]
```

Of these, only the mnemonic field is always required. The label and comment fields are always optional. The operand field applies only to instructions that require an operand; otherwise, you must omit it. (We show the label, operand, and comment fields in brackets here to identify them as optional; *don't* type the brackets into your programs.)

You may enter these fields anywhere on a line, but you must separate them with at least one space (or Tab). An assembly language instruction that uses all four fields is:

```
GETCOUNT:  MOV  CX,DI  ;Initialize count
```

Label Field

The label field assigns a *name* to an assembly language instruction. This lets other instructions in the program refer to the instruction. Thus, labels in assembly language programs serve the same purpose as line numbers in BASIC programs.

An instruction label can be up to 31 characters long and must end with a colon (:). It may consist of:

- The letters *A* through *Z* (or *a* through *z*, the assembler doesn't distinguish between lowercase and uppercase)
- The numeric digits *0* through *9*
- These special characters: ? . @ _ $

You can begin a label with any character except a digit, but if you use a period (.), it must be the first character. The symbols AH, AL, AX, BH, BL, BX, BP, CH, CL, CX, CS, DH, DL, DX, DI, DS, ES, SI, SP, and ST are register names; you can't use them as labels.

You can't put a space in a label, but you can get the same effect by using an underscore character (_). For example, you can write the previous sample statement as

```
GET_COUNT:  MOV  CX,DI  ;Initialize count
```

Clearly, GET_COUNT is more readable than GETCOUNT.

Selecting Label Names

Because the assembler lets you enter various combinations of letters, digits, and symbols, almost any label you can think of is acceptable. However, we recommend the following guidelines for selecting labels:

- Make the name as short as possible, while still being reasonable. Thus, MPH is preferable to MILES_PER_HOUR and CUR_YR is a reasonable abbreviation for CURRENT_YEAR.
- Make the name easy to type without errors. The usual typing problems are several identical letters in a row (such as HHHH) and similar-looking characters (such as the letter O and the number 0, letter I and number 1, and letter S and number 5). There is no reason to invite typing errors; most of us make enough of them anyway.
- Don't use labels that can be confused with each other. For example, avoid using things like XXXX and XXYX. There's no sense in tempting fate and Murphy's Law.

Mnemonic Field

The mnemonic field (the leading "m" in mnemonic is silent) contains the two- to seven-letter acronym for the instruction. For example, MOV is the acronym for a move instruction and ADD is the acronym for an add instruction. The assembler uses an internal table to translate each instruction mnemonic into its numeric equivalent.

In addition to the mnemonic, many instructions require you to specify either one or two operands. (For example, an add instruction must know which two terms it is to add.) The mnemonic tells the assembler how many operands, and which types, to obtain from the operand field.

Operand Field

The operand field tells the 80286 where to find the data it is to operate on. It is mandatory with some instructions and prohibited with others. If present, the operand field contains either one or two operands, separated from the mnemonic by at least one space or Tab. If two operands are required, you must put a comma between them.

In two-operand instructions, the first is the *destination operand* and the second is the *source operand*. The source operand specifies the value that the microprocessor should add to, subtract from, compare to, or store into the destination operand. For example, in this *Move* instruction:

```
MOV   CX,DX
```

CX,DX tells it to copy the contents of the source operand in the DX register into the destination operand in the CX register.

As you might have guessed, the source operand is never altered by the operation, while the destination operand is nearly always altered. In Chapter 3 we discuss the addressing characteristics for each instruction in the 80286's instruction set.

Comment Field

Like a REM in BASIC, this optional field lets you describe statements in the source program, to make the program easier to understand. You must precede a comment with a semicolon (;). It is also a good idea to separate it from the preceding field by at least one space or Tab, but you don't have to. The assembler ignores comments, but prints them when you list the program.

Put anything you want in a comment field, but to be useful, make comments describe what is happening in the program, not just restate the instruction. For example,

```
MOV   CX,0     ;Clear the count register
```

is more meaningful than

```
MOV   CX,0     ;Move 0 into CX
```

Stand-Alone Comments

You may also put a comment on a line by itself, to describe an entire block of instructions. To do this, enter a semicolon at the beginning of the line; the assembler recognizes it as the start of a comment line, and ignores whatever follows it.

2.5 Pseudo Operations

Pseudo operations, or *pseudo-ops*, are commands to the assembler, rather than to the microprocessor. Pseudo-ops can be used to set up segments and procedures (i.e., subroutines), define symbols, reserve memory for temporary storage, and perform a variety of other important "housekeeping" tasks. Unlike assembly language instructions, however, most pseudo-ops generate no object code.

Pseudo-op statements can have up to four fields:

```
[Name]  Pseudo-op  [Operand]  [;Comment]
```

As the brackets indicate, only the pseudo-op field is always required. A name is mandatory with some pseudo-ops, prohibited with others, and optional with the rest. The same applies to an operand. The comment field is always optional. As with assembly language instructions, you can put pseudo-op fields anywhere on a line, but you must separate them with at least one space or Tab.

The Macro Assembler provides about 60 different pseudo-ops. In this section we discuss the most common ones; we cover some advanced pseudo-ops in Section 2.10 and macro pseudo-ops in Chapter 10. Table 2-1 divides the common pseudo-ops into three groups: data, listing, and mode.

Table 2-1. Common pseudo-ops.

Type	Pseudo-Ops		
Data	ASSUME COMMENT DB DW DD END	ENDP ENDS EQU = (equal sign) EVEN EXTRN	INCLUDE ORG PROC PUBLIC SEGMENT
Listing	PAGE	SUBTTL	TITLE
Mode	.286C	.8086	

Note: Don't try to memorize the material in this section. Just read it casually, then come back to it later when you want to look up some detail.

Data Pseudo-Ops

We can divide the assembler's data pseudo-ops into five functional groups, as shown in Table 2-2.

Table 2-2. Data pseudo-ops.

Pseudo-Op	Function
Symbol Definition	
EQU	Format: `name EQU text` or `name EQU numeric-expression` Assigns *text* or value of *numeric-expression* to *name*, permanently.
=	Format: `name = numeric-expression` Assigns value of *numeric-expression* to *name*, but can be reassigned.
Data Definition	
DB	Format: `[name] DB expression[,...]` Defines a variable or initializes storage. DB allocates one or more bytes.
DW	Format: `[name] DW expression[,...]` Similar to DB, but allocates two-byte words.
DD	Format: `[name] DD expression[,...]` Allocates four-byte doublewords.
External Reference	
PUBLIC	Format: `PUBLIC symbol[,...]` Makes the defined *symbol*(s) available for use by other assembly modules that will be linked to this module.
EXTRN	Format: `EXTRN name:type[,...]` Specifies symbols defined in another assembly module.
INCLUDE	Format: `INCLUDE filespec` Merges the contents of the specified source file into the current source file.

Table 2-2. Data pseudo-ops (continued).

Pseudo-Op	Function
Segment/Procedure Specification	
SEGMENT	Format: `seg-name SEGMENT [align-type] [combine-type] ['class'] .. .. seg-name ENDS` Defines the boundaries of a segment. Each SEGMENT definition must end with an ENDS statement.
ASSUME	Format: `ASSUME seg-reg:seg-name[,...]` or `ASSUME seg-reg:NOTHING[,...]` Tells the assembler which segment register (CS, DS, ES, or SS) a segment belongs to. *ASSUME NOTHING* cancels any previous ASSUME for the specified register.
PROC	Format: `name PROC [NEAR]` or `name PROC FAR .. .. RET name ENDP` Assigns a *name* to a sequence of assembler statements. Every PROC definition must end with an ENDP statement.
Assembly Control	
END	Format: `END [entry-point label]` Marks the end of the source program.
EVEN	Format: `EVEN` Forces location counter to an even boundary.
ORG	Format: `ORG expression` Sets location counter to the value of *expression*. Assembler stores subsequent object code starting at that address.

Symbol Definition Pseudo-Ops

The symbol definition pseudo-ops assign a symbolic *name* to an *expression*. This may be a 16-bit constant, an address reference, another symbolic name, a segment identifier (prefix) and operand, or an instruction label. After assigning the name, you can use it anywhere you would normally use the expression.

The EQU (equate) and = (equal sign) pseudo-ops are similar, but:

1. You can redefine symbols defined with =, while symbols defined with EQU are permanent.
2. EQU can be used for either text or a numeric expression, while = can be used only for numeric expressions.

EQU is handy for assigning simple names to numbers, complex addressing combinations, and other things you don't want to enter over and over in your programs. Some examples are:

```
K       EQU   1024          ;Name a constant
TABLE   EQU   DS:[BP][SI]   ;Name an addressing combination
SPEED   EQU   RATE          ;Give an alternate name
COUNT   EQU   CX            ;Give a register a name
```

Being an expression, the operand can also include some simple math, where you let the assembler make the calculation. For example:

```
DBL_SPEED      EQU  2*SPEED
MINS_PER_DAY   EQU  60*24
```

Some examples of the = pseudo-op are:

```
CONST =  56        ;This is the same as CONST EQU 56, but
CONST =  57        ; now CONST may be redefined, or
CONST =  CONST+1   ; may refer to its previous definition
```

Data Definition Pseudo-Ops

Many programs use locations in memory to hold *variables*—named data items that can be changed as needed. The pseudo-ops we use to allocate space for variables are *DB* (Define Byte), *DW* (Define Word), and *DD* (Define Doubleword).

These differ in the amount of memory they allocate. DB allocates 8-bit bytes, DW allocates 2-byte words, and DD allocates 4-byte doublewords. When defining a variable, you can either give it a specific initial value or simply *reserve* the space and insert the value later.

The data definition pseudo-ops have the general formats

```
[name]  DB  expression[,...]
[name]  DW  expression[,...]
[name]  DD  expression[,...]
```

where [,...] means that you have the option of specifying several *expressions*.

An expression can take any of several forms, depending on how you want to define the variable. For example, it may be a *constant*. The following statements show the allowable maximum and minimum decimal values for byte- and word-size variables:

```
BU_MAX   DB   255      (maximum byte constant, unsigned)
BS_MAX   DB   127      (maximum byte constant, signed)
BS_MIN   DB   -128     (minimum byte constant, signed)
WU_MAX   DW   65535    (maximum word constant, unsigned)
WS_MAX   DW   32767    (maximum word constant, signed)
WS_MIN   DW   -32768   (minimum word constant, signed)
```

You can also use pseudo-ops to set up data tables in memory. To do this, simply list the table elements separated by commas. The following sequence sets up two 12-element tables, one made up of bytes and the other of words:

```
B_TABLE   DB   0,0,0,0,8,-13                (byte table)
          DB   -100,0,55,63,63,63
W_TABLE   DW   1025,567,-30222,0,90,-129   (word table)
          DW   17,645,26534,367,78,-17
```

Here we have arranged the elements as two lines of six values, but you may assign *any* number of values with one pseudo-op as long as you don't put more than 132 characters on a line.

Note that the first four elements and the last three elements of B_TABLE have the same value (0 and 63, respectively). The assembler has a *DUP* (duplicate) operator that allows you to repeat operands without entering them individually. Using DUP, we can set up B_TABLE with the shorter statement

```
B_TABLE   DB   4 DUP(0),8,-13,-100,0,55,3 DUP(63)
```

To define a variable without giving it an initial value, put a question mark (?) in the expression field. For example, the following statements reserve space for a byte and a word in memory, but don't store anything into them:

```
HIGH_TEMP    DB   ?
AVG_WEIGHT   DW   ?
```

Note that ? simply *reserves* space for HIGH_TEMP and AVG_WEIGHT; it does not initialize them in any way! Don't make the mistake of assuming they contain 0 or any other specific value.

You may also reserve space for an entire table. For example,

```
MONTHLY_SALES   DW   12 DUP(?)
```

reserves 12 words in memory. This does about the same thing as *DIM MONTHLY_SALES%(12)* in BASIC.

The DB (Define Byte) pseudo-op can also accept a *character string* as an expression. This lets you store error messages, table titles, and other text in memory. In this case, you must enclose the string in single or double quotes. Two examples are:

```
POLITE_MSG  DB   'The number you have entered is too large'
            DB   ' to be properly processed.  Please'
            DB   ' re-enter your data.'
RUDE_MSG    DB   'Try again, dummy!'
```

Variables are also useful for holding *memory addresses* that can be referenced by instructions in your program. As you know, each address has two components: a segment number and an offset. If a label lies in the same segment as the instruction that refers to it, you can specify only its offset. Since an offset is 16 bits long, we can use DW to hold it. For example,

```
HERE_NEAR  DW   HERE
```

assigns the 16-bit offset of the label HERE to the name HERE_NEAR. We refer to a variable that holds an offset as a *pointer*.

If a label lies in a different segment than the instruction that refers to it, the 80286 must know the label's segment number as well as its offset. You can provide both components with a DD (Define Doubleword) pseudo-op. For example,

```
LABEL_VECTOR  DD   FAR_LABEL
```

assigns the 16-bit offset and the 16-bit segment number of the label FAR_HERE to the 32-bit variable LABEL_VECTOR. A variable that holds both address terms is called a *vector*.

Segment/Procedure Specification Pseudo-Ops

The SEGMENT and ENDS pseudo-ops divide the source program into segments. As we mentioned earlier, a program may have up to four kinds of segments: data, code, extra, and stack. As Table 2-2 shows, SEGMENT can take three operands: *align-type*, *combine-type*, and *class*.

The *align-type* specifies at what kind of boundary the segment is to start when it is stored in memory. You can make it begin anywhere (BYTE), at an even-numbered address (WORD), or at an address that is divisible by either 16 (PARA) or 256 (PAGE).

The *combine-type* specifies how a segment is to be combined with others of the same name. Code, data, and extra segments may be joined (PUBLIC) or overlapped (COMMON). Stack segments must have the type STACK.

The *class* affects the order in which segments are stored. Segments having the same class name are stored consecutively, while those with different names are stored in the order the program-building program (the Linker) encounters them.

The Macro Assembler manual describes these options in detail, but in general you will be safe using the following combinations:

- For a data segment, use `SEGMENT PARA PUBLIC 'DATA'`
- For a code segment, use `SEGMENT PARA PUBLIC 'CODE'`
- For an extra segment, use `SEGMENT PARA PUBLIC 'EXTRA'`
- For a stack segment, use `SEGMENT PARA STACK 'STACK'`

For example, a data segment may look like this:

```
DSEG   SEGMENT   PARA PUBLIC 'DATA'
  A          DB   ?
  B          DB   ?
  SQUARES    DB   1,4,9,16,25,36,49,64
DSEG   ENDS
```

and a code segment may look like this:

```
CSEG   SEGMENT   PARA PUBLIC 'CODE'
       ..
       ..
       MOV   AX,BX
       MOV   CL,DH
       MOV   DI,CX
       ..
       ..
CSEG   ENDS
```

The words SEGMENT and ENDS simply mark the beginning and end of a segment; they don't tell the assembler which *kind* of segment is being defined. A separate pseudo-op, ASSUME, does that. ASSUME has the general format

```
ASSUME   seg-reg:seg-name[,...]
```

where *seg-reg* is either DS, CS, SS, or ES and *seg-name* is the name that precedes a SEGMENT pseudo-op. DS points to the data segment, CS to the code segment, SS to the stack segment, and ES to the extra segment.

ASSUME helps the assembler translate labels into addresses, by telling it which segment register you plan to use to address those labels. For example, the statement

```
ASSUME  DS:DSEG
```

tells the assembler, "DSEG is my data segment. Whenever you find a mention of a label in DSEG, tell the microprocessor to obtain the label's segment number from DS. In turn, *I* promise to make DS point to the beginning of DSEG."

The ASSUME belongs immediately after the code segment's SEGMENT statement. Thus, for the preceding two-segment program, the code segment would have this form:

```
CSEG    SEGMENT   PARA PUBLIC 'CODE'
        ASSUME    CS:CSEG,DS:DSEG
        MOV       AX,DSEG   ;Make DS point to DSEG
        MOV       DS,AX
        ..
        ..
        MOV       AX,BX
        MOV       CL,DH
        MOV       CX,DI
        ..
        ..
CSEG    ENDS
```

Again, note that we must explicitly load the data segment's address into DS; the ASSUME does not take care of this.

The PROC and ENDP pseudo-ops mark the beginning and end of a *procedure.* A procedure is a block of instructions that can be executed from various places in a program. Whenever your program calls a procedure, the 80286 executes it, then returns to the place where the call was made. Because you write a procedure just once in a program, it frees you from typing the sequence each time you need it, and thereby makes your programs shorter.

Every procedure must begin with a PROC and end with an ENDP. If it also contains a RET (Return from Procedure) instruction—and most do—we can call it a *subroutine.* The RET instruction makes the 80286 resume at the place where the subroutine was called, just as RETURN does in a BASIC subroutine.

A procedure always has one of two *distance* attributes: NEAR or FAR, as specified by the operand that follows PROC. Omitting the operand makes the procedure NEAR.

A NEAR procedure can only be called from within the code segment in which it is defined. For example:

```
CSEG   SEGMENT   PARA PUBLIC 'CODE
       ASSUME    CS:CSEG
CALLER   PROC
         ..
         CALL   CALLEE    (Call to a procedure)
         ..
         RET
CALLER   ENDP
CALLEE   PROC   NEAR      (Procedure that is called)
         ..
         ..
         RET
CALLEE   ENDP
CSEG   ENDS
```

Here, the called procedure (CALLEE) happens to be defined in the same segment as the CALL instruction. However, the two procedures may also be in different program modules (i.e., different disk files), as long as their code segments have the same name. Communicating between modules involves the EXTRN and PUBLIC pseudo-ops, which we discuss in the next section.

A FAR procedure can be called from any code segment. For example:

```
CSEG   SEGMENT   PARA PUBLIC 'CODE
       ASSUME    CS:CSEG
CALLER   PROC
         ..
         CALL   CALLEE    (Call to a procedure)
         ..
         RET
CALLER   ENDP
CSEG   ENDS

CSEG1   SEGMENT   PARA PUBLIC 'CODE'
        ASSUME    CS:CSEG1
CALLEE   PROC   FAR       (Procedure that is called)
         ..
         ..
         RET
CALLEE   ENDP
CSEG1   ENDS
```

When the 80286 calls a procedure, it pushes a return address onto the stack. It retrieves this address when it executes the RET instruction. If the procedure has a NEAR attribute, the 286 puts only an offset—the contents of the instruction pointer (IP)—on the stack. If the procedure has a FAR attribute, the 286 puts two things on the stack: a segment number—the contents of the code segment (CS) register—then an offset from IP.

When you assemble the program, the assembler translates each RET instruction into machine code that tells the 80286 how many return address words to retrieve from the stack. A RET in a NEAR procedure makes it remove only one word (IP contents) from the stack; a RET in a FAR procedure makes it remove two words (IP and CS contents).

If all this has you confused, here are some rules that will help you decide whether to make your procedures NEAR or FAR:

1. Your main procedure must be FAR. (This is only true for EXE programs. For COM program rules, see Section 2.9.)
2. If you always give your code segments the same name (e.g., CSEG), make all procedures NEAR except the main one.
3. If you are using a procedure that someone else created, you must know whether it is NEAR or FAR. (For example, the procedures on the supplemental disk for this book are all FAR.) We describe how to specify NEAR or FAR shortly, when we discuss the EXTRN pseudo-op.

External Reference Pseudo-Ops

These pseudo-ops allow you to share information between modules that you eventually link to form a program. They are a way to ask the linker (LINK) for help in constructing the final form of the program.

The PUBLIC pseudo-op makes one or more symbol(s) available to other modules that will eventually be linked to this one. It tells the linker, "Here is a list of items I have. If anyone needs access to them, you have my permission to tell them where to find them." A PUBLIC pseudo-op can list variable names, labels (including PROC labels), and names defined by an EQU or = pseudo-op.

EXTRN is the partner to PUBLIC. It tells the linker, "I want to use this item. I don't know where it is or what module has it, but I need to refer to it." EXTRN has the general form

```
EXTRN   name:type[,...]
```

where *name* is the symbol defined (and declared PUBLIC) in some other assembly module and *type* can be one of the following:

- If *name* is a symbol in a data segment or extra segment, then *type* can be BYTE, WORD, or DWORD.
- If *name* is a procedure label, then *type* can be NEAR or FAR.
- If *name* is a constant defined by an EQU or = pseudo-op, then *type* must be ABS.

PUBLIC and EXTRN are often used to share procedures. For example, to run a procedure called SORT from a main program, the module in which SORT is defined must include *PUBLIC SORT* and the main module (the one that refers to SORT) must contain *EXTRN SORT:NEAR* or *EXTRN SORT:FAR*.

The INCLUDE pseudo-op merges (reads) an entire file of source statements into the current source file at assembly time. For example, *INCLUDE B:OTHERFIL.ASM* reads the contents of the file OTHERFIL.ASM on Drive B into your source file, replacing the INCLUDE statement. You can also use INCLUDE to read macros into a program. We discuss this further in Chapter 10.

Assembly Control Pseudo-Ops

The assembler recognizes several assembly control pseudo-ops, but only END, EVEN, and ORG are frequently used.

The END pseudo-op marks the end of a program, and thus tells the assembler where to stop assembling. Therefore, *you must include END in every source program.* Its general form is

```
END  [entry-point label]
```

where *entry-point label* identifies the place where DOS started executing the program. For example,

```
END  MY_PROG
```

marks the end of the program MY_PROG.

Important: If your program consists of several modules, you must label the END in the main module, but omit it from the ENDs in secondary modules. For example, if your main program calls subroutines that are in separate modules, each subroutine module's END must be unlabeled.

The EVEN pseudo-op can make programs run faster! Here's why. Having a 16-bit data bus, the 80286 can transfer 16 bits of data in one operation. However, it takes longer to transfer data that starts at an odd-numbered address than data that starts at an even-numbered address. Therefore, in time-critical applications it is advantageous to store data at even-numbered addresses.

To keep data properly aligned, arrange it with doublewords (DDs) first, words (DWs) second, and bytes (DBs) last. If the data segment contains only byte pseudo-ops, put an EVEN ahead of each one except the first. For example:

```
DSEG  SEGMENT  PARA PUBLIC 'DATA'
     HOURS  DB  ?
     EVEN
```

```
    MESSAGE  DB  'Press any key to continue.'
DSEG  ENDS
```

EVEN only does its job if necessary. That is, if the location counter is already pointing to an even offset, EVEN does nothing. Otherwise, if the counter is pointing to an odd offset, the assembler replaces EVEN with a 00H byte to make the next location even. For example, if the location counter is pointing to offset 129H, EVEN makes the assembler store the next data unit at 12AH.

The ORG (Origin) pseudo-op alters the location counter, to make the assembler store data or instructions some place other than where it normally stores them. ORG is most often used in *COM* (Command) type programs, where you give the form

```
ORG  100H
```

This tells the assembler to start storing the program 256 bytes past the current location. We discuss COM programs in Section 2.9.

Listing Pseudo-Ops

Table 2-3 summarizes the listing pseudo-ops.

Table 2-3. Listing pseudo-ops.

Pseudo-Op	Function
PAGE	Format: `PAGE [lines][,columns]` Sets the length and width of the page.
TITLE	Format: `TITLE text` Specifies a title to be listed on the second line of each page.
SUBTTL	Format: `SUBTTL text` Specifies a subtitle to be listed on the third line of each page.

PAGE has the general format

```
PAGE  [lines][,columns]
```

where *lines* and *columns* set the length and width of the pages printed during assembly. Lines can range from 10 to 255; columns range from 60 to 132 characters. The defaults, 57 lines and 80 characters, are set up for standard $8\frac{1}{2}$ by 11-inch paper.

You can, for example, print on legal-size paper with a statement such as

```
PAGE 72
```

Or, to use standard wide computer printout paper, you want

```
PAGE  ,132
```

The assembler prints a chapter number and a page number at the top of each page, with a dash between them. It increases the page number when a page is full or when it encounters PAGE alone (no operands). It increases the chapter number only when it encounters *PAGE* + (this also resets the page number to 1). All three conditions make the printer advance to the next page.

The TITLE pseudo-op produces a left-justified title on the second line of each page; we use it to give the assembly module's filename and a short description of what the module does. We generally put the TITLE statement at the beginning of a program, but you can actually put it anywhere.

The SUBTTL pseudo-op produces a centered subtitle on the third line of the next page; this usually describes the contents of the page. For example, the beginning of a listing might have these headers:

```
TITLE   COUNT_ALL - Galaxy Census Program
SUBTTL  Venusian Data Segment
```

At the end of the first data segment, you could change the subtitle as follows:

```
SUBTTL  Plutonian Data Segment
PAGE
```

Titles and subtitles may be up to 60 characters long.

Mode Pseudo-Ops

As we mentioned earlier, the PC AT uses an Intel 80286 microprocessor, while the PC, XT, and Portable Computer use an Intel 8088. The 80286 includes all of the 8088 instructions, plus some additional ones of its own (we'll discuss them in Chapter 3). The mode pseudo-ops tell the assembler which microprocessor's instruction set to recognize. The first one,

```
.286C
```

tells it to accept 80286 instructions as well as 8086/8088 instructions. You need it only if your program includes any instructions that are unique to the 80286.

The second mode pseudo-op,

```
.8086
```

is the default. The assembler uses it if neither .8086 nor .286C is specified. This pseudo-op tells the assembler to accept only 8086/8088 instructions (and to produce an error if it encounters an 80286-only instruction). You can use .8086 to spot illegal instructions in a program that is designed to run on a regular IBM PC.

If you use .286C or .8086, put it at the beginning of the program, right after your listing pseudo-ops (if any).

2.6 Operators

Note: This is primarily a reference section. If you are a beginner, read it casually, then come back later if you need to look up details.

An operator is a modifier used in the operand field of an assembly language or pseudo-op statement. There are five kinds of operators: *arithmetic, logical, relational, value-returning,* and *attribute*. Table 2-4 summarizes them.

Table 2-4. Operators.

Pseudo-Op	Function
Arithmetic	
+	Format: `value1 + value2` Adds *value1* and *value2*.
-	Format: `value1 - value2` Subtracts *value2* from *value1*.
*	Format: `value1 * value2` Multiplies *value2* by *value1*.
/	Format: `value1 / value2` Divides *value1* by *value2*, and returns the quotient.
MOD	Format: `value1 MOD value2` Divides *value1* by *value2*, and returns the remainder.
SHL	Format: `value SHL expression` Shifts *value* left by *expression* bit positions.
SHR	Format: `value SHR expression` Shifts *value* right by expression bit positions.
Logical	
AND	Format: `value1 AND value2` Takes logical AND of *value1* and *value2*.

Table 2-3. Listing pseudo-ops (continued).

Pseudo-Op	Function
OR	Format: `value1 OR value2` Takes logical inclusive-OR of *value1* and *value2.*
XOR	Format: `value1 XOR value2` Takes logical exclusive-OR of *value1* and *value2.*
NOT	Format: `NOT value` Reverses the state of each bit in *value;* that is, it takes the one's complement.
Relational	
EQ	Format: `operand1 EQ operand2` True if the two operands are identical.
NE	Format: `operand1 NE operand2` True if the two operands are not identical.
LT	Format: `operand1 LT operand2` True if *operand1* is less than *operand2.*
GT	Format: `operand1 GT operand2` True if *operand1* is greater than *operand2.*
LE	Format: `operand1 LE operand2` True if *operand1* is less than or equal to *operand2.*
GE	Format: `operand1 GE operand2` True if *operand1* is greater than or equal to *operand2.*
Value-Returning	
$	Format: `$` Returns the current value of the location counter.
SEG	Format: `SEG variable` or `SEG label` Returns the segment value of *variable* or *label.*
OFFSET	Format: `OFFSET variable` or `OFFSET label` Returns the offset value of *variable* or *label.*
LENGTH	Format: `LENGTH variable` Returns the length in units (bytes or words) for any variable defined using DUP.
TYPE	Format: `TYPE variable` or `TYPE label`

Table 2-3. Listing pseudo-ops (continued).

Pseudo-Op	Function
	For variables, TYPE returns 1 (BYTE), 2 (WORD), or 4 (DOUBLEWORD). For labels, it returns -1 (NEAR) or -2 (FAR).
SIZE	Format: `SIZE variable` Returns the product of LENGTH times TYPE.
Attribute	
PTR	Format: `type PTR expression` Overrides the type (BYTE or WORD) or distance (NEAR or FAR) of a memory address operand. *type* is the new attribute and *expression* is the identifier whose attribute is to be overridden.

DS:
ES:
SS:
CS:
	Format: `seg-reg:addr-expr`
	or
	`seg-reg:label`
	or
	`seg-reg:variable`
	Overrides the segment attribute of a label, variable, or address expression.

SHORT	Format: `JMP SHORT label` Tells the assembler that the JMP target label is no farther than 127 bytes past the next instruction.
THIS	Format: `THIS attribute` or `THIS type` Creates a memory address operand of either distance attribute (NEAR or FAR) or either type attribute (BYTE or WORD) at an offset equal to the current value of the location counter and a segment attribute of the enclosing segment.
HIGH	Format: `HIGH value` or `HIGH expression` Returns the high-order byte of a 16-bit numeric value or address expression.
LOW	Format: `LOW value` or `LOW expression` Returns the low-order byte of a 16-bit numeric value or address expression.

Arithmetic Operators

The arithmetic operators combine numeric operands and produce a numeric result. The most common arithmetic operators are those that add (+), subtract (-), multiply (*), and divide (/).

The divide operator (/) returns the quotient produced by a divide operation. For example, the statement

```
PI_QUOT   EQU   31416/10000
```

returns the value 3.

The MOD operator returns the *remainder* of a divide operation. The statement

```
PI_REM   EQU   31416 MOD 10000
```

defines a constant called PI_REM that has the value 1416.

Finally, SHL and SHR displace a numeric operand to the left or right. About the only time you need this capability is if you set up "masks" that you'll apply to binary patterns in memory. For example, if you set up a mask with the statement

```
MASK   EQU   110010B
```

the statement

```
MASK_LEFT_2   EQU   MASK SHL 2
```

sets up a new constant with the value 11001000B. Similarly,

```
MASK_RIGHT_2   EQU   MASK SHR 2
```

sets up a new constant with the value 1100B.

Logical Operators

Like SHL and SHR in the preceding section, the logical operators are used primarily to manipulate binary values instead of decimal values. However, the logical operators manipulate individual bits, rather than an entire group of bits.

To draw an analogy, imagine a group of patients seated on a bench at a medical clinic. If the clinic operates in "shift" fashion, the nurse may order the first three patients to report to examination rooms and ask the remaining patients to shift left. In doing this, the nurse essentially performs an *SHL 3* operation.

Conversely, if the clinic operates in "logical" fashion, the nurse may order just certain patients (perhaps those with broken bones) to report for examination and tell the remaining patients to stay where they are.

The logical operators AND, OR, and XOR combine two operands to produce a result; NOT requires just one operand. Table 2-5 shows how AND, OR, and XOR operate.

Table 2-5. AND, OR, and XOR combinations.

		Result		
Operand #1	**Operand #2**	**AND**	**OR**	**XOR**
0	0	0	0	0
0	1	0	1	1
1	0	0	1	1
1	1	1	1	0

AND is convenient to filter, mask, or strip out certain bits. To do this, it sets the result bit to 1 for each bit position in which both operands contain a 1. For any other bit combination, AND clears the result bit to 0.

For example, the operation

```
00110100B AND 11010111B
```

produces 00010100B. As you can see, AND operates like a house with a double-lock door. If neither lock is engaged (1 = unlocked), you can enter the house, but if either or both locks are engaged (0 = locked), you are shut outside.

OR sets the result bit to 1 for each position in which either or both operands contain a 1. Conversely, for bit positions where both operands contain 0, OR clears the result bit to 0.

Using the preceding operand combination,

```
00110100B OR 11010111B
```

produces 11110111B. To make another door analogy, OR operates like a house with two doors. If either or both doors are unlocked (1), you can enter the house, but if both are locked (0), you are shut outside.

XOR is a variation of OR in which ones in both operands produce a 0 (rather than a 1) in the result. XOR is short for "exclusive-OR", because it excludes the 1-and-1 combination (to distinguish it from the "inclusive-OR" condition, OR.)

NOT reverses the state of each bit in the operand. That is, it changes each 1 to 0 and each 0 to 1. For example,

```
NOT 01101001B
```

produces 10010110B.

The 80286 also has assembly language instructions named AND, OR, XOR, and NOT, which we discuss in Chapter 3. The difference is that the logical operators do their job when the program *assembles;* the logical instructions do theirs when the program *executes.*

Relational Operators

Relational operators compare two numeric values or memory addresses in the same segment, and produce a numeric result. The result is always one of two numbers: 0 if the relationship is "false" or 0FFFFH if the relationship is "true."

For example, if CHOICE is a predefined constant,

```
MOV   AX,CHOICE LT 20
```

assembles as

```
MOV   AX,0FFFFH
```

if CHOICE is less than 20, and as

```
MOV   AX,0
```

if CHOICE is greater than or equal to 20.

Because the relational operators can only produce two values (0 or 0FFFFH), they are rarely used alone. Instead, they are usually combined with other operators to form a decision-making expression. For instance, suppose you want AX to contain 5 if CHOICE is less than 20 and contain 6 otherwise. A statement that performs this task is:

```
MOV   AX,((CHOICE LT 20) AND 5) OR ((CHOICE GE 20) AND 6)
```

Here, if CHOICE is less than 20, the clause (CHOICE LT 20) is "true" and the clause (CHOICE GE 20) is "false," so the intermediate form of the statement is

```
MOV   AX,(0FFFFH AND 5) OR (0 AND 6)
```

The assembler evaluates this as

```
MOV   AX,5
```

Conversely, if CHOICE is greater than or equal to 20, the clause (CHOICE LT 20) is "false" and (CHOICE GE 20) is "true," so the intermediate form of the statement is

```
MOV   AX,(0 AND 5) OR (0FFFFH AND 6)
```

The assembler evaluates this as

```
MOV   AX,6
```

Value-Returning Operators

Operators in this group provide information about variables or labels in a program.

The dollar sign ($) returns the value of the location counter; that is, it returns the offset of the current statement. This operator is handy for making the assembler calculate the length of a text string. For example, the following calculates the number of characters in the MESSAGE string and assigns this count to MESSAGEL:

```
MESSAGE    DB   'Press any key to continue.'
MESSAGEL   EQU  $-MESSAGE
```

When we want to display the message, we use the value MESSAGEL to tell our program how many characters to send to the screen.

SEG and *OFFSET* return the segment and offset values of a variable or label. For example, the statements

```
MOV   AX,SEG TABLE
MOV   BX,OFFSET TABLE
```

load the segment and offset values of TABLE into AX and BX, respectively. (Since both segment and offset are 16-bit values, they must be loaded into 16-bit registers.)

The *TYPE* operator returns a numeric value that indicates the type attribute of a variable (1 for BYTE or 2 for WORD) or the distance attribute of a label (-1 for NEAR or -2 for FAR).

The *LENGTH* and *SIZE* operators are only meaningful for variables you define with DUP. LENGTH returns the number of units (bytes or words) allocated for the variable. For example, the sequence

```
TABLE   DW    100 DUP(1)
        MOV   CX,LENGTH TABLE   ;Get no. of words in TABLE
```

loads 100 into CX. If you use LENGTH with any variable that was not defined with DUP, it returns 1.

SIZE returns the byte count of a variable. That is, it returns the product of LENGTH times TYPE. Using the variable TABLE we just defined, the statement

```
MOV   CX,SIZE TABLE   ;Get no. of bytes in TABLE
```

loads the value 200 into CX.

Attribute Operators

The pointer (PTR) operator overrides the type (BYTE or WORD) or distance (NEAR or FAR) attribute of an operand. For example, you can use PTR to refer to bytes in a table of words. If you define a table as

```
WORD_TABLE   DW   100 DUP(?)
```

the statement

```
FIRST_BYTE   EQU   BYTE PTR WORD_TABLE
```

assigns a name to the location of the first byte in WORD_TABLE. After that, you can name any other byte as easily as this:

```
FIFTH_BYTE   EQU   FIRST_BYTE+4
```

As we just mentioned, PTR can also change a label's distance attribute. For example, if we have this instruction in a program:

```
START:   MOV   CX,100
```

the label START has a NEAR attribute, which allows JMP (Jump) instructions in the same segment to refer to it. To let JMPs in other segments refer to this instruction as well, you must give it an alternate label that has a FAR attribute. This kind of statement does the job:

```
FAR_START   EQU   FAR PTR START
```

As we mentioned in Chapter 1, when the 80286 computes a memory address, it automatically assumes that SS is the segment register if the operand employs SP or BP to hold the offset. Similarly, it assumes that DS is the segment register if BX, SI, or DI holds the offset. The *segment override* operator (DS:, ES:, SS:, or CS:) overrides the segment attribute of a label, variable, or address expression. It lets you specify an alternate segment register. For example,

```
MOV   AX,ES:[BP]
```

tells the 286 to get its destination operand from the extra segment rather than from the stack segment.

The *SHORT* operator tells the assembler that a JMP target is no farther than 127 bytes past the next instruction. With this information, the assembler encodes JMP as a two-byte instruction, rather than a three-byte instruction, which saves memory. Here is an example:

```
          JMP   SHORT THERE
          ..
          ..
THERE:
```

The *THIS* operator creates a memory address operand of a specified type (BYTE or WORD) or distance (NEAR or FAR), and gives this operand the same segment and offset attributes as the next memory address available for allocation. For example, the sequence

```
FIRST_BYTE  EQU  THIS BYTE
WORD_TABLE  DW   100 DUP(?)
```

creates FIRST_BYTE, and gives it a BYTE-type attribute with the same address as WORD_TABLE. This does the same thing as the previous statement

```
FIRST_BYTE  EQU  BYTE PTR WORD_TABLE
```

You can also use THIS to define FAR instruction locations. Returning to an earlier example,

```
START  EQU  THIS FAR
       MOV  CX,100
```

gives the MOV instruction a FAR attribute, which allows JMP instructions in another segment to jump to START directly.

The *HIGH* and *LOW* operators return the high- or low-order byte of a 16-bit expression. For example, if you define a constant as

```
CONST  EQU  OABCDH
```

the statement

```
MOV  AH,HIGH CONST
```

loads the value OABH into the AH register.

2.7 Entering, Assembling, and Running a Program

Since we haven't discussed the details of the 80286's assembly language instruction set (that's coming in Chapter 3), you cannot yet write programs that add or subtract numbers, manipulate the registers, or perform the many other tasks you eventually want your computer to do. Still, you *do* have enough background to write a program that moves data with MOV instructions, and sets up the necessary segments with pseudo-ops.

In this section we develop a program that copies one four-byte data table in memory into another. To make it more interesting, we store the data into the "destination" table in the reverse order from how it is stored in the "source" table.

The details of the program are unimportant, however. The main point is that you will learn how to enter a program into the computer, how to assemble it, how to produce a listing file and a run module, and how to execute and debug it. In short, you will get hands-on experience with the basic steps. This helps you to proceed with confidence through more complex material in the rest of the book.

Creating a Working Assembler Disk

For assembly language work, we need several programs that are on the IBM DOS disks as well as those on the Macro Assembler disk. If you have a hard disk, simply copy the entire contents of the Macro Assembler disk into whatever directory contains DOS. Otherwise, if you have floppy disk drives, you should prepare a disk that contains all the necessary programs; this will save swapping disks.

To begin, use the DOS *FORMAT /S* command to format a blank disk. Onto it, copy the following programs:

- EDLIN.COM from the main DOS disk.
- DEBUG.COM, EXE2BIN.EXE, and LINK.EXE from the *Supplemental Programs* disk.
- MASM.EXE, CREF.EXE, SALUT.EXE, and LIB.EXE from the Macro Assembler disk.

From here on, we refer to this disk as the *assembler disk.*

Data Disk

For the procedures in this section, you also need another blank disk that has been formatted with plain old *FORMAT* (no /S). This serves as your data disk.

Example Program

Figure 2-1 lists our table-copying program. Note that it has a stack segment (STACK), a data segment (DSEG), and a code segment (CSEG). The stack segment will hold a return address that makes the 80286 return to DEBUG upon completing the program.

The data segment consists of just two pseudo-op statements. One sets up the source table (SOURCE), the other reserves space for the destination table (DEST).

The code segment has four groups of instructions:

- The first group puts an address on the stack that sends the computer back to DEBUG at the end of the program.
- The second group makes DS point to the data segment. *(Remember, ASSUME doesn't do this for you.)*
- The third group stores zeros in the four bytes of the DEST table. We do this so that when you check the final contents of DEST, you know you're seeing the program's effect on DEST, not the results of a previous run.
- The fourth group copies the table data, one byte at a time.

The instructions in the code segment are a single procedure enclosed by the pseudo-op statements *OUR_PROG PROC FAR* and *OUR_PROG ENDP.* We have given the procedure a FAR attribute so that the RET instruction at the end takes a two-word address off the stack (the one we put there at the start of the program) and sends the 80286 back to DEBUG. *For this same reason, you should set up the programs you write as procedures.*

Entering the Program

To enter the program into the computer, you can use EDLIN or, better yet, any editor or word processor that can produce standard ASCII (unformatted text that contains no control characters). For example, you can use WordStar's "non-document" (N) mode. Since we can't know which word processor you have (if any), we will use EDLIN. Table 2-6 summarizes the most useful EDLIN commands.

```
        PAGE    ,132
TITLE   EX_PROG - Example Program

STACK   SEGMENT PARA STACK 'STACK'
        DB      64 DUP('STACK   ')
STACK   ENDS

DSEG    SEGMENT PARA PUBLIC 'DATA'
SOURCE  DB      10,20,30,40     ;This table will be copied into
DEST    DB      4 DUP(?)        ; this table, in reverse order
DSEG    ENDS

CSEG    SEGMENT PARA PUBLIC 'CODE'
        ASSUME  CS:CSEG,DS:DSEG,SS:STACK
OUR_PROG PROC FAR

;   Set up the stack to contain the proper values so this
;   program can return to DEBUG.

        PUSH    DS              ;Put return seg. addr. on stack
        MOV     AX,0            ;Clear a register
        PUSH    AX              ;Put zero return addr. on stack

;   Initialize the data segment address.

        MOV     AX,DSEG         ;Initialize DS
        MOV     DS,AX

;   Initialize DEST with zeroes.

        MOV     DEST,0          ;First byte
        MOV     DEST+1,0        ;Second byte
        MOV     DEST+2,0        ;Third byte
        MOV     DEST+3,0        ;Fourth byte

;   Copy SOURCE table into DEST table, in reverse order.

        MOV     AL,SOURCE       ;Copy first byte
        MOV     DEST+3,AL
        MOV     AL,SOURCE+1     ;Copy second byte
        MOV     DEST+2,AL
        MOV     AL,SOURCE+2     ;Copy third byte
        MOV     DEST+1,AL
        MOV     AL,SOURCE+3     ;Copy fourth byte
        MOV     DEST,AL
        RET                     ;Far return to DEBUG
OUR_PROG ENDP
CSEG    ENDS
        END     OUR_PROG
```

Figure 2-1. Example program for editing and assembling.

Table 2-6. Common EDLIN commands.

Edit Lines
Format: *[line]*
Action: Displays a line for editing.
Comment: Pressing Return selects the next line.

C—Copy Lines
Format: *[start-line],[end-line],target-line C*
Action: Copies the specified lines to just ahead of *target-line.*
Example: *20, 25, 94 C* makes a copy of lines 20 through 25, and inserts the copy just ahead of line 94.
Comment: See also the Move Lines command.

D—Delete Lines
Format: *[start-line][,end-line] D*
Action: Deletes the specified lines.
16 D deletes line 16.
D deletes the current line.
Comment: EDLIN automatically renumbers all lines that follow the deletion.

E—End Edit
Format: *E*
Action: Saves the program on disk, then returns to DOS.
Comment: To exit EDLIN without saving changes, use the Quit command.

I—Insert Lines
Format: *[line] I*
Action: Inserts lines from the keyboard ahead of the specified line. Press Ctrl-Break to leave the insert mode.
Example: *20 I* inserts lines just ahead of line 20.
Comment: EDLIN automatically renumbers all lines that follow the insertion.

L—List Lines
Format: *[start-line][,end-line] L*
Action: Lists (displays) lines.

M—Move Lines
Format: *[start-line],[end-line],target-line M*
Action: Moves the specified lines to just ahead of *target-line.*
Comment: See also the Copy Lines command.

Q—Quit
Format: Q
Action: Returns to DOS without saving editing changes.
Comment: To save changes, use the End Edit command.

R—Replace Text
Format: *[start-line][,end-line] Rold-string[<F6>new-string]*
Action: Replaces *old-string* with *new-string* throughout the specified range.

Table 2-6. Common EDLIN commands (continued).

Examples: *1,40 RFINISH<F6>END* changes FINISH to END in lines 1 through 40.
1 RFINISH<F6>END changes FINISH to END throughout the program.
1 RFINISH deletes FINISH throughout the program.

S—Search for Text
Format: *[start-line][,end-line] Sstring*
Action: Searches for the specified string. If EDLIN locates the string, you may press S and Return to find the next occurrence.

Note: Brackets indicate that the item(s) inside them are optional.

Generally, we also assume that you have two floppy disk drives. (A single drive works, but you have to do some disk-swapping.) *If you have a hard disk,* ignore references to A> and B>, which are floppy disk prompts. Instead, mentally substitute C> wherever the book mentions A> or B>.

To enter the program using two floppies, proceed as follows:

1. Insert your new assembler disk in the top drive (A) and the blank data disk in the bottom drive (B), then switch the power on. Press Return when the computer asks for the date and time.
2. When the A> prompt appears, type **b:** and press Return to make the bottom drive active. (Hereafter, press Return after every command.)
3. Enter

   ```
   B>a:edlin ex_prog.asm
   ```

   Here, *ex_prog* is the name of the program we want to create. The extension *.asm* identifies it as an assembly language source code file.
4. When the computer displays

   ```
   New file
   *_
   ```

   press I to put EDLIN into the *insert* mode. The next prompt,

   ```
   1:*_
   ```

   indicates that EDLIN is waiting for the first line of text—in this case, the first statement in your source program.
5. Enter the source program shown in Figure 2-1, line by line. We have capitalized most words, but you may enter them in lowercase if you prefer. We have also aligned the fields to make the listing more readable, but feel free to enter them any way you like. Just be sure to put at least one space between them.

6. When you finish, press Ctrl-Break to take EDLIN out of the insert mode, then **E** to save the program on the data disk.

Now you can assemble this *source program* to produce an *object program.*

Assembling the Program

To assemble the program, type

```
B>a:masm ex_prog
```

Then respond to three prompts, as follows:

```
Object filename [EX_PROG.OBJ]: (press Return)
Source listing  [NUL.LST]: b:
Cross reference [NUL.CRF]: (press Return)
```

This tells the assembler to use the specified source file (EX_PROG.ASM) to create an object file with the name it has suggested (EX_PROG.OBJ) and a source listing file (EX_PROG.LST). The listing file contains the source instructions and their numeric codes—a handy, printable file that shows how the assembler interpreted your program.

If you followed the preceding steps exactly, the assembler will do its job, then display

```
nnnnn Bytes free

Warning  Severe
Errors   Errors
0        0
```

then return to DOS. If it reports errors, use EDLIN to correct them, then assemble EX_PROG.ASM again.

Listing the Source Program

To list the program on the screen, enter

```
B>type ex_prog.lst
```

A problem is that the instructions fly by so quickly you can't read them! To stop the scrolling temporarily, press Ctrl-Num Lock; press any key to resume. To print the listing, first set your printer "on-line," press Ctrl-PrtSc, then enter the Type command. The listing should look like Figure 2-2.

```
                                        PAGE     ,132
                                TITLE   EX_PROG - Example Program

0000                            STACK   SEGMENT PARA STACK 'STACK'
0000      40 [                          DB       64 DUP('STACK   ')
               53 54 41 43
               4B 20 20 20
                          ]

0200                            STACK   ENDS

0000                            DSEG    SEGMENT PARA PUBLIC 'DATA'
0000  0A 14 1E 28               SOURCE  DB       10,20,30,40       ;This table will be copied into
0004      04 [                  DEST    DB       4 DUP(?)          ; this table, in reverse order
               ??
                    ]

0008                            DSEG    ENDS

0000                            CSEG    SEGMENT PARA PUBLIC 'CODE'
                                ASSUME  CS:CSEG,DS:DSEG,SS:STACK
0000                            OUR_PROG PROC    FAR

                                ;  Set up the stack to contain the proper values so this
                                ;  program can return to DEBUG.

0000  1E                                PUSH     DS                ;Put return seg. addr. on stack
0001  B8 0000                           MOV      AX,0              ;Clear a register
0004  50                                PUSH     AX                ;Put zero return addr. on stack

                                ;  Initialize the data segment address.

0005  B8 ---- R                         MOV      AX,DSEG           ;Initialize DS
0008  8E D8                             MOV      DS,AX

                                ;  Initialize DEST with zeroes.

000A  C6 06 0004 R 00                   MOV      DEST,0            ;First byte
000F  C6 06 0005 R 00                   MOV      DEST+1,0          ;Second byte
0014  C6 06 0006 R 00                   MOV      DEST+2,0          ;Third byte
0019  C6 06 0007 R 00                   MOV      DEST+3,0          ;Fourth byte

                                ;  Copy SOURCE table into DEST table, in reverse order.

001E  A0 0000 R                         MOV      AL,SOURCE                 ;Copy first byte
0021  A2 0007 R                         MOV      DEST+3,AL
0024  A0 0001 R                         MOV      AL,SOURCE+1               ;Copy second byte
0027  A2 0006 R                         MOV      DEST+2,AL
002A  A0 0002 R                         MOV      AL,SOURCE+2               ;Copy third byte
002D  A2 0005 R                         MOV      DEST+1,AL
0030  A0 0003 R                         MOV      AL,SOURCE+3               ;Copy fourth byte
```

Figure 2-2. Assembly listing for the example program.

```
0033  A2 0004 R                       MOV     DEST,AL
0036  CB                              RET                             ;Far return to DEBUG
0037                                  OUR_PROG ENDP

IBM Personal Computer MACRO Assembler  Version 2.00   Page    1-2
EX_PROG - Example Program                                    06-04-85


0037                          CSEG    ENDS
                                      END     OUR_PROG

IBM Personal Computer MACRO Assembler  Version 2.00   Page    Symbols-1
EX_PROG - Example Program                                    06-04-85


Segments and Groups:

                N a m e               Size    Align  Combine Class

CSEG . . . . . . . . . . . . . .      0037    PARA   PUBLIC  'CODE'
DSEG . . . . . . . . . . . . . .      0008    PARA   PUBLIC  'DATA'
STACK. . . . . . . . . . . . . .      0200    PARA   STACK   'STACK'

Symbols:

                N a m e               Type    Value  Attr

DEST . . . . . . . . . . . . . .      L BYTE  0004   DSEG    Length =0004
OUR_PROG . . . . . . . . . . . .      F PROC  0000   CSEG    Length =0037
SOURCE . . . . . . . . . . . . .      L BYTE  0000   DSEG

50092 Bytes free

Warning Severe
Errors  Errors
0       0
```

Figure 2-2. Assembly listing for the example program (continued).

The first page in Figure 2-2 lists the source program instructions and their associated object code, in this order:

- The leftmost column shows the hexadecimal offset values (in bytes) from the beginning of the segment.
- The numeric columns show the object code for each statement. For the stack and data segments, these are the values in each memory location. For the code segment, the numbers represent the machine language codes that the 80826 executes.
- The text to the right is, of course, the source program.

The last page of the listing gives detailed summary information about the segments and symbols in the program. You can generally ignore these tables. In fact, the assembler provides an option (/N) that omits them entirely.

Finding the Program's Stopping Point

The main thing we want from this listing is the offset of the RET instruction at the end of the program. We will use this value later to execute the program until it reaches RET. There we will examine the final contents of the data tables. We must stop *before* executing RET because RET puts the 80286 back into DEBUG. When that happens, we won't be able to find the tables, because DEBUG uses a different data segment than our program.

To obtain RET's offset, enter **type ex_prog.lst**, then press Ctrl-Num Lock immediately to stop the scrolling. Using the space bar and Ctrl-Num Lock, work your way down to the RET instruction. When you see it, note that its offset (the leftmost number) is *0036*. Keep this number in mind for later reference.

Creating the Run File

DOS can store an object program at any convenient place in memory. To use this facility, you must create a *relocatable* run file.

The program that creates relocatable run files is called the *Linker,* because it can link several object files into one big run file. To run the Linker, enter

```
B>a:link ex_prog;
```

When B> appears, your data disk contains the run file *EX_PROG.EXE.*

Linking Multiple Object Modules

Our example program has only one object module (EX_PROG.OBJ). In later chapters you will create programs that have two or more object modules. You assemble these modules separately, then link them by listing their names connected with + symbols. For example,

```
B>a:link mod1+mod2+mod3;
```

combines object modules MOD1.OBJ, MOD2.OBJ, and MOD3.OBJ to create a run file called MOD1.EXE.

Running the Program

As we mentioned earlier, you may run the final form of a program (the EXE file) under DOS or DEBUG. You generally run it under DOS only when you're sure it is free of errors or it produces some visible or audible result. The example program is error-free (knock on formica), but it returns results in memory, where they are not visible. Hence, we will run it under DEBUG. Table 2-7 summarizes the most common DEBUG commands.

Table 2-7. Common DEBUG commands.

Execution Commands

G—Go

Format: *G [offset][,offset...]*

Action: Executes a program starting at the current location. Offset values are temporary breakpoints. Upon encountering a breakpoint instruction, the processor stops and displays registers and flags.

Examples: *G* executes to the end of the program.
G 4B executes to the instruction at offset 4BH.

Comment: The Trace and Proceed commands let you step through a program one or more instructions at a time.

T—Trace

Format: *T [instruction-count]*

Action: Executes one or more instructions and displays register and flag values for each of them.

Examples: *T* executes only the next instruction.
T 5 executes the next five instructions.

P—Proceed

Format: *P [instruction-count]*

Action: Same as Trace, but treats subroutine calls, interrupts, loop instruction, and repeat string instructions as a single instruction.

Quit Command

Q—Quit

Format: *Q*

Action: Exits DEBUG and returns to DOS.

Display/Change Commands

D—Dump

Format: *D seg:offset [offset]*

Action: Displays the numeric contents of memory locations and their character equivalents (if any).

Examples: *D DS:0* displays locations starting at the beginning of the data segment. A 40-column display shows eight bytes, an 80-column display shows 16 bytes.

Table 2-7. Common DEBUG commands (continued).

D ES:1A 1E displays locations 1AH through 1EH of the extra segment.

E—Enter Memory Values

Format: *E seg:offset [byte-list]*

Action: Enters one or more byte values into memory, starting at the specified address.

Example: *E DS:100 2B 10* changes the contents of locations 100H and 101H in the data segment to 2BH and 10H, respectively.

Comment: Omitting the list causes DEBUG to display the current value and wait for you to enter a new one.

R—Register

Format: *R [register-name [value]]*

Action: Displays contents of one or all 16-bit registers.

Examples: *R* displays all registers.
R AX displays the current contents of the AX register and prompts for a new value. (Press Return to keep current value.)
R AX FF loads 00FFH into the AX register.

U—Unassemble

Format: *U [seg:offset [offset]]*

Action: Translates (or unassembles) memory contents into instructions.

Examples: *U* unassembles the next 16 bytes on a 40-column display or the next 32 bytes on an 80-column display. *U F000:EF57 EF80* unassembles the bytes at offsets 0EF57H through 0EF80H of segment 0F000H.

Note: Brackets indicate that the item(s) inside them are optional.

To begin, load the example program into DEBUG by entering

```
a:debug ex_prog.exe
```

The computer shows DEBUG's hyphen (-) prompt.

Figure 2-3 shows a typical DEBUG session. Let's look at what's happening step by step. Don't pay much attention to the addresses, they may be different on your computer.

To begin, type **R** to display the registers. DEBUG's R (Registers) command shows the contents of each register, in hexadecimal form. (Note: *Everything* in DEBUG is hexadecimal.) It also summarizes the settings of the Flags register bits as a set of two-letter abbreviations. Table 2-8 tells what these abbreviations mean. For example, the abbreviations produced by this Register command tell you that all Flags bits are initially in the "clear" (0) state.

```
B>a:debug ex_prog.exe
-r
AX=0000  BX=0000  CX=0250  DX=0000  SP=0200  BP=0000  SI=0000  DI=0000
DS=0D70  ES=0D70  SS=0D85  CS=0D80  IP=0000   NV UP EI PL NZ NA PO NC
0D80:0000 1E            PUSH DS
-t


AX=0000  BX=0000  CX=0250  DX=0000  SP=01FE  BP=0000  SI=0000  DI=0000
DS=0D70  ES=0D70  SS=0D85  CS=0D80  IP=0001   NV UP EI PL NZ NA PO NC
0D80:0001 B80000        MOV AX,0000
-t


AX=0000  BX=0000  CX=0250  DX=0000  SP=01FE  BP=0000  SI=0000  DI=0000
DS=0D70  ES=0D70  SS=0D85  CS=0D80  IP=0004   NV UP EI PL NZ NA PO NC
0D80:0004 50            PUSH AX
-g36


AX=0D28  BX=0000  CX=0250  DX=0000  SP=01FC  BP=0000  SI=0000  DI=0000
DS=0D84  ES=0D70  SS=0D85  CS=0D80  IP=0036   NV UP EI PL NZ NA PO NC
0D80:0036 CB            RETF
-d ds:0
0D84:0000  0A 14 1E 28 28 1E 14 0A-00 00 00 00 00 00 00 00   ...((...........
0D84:0010  53 54 41 43 4B 20 20 20-53 54 41 43 4B 20 20 20   STACK   STACK
0D84:0020  53 54 41 43 4B 20 20 20-53 54 41 43 4B 20 20 20   STACK   STACK
0D84:0030  53 54 41 43 4B 20 20 20-53 54 41 43 4B 20 20 20   STACK   STACK
0D84:0040  53 54 41 43 4B 20 20 20-53 54 41 43 4B 20 20 20   STACK   STACK
0D84:0050  53 54 41 43 4B 20 20 20-53 54 41 43 4B 20 20 20   STACK   STACK
0D84:0060  53 54 41 43 4B 20 20 20-53 54 41 43 4B 20 20 20   STACK   STACK
0D84:0070  53 54 41 43 4B 20 20 20-53 54 41 43 4B 20 20 20   STACK   STACK
-q
```

Figure 2-3. DEBUG session with the example program.

Table 2-8. Flags abbreviations displayed by DEBUG.

Flag Name	Set	Clear
Overflow (yes/no)	OV	NV
Direction (decrement/increment)	DN	UP
Interrupt (enable/disable)	EI	DI
Sign (negative/positive)	NG	PL
Zero (yes/no)	ZR	NZ
Auxiliary Carry (yes/no)	AC	NA
Parity (even/odd)	PE	PO
Carry (yes/no)	CY	NC

The final line of the Register display shows which instruction the 80286 will execute next (*not* the instruction it just executed). Reading from left to right, you see that the instruction starts at address 0D80:0000 (these are the CS and IP values, respectively), its object code is 1E, and it is a PUSH DS. Everything must be working fine so far, because PUSH DS is indeed the first instruction in our example program.

Next we use T (Trace) commands to execute the *PUSH DS* and the *MOV AX,0000* instruction that follows it. Each time you enter T, the computer executes one instruction, then it displays the registers and lists the instruction it will execute next. Thus, tracing lets you see what the registers contain at any given time, and what the processor will do next. This information is invaluable in debugging a program.

Notice how some registers change as each instruction executes. After the first T, the Stack Pointer (SP) has decreased from 0200 to 01FE, because PUSH pushed a word—or two bytes—onto the stack. If you trace through the *PUSH AX* instruction, you will see SP decrease again.

Next we use the G (Go) command to execute down to the RET instruction. Specifically, we enter **g36** because (as the listing indicated) RET has an offset of 36 from the beginning of the code segment. This command says to DEBUG, "Execute down to the instruction at offset 36, then stop." DEBUG shows RET as *RETF*, because you are returning from a FAR procedure.

With the program completed, we must check to see whether it worked correctly—that is, whether it copied the SOURCE table to the DEST table in reverse order. To do this, we use the D (Dump) command to view the final contents of the tables. Enter

d ds:0

This tells DEBUG to display (d) the contents of the data segment (ds), starting at the beginning (offset 0).

The top line of the display shows

```
0A 14 1E 28 28 1E 14 0A
```

The first four values are the elements of SOURCE, the next four are the elements of DEST. These hexadecimal numbers represent the decimal values

```
10 20 30 40 40 30 20 10
```

As you can see, the program did its job.

Besides displaying numeric values for memory locations, the Dump command also shows their character equivalents (if any) in the right-hand column. This particular display shows the unused portion at the bottom of the stack segment, as repetitions of the word STACK. We made the stack display itself this way by defining the stack segment with the pseudo-op

```
DB   64 DUP('STACK    ')
```

Finally, use the Q (Quit) command to leave DEBUG and return to DOS.

Advanced Listing Options

If your program is long or complex, you can produce two other listings that provide additional information. These are the *cross-reference* and *map* listings.

Cross-Reference Listing

The cross-reference listing shows the line number where each symbol is defined and any other lines that refer to it. To generate a cross-reference listing, you must first produce a cross-reference (.CRF) file. To do this, enter the program name in response to the assembler's "Cross reference" prompt. For our example program, the correct response would be

```
Cross reference [NUL.CRF]: ex_prog
```

Besides creating the CRF file, entering a name in response to this prompt makes the assembler put line numbers in its regular assembly (.LST) listing.

Then, after assembling, type

```
B>a:cref ex_prog;
```

When the DOS prompt reappears, display the cross-reference listing by entering

```
type ex_prog.ref
```

As Figure 2-4 shows, you get the name of each symbol in the program, along with the line number where it is defined (marked with a #) and the line numbers of any other statements that refer to it.

Map Listing

The map listing summarizes the program's segments. For each segment, it shows the "start" and "stop" offsets, the length of the segment in bytes, and its class (CODE, DATA, EXTRA, or STACK).

The map listing file is a LINK option. You get it by entering the form

```
link progname,,;
```

(Note the two extra commas preceding the semicolon.)

```
EX_PROG - Example Program

 Symbol Cross Reference                    (# is definition)      Cref-1

CODE . . . . . . . . . . . . . .   20
CSEG . . . . . . . . . . . . . .   20#   21   55

DATA . . . . . . . . . . . . . .   12
DEST . . . . . . . . . . . . . .   14#   38   39   40   41   46   48   50   52
DSEG . . . . . . . . . . . . . .   12#   18   21   33

OUR_PROG . . . . . . . . . . . .   22#   54   56

SOURCE . . . . . . . . . . . . .   13#   45   47   49   51
STACK. . . . . . . . . . . . . .    4#    4   10   21

8 Symbols

62578 Bytes Free
```

Figure 2-4. Cross-reference listing for the example program.

To display the map listing, enter

type ex_prog.map

If you want to print the listing, first press Ctrl and PrtSc.

The listing should look like Figure 2-5. When it is done printing, press Ctrl and PrtSc again to make DOS stop sending screen text to the printer.

```
B>type ex_prog.map


Start  Stop   Length  Name                  Class
00000H 00036H 0037H  CSEG                  CODE
00040H 00047H 0008H  DSEG                  DATA
00050H 0024FH 0200H  STACK                 STACK

 Origin   Group

Program entry point at 0000:0000
```

Figure 2-5. Map listing for the example program.

2.8 Models for Constructing Programs

We now present generalized models that you can use to enter programs from this book or those you design. The models include the "boilerplate" that every program needs. All you have to do is fill in the data and instructions that apply to your particular program.

Main Program Module

Example 2-1 shows the model for a source module that will contain a complete program or that will be linked with one or more secondary modules to form a program. On the optional disk, it is named *MAINMOD.ASM*.

Example 2-1. Model for main program module.

```
        PAGE   ,132
TITLE  (Insert title here.)
(Insert EXTRN statement, if appropriate.)

STACK   SEGMENT PARA STACK 'STACK'
        DB     64 DUP('STACK   ')
STACK   ENDS

DSEG    SEGMENT PARA PUBLIC 'DATA'

(Insert data here.)

DSEG    ENDS

CSEG    SEGMENT PARA PUBLIC 'CODE'
        ASSUME  CS:CSEG,DS:DSEG,SS:STACK

ENTRY   PROC   FAR              ;Entry point

;Set up the stack to contain the proper values so this
;program can return to DOS or DEBUG.

        PUSH   DS
        SUB    AX,AX
        PUSH   AX

;Initialize the data segment address.

        MOV    AX,DSEG
        MOV    DS,AX

(Insert instructions here.)

        RET                     ;Return to DOS or DEBUG
ENTRY   ENDP
CSEG    ENDS
        END    ENTRY
```

Since the model is generalized, you may want to make one or more of the following changes:

1. Insert a TITLE. This normally indentifies the disk file; for example,

```
TITLE  SORT - Sort Program
```

2. If this module contains references to procedures or variables that are defined in a secondary module, it must include an EXTRN statement that lists them.
3. We have used the AX register to initialize the stack and the data segment address, but any other general 16-bit register works just as well. Thus, if your program obtains a user input value from AX, you *must* use some other register (say, DI) for the initialization.

Secondary Module

Example 2-2 shows the model for a secondary module that must be linked with the main module in Example 2-1 to form a program. On the optional disk it is named *SECMOD.ASM*.

Example 2-2. Model for secondary module.

```
        PAGE   ,132
TITLE (Insert title here.)

        PUBLIC  PNAME
(Insert PUBLIC for data variables, if appropriate.)

DSEG    SEGMENT PARA PUBLIC 'DATA'

(Insert data here.)

DSEG    ENDS

CSEG    SEGMENT PARA PUBLIC 'CODE'
        ASSUME  CS:CSEG,DS:DSEG

PNAME   PROC  NEAR

(Insert instructions here.)

        RET                     ;Return to calling program
PNAME   ENDP
CSEG    ENDS
        END
```

Among the possible changes are:

1. Because this module's code segment has the same name (CSEG) as the one in the main module, we have declared the PNAME procedure NEAR. To call PNAME from a code segment that has a different name, change it to FAR.
2. Because this module's data segment has the same name (DSEG) as the one in the main module, we did not initialize DS. There was no need to; instructions in the main module initialize it. However, if you use a different data segment name in your main module, insert DS-loading instructions in this secondary module.
3. We have represented the procedure name with the word PNAME. When you create your own module, replace PNAME with the name you want in three places: the PUBLIC statement at the top, the PROC statement in the middle, and the ENDP statement at the end.
4. This module has a PUBLIC statement that corresponds to the main module's EXTRN. If the main module contains a call to PNAME, it must include the statement *EXTRN PNAME:NEAR*.

Using the Models

If you don't have the optional disk, create these models just as you would any other program: using EDLIN, an editor, or a word processing program. Then, when you want to enter a program, copy the appropriate model and give the copy the name you want (e.g., **copy mainmod.asm newprog.asm**). Finally, use the editor to insert your instructions and data.

2.9 COM Files

DOS can actually work with two different kinds of assembly language program files. The kind we have been discussing so far is called an EXE (Execution) file; the other is called a COM (Command) file. In general, programmers use the EXE technique to create large programs—that is, programs that are more than 64K bytes long—and use COM files for smaller programs. In fact, *COM files are limited to 64K.* If your program is bigger, you must create it in EXE form.

You often encounter both kinds of files on purchased disks. For example, DOS 3's COMMAND, BASIC, and BASICA programs are COM files (they have COM extensions), while SORT, FIND, and LINK are EXE files (they have EXE extensions).

The programs in this book are based on the EXE approach (for reasons we discuss later), but it is worth spending a little time describing COM files, in case you want to use that approach or want to understand a COM program you have found in a magazine.

Rules for Creating COM Files

Creating COM files requires a different set of rules than creating EXE files. The Macro Assembler manual gives the full details, but here is a list of the most important points:

1. Omit all stack, data, and extra segments.
2. Define only a code segment, and put any data (as well as instructions) in it.
3. In the ASSUME pseudo-op, point all four segment registers to the code segment. For example,

```
CSEG  SEGMENT  PARA PUBLIC 'CODE'
      ASSUME   CS:CSEG,DS:CSEG,ES:CSEG,SS:CSEG
```

4. Precede the program entry point with

```
ORG  100H
```

which tells the computer to load the program 256 bytes past the beginning of the code segment. This is necessary because, in a COM program, the first 256 bytes are occupied by something called a *program segment prefix* (PSP). We won't go into detail here; they are well described in the Macro Assembler manual and the *DOS Technical Reference.*

5. Put any data ahead of the program instructions. Further, if data is included, start the program with a JMP (Jump) instruction that jumps to the first instruction. For example, to prepare our earlier table-moving program as a COM file, start it with

```
ENTRY:  JMP  OUR_PROG        ;Skip data area
SOURCE  DB   10,20,30,40
DEST    DB   4 DUP(?)
OUR_PROG  PROC  NEAR         ;Program instructions follow
```

6. Define all procedures as NEAR. That is, in the PROC statement, either type NEAR (as we did in rule 5) or omit the operator (the assembler assumes you want NEAR).
7. Follow the END pseudo-op with the label of the first instruction, as in

```
END  ENTRY
```

Rules for Secondary Modules

Those are the rules for the main program module. Any *secondary* module (one that contains a program the main module calls) must abide by the same rules, but note:

1. Give the secondary module's segment the same name as the main module. Hence, if you have named the main segment CSEG, you must also name the secondary segment CSEG.
2. As with EXE files, do not label the secondary module's END statement.

Example

Example 2-3 shows the COM version of our table-copyer, EX_PROG. Note that it is somewhat shorter than before, because it has no stack or data segment and no instructions that push a return address on the stack or that initialize DS. For this reason, the COM file also takes up less space on disk or in memory than the EXE version, and it runs faster. Note also that the program begins with an ORG 100H statement (the tipoff that it is of the COM, rather than the EXE, variety) and that the OUR_PROG procedure is NEAR instead of FAR.

Creating COM Files

To create an executable COM file, begin by producing an EXE file as before; that is, enter the program, assemble it, and link it. This time, however, LINK displays

```
Warning: No STACK segment.
```

Don't panic—this is just a warning, not an error message. There is no stack segment because you are working with a COM file, which does not allow a stack segment.

With an EXE file you would be done at this point. But creating a COM file requires one more step: you must convert the EXE file to a COM file, using the DOS *EXE2BIN* program.

Assuming your assembler disk is in drive A and your data disk is in drive B, run EXE2BIN by entering a command of the form

a:exe2bin *progname progname*.**com**

Example 2-3. COM version of table-copying program.

```
        PAGE   ,132
TITLE   EX_PROGC - Example Program, COM version

CSEG    SEGMENT PARA PUBLIC 'CODE'
        ASSUME  CS:CSEG,DS:CSEG,ES:CSEG,SS:CSEG

        ORG    100H           ;ORG required for COM file
ENTRY:  JMP    OUR_PROG       ;Skip data

SOURCE  DB     10,20,30,40    ;This table will be copied into
DEST    DB     4 DUP(?)       ; this table, in reverse order

OUR_PROG PROC NEAR

;   Initialize DEST with zeroes.

        MOV    DEST,0         ;First byte
        MOV    DEST+1,0       ;Second byte
        MOV    DEST+2,0       ;Third byte
        MOV    DEST+3,0       ;Fourth byte

;   Copy SOURCE table into DEST table, in reverse order.

        MOV    AL,SOURCE      ;Copy first byte
        MOV    DEST+3,AL
        MOV    AL,SOURCE+1    ;Copy second byte
        MOV    DEST+2,AL
        MOV    AL,SOURCE+2    ;Copy third byte
        MOV    DEST+1,AL
        MOV    AL,SOURCE+3    ;Copy fourth byte
        MOV    DEST,AL
        RET                   ;Return to DEBUG
OUR_PROG ENDP
CSEG    ENDS
        END    ENTRY
```

Once EXE2BIN has finished, erase the EXE file. It has been replaced with a COM file, so you no longer need it.

Now you can run the final COM program as you would run an EXE program, using either DOS or DEGUG. However, to view data tables under DEBUG, as you would want to do with our example program, you must look in a different place in a COM program than in an EXE program.

Viewing Data in COM Programs

As we mentioned in Section 2.7, to view data tables in an EXE program, you tell DEBUG to display the beginning of the data segment by entering

d ds:0. By contrast, in a COM program the data is included in the code segment, the only segment there is. To display it, you cannot simply ask DEBUG for **cs:0,** because the data does not start there. Instead, it starts past the program segment prefix (PSP) and the JMP instruction at the beginning of the program.

The PSP is 256 bytes long—or, in hexadecimal, 100H bytes (remember, that's the reason for the ORG 100H statement)—and the JMP instruction is three bytes long. Therefore, the data starts 103H bytes past the beginning of the code segment, and thus the correct DEBUG command to display it is

d cs:103

Remember this oddball number if you are working with COM files.

Models for COM Programs

In Section 2.8 we presented generalized models that you can use to enter EXE programs, one for a main module and the other for a secondary module. Examples 2-4 and 2-5 show the corresponding models for COM programs. On the optional disk, they are *MAINMODC.ASM* and *SECMODC.ASM*.

Example 2-4. Model for main COM module.

```
        PAGE   ,132
TITLE (Insert title here.)
(Insert EXTRN statement, if appropriate.)

CSEG    SEGMENT PARA PUBLIC 'CODE'
        ASSUME  CS:CSEG,DS:CSEG,ES:CSEG,SS:CSEG

        ORG     100H            ;Skip to end of the PSP
ENTRY:  JMP     START           ;Skip data

(Insert data here.)

START   PROC    NEAR

(Insert instructions here.)

        RET                     ;Return to DOS or DEBUG
START   ENDP
CSEG    ENDS
        END     ENTRY
```

Example 2-5. Model for secondary COM module.

```
        PAGE  ,132
TITLE (Insert title here.)

        PUBLIC  PNAME
(Insert PUBLIC for data variables, if appropriate.)

CSEG    SEGMENT PARA PUBLIC 'CODE'
        ASSUME  CS:CSEG,DS:CSEG,ES:CSEG,SS:CSEG

(Insert data here.)

PNAME   PROC  NEAR

(Insert instructions here.)

        RET                     ;Return to calling program
PNAME   ENDP
CSEG    ENDS
        END
```

Pros and Cons of COM Files

Designing a program as a COM file has certain advantages over designing it as an EXE file. Then again, it has certain disadvantages. Among the advantages of COM files are:

1. They are inherently shorter than EXE files.
2. They generally load faster than EXE files.
3. They are somewhat easier to write, because you don't initialize the stack, the DS register, or the ES register.

COM files also have the following drawbacks:

1. They can be no longer than 64K bytes.
2. They require stricter (albeit simpler) coding methods.
3. They can only have one segment, and thus do not provide a clean separation between data and instructions.
4. They cannot access procedures or data that are in another segment. This makes it particularly difficult to use modules that were constructed by other programmers, who may have named their segment different than you have named yours.

Because of this last reason, I have designed every example in this book as an

EXE. You can, of course, use whichever approach you prefer in your own programs.

2.10 Advanced Pseudo-Ops

In Section 2.5 we discussed the assembler pseudo-ops that you will probably use most often. This section describes additional pseudo-ops that are less common, or used by advanced programmers. Table 2-9 lists these advanced pseudo-ops in three groups: data, conditional, and listing.

Table 2-9. Advanced pseudo-ops.

Type	Pseudo-Ops		
Data	GROUP	LABEL	

Conditional	ELSE
	ENDIF
	IF
	IFDEF
		IFNDEF
		IFDIF
		IFE
		IFIDN
			IF1
			IF2

Listing	.CREF .LFCOND .LIST	%OUT .SFCOND .XREF	.XLIST

Data Pseudo-Ops

Table 2-10 describes the assembler's advanced data pseudo-ops.

Table 2-10. Advanced data pseudo-ops.

Pseudo-Op	Function
GROUP	Format: `name GROUP seg-name[,...]` Collects the specified segments under one name, so they all reside within a 64K-byte physical segment.
LABEL	Format: `name LABEL type` Defines the attributes of *name*.

The GROUP pseudo-op gives a name to a collection of segments. This makes all elements in those segments addressable with one setting of a segment register. If you follow the rules that are outlined in the *Macro Assembler Reference* manual, you can also ensure that your GROUPed segments are all stored within one 64K physical segment.

You can, for instance, use GROUP to create a COM file that has separate code and data segments, rather than one segment with a JMP over the data. The GROUP description in the *Macro Assembler Reference* shows an example of this.

As another application, suppose you want to use two procedures that are in external disk files. The problem is that both procedures are NEAR, but they are in code segments that have different names than your code segment. Specifically, PROC1 is in CODESEG and its data is in DATASEG, while PROC2 is in CODE_SEG and its data is in DATA_SEG. Since NEAR procedures can only be called from within the same segment, it looks like you're out of luck. GROUP to the rescue! Your calling program can reach these foreign beasts with the kind of approach shown in Example 2-6.

Example 2-6. Example of groups.

```
; Define externally-used segments

CODESEG  SEGMENT  PARA PUBLIC 'CODE
         EXTRN    PROC1:NEAR
CODESEG  ENDS
CODE_SEG  SEGMENT  PARA PUBLIC 'CODE
          EXTRN    PROC1:NEAR
CODE_SEG  ENDS
DATASEG  SEGMENT  PARA PUBLIC 'DATA'
DATASEG  ENDS
DATA_SEG  SEGMENT  PARA PUBLIC 'DATA'
DATA_SEG  ENDS

; Define code and data groups

CGROUP  GROUP  CSEG,CODESEG,CODE_SEG
DGROUP  GROUP  DATASEG,DATA_SEG

;  The main program follows

CSEG  SEGMENT  PARA PUBLIC 'CODE'
      ASSUME   CS:CGROUP,DS:DGROUP,SS:STACK
ENTRY  PROC  FAR
       ..
       ..
       MOV   AX,DGROUP    ;Make DS point to DGROUP
       MOV   DS,AX
       ..
       ..
       CALL  PROC1        ;Call external procedures
       CALL  PROC2
       ..
       ..
       RET
ENTRY  ENDP
CSEG  ENDS
      END  ENTRY
```

Here, we set up dummy definitions for the segments that are being grouped, and put EXTRNs for the procedures within the code segments in which they appear (this helps the Linker find them). Next we define two groups, CGROUP for code segments and DGROUP for data segments. Finally, we set up the calling program. Note that its ASSUME points to the groups rather than to individual segments, and that we make DS point to DGROUP.

A hazard of using GROUP is in instructions like *MOV DX,OFFSET MESSAGE,* since the offset used is the offset within its segment, not the offset from where the segment register is based. To make it work, you must enter it as *MOV DX,OFFSET CGROUP:MSG.* The Macro Assembler manuals describe a few other potential GROUP hazards.

The LABEL pseudo-op defines the *segment, offset,* and *type* attributes of *name.* You can use LABEL to give an instruction a FAR attribute, so that a jump instruction in another segment can transfer to it. For example,

```
HERE  LABEL   FAR
      MOV     DX,0
```

labels the MOV instruction *HERE.*

You can also use LABEL to access bytes in a table of word values, or vice versa. For example, the 80286 recognizes the following as either a byte table called B_TABLE or a word table called W_TABLE:

```
B_TABLE  LABEL  BYTE
W_TABLE  DW     2F24H,36AH,0817H,3
```

Conditional Pseudo-Ops

Conditional pseudo-ops cause the assembler to either assemble or skip a set of source statements, based on whether a specified condition is "true" or "false" at assembly time. This selective assemble/don't-assemble capability lets you place diagnostics or special conditions in test runs, or create specialized versions of a multipurpose program.

To "conditionally assemble" a portion of a program, precede it with an *IF* pseudo-op (see Table 2-11) and follow it with an *ENDIF* pseudo-op. In each case, if the test condition evaluates as "true," the enclosed code is assembled; if the condition evaluates as "false," the assembler skips the code and continues with the statement that follows ENDIF.

We can group the eight IF pseudo-ops into four pairs, as follows:

- IFE is true if *expression* is 0; IF is true if *expression* is not 0.

Table 2-11. Conditional pseudo-ops.

Pseudo-Op	Function
IFE	Format: IFE expression True if *expression* is 0.
IF	Format: IF expression True if *expression* is not 0.
IF1	Format: IF1 True if assembler is executing pass 1.
IF2	Format: IF2 True if assembler is executing pass 2.
IFDEF	Format: IFDEF symbol True if *symbol* is defined or has been declared external by an EXTRN pseudo-op.
IFNDEF	Format: IFNDEF symbol True if *symbol* is undefined or not declared external by an EXTRN pseudo-op.
IFIDN	Format: IFIDN <string1>,<string2> True if *string1* and *string2* are identical. Angle brackets required.
IFIDF	Format: IFIDF <string1>,<string2> True if *string1* and *string2* are different. Angle brackets are required.

- IF1 is true when the assembler is executing pass 1; IF2 is true when it is executing pass 2.
- IFDEF is true if *symbol* is defined or has been declared external by an EXTRN pseudo-op; otherwise, IFNDEF is true.
- IFIDN is true if strings *argument-1* and *argument-2* are identical; IFIDF is true if they are different.

For example, to include diagnostic routines in a test run, you could enclose them with IFE and ENDIF, and set up a constant called FOR_TEST_ONLY. At assembly time, the assembler checks the value of FOR_TEST_ONLY. If it is 0, the diagnostics are included in (assembled into) the program. If FOR_TEST_ONLY has any other value, the diagnostics are omitted. The program might have this form:

```
        IFE   FOR_TEST_ONLY
DIAG1:  ..        (diagnostic test instructions)
        ..
        ENDIF
```

The instructions between DIAG1 and ENDIF are assembled only if a statement such as

```
FOR_TEST_ONLY   =  0
```

appears earlier in the program. A statement such as

```
FOR_TEST_ONLY   =  1
```

makes the assembler skip the instructions between DIAG1 and ENDIF.

ELSE Option

You can also include an ELSE term to generate an *alternate* set of instructions for the "false" case. The general format is:

```
IFxx  [argument]
  ..     (statements for "true" case)
  ..
[ELSE]
  ..     (statements for "false" case)
  ..
ENDIF
```

The ELSE option allows you, for example, to produce two versions of a program: one that displays prompts and messages in English and another that displays them in Spanish. To do this, you could set up a constant called LANGUAGE to select the instructions that deal with each language. If LANGUAGE is 0, the assembler produces the English version; if LANGUAGE is 1, it produces the Spanish version. A message-related section of the program may then have this form:

```
IFE  LANGUAGE
  ..          (English-producing statements)
  ..
ELSE
  ..          (Spanish-producing statements)
  ..
ENDIF
```

Nesting Conditionals

You can give the assembler more than two options by *nesting* conditional clauses. For example, suppose the Spanish version of your program really caught on, and you decide to produce other versions that display messages and prompts in French and German. To do this, you could modify the program so the assembler selects the language based on whether LANGUAGE has a value of 0, 1, 2, or 3 (for English, Spanish, French, or German). Now the message section may have this form:

```
IFE  LANGUAGE
  ..          (English-producing statements)
  ..
ELSE
  IFE  LANGUAGE-1
    ..        (Spanish-producing statements)
    ..
  ELSE
    IFE  LANGUAGE-2
      ..      (French-producing statements)
      ..
    ELSE
      ..      (German-producing statements)
      ..
    ENDIF
  ENDIF
ENDIF
```

Note that we need three separate ENDIFs to balance the preceding IFEs. Note also that we have indented the IFE-ENDIF pairs to make the program easier to read.

Listing Pseudo-Ops

Listing pseudo-ops tell the assembler what to print and how to format it. Table 2-12 summarizes them as four functional groups.

Listing Control Pseudo-Ops

Pseudo-ops .XCREF and .CREF let you exclude portions of a program from the cross-reference file (.CREF), while .XLIST and .LIST let you exclude them from the assembler listing file (.LST). You can use .LIST and .XLIST to print selected procedures within a long program; put .LIST at the beginning of a procedure and .XLIST at the end.

Display Status Message Pseudo-Op

The %OUT pseudo-op displays a message while a program is being assembled. This is useful for reporting on the progress of a long assembly. For example, the following tells you when the assembler has reached the halfway point in its two-pass assembly procedure.

```
IF2
  %OUT  Starting assembly pass 2
ENDIF
```

Table 2-12. Listing pseudo-ops.

Pseudo-Op	Function
Listing Control	
.XCREF	Format: `.XRCEF` Turns off cross-reference listing between here and the next .CREF (if any).
.CREF	Format: `.CREF` Restores cross-reference listing.
.XLIST	Format: `.XLIST` Turns off assembly listing between here and the next .LIST (if any).
.LIST	Format: `.LIST` Restores assembly listing.
Display Status Message	
%OUT	Format: `%OUT   text` Displays the *text* message.
False Conditional Block Control	
.LFCOND	Format: `.LFCOND` Lists all conditional blocks. This is the default setting.
.SFCOND	Format: `.SFCOND` Omits "false" conditional blocks from the listing.

If you see the message, wait; otherwise, take a walk out to the coffee machine.

False Conditional Block Control Pseudo-Ops

From our discussion of conditional assembly, you know that if an IF pseudo-op evaluates as "false," the assembler ignores everything between IF and the next ENDIF. However, you will probably want to *list* those unassembled statements eventually, so you can see your program in its entirety.

.LFCOND and .SFCOND control the listing of conditional blocks. Quite simply, .LFCOND causes everything in conditional blocks to be listed, while .SFCOND omits false conditional blocks from the listing.

2.11 Key Point Summary

Following are the keys points you learned in this chapter:

1. Lines in a program, or *statements*, can represent either assembly language instructions or pseudo-ops. Assembly language instructions are commands to the computer's microprocessor, while pseudo-ops are commands to the assembler.
2. Each assembly language statement can have up to four fields, as follows:

   ```
   [Label:]  Mnemonic  [Operand]  [;Comment]
   ```

   The label field assigns a name to an instruction, which lets other instructions refer to this instruction. Every label must be followed with a colon. The mnemonic field contains the two- to seven-letter acronym for the instruction. The operand field tells the 80286 where to find the data it is to operate on. The comment field lets you include a short description of the instruction; it must be preceded by a semicolon.
3. Each pseudo-op statement can have up to four fields, as follows:

   ```
   [Name]  Pseudo-op  [Operand]  [;Comment]
   ```

4. The most frequently-used pseudo-ops can be divided into three groups: data, listing, and mode.
5. *Data pseudo-ops* can be divided into five groups: symbol definition, data definition, external reference, segment/procedure specification, and assembly control.
6. There are two *symbol definition pseudo-ops,* EQU and = EQU assigns a name to an expression permanently, while = assigns one temporarily; you can redefine it later.
7. There are three *data definition pseudo-ops*: DB (Define Byte), DW (Define Word), and DD (Define Doubleword). DB and DW are generally used to allocate memory space for variables, while DD is used to allocate space for an address. In all three cases, you can either specify an initial value or simply reserve space in memory; to reserve space, put ? in the operand field.

   To set up a table, enter the elements with commas between them. To make the assembler repeat a value, tell it how many times to repeat using a DUP operator.
8. The *segment/procedure specification pseudo-ops* include SEGMENT and ENDS, which are used to define segments, PROC and ENDP, which are used to define procedures, and ASSUME, which identifies the kinds of segments (code, data, extra, or stack) you are using.

Procedures can be NEAR or FAR. NEAR procedures can be called only from within the code segment, while FAR procedures can be called from other code segments.

9. *External reference pseudo-ops* allow you to use information (e.g., a procedure or a variable) that is in a file elsewhere in the system. PUBLIC makes symbols available to other modules that are eventually linked to this one. Its opposite, EXTRN, specifies the external symbols a module refers to. INCLUDE merges an external file into the current source file at assembly time.
10. The *assembly control pseudo-ops* are END and EVEN. END marks the end of a source module, so it must appear in every module. EVEN can be used to align variables on an even-numbered boundary; this makes data accesses execute faster.
11. The *listing pseudo-ops* control the format of assembly listings. PAGE specifies the length and width of the page, while TITLE and SUBTTL are used to insert a title or subtitle.
12. The assembler assumes that your program contains only 8086/8088 instructions. To use any instructions that are unique to the 80286, give a .286C pseudo-op.
13. There are five kinds of *operators*: arithmetic, logical, relational, value-returning, and attribute.
14. *Arithmetic operators* include the standard ones for addition, subtraction, multiplication, and division (+, -, *, and /), plus MOD, which returns the remainder of a division.
15. The *logical operators* AND, OR, XOR, and NOT let you manipulate individual bits in a binary number.
16. The *relational operators* compare the magnitude of two operands with tests for equal (EQ), not equal (NE), less than (LT), greater than (GT), less than or equal to (LE), or greater than or equal to (GE).
17. The two most common *value-returning operators* are SEG and OFFSET, which return the segment or offset value of a variable or label.
18. The most useful *attribute operators* are DS:, ES:, SS:, and CS:. They let you specify a segment that is different from the one the processor normally uses to transfer data to or from a memory location.
19. There are two kinds of program structures, EXE and COM. EXE programs contain multiple segments and may be any length. COM programs contain only one segment and may be up to 64K bytes long.
20. To develop a program, you must enter it into the computer (using EDLIN or a word processor), then assemble it and link it. A COM program must also be converted to COM format. Assuming your assembler disk is in drive A and your data disk is in drive B, and that B is active, the general command forms are:

a:edlin *progname*.**asm**	(edit)
a:masm *progname*;	(assemble)
a:link *progname*;	(link)

a:exe2bin ***progname progname*.com** (convert, for COM)

To link several modules, list their names, separated with + signs (e.g., link mod1+mod2).

21. You may run a program under DEBUG or DOS. Use DEBUG if the program does not produce visible results. The general command form for DEBUG is:

```
a:debug progname.exe (or .com)
then g [offset]
```

The general form for DOS is:

progname

Study Exercises (answers on page 400)

1. How many *bytes* does the following sequence allocate in memory?

```
VAR1  DB  ?
VAR2  DW  4 DUP(?),20
VAR3  DB  10 DUP(?)
```

2. What value does the assembler put into VAR1 in Exercise 1?
3. How do the following statements differ?

```
K  EQU  1024
K  =    1024
```

4. What is wrong with this sequence?

```
CONST  DB    ?
       MOV   CONST,256
```

5. Which pseudo-ops mark the beginning and end of every procedure?
6. What is the difference between a NEAR procedure and a FAR procedure?
7. What does the following ASSUME statement do?

```
ASSUME  CS:CSEG
```

8. What does the Linker program do?

3

80286 Instruction Set

In Chapter 2 you became acquainted with Move and a few other rudimentary instructions. In this chapter we describe the 80286's entire instruction set. The 80286 has a few instructions and features that the 8088 does not have. For the benefit of readers who have programmed the IBM PC, XT, or some other 8088- or 8086-based computer, we will note the differences. We will also discuss the techniques the 80286 uses to obtain data that instructions will operate on; these are called its *operand addressing modes.*

Some books cover the instructions individually, discussing them in alphabetical order. Although this approach is suitable for reference manuals, it tends to leave readers bored and bewildered after the fifth or sixth instruction.

In this book we group instructions by function, describing similar instructions together. For example, we group add instructions with subtract instructions, shifts with rotates, and so on. This should help you understand the instruction set and appreciate how individual instructions relate to each other, so you don't learn them as just a lot of disjointed entities.

Later, after running a few programs, you will need to refer to this chapter only occasionally, to look up details of specific instructions. Generally, you should be able to resolve most questions by referring to Appendix D, where the instructions are summarized alphabetically. Appendix C is also useful; it tells you how long each instruction takes to execute.

3.1 Addressing Modes

The 80286 (or "286" for short) provides a variety of ways to obtain the operands your programs are to operate on. It can obtain them from a register, from within the instruction itself, or from a memory location or an I/O port. Some people claim that the 286 has 24 operand addressing modes—and perhaps they are right if you consider all the possible operand combinations. In this book, however, we divide the addressing modes into seven groups:

1. Register addressing
2. Immediate addressing
3. Direct addressing
4. Register indirect addressing
5. Base relative addressing
6. Direct indexed addressing
7. Base indexed addressing

The microprocessor determines *which* of the seven addressing modes to use by examining the contents of a "mode field" in the instruction. The assembler sets up the mode field based on how the operand(s) appear in your source program. For instance, if you write

```
MOV   AX,BX
```

the assembler encodes both operands (*AX* and *BX*) for the register addressing mode. However, if you put brackets around the source operand, and write

```
MOV   AX,[BX]
```

the assembler encodes the source operand (BX) for the register *indirect* addressing mode.

Table 3-1 shows the assembler format, and which segment register is used to calculate the physical address, for the 286's seven operand addressing modes. Note that all modes assume that you are referring to data in the data segment (DS is the segment register) except those that involve BP, in which case the stack segment is assumed (SS is the segment register).

Note: The 286's string instructions (described in Section 3.7) assume that DI points to a location in the extra segment rather than the data segment. Hence, they use ES as the segment register. All other instructions use the assignments shown in Table 3-1.

In the sections that follow, each time we describe an addressing mode, we will illustrate its usage with an example. Generally, we employ the 286's *MOV* (Move) instruction to illustrate it.

Table 3-1. 80286 addressing modes.

Addressing Mode	Operand Format	Segment Register
Register	reg	None
Immediate	data	None
Direct	disp	DS
	label	DS
Register indirect	[BX]	DS
	[BP]	SS
	[DI]	DS
	[SI]	DS
Base relative	[BX]+disp	DS
	[BP]+disp	SS
Direct indexed	[DI]+disp	DS
	[SI]+disp	DS
Base indexed	[BX][SI]+disp	DS
	[BX][DI]+disp	DS
	[BP][SI]+disp	SS
	[BP][DI]+disp	SS

Notes: 1. *disp* is optional for base indexed addressing.
2. *reg* can be any 8- or 16-bit register, except IP.
3. *data* can be an 8- or 16-bit constant value.
4. *disp* can be an 8- or 16-bit signed displacement value.

Register and Immediate Addressing

In *register addressing,* the 286 fetches an operand from (or loads it into) a register. For example, the instruction

```
MOV   AX,CX
```

copies the 16-bit contents of the count register (CX) into the accumulator register (AX). It does not alter the contents of CX. Here, the 286 uses register addressing to fetch the source operand from CX and to load it into the destination register, AX.

Immediate addressing lets you specify an 8- or 16-bit constant value as a source operand. This constant is contained in the instruction (where it was put by the assembler), rather than in a register or memory location. For example,

```
MOV   CX,500
```

loads the decimal value 500 into the CX register and

```
MOV   CL,-30
```

loads -30 into the CL register.

The immediate operand may also be a symbol that was defined by an EQU directive, so this kind of form is valid:

```
K EQU   1024
  ..
  ..
  MOV   CX,K
```

To avoid problems, remember that 8-bit signed numbers can range from 127 (7FH) to -128 (80H) and that 16-bit signed numbers can range from 32767 (7FFFH) to -32768 (8000H). The maximum 8- and 16-bit unsigned values are 255 (0FFH) and 65535 (0FFFFH), respectively.

Immediate Values Are Sign-Extended

The assembler always *sign-extends* immediate values in the destination. That is, it duplicates the most-significant bit of the source value to fill the 8 or 16 bits of the destination operand.

For example, if you enter *MOV CX,500*, the assembler sees the source value, decimal 500, as the 10-bit binary pattern 0111110100. To load this value into the 16-bit destination register (CX), it extends the pattern to 16 bits by preceding it with six copies of the "sign" bit value (0). Therefore, CX ends up containing binary *000000*0111110100. In the second example, the 286 loads the 8-bit binary pattern for -30 (11100010) into CL.

Memory Addressing Modes

As we mentioned in Chapter 1, accessing memory involves a joint effort by the 286's Execution Unit (EU) and Bus Unit (BU). When the EU needs to read or write a memory operand, it passes an offset value to the BU. The BU adds this offset to the contents of a segment register (with four zeros appended) to produce a 20-bit physical address, then it uses that address to access the operand.

The Effective Address (EA)

The offset that the Execution Unit calculates for a memory operand is called the *effective address* (EA). The EA is the distance in bytes from the beginning of the segment to the operand's location. Being a 16-bit unsigned value, the EA can refer to operands that lie anywhere in a segment; that is, up to 65,535 (or 64K) bytes past the beginning of the segment.

The amount of time the Execution Unit takes to calculate the EA is a prime factor in determining how long an instruction takes to execute. Depending on which addressing mode you are using, obtaining the EA may involve something as simple as fetching a displacement from within the instruction. Then again, it may require some lengthy calculation, such as adding a displacement, a base register, and an index register. Regardless of whether execution time is critical in your programs, you should appreciate these time factors as you read the addressing mode descriptions that follow.

Direct Addressing

With direct addressing, the EA is contained in the instruction (just as immediate data values are contained in instructions). The 286 adds the EA to the (shifted) contents of the Data Segment (DS) register to produce the operand's 20-bit physical address.

The direct addressing operand is generally a label. For example, the instruction

```
MOV   AX,TABLE
```

loads the contents of data memory location TABLE into the AX register. Figure 3-1 shows how this instruction works.

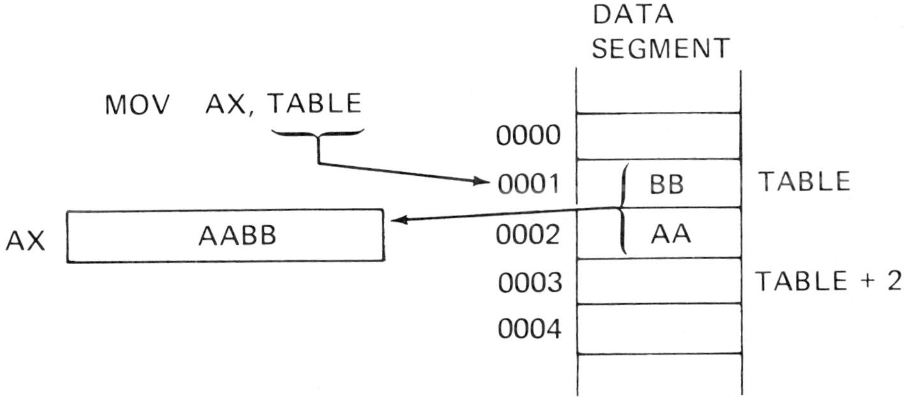

Figure 3-1. Direct addressing.

Note that the 286 stores data in memory in the reverse order you would expect: it puts the high-order byte *after* (rather than before) the low-order byte. To keep this straight, just remember that *the high (most-significant) part of the data is in the highest memory address.*

Register Indirect Addressing

With register indirect addressing, the effective address of the operand is contained in base register BX, base pointer BP, or an index register (SI or DI). You must enclose register indirect operands in square brackets to distinguish them from register operands. For example, the instruction

```
MOV   AX,[BX]
```

loads the contents of the memory location addressed by BX into the AX register. Figure 3-2 illustrates this example.

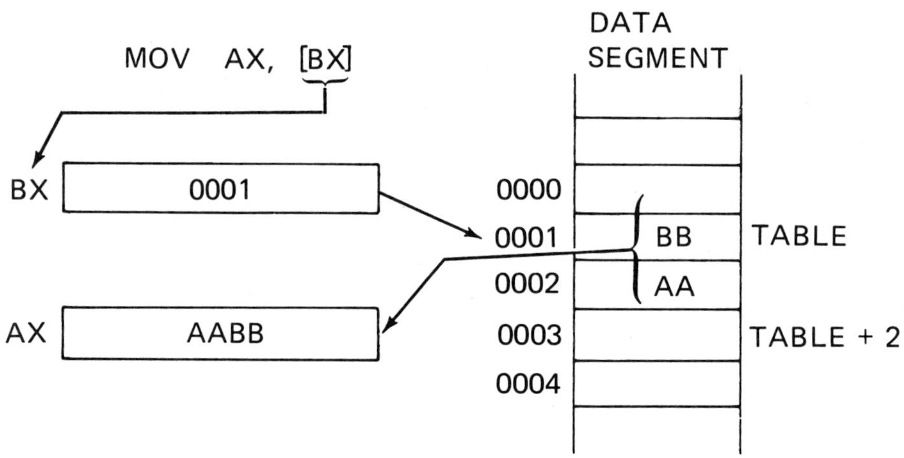

Figure 3-2. Register indirect addressing.

How do you put an offset into BX? One way is by entering an OFFSET prefix ahead of the memory address. For example, to load the word at location *TABLE* into AX, use the sequence

```
MOV   BX,OFFSET TABLE
MOV   AX,[BX]
```

These two instructions do the same job as the single instruction

```
MOV   AX,TABLE
```

except that they destroy the previous contents of BX. If you want to access just one memory location (the contents of TABLE here), this single-instruction approach makes more sense. However, to access *several* locations, starting at some base address, having the effective address in a register is better. Why? Because you can manipulate the contents of the register without fetching a new address each time.

Base Relative Addressing

With base relative addressing, the assembler calculates the effective address by adding a displacement value to the contents of the BX or BP register.

The BX form gives you a convenient way to access data structures that are located in different parts of memory. To do this, you put the base address of the structure into the base register and refer to elements of the structure by their displacement from the base. After that, you can access different records in the structure by simply changing the base register.

For example, suppose you have read some personnel records from disk, where each record contains an employee's identification number, department number, division number, age, pay rate, etc. If the division number is stored in the fifth and sixth bytes of the record, and the starting address of the record is in BX, the instruction

```
MOV   AX,[BX]+4
```

loads the employee's division number into AX. (The displacement is 4, rather than 5, because the first byte is numbered 0.) Figure 3-3 illustrates this example.

The IBM Macro Assembler lets you specify the base relative operand in three different ways. The following are equivalent instructions:

```
MOV   AX,[BP]+4    ;This is the standard form, but you may
MOV   AX,4[BP]     ; put the displacement first
MOV   AX,[BP+4]    ; or within the brackets.
```

Direct Indexed Addressing

With direct indexed addressing, the effective address is the sum of a displacement and an index register, either DI or SI. This type of addressing is convenient for accessing elements in a table; the displacement points to the beginning of the table and the index register points to an element in it.

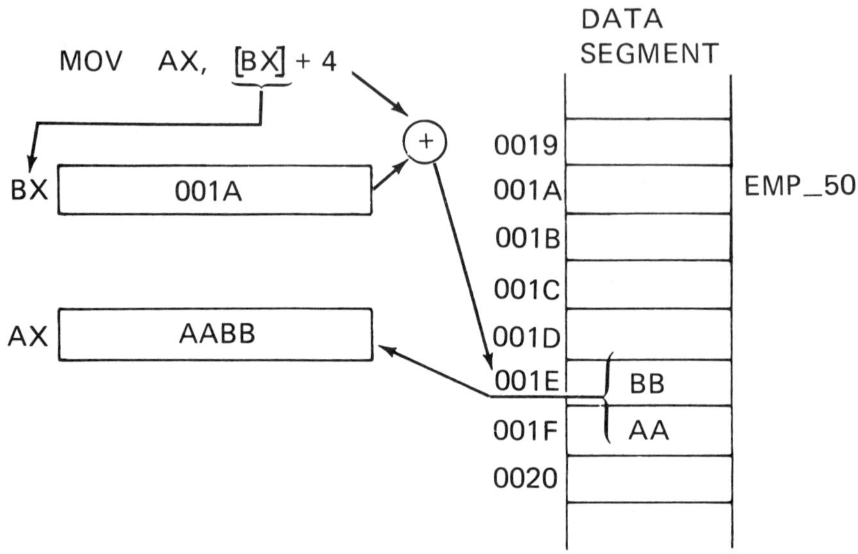

Figure 3-3. Base relative addressing.

For example, if we have a byte table called B_TABLE, the instruction sequence

```
MOV  DI,2
MOV  AL,B_TABLE[DI]
```

loads the third element into the AL register.

In a word table, the elements are two bytes apart, so you must *double the element number* to get its index value. With a word table called TABLE, the instruction sequence

```
MOV  DI,4
MOV  AX,TABLE[DI]
```

loads the third element into the AX register. Figure 3-4 illustrates this example.

Base Indexed Addressing

With base indexed addressing, the EA is the sum of a base register, an index register, and (optionally) a displacement.

Because it accepts two separate offsets, this mode is useful for accessing two-dimensional arrays. Here, the base register holds the starting address of the array, and the displacement and index register provide row and column offsets.

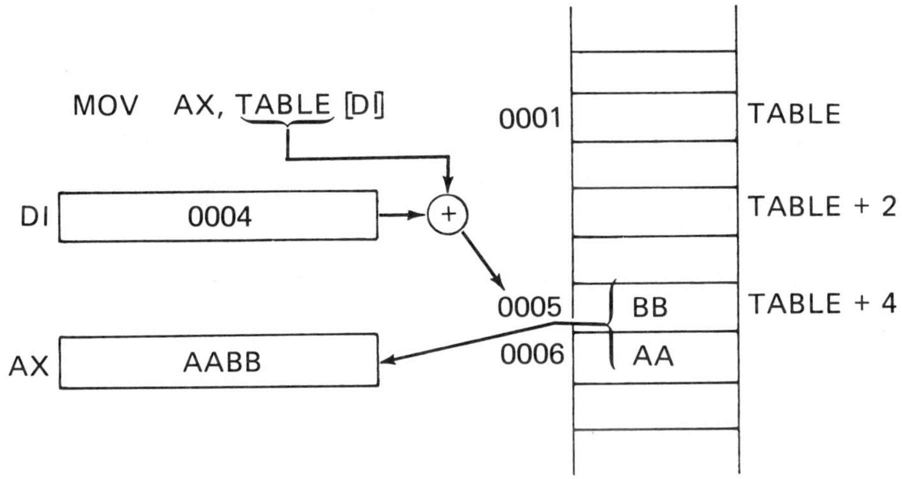

Figure 3-4. Direct indexed addressing.

For example, suppose your computer monitors six pressure valves in a chemical processing plant. It reads the valve settings every half-hour and records them in memory. In one week, these readings form an array that has 336 blocks (48 readings per day for seven days) of six elements each, a total of 2,016 data values.

If the starting address of the array is in BX, the block displacement (reading number times 12) is in DI, and the valve number displacement is defined by the variable VALVE, you can use the instruction

```
MOV   AX,VALVE[BX][DI]
```

to load any selected pressure valve reading into AX. In Figure 3-5, this instruction extracts the third reading (Reading 2) of valve 4 from an array that has a data segment offset of 100H.

Here are some other legal formats for base indexed addressing operands:

```
MOV   AX,[BX+2+DI]    ;You may put all three terms in brackets
MOV   AX,[DI+BX+2]    ; in any order.
MOV   AX,[BX+2][DI]   ;Or you may combine the displacement
MOV   AX,[BX][DI+2]   ; with either register.
```

3.2 Instruction Types

As we mentioned earlier, the 80286 has nearly 100 instruction types. Table 3-2 shows their assembler mnemonics and tells you what each mnemonic stands for. The shaded instructions are new with the 80286; they are not available with the 8088 or 8086.

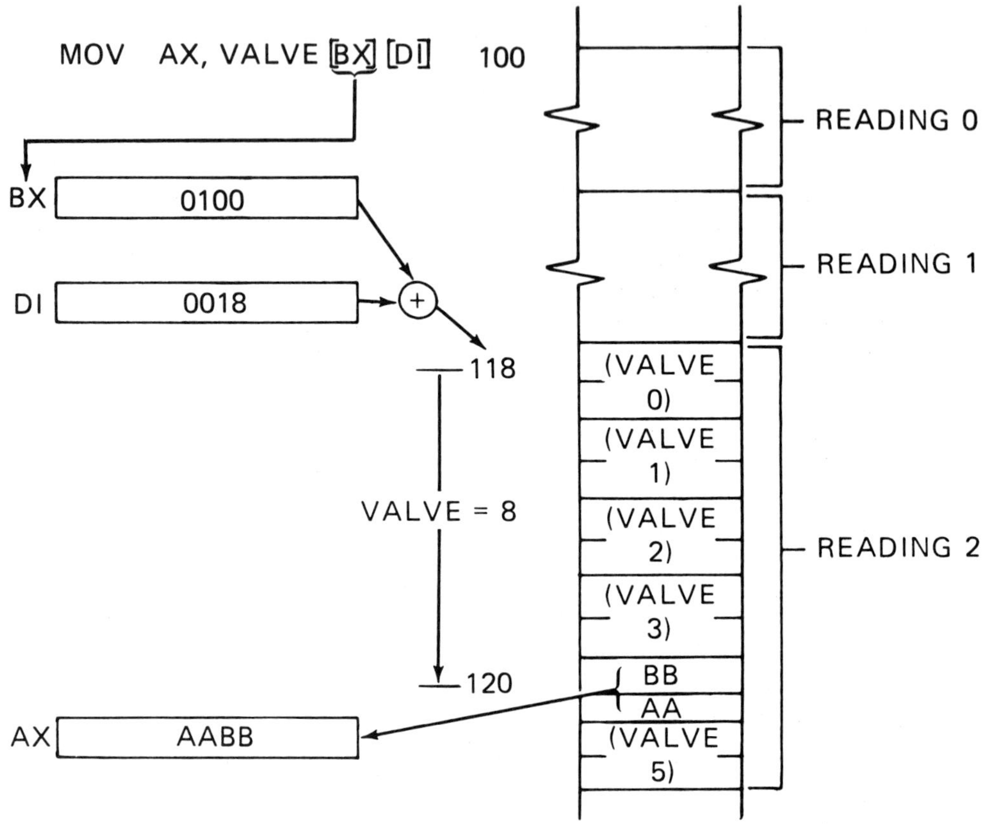

Figure 3-5. Extracting a data value from a two-dimensional array.

Table 3-2. 80286 instruction set.

Mnemonic	Description
AAA	ASCII Adjust for Addition
AAD	ASCII Adjust for Division
AAM	ASCII Adjust for Multiplication
AAS	ASCII Adjust for Subtraction
ADC	Add with Carry
ADD	Add (without Carry)
AND	Logical AND
BOUND	Check Array Index Against Bounds
CALL	Call a Procedure
CBW	Convert Byte to Word
CLC	Clear Carry Flag
CLD	Clear Direction Flag
CLI	Clear Interrupt Flag

Table 3-2. 80286 instruction set (continued).

Mnemonic	Description
CMC	Complement Carry Flag
CMP	Compare Destination to Source
CMPS, CMPSB, or **CMPSW**	Compare Byte or Word Strings
CWD	Convert Word to Doubleword
DAA	Decimal Adjust for Addition
DAS	Decimal Adjust for Subtraction
DEC	Decrement Destination by One
DIV	Divide, Unsigned
ENTER	Make Stack Frame for High-Level Procedure
ESC	Escape
HLT	Halt the Processor
IDIV	Integer Divide, Signed
IMUL	Integer Multiply, Signed
IN	Input Byte or Word
INC	Increment Destination by One
INS, INSB, or **INSW**	Input String
INT	Interrupt
INTO	Interrupt If Overflow
IRET	Interrupt Return
JA or **JNBE**	Jump If Above/If Not Below nor Equal
JAE, JNB, or **JNC**	Jump If Above or Equal/If Not Below/If No Carry
JB, JNAE, or **JC**	Jump If Below/If Not Above nor Equal/If Carry
JBE or **JNA**	Jump If Below or Equal/If Not Above
JCXZ	Jump If CX Is Zero
JE or **JZ**	Jump If Equal/If Zero
JG or **JNLE**	Jump If Greater/If Not Less nor Equal
JGE or **JNL**	Jump If Greater or Equal/If Not Less
JL or **JNGE**	Jump If Less/If Not Greater Nor Equal
JLE or **JNG**	Jump If Less or Equal/If Not Greater
JMP	Jump
JNE or **JNZ**	Jump If Not Equal/If Not Zero
JNO	Jump If No Overflow
JNP or **JPO**	Jump If No Parity/If Parity Odd
JNS	Jump If No Sign (If Positive)
JO	Jump On Overflow
JP or **JPE**	Jump On Parity/If Parity Even
JS	Jump On Sign
LAHF	Load AH from Flags
LDS	Load Pointer Using DS
LEA	Load Effective Address

Table 3-2. 80286 instruction set (continued).

Mnemonic	Description
LEAVE	Exit High-Level Procedure
LES	Load Pointer Using ES
LOCK	Lock the Bus
LODS, LODSB, or LODSW	Load Byte or Word String
LOOP	Loop Until Count Complete
LOOPE or LOOPZ	Loop While Equal/While Zero
LOOPNE or LOOPNZ	Loop While Not Equal/While Not Zero
MOV	Move
MOVS, MOVSB, or MOVSW	Move Byte or Word String
MUL	Multiply, Unsigned
NEG	Negate (Form Two's-Complement)
NOP	No Operation
NOT	Logical NOT
OR	Logical Inclusive-OR
OUT	Output Byte or Word
OUTS, OUTSB or OUTSW	Output String
POP	Pop Word Off Stack
POPA	Pop All General Registers
POPF	Pop Flags Off Stack
PUSH	Push Word onto Stack
PUSHA	Push All General Registers
PUSHF	Push Flags onto Stack
RCL	Rotate Left through Carry
RCR	Rotate Right through Carry
REP, REPE, or REPZ	Repeat String Operation/While Equal/While Zero
REPNE or REPNZ	Repeat String Operation While Not Equal/While Not Zero
RET	Return from Procedure
ROL	Rotate Left
ROR	Rotate Right
SAHF	Store AH into Flags
SAL or SHL	Shift Arithmetic Left/Logical Left
SAR	Shift Arithmetic Right
SBB	Subtract with Borrow
SCAS, SCASB, or SCASW	Scan Byte or Word String
SHR	Shift Logical Right

Table 3-2. 80286 instruction set (continued).

Mnemonic	Description
STC	Set Carry Flag
STD	Set Direction Flag
STI	Set Interrupt Enable Flag
STOS, STOSB, or STOSW	Store Byte or Word String
SUB	Subtract (without Borrow)
TEST	Test (Logically Compare Two Operands)
WAIT	Wait
XCHG	Exchange Two Operands
XLAT	Translate
XOR	Logical Exclusive-OR

We can divide the instruction set into eight functional groups:

1. *Data transfer instructions* move information between registers and memory locations or I/O ports.
2. *Arithmetic instructions* perform add, subtract, multiply, and divide operations on binary or binary-coded decimal (BCD) numbers.
3. *Bit manipulation instructions* perform shift, rotate, and logical operations on memory locations and registers.
4. *Control transfer instructions* can change the sequence in which a program executes; they include jumps and transfers to and from procedures.
5. *String instructions* operate on consecutive units, or strings.
6. *Interrupt instructions* interrupt the microprocessor to make it service some specific condition.
7. *Processor control instructions* set and clear status flags, and change the microprocessor's execution state.
8. *High-level instructions* let you communicate with programs that are written in "block-oriented" high-level languages such as Pascal.

In the following sections we describe the 80286 instruction set according to these groups. Let us begin with the data transfer group, which includes the ubiquitous MOV instruction.

3.3 Data Transfer Instructions

Data transfer instructions move data and addresses between registers and memory locations or I/O ports. Table 3-3 summarizes these instructions in four groups: general-purpose, input/output, address transfer, and flag transfer.

Table 3-3. Data transfer instructions.

Mnemonic	Assembler Format		Flags								
			OF	DF	IF	TF	SF	ZF	AF	PF	CF
General-Purpose											
MOV	MOV	destination,source	-	-	-	-	-	-	-	-	-
PUSH	PUSH	source	-	-	-	-	-	-	-	-	-
PUSH	PUSH	immediate	-	-	-	-	-	-	-	-	-
PUSHA	PUSHA		-	-	-	-	-	-	-	-	-
POP	POP	destination	-	-	-	-	-	-	-	-	-
POPA	POPA		-	-	-	-	-	-	-	-	-
XCHG	XCHG	destination,source	-	-	-	-	-	-	-	-	-
XLAT	XLAT	source-table	-	-	-	-	-	-	-	-	-
Input/Output											
IN	IN	accumulator,port	-	-	-	-	-	-	-	-	-
OUT	OUT	port,accumulator	-	-	-	-	-	-	-	-	-
Address Transfer											
LEA	LEA	reg16,mem16	-	-	-	-	-	-	-	-	-
LDS	LDS	reg16,mem32	-	-	-	-	-	-	-	-	-
LES	LES	reg16,mem32	-	-	-	-	-	-	-	-	-
Flag Transfer											
LAHF	LAHF		-	-	-	-	-	-	-	-	-
SAHF	SAHF		-	-	-	-	*	*	*	*	*
PUSHF	PUSHF		-	-	-	-	-	-	-	-	-
POPF	POPF		*	*	*	*	*	*	*	*	*

Notes: (1) * means changed and - means unchanged.
(2) Shaded instructions are new with the 80286; they are not available with the 8088 or 8086.

General-Purpose Instructions

Move (MOV)

The most common general-purpose instruction, *Move (MOV)*, can transfer a byte or word between a register and a memory location, or between two registers. It can also copy an immediate value (constant) into a register or memory location. The Move instruction has the general form

```
MOV   destination,source
```

Most operand combinations are legal. Here are some examples:

```
MOV   AX,TABLE      ;Move from memory into a register
MOV   TABLE,AX      ; or vice versa
MOV   ES:[BX],AX    ;Override the segment assignment
MOV   DS,AX         ;Move between 16-bit registers
MOV   BL,AL         ; or 8-bit registers
MOV   CL,-30        ;Move a constant into a register
MOV   DEST,25H      ; or into memory
```

There are a few things you *cannot* do with a Move instruction:

1. You cannot move data between two memory locations directly. Instead, you must move the source data into a general-purpose register, then move *that* register into the destination. For example, if POUNDS and WEIGHT are variables in memory, you can give them the same value with:

   ```
   MOV   AX,POUNDS
   MOV   WEIGHT,AX
   ```

2. You cannot load an immediate value into a segment register directly. As with rule 1, you must transfer it through a general-purpose register. For example, the following loads the number of the data segment (DATA_SEG here) into DS:

   ```
   MOV   AX,DATA_SEG
   MOV   DS,AX
   ```

   These instructions tell the 286 which segment in your program is the data segment. You use similar instructions after the ASSUME statement in a code segment.
3. You cannot move the contents of one segment register into another directly. As before, you must transfer through a general-purpose register. For example, to make DS point to the same segment as ES, use

   ```
   MOV   AX,ES
   MOV   DS,AX
   ```

   (You can also use PUSH and POP instructions to perform this operation, as you will see in the next section.)
4. You cannot use the CS register as the destination of a Move instruction.

Push Word onto Stack (PUSH) and Pop Word Off Stack (POP)

We mentioned earlier that the stack holds return addresses while the 286 is executing a procedure. The Call (CALL) instruction puts an address onto the stack and a Return (RET) instruction retrieves it at the conclusion of the procedure. In both cases, the processor uses the stack *automatically;* you don't have to tell it to do so.

The stack is also a convenient place to temporarily deposit data—register and memory operands—from your program. For example, you might want to save the contents of the AX register while you put AX to some other use. Two instructions that let you use the stack are *Push Word onto Stack (PUSH)* and *Pop Word Off Stack (POP).*

PUSH puts the contents of a word-sized (16-bit) register or memory operand on the top of the stack. Conversely, POP retrieves a word from the top of the stack and puts it into a memory location or register. The PUSH and POP instructions have these general formats:

```
PUSH  source
POP   destination
```

There is also a form of PUSH (new with the 80286) that lets you push an immediate value onto the stack. The general form is

```
PUSH  immediate
```

If the value is byte-sized, the 286 sign-extends it to a word before pushing it onto the stack.

Here are some examples:

```
PUSH  SI               ;You can save a general-purpose register
PUSH  DS               ; or a segment register,
PUSH  CS               ; including CS.
PUSH  147EH            ;You can also save a constant
PUSH  TABLE[BX][DI]    ; or the contents of a memory location.
```

Because PUSH and POP are complementary instructions, we generally use them in pairs. That is, we balance each PUSH in a program with a later POP. For example, to preserve the contents of AX on the stack, your program has this form:

```
PUSH  AX   ;Save AX on top of the stack
..           (Other operations are being performed
..            with AX here.)
POP   AX   ;Retrieve AX from top of the stack
```

By "top" of the stack, we mean the location in the stack segment the stack pointer (SP) is pointing to. Since the stack "builds" downward in memory (toward location 0), the first word pushed onto the stack is stored at the end of the stack segment, the next is stored two bytes lower, and so on.

The SP always points to the word that was last pushed onto the stack. Therefore, PUSH subtracts two from the stack pointer before it copies the source word onto the stack. Conversely, POP copies the word addressed by SP to the destination operand, then adds two to the SP.

Figure 3-6 shows the stack and stack pointer before and after a PUSH, and after a POP. Following the PUSH (Figure 3-6B), the stack pointer points two bytes lower in memory and those previously-unused bytes now hold the contents of AX. Following the POP (Figure 3-6C), the SP has its original value. (Note that although AX is still stored at the same location in memory, we no longer consider it as being "on the stack.")

Of course, you can also save several words on the stack by doing a series of pushes. Just remember that because each PUSH puts its data on top of the stack, *you must always POP words in the reverse order you PUSHed them.* For example, the following sequence pushes four registers onto the stack, and later restores them:

```
PUSH  AX   ;Save AX,
PUSH  ES   ; ES,
PUSH  DI   ; DI,
PUSH  SI   ; and SI
..
..
POP   SI   ;Restore SI
POP   DI   ; DI,
POP   ES   ; ES,
POP   AX   ; and AX
```

The 80286 also provides instructions called PUSHA and POPA that transfer all of the general registers. We will discuss them shortly.

PUSH and POP are also convenient for copying one segment register into another. For example, you can copy ES into DS as follows:

```
PUSH  ES
POP   DS
```

The advantage of this technique is that it doesn't require you to use a general-purpose register for intermediate storage (see the preceding section); the drawback is that the PUSH-POP combination takes 10 clock cycles to execute, versus four cycles for a pair of MOV instructions.

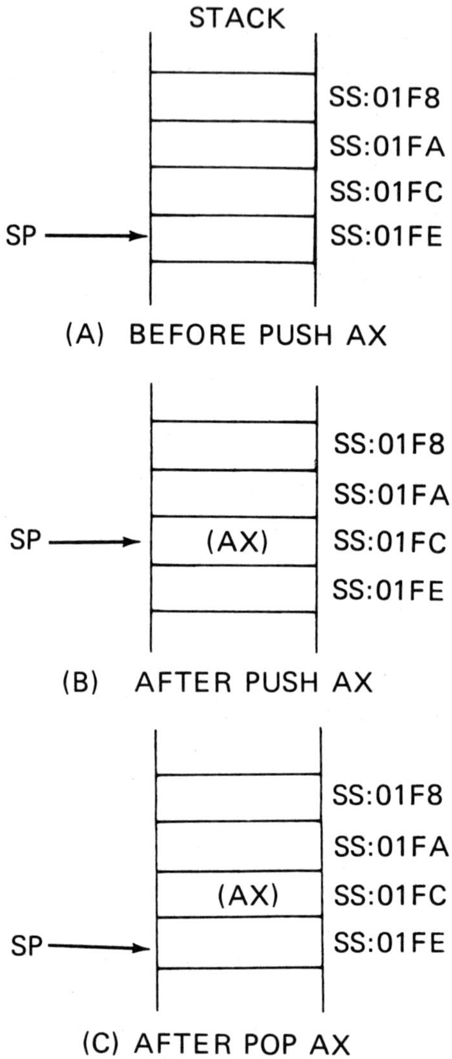

Figure 3-6. How a PUSH and a POP affect the stack.

There are also special instructions that push and pop the contents of the flags register. We'll look at them in the *Flag Transfer* portion of this section.

Push and Pop All General Registers (PUSHA and POPA)

These two instructions, new with the 80286, let you push or pop all of the general registers with one operation. PUSHA transfers them in this order: AX, CX, DX, BX, original SP, BP, SI, and DI. (Note that is does not push the segment registers or the flags register.) POPA restores these registers in the opposite order.

Besides saving you from entering eight PUSH or POP instructions, PUSHA and POPA also make your program easier to read and run faster. PUSHA executes in 17 clock cycles, versus 24 cycles for eight PUSHes; POPA executes in 19 cycles, versus 45 cycles for eight POPs.

Exchange (XCHG)

Exchange (XCHG) swaps the contents of the source and destination operands, either bytes or words. You can swap two registers (except segment registers) or a register and a memory location. Some examples are:

```
XCHG  AX,BX        ;Exchange two word registers
XCHG  AL,BH        ; or two byte registers.
XCHG  WORD_LOC,DX  ;Exchange a memory location
XCHG  DL,BYTE_LOC  ; and a register.
```

Translate (XLAT)

Translate (XLAT) looks up a value in a byte table and loads it into AL. The table may be up to 256 bytes long. XLAT's general format is

```
XLAT  source-table
```

where *source-table* is the name of the look-up table. Before executing XLAT, you must load the table's starting address into BX and the index value of the desired byte into AL.

This sequence looks up the tenth byte in the table S_TAB:

```
MOV   AL,10              ;Load index value into AL
MOV   BX,OFFSET S_TAB    ;Load offset into BX
XLAT  S_TAB              ;Fetch table value into AL
```

XLAT is convenient for making conversions that take a lot of time to calculate, such as finding the ASCII display code for a hexadecimal digit.

Input and Output Instructions

The Input and Output instructions are used to communicate with peripheral devices in the system. They have the general formats

```
IN   accumulator,port
OUT  port,accumulator
```

where *accumulator* is AL for byte transfers and AX for word transfers. The *port* operand is a decimal value between 0 and 255, which refers to one of 256 devices in the system.

The alternate forms

```
IN    accumulator,DX
OUT   DX,accumulator
```

let you use the DX register to hold the port number, giving you access to 64K different ports. Using DX lets you change the port number easily, perhaps to send the same data to several different ports.

Here are a few examples of the IN and OUT instructions:

```
IN    AL,200          ;Input a byte from Port 200
IN    AL,PORT_VAL     ; or from a port named by a constant
OUT   30H,AX          ;Output a word to Port 30H
OUT   DX,AX           ; or to the port specified by DX
```

Address Transfer Instructions

Address transfer instructions move the *addresses* of variables, rather than their contents.

Load Effective Address (LEA)

LEA transfers the offset of a memory operand into any 16-bit general, pointer, or index register. It has the general format

```
LEA   reg16,mem16
```

where *mem16* must have a type attribute of WORD.

Unlike MOV with an OFFSET operator, the memory operand for LEA can be subscripted, which gives you a lot more addressing flexibility. For example, if the DI register contains 5, the instruction

```
LEA   BX,TABLE[DI]
```

loads the offset of TABLE+5 into BX.

We discuss LEA instructions extensively in Section 3.7, where we perform operations on strings.

Load Pointer Using DS (LDS)

The LDS instruction reads a 32-bit doubleword from memory, and loads the low-order 16 bits into a specified register and the high-order 16 bits into DS. The general format is

```
LDS   reg16,mem32
```

where *reg16* is any 16-bit general register and *mem32* is a memory location with a DOUBLEWORD type attribute.

Generally, the *mem32* operand is defined with the Define Doubleword (DD) data definition directive we discussed in Section 2.5. Using the example in that section,

```
HERE_FAR   DD   HERE
```

we can get the offset and segment number of HERE into BX and DS, respectively, with the instruction

```
LDS   BX,HERE_FAR
```

Note that LDS is a one-instruction replacement for a sequence such as

```
MOV   BX,OFFSET HERE
MOV   AX,SEG HERE
MOV   DS,AX
```

Note also that LDS eliminates the need for a third 16-bit register (AX, in this example).

Load Pointer Using ES (LES)

The LES instruction is identical to LDS, except LES transfers the segment number into ES instead of DS.

Flag Transfer Instructions

Load AH from Flags (LAHF) and Store AH into Flags (SAHF)

The LAHF instruction copies the flags register's 8080/8085 flags into AH. Specifically, it copies CF, PF, AF, ZF, and SF into the corresponding bits of AH (0, 2, 4, 6, and 7, respectively). SAHF performs the reverse operation; it loads the five bits of AH we just mentioned into the flags register.

Intel provides LAHF and SAHF for the convenience of those who want to convert 8080 or 8085 programs for use on the later microprocessors. Chances are, you will never use either instruction.

Push Flags onto Stack (PUSHF) and Pop Flags Off Stack (POPF)

These instructions transfer the contents of the flags register to or from the stack. Note that unlike the PUSH and POP instructions, PUSHF and POPF require no operands; they reference the flags register implicitly.

As with PUSH and POP, you must always use PUSHF and POPF in pairs. That is, every PUSHF must have a corresponding POPF later in the program, like this:

```
PUSHF           ;Save flags on stack
..      (Other flag-altering instructions are executed here)
..
POPF            ;Restore flags from stack
```

Note that with PUSH, PUSHA, PUSHF, POP, POPA, and POPF, you can save any or all registers while a procedure or interrupt routine is executing. For example, suppose you have valuable data in AX, DI, and SI, and need to call a procedure named SORT that uses these registers. Suppose also that you have just performed an arithmetic operation, and need to have the flags intact after the procedure. This sequence does the job:

```
PUSH    AX      ;Save the three registers
PUSH    DI
PUSH    SI
PUSHF           ; and the flags
CALL    SORT    ;Call the procedure
POPF            ;Upon return, restore the flags
POP     SI      ; and the three registers
POP     DI
POP     AX
```

An even better idea is to put all required PUSHes and POPs *inside* the procedure, so you don't have to repeat them every time you call it. Hence, for the preceding example, the four PUSHes and four POPs should be the first and last instructions in the SORT procedure. Then you can simply CALL SORT without worrying about which registers are destroyed or preserved.

3.4 Arithmetic Instructions

The 80286 can perform arithmetic operations on signed or unsigned binary numbers and on decimal numbers (either packed or unpacked). As Table 3-4 shows, there are instructions for the four standard arithmetic functions—addition, subtraction, multiplication, and division. There are also instructions that "sign-extend" operands; these let you combine data of different sizes (e.g., they let you add a byte to a word). Before discussing the instructions, let's look at the formats of binary and decimal numbers.

Data Formats

Binary Numbers

Binary numbers may be 8 or 16 bits long, and may be either unsigned or signed. In an *unsigned* number, all bits represent data. Therefore, unsigned numbers can range from 0 to 255 (8 bits) or 65535 (16 bits). In a *signed* number, the high-order bit—7 or 15—specifies the sign of the number; the rest hold data. Therefore, signed numbers can range from 127 to -128 (8 bits) or from 32767 to -32768 (16 bits).

Decimal Numbers

The 286 stores decimal numbers as a series of unsigned byte-size values in either "packed" or "unpacked" form. In a packed decimal number, each byte holds two *binary-coded decimal (BCD)* digits, with the most-significant digit in the upper four bits. Therefore, a packed decimal byte can hold values from 00 to 99.

In an unpacked decimal number, each byte holds just one BCD digit, in the lower four bits. Therefore, a byte can hold values from only 0 to 9. The upper four bits must be zero for multiplication and division, but may be any value for addition or subtraction.

How does the 286 know *which* kind of data you are operating on? For example, if you tell it to add two bytes, how does it know whether they represent signed binary numbers, unsigned binary numbers, packed decimal numbers, or unpacked decimal numbers? The truth is that the 286 neither knows nor cares what the data represents; it treats *all* operands as binary numbers.

Table 3-4. Arithmetic instructions.

Mnemonic	Assembler Format	Flags OF	DF	IF	TF	SF	ZF	AF	PF	CF
Addition										
ADD	ADD destination,source	*	-	-	-	*	*	*	*	*
ADC	ADC destination,source	*	-	-	-	*	*	*	*	*
AAA	AAA	?	-	-	-	?	?	*	?	*
DAA	DAA	?	-	-	-	*	*	*	*	*
INC	INC destination	*	-	-	-	*	*	*	*	-
Subtraction										
SUB	SUB destination,source	*	-	-	-	*	*	*	*	*
SBB	SBB destination,source	*	-	-	-	*	*	*	*	*
AAS	AAS	?	-	-	-	?	?	*	?	*
DAS	DAS	?	-	-	-	*	*	*	*	*
DEC	DEC destination	*	-	-	-	*	*	*	*	-
NEG	NEG destination	*	-	-	-	*	*	*	*	*
CMP	CMP destination,source	*	-	-	-	*	*	*	*	*
Multiplication										
MUL	MUL source	*	-	-	-	?	?	?	?	*
IMUL	IMUL source	*	-	-	-	?	?	?	?	*
IMUL	IMUL reg16,immediate	*	-	-	-	?	?	?	?	*
IMUL	IMUL reg16,source,immediate	*	-	-	-	?	?	?	?	*
AAM	AAM	?	-	-	-	*	*	?	*	?
Division										
DIV	DIV source	?	-	-	-	?	?	?	?	?
IDIV	IDIV source	?	-	-	-	?	?	?	?	?
AAD	AAD	?	-	-	-	*	*	?	*	?
Sign-Extension										
CBW	CBW	-	-	-	-	-	-	-	-	-
CWD	CWD	-	-	-	-	-	-	-	-	-

Notes: (1) * means changed, - means unchanged and ? means undefined.
(2) Shaded instructions are new with the 80286; they are not available with the 8088 or 8086.

This is fine if your operands are indeed binary, but if they happen to be decimal, the results will be incorrect (obviously). To compensate, the 286 has a group of "adjust" instructions that make decimal operations give the proper result. We will discuss these instructions at the appropriate places in this section.

How Numbers Are Stored in Memory

As we mentioned earlier, the 80286 stores 16-bit numbers in the opposite order you might expect: with the least-significant byte at the lower address. For example, when storing 1234H at a location called NUM, it puts 34H at NUM and 12H at NUM+1. Keep this backward storage scheme in mind when you display the contents of memory. Just remember "low data, low address; high data, high address."

Addition Instructions

Add (ADD) and Add With Carry (ADC)

The ADD and ADC instructions can add 8- or 16-bit operands. ADD adds a source and destination operand and puts the result in the destination. Symbolically, we can represent this as

```
destination = destination + source
```

ADC does the same thing as ADD, except it includes the Carry Flag (CF) in the addition, like this:

```
destination = destination + source + Carry
```

You may not be familiar with the concept of *carry* as applied to computers, but you have certainly encountered it before in adding decimal numbers with pencil and paper. For instance, the following addition produces two carries:

$$\begin{array}{r} 98 \\ 13 \\ +79 \\ \hline 190 \end{array}$$

Adding the "ones" column produces an excess of 2, which gets carried into the "tens" position. Then, adding the tens column along with the carry produces another carry (1), which goes into the "hundreds" column. A carry is produced whenever a column cannot hold the sum of all the digits in it.

Similarly, when the computer adds binary numbers, it generates a carry whenever the destination operand cannot hold a sum. For example, we know that an 8-bit register can hold unsigned values between 0 and 255 (decimal). If we perform a binary addition of 250 and 10, we get

```
  1111 1010    (Binary representation of 250)
 +0000 1010    (Binary representation of 10)
1 0000 0100    (Answer = 260 decimal)
```

The sum is correct, but it takes nine bit positions to represent it! If we are using 8-bit registers, the lower eight bits are returned in the destination register, and the ninth bit is returned in the *Carry Flag (CF)*.

Now you can see why the 286 has two separate add instructions. One instruction, ADD, can add single-byte or single-word numbers and the low-order terms of multi-precision numbers. The other, ADC, is used to add the higher-order terms of two multi-precision numbers.

For example,

```
ADD   AX,CX
```

adds the 16-bit contents of AX and CX and returns the result in AX. If your operands are longer than 16 bits, you can use this kind of sequence:

```
ADD   AX,CX    ;Add low-order 16 bits,
ADC   BX,DX    ; then high-order 16 bits
```

which adds the 32-bit number in CX and DX to the one in AX and BX. Here, the ADC instruction includes any carry out of (CX)+(AX) into (DX)+(BX).

You may also add a memory operand to a general register (or vice versa) or add an immediate value to a register or to memory. Some examples are:

```
ADD   AX,MEM_WORD      ;Add a memory operand to a register
ADD   MEM_WORD,AX      ; or vice versa
ADD   AL,10            ;Add a constant to a register
ADD   MEM_BYTE,0FH     ; or to a memory location
```

Note that most combinations are legal, but you may not add memory-to-memory, nor may you use an immediate value as a destination.

ADD and ADC can affect six flags:

- The Carry Flag (CF) is 1 if the result cannot be contained in the destination operand; otherwise, CF is 0.
- The Parity Flag (PF) is 1 if the result has an even number of 1 bits; otherwise, PF is 0.
- The Auxiliary Carry Flag (AF) is 1 if the result of a decimal addition needs to be adjusted; otherwise, AF is 0.
- The Zero Flag (ZF) is 1 if the result is zero; otherwise, ZF is 0.
- The Sign Flag (SF) is 1 if the result is negative (the high-order bit is a 1); otherwise, SF is 0.
- The Overflow Flag (OF) is 1 if adding two like-signed numbers (both positive or both negative) gives a result that exceeds the two's-comple-

ment range of the destination, which changes the sign; otherwise, OF is 0.

SF and OF are pertinent only when you add signed numbers. AF is pertinent only when you add decimal numbers.

The 286 has instructions that test flags and base an execution decision on the outcome. For instance, a negative result (SF=1) may cause it to execute one set of instructions, while a non-negative result (SF=0) causes it to execute a different set. We discuss these "decision-making" instructions later in this chapter.

ASCII and Decimal Adjust for Addition (AAA and DAA)

As we mentioned earlier, the 286 always adds numbers as if they were binary. What happens if they are binary-coded decimal (BCD) numbers? Let's find out by looking at an example. If you add the packed BCD numbers 26 and 55, the 286 performs this binary addition:

```
  0010 0110    (= BCD 26)
 +0101 0101    (= BCD 55)
  0111 1011    (= ??)
```

Instead of the correct answer (BCD 81), the result has a high digit of 7 and a low digit of hexadecimal B. Does this mean you can't add decimal numbers? No, but it means that you must *adjust* the result to put it into BCD form.

The instructions ASCII Adjust for Addition (AAA) and Decimal Adjust for Addition (DAA) adjust the result of a decimal addition. Neither takes an operand; they both assume that the value that needs adjusting is in the AL register.

AAA converts the contents of AL to a valid *unpacked* decimal digit in the lower four bits of AL (and it puts zeros in the upper four bits). You use it in this context:

```
ADD  AL,BL    ;Add unpacked BCD numbers in AL and BL
AAA           ; and make the result an unpacked number
```

If ADD produces a result that exceeds 9, AAA adds 1 to AH (to reflect the excess digit) and sets CF to 1; otherwise, it clears CF to 0. AAA also updates AF and leaves PF, ZF, SF, and OF undefined. But since only CF is pertinent, consider these other statuses destroyed.

DAA converts the value in AL to two valid *packed* decimal digits. You use it in this context:

```
ADD  AL,BL    ;Add packed BCD numbers in AL and BL
DAA           ; and make the result a packed number
```

If the ADD result exceeds 99 (the packed BCD limit), DAA adds 1 to AH and sets CF to 1. DAA also updates PF, AF, ZF, and SF, and leaves OF undefined. But since only CF is pertinent, consider these other five statuses destroyed.

Increment Destination by One (INC)

The INC instruction adds 1 to a register or memory operand but, unlike ADD, does not affect the Carry Flag (CF). INC is convenient for increasing loop counters. It can also be used to increase an index register or pointer when you are accessing consecutive locations in memory. Examples are:

```
INC  CX              ;Increment a word register
INC  AL              ; or a byte register
INC  MEM_BYTE        ;Increment a byte in memory
INC  MEM_WORD[BX]    ; or a word in memory
```

Subtraction Instructions

How the 80286 Subtracts

Like every other general-purpose microprocessor, the 286 has no internal subtraction unit. However, it *does* have an *addition* unit—an adder—and can subtract numbers by adding them. Strange as this seems, the concept is "elementary," as Mr. Holmes would say.

To see how to subtract by adding, consider how you subtract 7 from 10. In elementary school you learned to write this as

$$10 - 7$$

However, later (in Algebra 101, perhaps) you learned that another way to write this is

$$10 + (-7)$$

The first form—the straight subtraction—can be performed by a processor that has a subtraction unit. Since the 286 has no such unit, it subtracts in two steps. First, it changes the sign of, or *complements*, the second number (the subtrahend). Then it adds the minuend and complemented subtrahend to produce the result. Because the 286 works with base 2 (binary) numbers, the complement is a *two's*-complement.

To obtain the two's-complement of a binary number, we take its positive form and reverse each bit (change each 1 to 0 and each 0 to 1), then add 1 to the result.

Applying this to our "10 − 7" example, the 8-bit binary representations of 10 and 7 are 00001010B and 00000111B, respectively. Take the two's-complement of 7 as follows:

```
  1111 1000    (Reverse all bits)
+         1    (Add 1)
  ---------
  1111 1001    (Two's-complement of 7, or -7)
```

Now the subtraction operation becomes

```
  0000 1010    (=  10)
+ 1111 1001    (= -7)
  ---------
  0000 0011    (Answer = 3)
```

Eureka! We got the right answer!

Since the 286 does the two's-complementing automatically, there aren't many occasions when you will want to do it yourself. Later in this section, however, we study an instruction called NEG that takes a two's-complement, in case you ever need it.

Subtract (SUB) and Subtract With Borrow (SBB)

SUB and SBB are similar to their addition counterparts (ADD and ADC), but with subtraction, the Carry Flag (CF) acts as a *borrow* indicator. SUB subtracts a source operand from a destination operand and returns the result in the destination. That is,

```
destination = destination - source
```

SBB does the same thing, except it also subtracts out the Carry Flag (CF), like this:

```
destination = destination - source - Carry
```

As with addition, the subtraction instructions perform two separate functions. One instruction, SUB, subtracts single-byte or single-word numbers, or the low-order terms of multi-precision numbers. The other, SBB, subtracts the higher-order terms of two multi-precision numbers.

For example, the instruction

```
SUB   AX,CX
```

subtracts CX from AX and returns the result in AX.

For operands longer than 16 bits, use this kind of sequence:

```
SUB   AX,CX     ;Subtract low-order 16 bits
SBB   BX,DX     ; then high-order 16 bits
```

Here we subtract the 32-bit number in CX and DX from the one in AX and BX. When SBB subtracts DX from BX, it includes any borrow out of the first subtraction.

You may also subtract a memory operand from a register (or vice versa) or an immediate value from a register or memory location. You may not subtract one memory value from another directly, nor may you use an immediate value as a destination. Examples of legal forms are:

```
SUB    AX,MEM_WORD          ;Subtract memory from a register
SUB    MEM_WORD[BX],AX      ; or vice versa
SUB    AL,10                ;Subtract constant from a register
SUB    MEM_BYTE,0FH         ; or from a memory location
```

SUB and SBB can affect six flags:

- The Carry Flag (CF) is 1 if a borrow was needed; otherwise, it is 0.
- The Parity Flag (PF) is 1 if the result has an even number of 1 bits; otherwise, it is 0.
- The Auxiliary Carry Flag (AF) is 1 if the result of a decimal subtraction adjusting; otherwise, it is 0.
- The Zero Flag (ZF) is 1 if the result is zero; otherwise, it is 0.
- The Sign Flag (SF) is 1 if the result is negative (high-order bit is 1); otherwise, it is 0.
- The Overflow Flag (OF) is 1 if you subtract a positive number from a negative (or vice versa) and the result exceeds the two's-complement capacity of the destination, which changes the sign; otherwise, OF is 0.

SF or OF are pertinent only when you subtract signed binary numbers. AF is pertinent only when you subtract decimal numbers.

ASCII and Decimal Adjust for Subtraction (AAS and DAS)

As with addition, the 286 subtracts as if the operands were binary numbers. This means that if you subtract binary-coded decimal (BCD) numbers, your answer may be incorrect. For example, suppose you want to subtract

BCD 26 from BCD 55. The 286 performs a binary subtraction by taking the two's-complement of 26, then doing this addition:

```
   0101 0101    (= BCD 55)
 + 1101 1010    (= two's-complement of BCD 26)
 1 0010 1111    (= ??)
```

Instead of the correct answer (BCD 29), the result has a high digit of 2, a low digit of hexadecimal F, and a carry. Clearly, this result sorely needs adjusting.

The instructions ASCII Adjust for Subtraction (AAS) and Decimal Adjust for Subtraction (DAS) adjust the result after you subtract two decimal numbers. Both assume that the number to be adjusted is in the AL register.

AAS converts the contents of AL to a valid *unpacked* decimal digit in the lower four bits of AL (and it puts zeros in the higher four bits). Use AAS in this context:

```
SUB   AL,BL   ;Subtract BCD number in BL from AL
AAS           ; and make the result an unpacked number
```

If the result exceeds 9, AAS subtracts 1 from AH and sets CF to 1; otherwise, it clears CF to 0. AAS also updates AF and leaves PF, ZF, SF, and OF undefined. But since only CF is pertinent, consider these other statuses destroyed.

DAS converts the contents of AL to two valid *packed* decimal digits. Use it in this context:

```
SUB   AL,BL    ;Subtract packed BCD number in BL from AL
DAS            ; and make the result a packed number
```

If the result exceeds 99 (the packed BCD limit), DAS subtracts 1 from AH and sets CF to 1; otherwise, it clears CF to 0. DAS also updates PF, AF, ZF, and SF, and leaves OF undefined. But since only CF is pertinent, consider these other statuses destroyed.

Decrement Destination by One (DEC)

The DEC instruction subtracts 1 from a register or memory operand, but unlike SUB, does not affect the Carry Flag (CF). DEC is often used to decrement a loop counter until it becomes zero or negative. It can also be used to decrease an index register or pointer when you access consecutive memory locations. Some examples are:

```
DEC  CX             ;Decrement a word register
DEC  AL             ; or a byte register
DEC  MEM_BYTE       ;Decrement a byte in memory
DEC  MEM_WORD[BX]   ; or a word in memory
```

Negate (NEG)

The NEG instruction subtracts the destination operand from zero, thus forming the operand's two's-complement. NEG affects the flags in the same way as SUB. However, since one operand is zero, we can be more explicit about the conditions that set individual flags. Therefore, for NEG:

- The Carry Flag (CF) and the Sign Flag (SF) are 1 if the operand is a nonzero positive number; otherwise, they are 0.
- The Parity Flag (PF) is 1 if the result has an even number of 1 bits; otherwise, it is 0.
- The Zero Flag (ZF) is 1 if the operand is zero; otherwise, it is 0.
- The Overflow Flag (OF) is 1 if the operand has the value 80H (byte) or 8000H (word); otherwise, it is 0.

NEG is useful for subtracting a register or memory operand from an immediate value. For instance, you may want to subtract the value in AL from 100. Since an immediate value can't serve as a destination, the form *SUB 100,AL* is illegal. As an alternative, you can negate AL and *add* 100 to the result, like this:

```
NEG  AL
ADD  AL,100
```

Compare Destination to Source (CMP)

Most programs don't execute instructions in the exact order they are stored in memory. Instead, they usually include jumps, loops, subroutine calls, and other factors that make the 286 transfer to different parts of a program. We discuss the instructions that actually produce these transfers later in this chapter, when we discuss the control transfer instructions. But now we will discuss the CMP instruction, which is used to help the control transfer instructions make their transfer/no-transfer "decisions."

Like the SUB instruction, CMP subtracts a source from a destination and sets or clears the flags based on the result (see Table 3-5). But unlike SUB, *CMP does not save the result of the subtraction;* that is, it doesn't alter the destination. CMP's sole purpose is to set up the flags for decision-making by conditional jump instructions.

Table 3-5. CMP instruction results.

Condition	OF	SF	ZF	CF
Unsigned Operands				
Source < Destination	D	D	0	0
Source = Destination	D	D	1	0
Source > Destination	D	D	0	1
Signed Operands				
Source < Destination	0/1	0	0	D
Source = Destination	0	0	1	D
Source > Destination	0/1	1	0	D

Note: "D" means Don't Care; "0/1" means the flag may be either 0 or 1, depending on the values of the operands.

Multiplication Instructions

If you have ever endured the agony of writing a multiplication program for the Z80, 6502, or any other conventional 8-bit microprocessor, you will be happy to hear that the 80286 has built-in multiplication instructions. Multiply (MUL) multiplies unsigned numbers and Integer Multiply (IMUL) multiplies signed numbers. Both can multiply bytes or words.

Multiply, Unsigned (MUL) and Integer Multiply, Signed (IMUL)

The 286's multiply instructions have the general forms

```
MUL   source
IMUL  source
```

where *source* is a byte- or word-length general register or memory location. For the second operand, MUL and IMUL use the contents of AL (for byte operations) or AX (for word operations). They return double-length products as follows:

- Multiplying *bytes* produces a 16-bit product in AH (high byte) and AL (low byte).
- Multiplying *words* produces a 32-bit product in DX (high word) and AX (low word).

Upon completion, the Carry and Overflow Flags (CF and OF) tell how much of the product is relevant. For MUL, if the high-order half of the product is zero, CF and OF are 0; otherwise, they are 1. For IMUL, if the high-order half of the product is just a sign-extension of the low-order half, CF and OF are 0; otherwise, they are 1.

Here are some multiplication examples:

```
MUL   BX        ;Unsigned multiply of BX times AX
MUL   MEM_BYTE  ;Unsigned multiply of memory times AL
IMUL  DL        ;Signed multiply of DL times AL
IMUL  MEM_WORD  ;Signed multiply of memory times AX
```

Multiplying By Immediate Values

There is a variation of IMUL that lets you multiply a 16-bit signed *or unsigned* operand by an immediate value directly. (This is new with the 80286; with an 8086 or 8088, you must first put the immediate value in a register or memory location.) Its general forms are:

```
IMUL  reg16,immediate
IMUL  reg16,source,immediate
```

Here, *reg16* is the general register in which the result is to be placed and *source* is a 16-bit register or memory location. If you don't specify a *source*, the 286 obtains the second operand from the *reg16* register.

Note that although multiplying two 16-bit numbers produces a 32-bit result, IMUL returns only the low 16-bits in *reg16*; it simply discards the high 16 bits. In fact, IMUL limits you to a 16-bit result. If the result exceeds 16 bits, IMUL sets the Carry and Overflow Flags (CF and OF) to 1; otherwise, it makes them 0. Generally, you follow IMUL with an instruction that jumps to an error-handling routine if CF or OF is 1. This kind of job requires a conditional transfer instruction, which we'll discuss later in this chapter.

Examples are

```
IMUL  BX,10      ;Multiply BX by 10
IMUL  BX,DX,-10  ;Multiply DX by -10, put result in BX
```

ASCII Adjust for Multiplication (AAM)

The AAM instruction converts the product of a preceding byte multiplication into two valid unpacked decimal operands. It assumes that the double-length product is in AH and AL, and returns the unpacked operands in AH and AL. For AAM to work correctly, the original multiplier and multiplicand must have been valid unpacked bytes.

To make the conversion, AAM divides the AL register by 10 and stores the resulting quotient and remainder in AH and AL, respectively. It also updates the Parity Flag (PF), the Zero Flag (ZF), and the Sign Flag (SF) to reflect the contents of AL. The Carry Flag (CF), Auxiliary Carry Flag (AF), and Overflow Flag (OF) are undefined.

To see how AAM works, assume AL contains 9 (00001001B) and BL contains 7 (00000111B) and you execute

```
MUL   BL
AAM
```

The instruction *MUL BL* multiplies AL by BL and returns a 16-bit result in AH and AL. In this case, it returns 0 in AH and 00111111B (decimal 63) in AL. Then *AAM* divides AL by 10 and returns a quotient of 00000110B in AH and a remainder of 00000011B in AL. This double-length result is indeed correct—BCD 63, in unpacked form.

The 286 cannot multiply *packed* decimal numbers directly. To do this, you must unpack them using AAM, multiply, then pack the result.

Division Instructions

Just as the 286 has two separate multiplication instructions, it also has two separate division instructions. Divide (DIV) performs an unsigned division, while Integer Divide (IDIV) performs a signed division.

Divide, Unsigned (DIV) and Integer Divide, Signed (IDIV)

DIV and IDIV have the general forms

```
DIV    source
IDIV   source
```

where *source* is a byte- or word-sized general register or memory location that contains the divisor (the value by which you want to divide). The dividend is a double-length operand contained in either AH and AL (for byte operations) or DX and AX (for word operations).

DIV and IDIV produce the following results:

- If the source operand is a *byte*, the quotient is returned in AL and the remainder in AH.
- If the source operand is a *word*, the quotient is returned in AX and the remainder in DX.

Both instructions leave the flags undefined. However, if the quotient cannot fit in the destination register (AL or AX)—that is, if it *overflows* the destination—the 286 has a dramatic way of telling you that the result is invalid: it generates a *type 0 (divide by 0) interrupt.*

The following conditions cause a divide overflow:

1. The divisor is zero.
2. For an unsigned byte divide, the dividend is at least 256 times larger than the divisor.
3. For an unsigned word divide, the dividend is at least 65,536 times larger than the divisor.
4. For a signed byte divide, the quotient exceeds +127 or -128.
5. For a signed word divide, the quotient exceeds +32,767 or -32,768.

Here are some typical division operations:

```
DIV   BX        ;Divide DX:AX by BX, unsigned
DIV   MEM_BYTE  ;Divide AH:AL by memory, unsigned
IDIV  DL        ;Divide AH:AL by DL, signed
IDIV  MEM_WORD  ;Divide DX:AX by memory, signed
```

Neither DIV nor IDIV lets you divide by an immediate value directly; you must put it in a register or memory location. For instance,

```
MOV  BX,20
DIV  BX
```

divides DX:AX by 20.

ASCII Adjust for Division (AAD)

The decimal adjust instructions we previously described (AAA, DAA, AAS, DAS, and AAM) all operate on the *result* of an operation. By contrast, you must apply the AAD instruction *before* you do a divide operation.

AAD converts an unpacked dividend to a binary value in AL. In doing this, it multiplies the high-order digit of the dividend (the contents of AH) by 10 and adds the result to the low-order digit in AL. Then it zeros the contents of AH.

This sequence shows a typical use of AAD:

```
AAD      ;Adjust the unpacked dividend in AH:AL
DIV  BL  ; then perform the division
```

Sign-Extension Instructions

Two instructions let you operate on mixed-size data, by doubling the length of a signed operand. Convert Byte to Word (CBW) reproduces bit 7 of

AL throughout AH, while Convert Word to Doubleword (CWD) reproduces bit 15 of AX throughout DX. Figure 3-7 illustrates these operations.

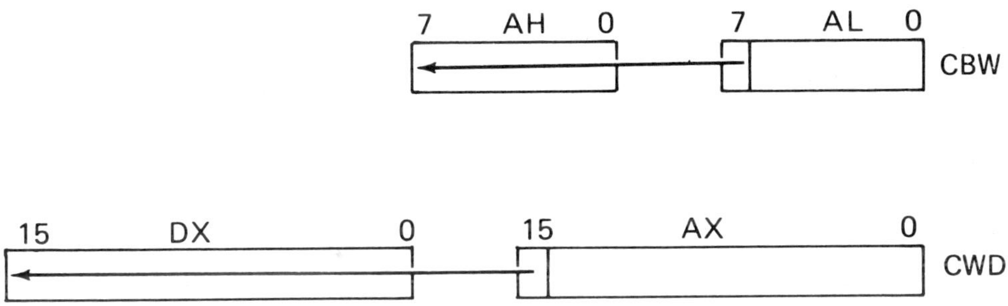

Figure 3-7. How CBW and CWD sign-extend data.

Thus, CBW lets you add a byte to a word, subtract a word from a byte, and so forth. Similarly, CWD lets you divide a word by a word. Here are some examples:

```
CBW             ;Add a byte in AL to a word in BX
ADD    BX,AX

CBW             ;Multiply a byte in AL by a word in BX
IMUL   BX

CWD             ;Divide a word in AX by a word in BX
IDIV   BX
```

3.5 Bit Manipulation Instructions

These instructions manipulate bit patterns within registers and memory locations. Table 3-6 divides them into three groups: logical, shift, and rotate.

Logical Instructions

Logical instructions are so named because they operate according to the rules of formal logic, rather than those of mathematics. For example, the rule of logic that states, "If A is true and B is true, then C is true" has a 80286 counterpart in the AND instruction. AND applies this rule to corresponding bits in two operands.

Specifically, for each bit position where both operands are 1 (true), AND sets the corresponding bit in the destination operand to 1. Conversely, for

Table 3-6. Bit manipulation instructions.

Mnemonic	Assembler Format	OF	DF	IF	TF	SF	ZF	AF	PF	CF
Logical										
AND	AND destination,source	0	-	-	-	*	*	?	*	0
OR	OR destination,source	0	-	-	-	*	*	?	*	0
XOR	XOR destination,source	0	-	-	-	*	*	?	*	0
NOT	NOT destination	-	-	-	-	-	-	-	-	-
TEST	TEST destination,source	0	-	-	-	*	*	?	*	0
Shift										
SAL/SHL	SAL destination,1	*	-	-	-	*	*	?	*	*
SAL/SHL	SAL destination,CL	?	-	-	-	*	*	?	*	*
SAL/SHL	SAL destination,count	?	-	-	-	*	*	?	*	*
SAR	SAR destination,1	0	-	-	-	*	*	?	*	*
SAR	SAR destination,CL	?	-	-	-	*	*	?	*	*
SAR	SAR destination,count	?	-	-	-	*	*	?	*	*
SHR	SHR destination,1	*	-	-	-	0	*	?	*	*
SHR	SHR destination,CL	?	-	-	-	0	*	?	*	*
SHR	SHR destination,count	?	-	-	-	0	*	?	*	*
Rotate										
ROL	ROL destination,1	*	-	-	-	-	-	-	-	*
ROL	ROL destination,CL	?	-	-	-	-	-	-	-	*
ROL	ROL destination,count	?	-	-	-	-	-	-	-	*
ROR	ROR destination,1	*	-	-	-	-	-	-	-	*
ROR	ROR destination,CL	?	-	-	-	-	-	-	-	*
ROR	ROR destination,count	?	-	-	-	-	-	-	-	*
RCL	RCL destination,1	*	-	-	-	-	-	-	-	*
RCL	RCL destination,CL	?	-	-	-	-	-	-	-	*
RCL	RCL destination,count	?	-	-	-	-	-	-	-	*
RCR	RCR destination,1	*	-	-	-	-	-	-	-	*
RCR	RCR destination,CL	?	-	-	-	-	-	-	-	*
RCR	RCR destination,count	?	-	-	-	-	-	-	-	*

Notes: (1) * means changed, - means unchanged, and ? means undefined.
(2) Shaded instructions are new with the 80286; they are not available with the 8088 or 8086.

any bit position where the two operands have any other combination—both are 0 or one is 0 and the other is 1—AND sets the bit in the destination to 0.

Since logical operations reference bits within an operand, we generally use hexadecimal numbering for the operands. The 286's logical instructions can operate on either bytes or words, so you normally deal with either two or four hexadecimal digits.

To help you construct the correct "mask" value for a logical operation, Table 3-7 shows the hexadecimal representation of a 1 in 16 different bit positions. For example, to operate on bit 2, the correct mask value is 4H; to operate on bits 2 and 3, the mask is 0CH (hex 4 + hex 8); and so on.

Table 3-7. Hexadecimal values for bit positions.

Bit Number	Hex. Value	Bit Number	Hex. Value
0	0001	8	0100
1	0002	9	0200
2	0004	10	0400
3	0008	11	0800
4	0010	12	1000
5	0020	13	2000
6	0040	14	4000
7	0080	15	8000

Logical AND (AND), Inclusive-OR (OR), and Exclusive-OR (XOR)

You encountered AND, OR, and XOR in Section 2.7, where we discussed logical operators of the same names. However, operators do their work when the program is *assembled*, while instructions do theirs when the program is *executed*. Still, these operators and instructions have the same names because they function in the same way. Although we describe the AND, OR, and XOR instructions here for the sake of completeness, you might want to refer to Section 2.7 for explanations of how they operate.

AND, OR, and XOR operate on byte or word operands. They let you combine two registers, a register with a memory location, or an immediate value with a register or memory location. Table 3-8 shows what effect these instructions have.

Table 3-8. AND, OR, and XOR bit combinations.

		Result		
Source	Destination	AND	OR	XOR
0	0	0	0	0
0	1	0	1	1
1	0	0	1	1
1	1	1	1	0

The *AND* instruction masks out (zeros) certain bits so you can do some kind of processing on the remaining bits. As we just mentioned, for each bit position in which both operands contain 1, the corresponding bit in the destination is also 1. All other operand bit combinations put a 0 in the destination bit. Note that *any bit ANDed with 0 becomes 0, and any bit ANDed with 1 retains its original value.*

Some examples of AND are:

```
AND  AX,BX              ;AND two registers
AND  AL,MEM_BYTE        ;AND register with memory
AND  MEM_BYTE,AL        ; or vice-versa
AND  BL,1101B           ;AND a constant with a register
AND  TABLE[BX],MASK3    ; or with memory
```

To see how AND works, suppose port 200 is connected to the 16-bit status register of an external device in the system, and bit 6 indicates whether that device is on (1) or off (0). If your program requires the device to be on before continuing, it might include the following loop:

```
CHK_PWR: IN   AX,200        ;Read device status
         AND  AX,1000000B   ;Isolate the power indicator
         JZ   CHK_PWR       ;Wait until power is on,
         ..                 ; then continue
         ..
```

The JZ (Jump If Zero) instruction, which we have not yet discussed, makes the 286 jump back to the IN instruction at CHK_PWR if the Zero Flag (ZF) is 1, or continue to the next instruction otherwise. Here, ZF is 1 only when the power indicator—bit 6—is 1, because the AND instruction already zeroed the rest of the bits in AX.

The *OR* instruction produces a 1 result in the destination for each bit position in which either or both operands contain 1. OR is generally used to force specific bits to 1. For example,

```
OR   BX,0C000H
```

sets the two most-significant bits (14 and 15) of BX to 1 and leaves all other bits unchanged.

The *XOR* instruction can be used to determine which bits differ between two operands or to reverse the settings of selected bits. XOR puts a 1 in the destination for every bit position in which the operands differ (one operand has 0 and the other has 1). If both operand's bits are either 0 or 1, XOR clears the destination bit to 0. For example,

```
XOR  BX,0C000H
```

reverses the state of the two most-significant bits of BX (14 and 15) and leaves all other bits as they were.

Logical NOT (NOT)

The NOT instruction reverses the state of each bit in a register or memory operand without affecting any flags. That is, NOT changes each 1 to 0 and each 0 to 1. In other words, it takes the *one's-complement* of an operand.

Test (TEST)

The TEST instruction ANDs two operands, but affects only the flags; it doesn't alter either operand. TEST does the same as AND: it clears CF and OF to 0, updates PF, ZF, and SF, and leaves AF undefined.

If you follow TEST with a JNZ (Jump If Not Zero) instruction, the 286 will make the jump if there are any corresponding 1 bits in both operands.

Shift and Rotate Instructions

The 80286 has seven instructions that displace the contents of an 8- or 16-bit general register or memory location one or more positions to the left or right. Three of these instructions "shift" the operand, the other four "rotate" it.

For all seven instructions, the Carry Flag (CF) acts as a "9th bit" or "17th bit" extension of the operand. That is, CF receives the value of the bit that has been displaced out of one end of the operand. A right shift or rotate puts the value of bit 0 into CF; a left shift or rotate puts the value of bit 7 (byte) or bit 15 (word) into it.

Shift and rotate instructions fall into two groups. *Logical* shifts and rotates displace an operand without regard to its sign; they are used to operate on unsigned numbers and non-numbers such as masks. *Arithmetic* shifts and rotates preserve the most-significant bit of the operand, the sign bit; they are used to operate on signed numbers. Figure 3-8 shows how these instructions work.

Shift and rotate instructions take two operands: a *destination* and a *count*. The destination may be an 8- or 16-bit general register or memory location. The count may be a value between 1 and 31 in either the instruction itself or in the CL register. (Note that Table 3-6 lists the form that has a count of "1" separately. I did this to illustrate a difference between the 80286 and the 8086/8088. In these earlier microprocessors, 1 is the only legal immediate value; to use a larger count, you had to put it in CL.)

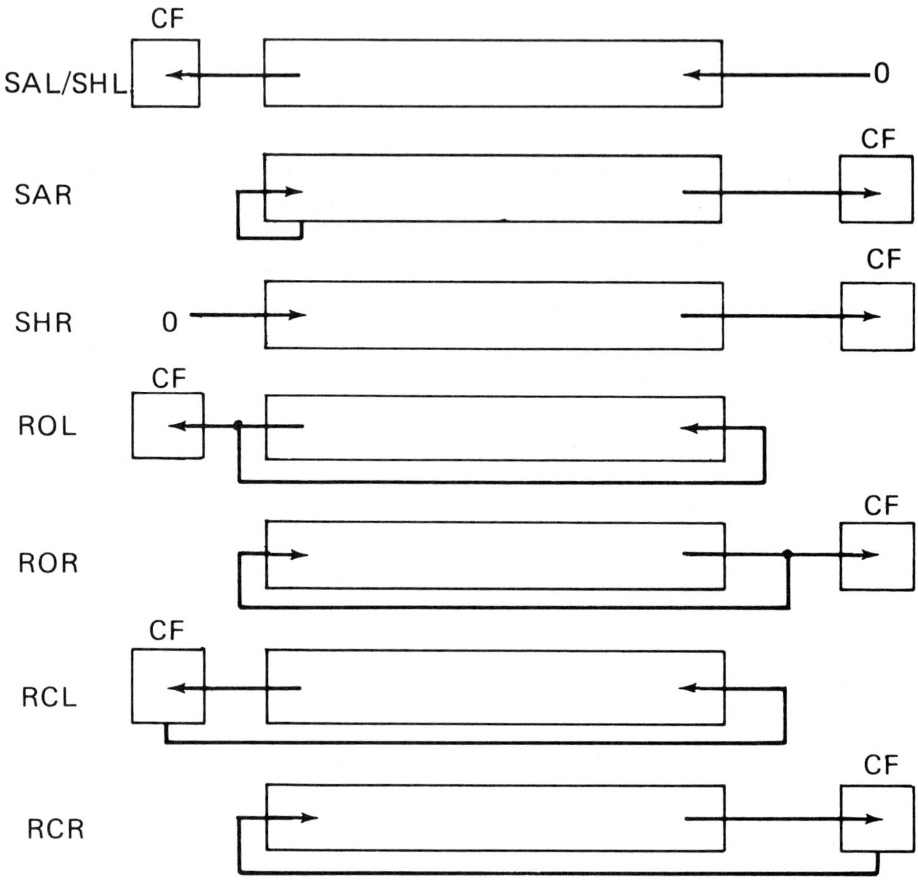

Figure 3-8. Shift and rotate operations.

Shift Instructions

Shift Arithmetic Left (SAL) and *Shift Arithmetic Right (SAR)* shift signed numbers. SAR preserves the sign of the operand by replicating the sign bit throughout the shift operation. SAL does not preserve the sign, but it puts 1 in the Overflow Flag (OF) if the sign ever changes. Whenever SAL shifts an operand, the vacated bit 0 position receives 0.

Shift Logical Left (SHL) and *Shift Logical Right (SHR)* shift unsigned numbers. SHL does the same thing as SAL. SHR is similar to SHL, but it shifts operands right instead of left. Whenever SHR shifts an operand, the vacated high-order bit position (bit 7 in a byte, bit 15 in a word) receives 0.

Besides CF and OF, the shift instructions update PF, ZF, and SF, and leave AF undefined.

To see how the shift instructions work, assume the AL register contains 0B4H and the Carry Flag is 1. In binary,

AL = 10110100 CF = 1

Here is how the four shift instructions affect AL and CF:

After *SAL AL,1*: AL = 01101000 CF = 1
After *SAR AL,1*: AL = 11011010 CF = 0
After *SHL AL,1*: AL = 01101000 CF = 1
After *SHR AL,1*: AL = 01011010 CF = 0

The shift instructions have some interesting uses. For example, the following converts two unpacked BCD digits in BL (high) and AL (low) to a packed BCD number in AL:

```
SHL  BL,4   ;Shift high digit into high four bits of BL
OR   AL,BL  ;Merge AL and BL to form packed BCD number
```

Multiplying and Dividing with Shifts

The shift instructions can also serve as fast-executing multiply and divide instructions, because *shifting an operand one bit position to the left doubles its value (multiplies it by two) and shifting it one bit position to the right halves its values (divides it by two).*

This multiply and divide capability is most often used for working with tables of word values, to access a particular element in the table. The address of any element is equal to the starting address of the table plus the distance of the element into the table (its *index*). That is,

Element address = Starting address + index

In a byte table, the index is simply the element number. In a word table, however, each element occupies two bytes in memory, so *the index is the element number times two.* That is,

Element address = Starting address + (element number × 2)

We can, of course, use the standard MUL instruction to double the element number, but it is much easier to shift it one position to the left using SHL. For example, suppose you have a word table called TABLE1, and want to read into AL the value of the element whose number is in BX. The instructions are:

```
SHL  BX,1            ;Convert element number to byte index
MOV  AL,TABLE1[BX]   ;Read the element
```

Similarly, you can use SHR to convert an index in bytes to an element number in words.

Rotate Instructions

The rotate instructions are similar to the shifts, but rotates *preserve* displaced bits by putting them back into the operand. As with the shift instructions, bits displaced out of the operand enter the Carry Flag (CF).

For Rotate Left (ROL) and Rotate Right (ROR), the bit displaced out of one end of the operand enters the opposite end. For Rotate Left through Carry (RCL) and Rotate Right through Carry (RCL), the value of *CF* goes into the opposite end of the operand. The rotate instructions affect only CF and OF.

To see how the rotate instructions work, let's use our shift example:

AL = 10110100 CF = 1

Here is how the four rotate instructions affect AL and CF:

After *ROL AL,1*: AL = 01101001 CF = 1
After *ROR AL,1*: AL = 01011010 CF = 0
After *RCL AL,1*: AL = 01101001 CF = 1
After *RCR AL,1*: AL = 11011010 CF = 0

3.6 Control Transfer Instructions

As we mentioned earlier, instructions are stored consecutively in memory, but programs rarely execute in that exact order. All but the simplest programs include jumps and procedure calls that alter the execution path the microprocessor takes.

The control transfer instructions can make the 286 transfer from one part of a program to another. Table 3-9 divides them into three groups: unconditional transfer, conditional transfer, and loop. Note that none of these instructions affect the flags.

Table 3-9. Control transfer instructions.

Mnemonic	Assembler Format		Flags								
			OF	DF	IF	TF	SF	ZF	AF	PF	CF
Unconditional Transfer											
CALL	CALL	target	-	-	-	-	-	-	-	-	-
RET	RET	[pop-value]	-	-	-	-	-	-	-	-	-
JMP	JMP	target	-	-	-	-	-	-	-	-	-
Conditional Transfer											
JA/JNBE	JA	short-label	-	-	-	-	-	-	-	-	-
JAE/JNB	JAE	short-label	-	-	-	-	-	-	-	-	-
JB/JNAE/JC	JB	short-label	-	-	-	-	-	-	-	-	-
JBE/JNA	JBE	short-label	-	-	-	-	-	-	-	-	-
JCXZ	JCXZ	short-label	-	-	-	-	-	-	-	-	-
JE/JZ	JE	short-label	-	-	-	-	-	-	-	-	-
JG/JNLE	JG	short-label	-	-	-	-	-	-	-	-	-
JGE/JNL	JGE	short-label	-	-	-	-	-	-	-	-	-
JL/JNGE	JL	short-label	-	-	-	-	-	-	-	-	-
JLE/JNG	JLE	short-label	-	-	-	-	-	-	-	-	-
JNC	JNC	short-label	-	-	-	-	-	-	-	-	-
JNE/JNZ	JNE	short-label	-	-	-	-	-	-	-	-	-
JNO	JNO	short-label	-	-	-	-	-	-	-	-	-
JNP/JPO	JNP	short-label	-	-	-	-	-	-	-	-	-
JNS	JNS	short-label	-	-	-	-	-	-	-	-	-
JO	JO	short-label	-	-	-	-	-	-	-	-	-
JP/JPE	JP	short-label	-	-	-	-	-	-	-	-	-
JS	JS	short-label	-	-	-	-	-	-	-	-	-
Loop											
LOOP	LOOP	short-label	-	-	-	-	-	-	-	-	-
LOOPE/ LOOPZ	LOOPE	short-label	-	-	-	-	-	-	-	-	-
LOOPNE/ LOOPNZ	LOOPNE	short-label	-	-	-	-	-	-	-	-	-

Note: - means unchanged.

Unconditional Transfer Instructions

Sometimes you will want to perform a specific operation (say, display a message) at more than one place in your program. One way to do that is to duplicate the entire set of instructions everywhere you need it. Clearly, duplicating instructions at many places in a program would be frustrating and time-consuming. It would also make programs much longer than they would be if you could avoid this duplication. As a matter of fact, you *can* eliminate needless duplicating if you define the repeated instructions as a *procedure*.

Procedures

Like a subroutine in BASIC, a procedure is a block of instructions that you write just once, but which you can execute as needed at any point in a program. The process of transferring control from the main part of a program to a procedure is defined as "calling." When you *call* a procedure, the 286 executes the instructions in it, then returns to the place where the call was made.

This invites two questions: "How do you call a procedure?" and, "How does the 286 return to the proper place in the program?" The answers involve two procedure-related instructions, CALL and RET.

Call a Procedure (CALL) and Return from Procedure (RET)

Instructions that execute procedures must perform three tasks:

1. They must include some provision for saving the contents of the Instruction Pointer (IP). Once the procedure has been executed, this address is used to return the 286 to the calling point. Hence, we call it a *return address*.
2. They must make the microprocessor begin executing the procedure.
3. They must use the stored contents of the IP to return to the program, and continue executing at this point.

These three tasks are performed by two instructions: *Call a Procedure (CALL)* and *Return from Procedure (RET)*. They are essentially the assembly language equivalents of GOSUB and RETURN in BASIC.

CALL performs the return address-storing and begin-executing tasks (1 and 2). The return address it pushes onto the stack is 16 bits long if you defined the procedure as NEAR or 32 bits if you defined it as FAR (see Section 2.4). NEAR procedures can be called only from within the segment in which they reside; FAR procedures can be called from a different segment.

CALL has the general format

```
CALL  target
```

where *target* is the name of the procedure being called. If *target* is NEAR, CALL pushes the offset of the next instruction onto the stack. If *target* is FAR, it pushes the contents of the CS register, then the offset.

After saving the return address, CALL loads the offset address of the target label into IP. If the procedure is FAR, it also loads the label's segment number into CS.

The RET instruction makes the 286 leave the procedure and return to the calling program. It does this by "undoing" everything CALL did. RET must always be the last procedure instruction that the processor executes. (This doesn't mean that RET must be the last instruction in the procedure—although it often is—just the last one the 286 *executes*.)

RET pops the return address off the stack. If the procedure is NEAR (in the same code segment as the CALL), RET pops one word and loads it into the Instruction Pointer (IP). If the procedure is FAR (in a different code segment), RET pops *two* words off the stack: an offset for IP, then a segment number for CS.

For example, to call a NEAR procedure named MY_PROC at some point, your program might execute the following sequence (offsets are also listed):

```
04F0              CALL   MY_PROC    ;Call the procedure
04F3   NEXT:      MOV    AX,BX      ;Return here after the procedure
                  ..
                  ..
0500   MY_PROC    PROC              (start of procedure)
0500              MOV    CL,6       ;First instruction of procedure
                  ..                (additional instructions)
                  ..
051E              RET               ;Return to calling program
                  ..
051F   MY_PROC    ENDP              (end of procedure)
```

When the 286 executes CALL, it pushes the offset of NEXT (04F3H) onto the stack, then loads the offset of MY_PROC (0500H) into the Instruction Pointer (IP). Since the PROC directive has no distance operand, MY_PROC is (by default) a NEAR procedure.

Since IP has changed, the 286 begins executing at that new offset. In our example, the first instructions happens to be *MOV CL,6*. When the microprocessor encounters the RET instruction, it pops the return address off the stack and puts it in IP. This makes it resume at the instruction labeled NEXT. Figure 3-9 shows the stack, the Stack Pointer (SP), and the Instruction Pointer (IP) before and after the CALL, and after RET.

Indirect Calls to Procedures

So far we have discussed just one form of the CALL instruction: a *direct* call, in which the operand is a label. You may also make an *indirect* call to a procedure through a register or memory location. With indirect calls through

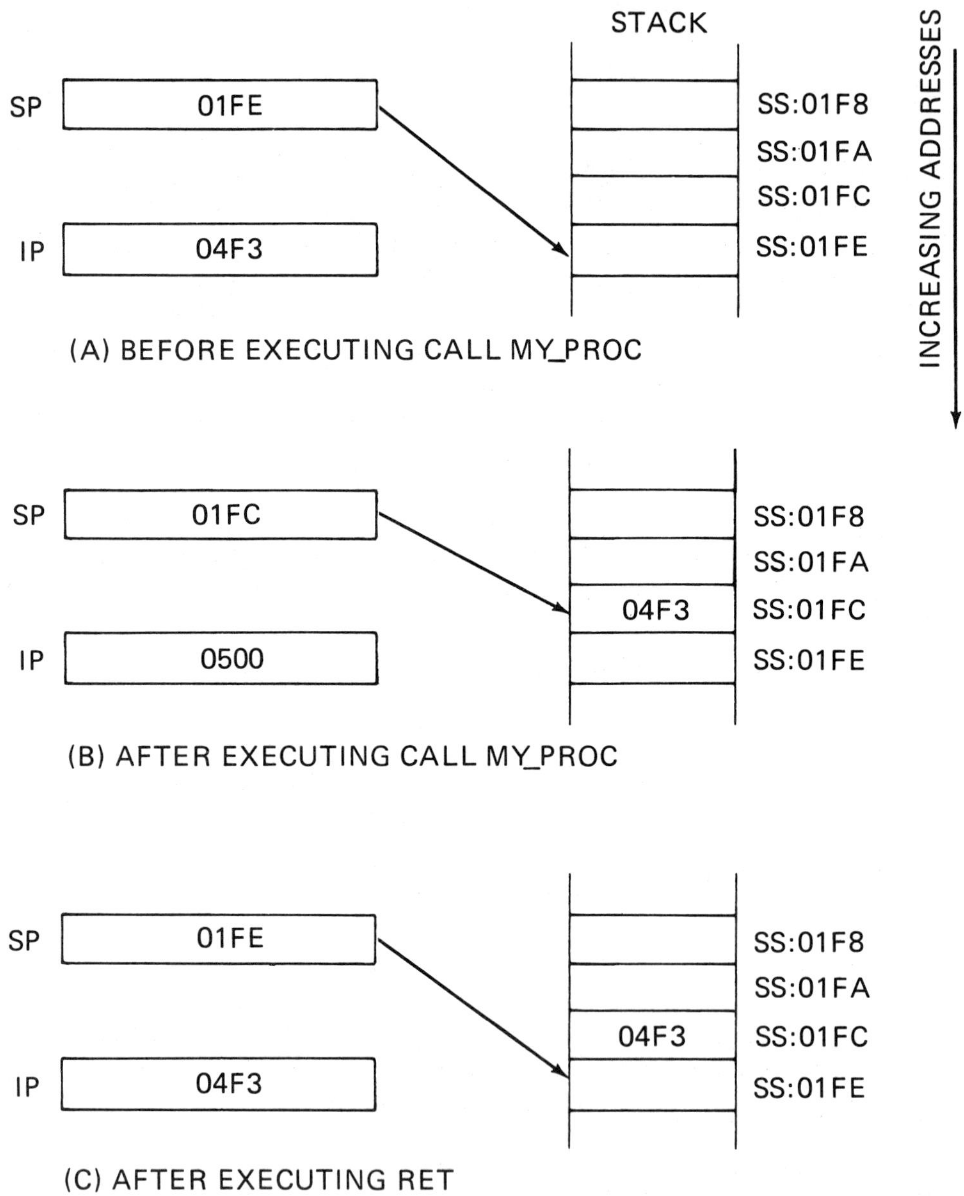

Figure 3-9. How a procedure affects the stack.

memory, the 286 fetches the procedure's offset from the data segment unless you use BP or specify an override. If you use BP to address memory, the 286 fetches the offset from the stack segment.

You may call a NEAR procedure through a register, like this:

```
CALL  BX
```

Here, BX holds the procedure's offset relative to CS. When the 286 executes this instruction, it copies the contents of BX into IP and then transfers to the instruction addressed by the CS:IP combination. For example, if BX holds 1ABH, the 286 continues executing at location 1ABH in the code segment.

You may also call a NEAR procedure through a word-size variable, as in these examples:

```
CALL  WORD PTR [BX]
CALL  WORD PTR [BX][SI]
CALL  WORD PTR VARIABLE_NAME[BX]
CALL  MEM_WORD
CALL  WORD PTR ES:[BX][SI]
```

The last CALL gets its procedure address from a location in the extra segment (because of the ES override), the rest get their address from the data segment.

You may also call a FAR procedure indirectly through a doubleword-size variable, as in these examples:

```
CALL  DWORD PTR [BX]
CALL  MEM_DWORD
CALL  DWORD PTR SS:VARIABLE_NAME[SI]
```

The first two CALLs get their procedure address from the data segment; the last gets its address from the stack segment.

Nesting Procedures

A procedure may itself call other procedures. For example, a subroutine that reads a character from the keyboard may well decode the character and then call one of several other procedures based on the result. Calling one procedure from within another is referred to as *nesting*. Figure 3-10 shows the CALL and RET instructions for a program in which PROC_1 calls PROC_1 (i.e., PROC_2 is nested inside PROC_1).

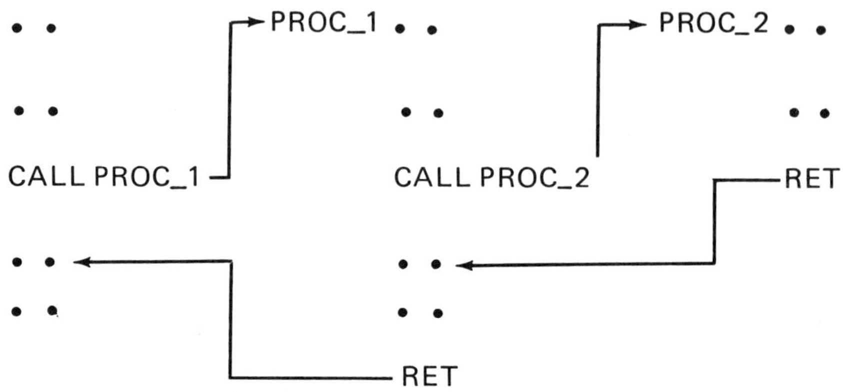

Figure 3-10. Nested procedures.

Programmers usually describe nesting in terms of *levels*. An application like the one in Figure 3-10, where the nesting extends only to the CALL to PROC_2 (PROC_2 does not call another procedure), is said to have one level of nesting. However, PROC_2 might well have called a third procedure (PROC_3), with PROC_3 calling PROC_4, and so on.

Because each CALL instruction pushes a return address onto the stack, nesting is limited only by the capacity of the stack segment. Since a stack segment can be up to 64K bytes long, your nesting capabilities are virtually unlimited.

Jump (JMP)

The JMP instruction is the assembly language equivalent of GOTO in BASIC; it makes the 286 take its next instruction from some place other than the next consecutive memory location. JMP has the general form

```
JMP   target
```

where *target* follows the same rules as the CALL operand. That is, it can be NEAR or FAR, direct or indirect. For direct jumps, JMP is three bytes long if the label is NEAR or five bytes long if it is FAR. For instance,

```
JMP   THERE
```

is three bytes long if *THERE* is in the same segment or five bytes long if it is in a different segment. (For the latter case, *EXTRN THERE:FAR* must precede the segment that contains the JMP and *PUBLIC THERE* must precede the target segment.)

If the label lies within -128 or +127 bytes of the JMP instruction, you can force the assembler to make JMP a *two-byte* instruction by declaring the label SHORT. For example,

```
JMP   SHORT NEAR_LABEL
```

is a two-byte instruction. It executes in the same amount of time as

```
JMP   NEAR_LABEL
```

but occupies one less byte in memory.

We often use JMP to bypass a group of instructions that are executed from some other part of the program. For example, you may see JMP used like this:

```
        ..
        ..
        MOV   AX,BX
        ADD   DX,AX
        JMP   THERE
HERE    MOV   MEM_WORD,DX
        ..
        ..
THERE   MOV   SAVE_DX,DX
        ..
        ..
```

Conditional Transfer Instructions

There are 17 different instructions that let the 286 make an execution "decision" based on some prescribed condition, such as a register value being zero or CF being set to 1. If the condition is satisfied, the 286 makes the jump; otherwise, it continues to the next instruction in the program.

As Table 3-9 shows, the assembler recognizes some conditional transfer instructions by two or three different mnemonics. (With these alternate mnemonics, one might well claim that the 286 has *31* conditional transfer instructions. If you think that way, you should seriously consider a career in marketing!) For example, the assembler treats JA LABEL and JNBE LABEL as the same instruction. These particular instructions refer to the result of a preceding Compare (CMP) or Subtract (SUB or SBB) instruction.

The first mnemonic, JA, tells the 286 to make the jump if the destination is "Above" (that is, greater than) the source. The second, JNBE, tells it to make the jump if the destination is "Not Below Nor Equal" to the source. Thus, JA and JNBE say exactly the same thing, but in different ways. They exist strictly for your convenience, so you can write programs that are more readily understandable.

The conditional transfer instructions have the general format

```
Jx   short-label
```

where *x* is a one- to three-letter modifier. The operand form *short-label* tells you that the target label of the jump must be no more than -128 or +127 bytes away from the conditional transfer instruction. Compare this with the Jump (JMP) instruction, which can transfer anywhere in memory.

Table 3-10 summarizes the conditional transfer instructions, and shows which conditions cause a jump. We have listed the mnemonics individually to save you from searching through a list of alternates.

Conditional transfer instructions occupy two bytes in memory; the first holds the operation code, the second holds the relative displacement. These instructions execute in 7+m clock cycles if the jump is taken (*m* is the number of bytes in the next instruction) and in 3 clock cycles if it is not taken. Because of this time difference, construct your programs so that, whenever possible, the expected case executes if the jump is *not taken.*

Here are some examples of conditional transfer instructions:

1. The sequence

   ```
   ADD  AL,BL
   JC   TOOBIG
   ```

   jumps to TOOBIG if the addition produces a carry.
2. The sequence

   ```
   SUB  AL,BL
   JZ   ZERO
   ```

   jumps to ZERO if the subtraction produces a zero result in AL.
3. The sequence

   ```
   CMP  AL,BL
   JE   ZERO
   ```

   jumps to ZERO if AL and BL hold the same value. (We could have used the equivalent mnemonic JZ used here, but JE—for "Jump if Equal"—is more meaningful in this case.)
4. Some tests require you to choose between two different conditional transfer instructions, based on whether you are testing the result of a signed or unsigned operation. For example, suppose you want to jump to label BXMORE if the contents of BX are higher-valued than those of AX.

Table 3-10. Conditional transfer instructions.

Instruction	Description	Jump if...
JA	Jump If Above	CF = 0 and ZF = 0
JAE	Jump If Above or Equal	CF = 0
JB	Jump If Below	CF = 1
JBE	Jump If Below or Equal	CF = 1 or ZF = 1
JC	Jump If Carry	CF = 1
JCXZ	Jump If CX is Zero	(CX) = 0
JE	Jump If Equal	ZF = 1
*JG	Jump If Greater	ZF = 0 and SF = OF
*JGE	Jump If Greater or Equal	SF = OF
*JL	Jump If Less	SF not = OF
*JLE	Jump If Less or Equal	ZF = 1 or SF not = OF
JNA	Jump If Not Above	CF = 1 or ZF = 1
JNAE	Jump If Not Above nor Equal	CF = 1
JNB	Jump If Not Below	CF = 0
JNBE	Jump If Not Below nor Equal	CF = 0 and ZF = 0
JNC	Jump If No Carry	CF = 0
JNE	Jump If Not Equal	ZF = 0
*JNG	Jump If Not Greater	ZF = 1 or SF not = OF
*JNGE	Jump If Not Greater nor Equal	SF not = OF
*JNL	Jump If Not Less	SF = OF
*JNLE	Jump If Not Less nor Equal	ZF = 0 and SF = OF
*JNO	Jump If No Overflow	OF = 0
JNP	Jump If No Parity (Odd)	PF = 0
*JNS	Jump If No Sign	SF = 0
JNZ	Jump If Not Zero	ZF = 0
*JO	Jump On Overflow	OF = 1
JP	Jump On Parity (Even)	PF = 1
JPE	Jump If Parity Even	PF = 1
JPO	Jump If Parity Odd	PF = 0
*JS	Jump On Sign	SF = 1
JZ	Jump If Zero	ZF = 1

*Pertinent for signed (two's-complement) arithmetic.

The sequence

```
CMP  BX,AX
JA   BXMORE
```

applies if the operands are *unsigned,* whereas

```
CMP  BX,AX
JG   BXMORE
```

applies if the operands are *signed.*

Using Conditional Transfers with Compare (CMP)

You can precede conditional transfer instructions with any instruction that alters the flags, but you normally precede them with a Compare (CMP) instruction. Table 3-5 in Section 3.4 shows how CMP affects the flags for various source and destination relationships. Now, with the wide variety of conditional transfer instructions at your disposal, it is worthwhile to look at a more practical table—one that shows which conditional transfer to use for all possible combinations of source and destination. Table 3-11 is the one you need.

Table 3-11. Using conditional transfers with Compare (CMP).

To Jump If	Follow CMP with	
	For unsigned numbers	**For signed numbers**
Destination is greater than Source	JA	JG
Destination is equal to Source	JE	JE
Destination is not equal to Source	JNE	JNE
Destination is less than Source	JB	JL
Destination is less than or equal to Source	JBE	JLE
Destination is greater than or equal to Source	JAE	JGE

To illustrate a typical application for a conditional transfer/compare combination, Example 3-1 shows a program that arranges two unsigned numbers in memory in increasing order. The data segment offsets of these numbers are assumed to be in BX and DI, respectively. Note that whenever two numbers need to be exchanged, one of them must be loaded into a register, because the 286 has no memory-to-memory Move instruction.

Example 3-1. Arranging two numbers in increasing order.

```
;  This sequence arranges two unsigned 16-bit numbers in
;  memory in order of magnitude, with the lesser value in
;  the lower address.  The offsets of numbers are in BX
;  and DI.
```

```
        MOV    AX,[BX]   ;Load first number into AX
        CMP    AX,[DI]   ;Compare it with second number
        JBE    DONE      ;Is first below or equal to second?
        XCHG   AX,[DI]   ; If not, swap the numbers
        MOV    [BX],AX
DONE:   ..
        ..
```

You can also combine a single Compare instruction with two conditional transfer instructions to test the "less than," "equal to," and "greater than" cases separately. Example 3-2 shows a sequence that executes any of three groups of instructions, based on whether the value in AL is below, equal to, or above 10.

Example 3-2. Three-way decision sequence.

```
;  This sequence executes one of three different groups of
;  instructions, based on whether the unsigned number in
;  AL is below, equal to, or above 10.

        CMP  AL,10    ;Compare AL to 10
        JAE  AE10
        ..            ;Instructions for AL < 10
        ..
AE10:   JA   A10
        ..
                      ;Instructions for AL = 10
        ..
A10:    ..            ;Instructions for AL > 10
        ..
```

This sequence uses a JAE instruction to determine whether AL is above or equal to 10. If it is, the 286 jumps to the label AE10. A JA instruction then determines whether AL is above 10. If it is, the 286 jumps to A10. Normally, the last instruction in the first two groups is a JMP, to skip the unused options.

Loop Instructions

The loop instructions can make the 286 repeat sections of a program like a FOR-NEXT structure does in BASIC. Here, the Count register (CX) serves as the repetition counter. Each loop instruction decrements CX by 1, then makes a jump/no-jump decision based on its new value.

The basic instruction of this group, *Loop until Count Complete (LOOP),* decrements CX by 1 and transfers control to a *short-label* target operand if CX is not zero. For example, to repeat a block of instructions 100 times, you might use this kind of sequence:

```
        MOV    CX,100    ;Load repetition count into CX
START:  ..               (The instructions to be repeated go here)
        ..
        LOOP   START     ;If CX is not zero, jump to START
        ..               ;Otherwise continue here
```

LOOP terminates the loop only if CX has been decremented to zero. However, many applications involve loops that must also terminate if something takes place before CX reaches zero. The instructions that provide an alternate escape route are *Loop If Equal (LOOPE)* and *Loop If Not Equal (LOOPNE)*.

LOOPE, which has the alternate form *Loop If Zero (LOOPZ)*, decrements CX by 1, then jumps if CX is not zero and the Zero Flag (ZF) is 1. Thus, looping continues until CX is zero or ZF is 0, or both. You normally use LOOPE to find the first nonzero result in a series of operations. To illustrate, Example 3-3 shows a sequence that finds the first nonzero byte in a block of memory. The offsets of the first and last bytes are in BX and DI, respectively.

Example 3-3. Find a nonzero byte in memory.

```
;   This sequence finds the first nonzero byte in a specified
;   block of memory.
;   Inputs: BX = Offset of the starting address
;           DI = Offset of the ending address
;   Results: BX = Offset of nonzero (if found)
;                = DI (if not found)

            SUB  DI,BX               ;Byte count =
            INC  DI                  ; (DI) - (BX) + 1
            MOV  CX,DI               ;Move byte count into CX
            DEC  BX
NEXT:       INC  BX                  ;Point to next location
            CMP  BYTE PTR [BX],0     ;and compare it to 0
            LOOPE  NEXT              ;Go compare next byte
            JNZ  NZ_FOUND            ;Nonzero byte found?
            ..                       ; No.  (BX) = (DI)
            ..
NZ_FOUND:   ..                       ; Yes.  Offset of the
            ..                       ; nonzero entry is in BX.
```

LOOPNE, which has the alternate form *Loop If Not Zero (LOOPNZ)*, decrements CX by 1, then jumps if CX is not zero and the Zero Flag (ZF) is 0. Thus, looping continues until CX is zero or ZF is 1, or both. LOOPNE is normally used to find the first zero result in a series of operations. If you replace LOOPE with LOOPNE in Example 3-3, the sequence will find the first *zero* byte in a block of memory rather than the first nonzero byte.

3.7 String Instructions

The string instructions let you operate on blocks of consecutive bytes or words in memory. These blocks, or *strings*, may be up to 64K bytes long and may consist of numeric values (either binary or BCD) or alphanumeric values (such as text characters).

The string instructions provide seven basic operations, called *primitives*, that process strings one element (byte or word) at a time. These primitives—move, compare, scan, load, store, input, and output—are summarized in Table 3-12.

Table 3-12. String instructions.

		Flags								
Mnemonic	**Assembler Format**	**OF**	**DF**	**IF**	**TF**	**SF**	**ZF**	**AF**	**PF**	**CF**
Direction										
CLD	CLD	-	0	-	-	-	-	-	-	-
STD	STD	-	1	-	-	-	-	-	-	-
Repeat Prefixes										
REP	REP	-	-	-	-	-	-	-	-	-
REPE/REPZ	REPE	-	-	-	-	-	-	-	-	-
REPNE/ REPNZ	REPNE	-	-	-	-	-	-	-	-	-
Move										
MOVS	MOVS dest-string, source-string	-	-	-	-	-	-	-	-	-
MOVSB	MOVSB	-	-	-	-	-	-	-	-	-
MOVSW	MOVSW	-	-	-	-	-	-	-	-	-
Compare										
CMPS	CMPS dest-string, source-string	*	-	-	-	*	*	*	*	*
CMPSB	CMPSB	*	-	-	-	*	*	*	*	*
CMPSW	CMPSW	*	-	-	-	*	*	*	*	*

Table 3-12. String instructions (continued).

Mnemonic	Assembler Format		Flags OF	DF	IF	TF	SF	ZF	AF	PF	CF
Scan											
SCAS	SCAS	dest-string	*	-	-	-	*	*	*	*	*
SCASB	SCASB		*	-	-	-	*	*	*	*	*
SCASW	SCASW		*	-	-	-	*	*	*	*	*
Load and Store											
LODS	LODS	source-string	-	-	-	-	-	-	-	-	-
LODSB	LODSB		-	-	-	-	-	-	-	-	-
LODSW	LODSW		-	-	-	-	-	-	-	-	-
STOS	STOS	dest-string	-	-	-	-	-	-	-	-	-
STOSB	STOSB		-	-	-	-	-	-	-	-	-
STOSW	STOSW		-	-	-	-	-	-	-	-	-
Input/Output											
INS	INS	dest-string,DX	-	-	-	-	-	-	-	-	-
INSB	INSB		-	-	-	-	-	-	-	-	-
INSW	INSW		-	-	-	-	-	-	-	-	-
OUTS	OUTS	DX,source-string	-	-	-	-	-	-	-	-	-
OUTSB	OUTSB		-	-	-	-	-	-	-	-	-
OUTSW	OUTSW		-	-	-	-	-	-	-	-	-

Notes: (1) - means unchanged and * means changed.
(2) Shaded instructions are new with the 80286; they are not available with the 8088 or 8086.

Note that each primitive has three different instruction forms. The first form takes one or two operands (e.g., MOVS takes a source string and a destination string), while the "B" and "W" forms (e.g., MOVSB and MOVSW) take no operands. The 286 can execute only the no-operand forms. If you use the more general operand form, the assembler will convert it to one of these two instructions.

The 286 assumes that the destination string is in the extra segment and that the source string is in the data segment. Further, it uses DI to point to the destination string and SI to point to the source string. For example, MOVSB copies the data segment byte addressed by SI into the extra segment location addressed by DI. Note that DI and SI are reasonable choices here because they are easy-to-remember abbreviations for Destination Index (DI) and Source Index (SI).

Incidentally, although the 286 assumes that the destination string is in the extra segment and the source string is in the data segment, you *can* use other combinations. We will show you how later.

Direction Instructions

Because the string instructions are designed to operate on a *series* of elements, they automatically update the pointer(s) to address the next element in the string. For example, each time MOVS moves an element it increases or decreases both the source and destination string pointer (SI and DI).

The Direction Flag (DF) bit in the flags register determines whether SI and DI increments or decrements at the end of a string instruction. If DF is 0, the 286 *increments* SI and DI, thereby addressing the next string element. If DF is 1, it *decrements* SI and DI, thereby addressing the preceding string element. Two instructions let you control the setting of DF: *Clear Direction Flag (CLD)* makes it 0 and *Set Direction Flag (STD)* makes it 1.

Repeat Prefixes

To make a single string instruction operate on a number of consecutive elements, you can precede it with a *repeat prefix*. These are not instructions, but one-byte modifiers that make the 286 hardware repeat a string instruction based on a count in the CX register. With a prefix, the 286 processes long strings much faster than it could with a software loop. For example, the sequence

```
      MOV   CX,500
REP   MOVS  DEST,SOURCE
```

makes it execute the MOVS instruction 500 times (we'll discuss MOVS momentarily) and decrement the CX register after each repetition. In effect, the REP prefix says "repeat while not end-of-string"; that is, repeat while CX is not 0.

The remaining repeat prefixes involve the Zero Flag (ZF) in the repeat/exit decision. Therefore, they apply only to the Compare String and Scan String instructions, which affect ZF. Repeat While Equal (REPE), which has the alternate name Repeat While Zero (REPZ), repeats the instruction as long as ZF is 1 and CX is not zero. If you attach an REPE prefix to a Compare String (CMPS) instruction, the compare operation repeats until a mismatch occurs. For example,

```
      MOV   CX,100
REPE  CMPS  DEST,SOURCE
```

compares the elements of the strings SOURCE and DEST until 100 elements have been compared or until the 286 finds an element in DEST that doesn't match the corresponding element in SOURCE.

Repeat While Not Equal (REPNE), which has the alternate name Repeat While Not Zero (REPNZ), has the opposite effect of REPE. That is, REPNE causes the prefixed instruction to be repeated while ZF is 0 and CX is not zero. For example, the sequence

```
        MOV    CX,100
REPNE   CMPS   DEST,SOURCE
```

compares SOURCE to DEST until 100 elements have been compared or until the 286 finds an element in DEST that *matches* the corresponding element in SOURCE.

Move String Instructions

Move String (MOVS)

MOVS copies a byte or word from one part of memory to another. It has the general format

```
MOVS  dest-string,source-string
```

where *source-string* is in the data segment and *dest-string* is in the extra segment. As with CMPS, the 286 uses SI to address the data segment and DI to address the extra segment. So *MOVS copies a byte or word from the data segment to the extra segment.*

You may override the segment assignment for SI, but not for DI. For instance, you might override SI to copy a string from one part of the extra segment to another.

Although MOVS moves only one element, you can move a string of up to 64K bytes (32K words) by applying the REP prefix. Example 3-4 shows a sequence that copies a 100-byte string called SOURCE in the data segment into the extra segment, where it is called DEST.

Example 3-4. Multi-byte move operation.

```
;  This sequence copies 100 bytes from the string SOURCE
;  in the data segment to the string DEST in the extra
;  segment.
CLD                           ;Set DF = 0, to move forward
LEA    SI,SOURCE              ;Load SOURCE offset into SI
LEA    DI,ES:DEST             ; and DEST offset into DI
MOV    CX,100                 ;Load element count into CX
REP  MOVS   DEST,SOURCE       ;Move the bytes
```

As Example 3-4 demonstrates, every multi-element MOVS operation takes five steps:

1. Clear DF (with CLD) or set DF (with STD), depending on whether you want the move to progress toward higher or lower addresses in memory, respectively.
2. Load the offset of the source string into SI.
3. Load the offset of the destination string into DI.
4. Load the element count (number of bytes or words to be moved) into CX.
5. Execute the MOVS instruction, with a REP prefix.

Of course, your program must include an *extra segment* that holds the source string. Generally, you reserve space for the destination string with a statement such as

```
DEST   DB   100 DUP(?)
```

How does the assembler know whether you are moving bytes or words? It determines this based on the *type* of the source and destination labels in the operand field. If you have set these labels with DB directives, the assembler converts MOVS to a MOVSB instruction. Conversely, if the labels were set up with DW directives, the assembler converts MOVS to a MOVSW instruction. Therefore, if you define SOURCE and DEST with DW directives, the sequence in Example 3-4 copies 100 words instead of 100 bytes.

Move Byte String (MOVSB) and Move Word String (MOVSW)

Besides reminding you which strings are involved in the move, of what value are the MOVS instruction's operands? That is, what do they tell the assembler? They simply tell it to translate MOVS into one of the two forms the 80286 can execute, MOVSB (Move Byte String) or MOVSW (Move Word String). To make this translation, the assembler doesn't need to know *which* strings are affected (that information is in SI and DI), but only what size elements they have.

Since element size is the only thing the assembler finds out from MOVS, there is no reason we can't use the size-specific instructions MOVSB and MOVSW instead of the general instruction MOVS. In fact, MOVSB and MOVSW are preferable to MOVS because they save the assembler from looking up the size of the operands. Thus, for example, we can write the instructions in Example 3-4 as follows:

```
        CLD
        LEA     SI,SOURCE
```

```
      LEA    DI,ES:DEST
      MOV    CX,100
REP   MOVSB
```

Overriding the Segment Assignments

SI normally addresses the data segment, but you can use a different segment by applying a *segment override* prefix to the source operand. For example,

```
LEA      SI,ES:HERE
LEA      DI,ES:THERE
MOVSB
```

copies a byte from HERE to THERE, where both strings are in the extra segment.

Since you can't override DI, it appears the destination must always be a string in the extra segment. Does this mean you can't copy a string into the data segment? No, you *can* copy into the data segment, but it takes some trickery.

To copy a string into the data segment, you must give the extra segment register (ES) the same value as the data segment register (DS). Then, when you execute MOVS, the 286 will think it is copying a string from the data segment to the extra segment, as usual, but *you* know that it is actually copying from one part of the data segment to another!

Example 3-5 shows this trick being used to copy 100 bytes from SOURCE_D to DEST_D, where both strings are in the data segment. Note that except for the first two instructions, this sequence is identical to Example 3-4. You can also apply this technique to the other string instructions we discuss in this section.

Example 3-5. Moving a string in the data segment.

```
;   This sequence copies 100 bytes from a string called
;   SOURCE_D to one called DEST_D, where both strings are
;   in the data segment.
      PUSH  DS               ;Make ES point to data segment
      POP   ES
      CLD                    ;Set DF = 0, to move forward
      LEA   SI,SOURCE_D      ;Load SOURCE_D SOURCE_D into SI
      LEA   DI,DEST_D        ; and DEST_D offset into DI
      MOV   CX,100           ;Load element count into CX
REP   MOVSB                  ;Move the bytes
```

Compare String Instructions

Compare Strings (CMPS)

Like the Compare (CMP) instruction we discussed in Section 3.4, the Compare Strings (CMPS) instruction compares a source operand to a destination operand, and returns the results in the flags. CMPS, like CMP, affects neither operand.

The general form of CMPS is:

```
CMPS  dest-string,source-string
```

where *source-string* is a string in the data segment addressed by SI and *dest-string* is a string in the extra segment addressed by DI. Therefore, CMPS compares an element (byte or word) in the data segment with an element in the extra segment.

Like the CMP instruction, CMPS compares the operands by subtracting them. However, CMP subtracts the source operand from the destination operand, whereas, *CMPS subtracts the destination operand from the source operand!* This means the conditional transfer instructions that follow a CMPS instruction must be different than those that follow a CMP. Table 3-13 is the one you need with CMPS.

Table 3-13. Using conditional transfers with CMPS.

To Jump If	Follow CMPS with	
	For unsigned numbers	**For signed numbers**
Source is greater than Destination	JA	JG
Source is equal to Destination	JE	JE
Source is not equal to Destination	JNE	JNE
Source is less than Destination	JB	JL
Source is less than or equal to Destination	JBE	JLE
Source is greater than or equal to Destination	JAE	JGE

To compare more than one element, you must apply an REPE or REPNE prefix to the CMPS instruction. (The REP prefix is useless here, because the flags it returns reflect comparing only the two final elements.) REPE makes the 286 compare the strings until either (CX) is zero or it finds two mismatched elements. For example,

```
       CLD
       MOV    CX,100
REPE   CMPS   DEST,SOURCE
```

compares up to 100 elements of SOURCE and DEST in an attempt to find two elements that are different.

REPNE makes the 286 compare the strings until either (CX) is zero or it finds two identical elements. For example,

```
        CLD
        MOV    CX,100
REPNE   CMPS   DEST,SOURCE
```

compares up to 100 elements of SOURCE and DEST in an attempt to find two elements that are alike.

As with MOVS, the Direction Flag (DF) determines whether the operation proceeds forward (DF = 0) or backward (DF = 1) in memory, and SI and DI are updated after each operation.

Checking Results

Since repeated compare operations can terminate in two ways—CX contains zero or ZF has changed to 0 (REPE) or 1 (REPNE)—you will want to know which condition was responsible. The easiest way to find out what stopped a compare is to follow CMPS with a conditional transfer instruction that tests ZF: either JE (JZ) or JNE (JNZ).

For example, the following makes the 286 jump to NOT_FOUND if none of the first 100 elements of DEST and SOURCE match:

```
            CLD
            MOV    CX,100
REPNE       CMPS   DEST,SOURCE    ;Search for a match
            JNE    NOT_FOUND      ;Matching elements found?
            ..                    ; Yes.  Continue here.
            ..
NOT_FOUND:  ..                    ; No.  Continue here.
            ..
```

Compare Byte Strings (CMPSB) and Compare Word Strings (CMPSW)

The assembler translates CMPS to either CMPSB (for bytes) or CMPSW (for words). You are encouraged to use these size-specific, no-operand forms instead of CMPS.

Scan String Instructions

The Scan String instructions let you search a string in the extra segment for a specific value, starting at the offset value in DI. To scan a byte string, you must put the search value in AL; to scan a word string, you must put it in AX. A scan operation is nothing more than a compare-with-accumulator operation, so it affects the flags in the same way as the Compare String instructions.

Scan String (SCAS)

The basic instruction in this group, Scan String (SCAS), has the general form

```
SCAS  dest-string
```

where *dest-string* is a string in the extra segment whose offset is in DI. This operand tells the 286 whether the search value is a byte in AL or a word in AX.

As with CMPS, to operate on more than one string element, apply the repeat prefix REPE (REPZ) or REPNE (REPNZ). For example, this sequence

```
      CLD
      LEA   DI,ES:B_STRING
      MOV   AL,' '
      MOV   CX,100
REPE  SCAS  B_STRING
```

searches up to 100 elements of the byte string *B_STRING*, looking for an element other than a space. If it finds such an element, it returns the offset of the *next* element in DI and sets ZF to 0. A subsequent JCXZ instruction indicates whether the element was found (jump not taken) or not found (jump taken).

Scan Byte String (SCASB) and Scan Word String (SCASW)

The assembler translates SCAS to either SCASB (for bytes) or SCASW (for words). Use these size-specific, no-operand forms instead of SCAS.

Load String and Store String Instructions

Once you have located a string element with a Compare String or Scan String instruction, you normally want to perform some operation on it. You may want to change it or read it into a register (perhaps to determine its exact value). The Load String and Store String instructions provide these operations.

Load String (LODS)

Load String (LODS) transfers a *source-string* element addressed by SI from the data segment to AL (byte operation) or AX (word operation), then adjusts SI to point to the next element. LODS increments SI if DF is 0 or decrements it if DF is 1.

For example, the following sequence compares the 500-byte strings DEST and SOURCE to find the first non-matching elements. If it encounters a mismatch, it loads the SOURCE string element into AL.

```
        CLD
        LEA     DI,ES:DEST          ;Get offset of DEST
        LEA     SI,SOURCE           ; and SOURCE
        MOV     CX,500              ;Element count
REPE    CMPSB                       ;Search for a mismatch
        JCXZ    MATCH               ;Mismatch found?
        DEC     SI                  ; Yes.  Adjust SI,
        LODS    SOURCE              ;  read element into AL,
        ..                          ;  and process it
        ..
MATCH:  ..                          ; No mismatch.  Continue
        ..                          ;  here.
```

Because this is a byte operation, the LODS instruction either increments SI by 1 (if DF = 0) or decrements SI by 1 (if DF = 1). As usual, LODS has the optional shorter forms Load Byte String (LODSB) and Load Word String (LODSW).

Store String (STOS)

Store String (STOS) transfers the byte in AL or word in AX to the *destination-string* operand in the extra segment, addressed by DI, then adjusts DI to point to the next element. DI is incremented if DF is 0 or decremented if DF is 1.

As a repeated operation, STOS is convenient for filling a string with a given value. For instance, the following sequence scans the 200-word string *W_STRING* for the first nonzero element. If such an element is found, this word and the next five are filled with zeros.

```
        CLD
        LEA     DI,ES:W_STRING      ;Address string
        MOV     AX,0                ;Search value is 0
        MOV     CX,200              ;Search count is 200 words
REPNE   SCASW                       ;Search the string
        JCXZ    ALLO                ;Non-zero word found?
        SUB     DI,2                ; Yes.  Adjust DI,
```

```
        MOV     CX,6                    ;    then fill six words
REP     STOS    W_STRING                ;    with 0
ALLO:   ..                              ;No.  Continue here
        ..
```

Input/Output String Instructions

These instructions, new with the 80286, are similar to IN and OUT (see Section 3.3), except they transfer data to or from memory rather than a register. The general forms of INS is

```
INS   destination-string,DX
```

where *destination-string* is a string in the extra segment and DX contains the port number. The 286 uses the string name only to make sure it is valid and to determine whether you are transferring a byte or a word. It obtains the string's starting address from the DI register. You may not override the segment assignment, but of course you can trick the 286 by making ES point to the data segment.

The general form of OUTS is

```
OUTS  DX,source-string
```

where *source-string* is in the data segment and DX contains the port number. The 286 obtains the string's starting address from the SI register. With OUTS, you may override the segment assignment.

Like the other string instructions, INS and OUTS are available in the more specific "B" and "W" forms (INSB, INSW, OUTSB, and OUTSW, in this case).

To transfer a block of bytes or words, precede the instruction with a REP prefix. For example, the following transfers 100 bytes from port 10 to a block called B_STRING in the extra segment:

```
      CLD
      LEA  DI,ES:B_STRING  ;Get the starting address
      MOV  DX,10           ;Point to port 10
      MOV  CX,100          ;Ask for 100 bytes
REP   INSB                 ;Perform the transfer
```

3.8 Interrupt Instructions

Like a procedure call, an interrupt makes the 286 save return information on the stack, then jump to an instruction sequence that is somewhere else in memory. However, a procedure call makes the 286 execute a procedure, while an interrupt makes it execute an *interrupt service routine*.

Unlike procedure calls, which can be NEAR or FAR and direct or indirect, an interrupt always makes an indirect jump to its service routine. It does this by obtaining the address of the routine from an *interrupt vector,* a 32-bit location in memory. Moreover, procedure calls save only an address on the stack, while interrupts also save the flags (as a PUSHF instruction does).

Interrupts can be activated by external devices in the system or by special interrupt instructions within a program. The 286 has three different interrupt instructions—two "calls" and one "return"—as summarized in Table 3-14.

Table 3-14. Interrupt instructions.

		Flags								
Mnemonic	**Assembler Format**	**OF**	**DF**	**IF**	**TF**	**SF**	**ZF**	**AF**	**PF**	**CF**
INT	INT interrupt-type	-	-	0	0	-	-	-	-	-
INTO	INTO	-	-	0	0	-	-	-	-	-
IRET	IRET	*	*	*	*	*	*	*	*	*

Note: - means unchanged and * means changed.

Interrupt (INT)

The INT instruction has the general form

```
INT  interrupt-type
```

where *interrupt-type* is the identification number of one of 256 different vectors in memory. (One vector for each of the 256 interrupts we discussed in Chapter 1.)

When the 286 executes INT, it does the following:

1. Push the Flags register onto the stack.
2. Clear the Trap Flag (TF) and the Interrupt Enable/Disable Flag (IF), to disable single-stepping and "lock out" other maskable interrupts.
3. Push the CS register onto the stack.
4. Calculate the address of the interrupt vector, by multiplying *interrupt-type* by 4.
5. Load the second word of the interrupt vector into CS.
6. Push the IP onto the stack.
7. Load the first word of the interrupt vector into IP.

In summary, after INT has executed, the flags, CS, and IP are on the stack, TF and IF are 0, and the CS:IP combination points to the starting address of the interrupt service routine. Now the 286 begins executing that service routine.

As we mentioned in Chapter 1, the 256 interrupt vectors are located in the lowest locations in memory. Each vector is four bytes long, so they occupy the first 1K bytes—absolute addresses 0 through 3FFH. For example, the instruction

```
INT   1AH
```

makes the 286 calculate the vector address 68H (4 x 1AH). Thus, it obtains the 16-bit IP and CS values of the interrupt service routine from locations 68H and 6AH, respectively.

Figure 3-11 shows the stack, the Stack Pointer (SP), the Code Segment (CS) register, and the Instruction Pointer (IP) before and after this instruction is executed. In this example, we assume that the interrupt vector holds the address F000:FE6E, so that is where the 286 begins executing.

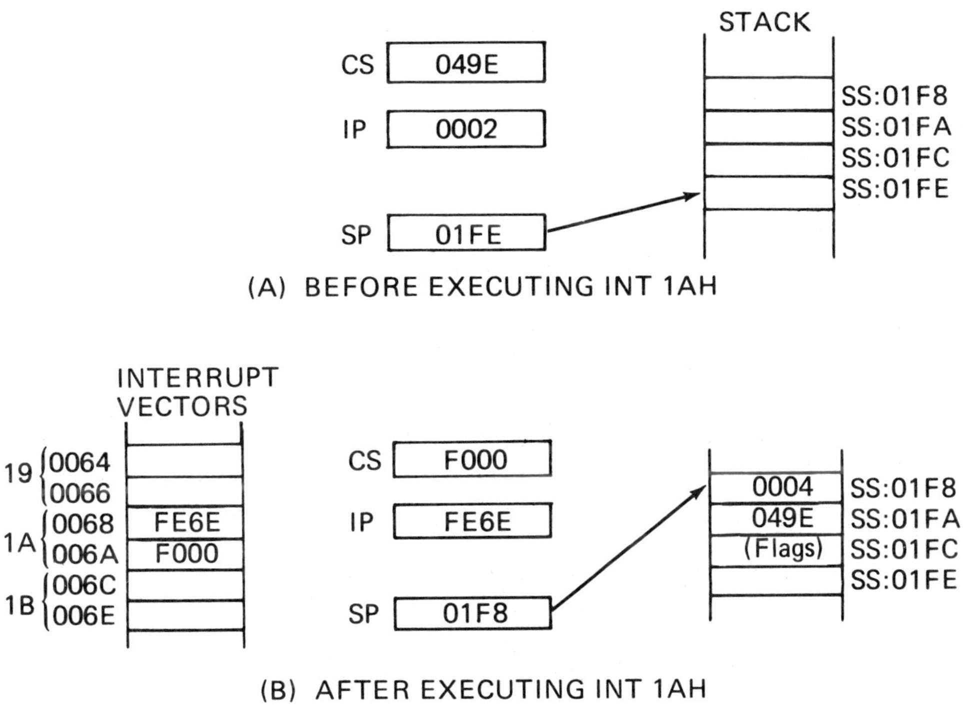

Figure 3-11. How an interrupt affects the stack.

Of the 256 interrupt types, Intel has reserved the first five (Types 0 through 4) for internal interrupts. In the PC AT, many of the others are reserved for the computer's *Basic I/O System (BIOS)*, and for DOS and BASIC. We discuss these interrupts in more detail in Chapter 6.

Interrupt If Overflow (INTO)

Interrupt If Overflow (INTO) is a *conditional* interrupt instruction; it generates an interrupt only if the Overflow Flag (OF) is 1. When that happens, INTO transfers control to an interrupt service routine with an indirect call through interrupt vector 4. (In other words, INTO activates a Type 4 interrupt.)

Interrupt Return (IRET)

Interrupt Return (IRET) is to interrupts what RET is to procedure calls. That is, it undoes the work of the original operation and makes the 286 return to the main program. For this reason, IRET must be the last instruction the 286 executes in an interrupt service routine.

IRET pops three 16-bit values off the stack and loads them into the Instruction Pointer (IP), Code Segment (CS) register, and Flags register, respectively. Other program registers may be destroyed unless the interrupt service routine explicitly saves them.

3.9 Processor Control Instructions

These instructions let you regulate the operation of the 286 from within a program. As Table 3-15 shows, there are three kinds of processor control instructions: flag operations, external synchronization, and the "do-nothing" instruction, No Operation (NOP).

Flag Operations

The 286 has seven instructions that let you change the Carry Flag (CF), Direction Flag (DF), and Interrupt Enable Flag (IF). In Section 3.7 we discussed Clear Direction Flag (CLD) and Set Direction Flag (STD), the instructions that control DF, but we have also included them here for completeness.

Clear Carry Flag (CLC) and *Set Carry Flag (STC)* force CF to a 0 or 1 state, respectively. These are useful to prepare CF for an RCL or RCR rotate-with-

Table 3-15. Processor control instructions.

Mnemonic	Assembler Format	OF	DF	IF	TF	SF	ZF	AF	PF	CF
		Flags								
Flag Operations										
CLC	CLC	-	-	-	-	-	-	-	-	0
STC	STC	-	-	-	-	-	-	-	-	1
CMC	CMC	-	-	-	-	-	-	-	-	*
CLD	CLD	-	0	-	-	-	-	-	-	-
STD	STD	-	1	-	-	-	-	-	-	-
CLI	CLI	-	-	0	-	-	-	-	-	-
STI	STI	-	-	1	-	-	-	-	-	-
External Synchronization										
HLT	HLT	-	-	-	-	-	-	-	-	-
WAIT	WAIT	-	-	-	-	-	-	-	-	-
ESC	ESC ext-opcode,source	-	-	-	-	-	-	-	-	-
LOCK	LOCK	-	-	-	-	-	-	-	-	-
No Operation										
NOP	NOP	-	-	-	-	-	-	-	-	-

Note: - means unchanged and * means changed.

carry operation. *Complement Carry Flag (CMC)* make CF a 0 if it is a 1, or vice versa.

Clear Interrupt Flag (CLI) puts 0 in IF, which makes the 286 ignore maskable interrupts from external devices in the system. You generally disable interrupts when the processor is performing some time-critical or high-priority task that cannot be interrupted. However, the processor will still process *nonmaskable* interrupts while IF is 0.

Set Interrupt Flag (STI) sets IF to 1, which lets the 286 respond to maskable interrupts from external devices.

External Synchronization Instructions

These instructions are used primarily to synchronize the 286 with external events.

Halt (HLT) puts the 286 into a halt state, in which it sits idle and executes no instructions. The 286 leaves the halt state only if you reset it or it receives an external interrupt, either nonmaskable or (if IF is 1) maskable. You can use HLT to make the processor wait for an interrupt (e.g., a character from the keyboard) before proceeding.

Wait (WAIT) puts the 286 into an idle state in which it halts, but also checks an input line called TEST at five-clock intervals. The 286 services interrupts while it is waiting, but it goes idle again upon returning from the interrupt service routine. If TEST is active, the 286 proceeds to the instruction that follows WAIT. WAIT's purpose is to stop the processor until some external device has completed its activity.

After reading how HLT and WAIT stop the processor, you might expect *Escape (ESC)* to send it on vacation! Not true. ESC simply makes the 286 fetch the contents of a specified operand and put that operand on its data bus. Thus, ESC provides a way for other processors in the system to receive their instructions from the instruction stream.

The general form for ESC is:

```
ESC   ext-opcode,source
```

where *ext-opcode* is a 6-bit immediate number and *source* is a register or a memory variable. For example, if your computer has an 80287 Math Coprocessor, you can send it instructions with ESCs (more about this in Chapter 13). Here, the 80287's op-code is *ext-opcode* and its operand is the contents of *source*.

Lock the Bus (LOCK) is a one-byte prefix that may precede any instruction. LOCK makes the 286 activate its bus LOCK signal for as long as the LOCKed instruction takes to execute. While the LOCK signal is active, no other processor in the system can use the bus.

No Operation Instruction

No Operation (NOP) is the simplest instruction of all, because it does exactly what its name implies: it performs no operation whatsoever. NOP affects no flags, registers, or memory locations; it only advances the Instruction Pointer (IP).

Surprisingly, NOP has a variety of uses. For example, you can use its op-code (90H) to "patch" object code when you want to delete an instruction without reassembling the program. NOP is also convenient for testing sequences of instructions. That is, you can make NOP the last instruction in a test program—a convenient spot at which to stop a trace. You may find other uses for this innocuous, but handy, instruction.

3.10 High-Level Instructions

There are three instructions that are intended to be used by programmers who are writing compilers and interpreters for high-level languages such as BASIC and Pascal (see Table 3-16). Since they aren't of much use to the average person, we won't spend much time on them.

Table 3-16. High-level instructions.

Mnemonic	Assembler Format		OF	DF	IF	TF	SF	ZF	AF	PF	CF
			Flags								
ENTER	ENTER	immed16,immed8	-	-	-	-	-	-	-	-	-
LEAVE	LEAVE		-	-	-	-	-	-	-	-	-
BOUND	BOUND	reg16,source	-	-	-	-	-	-	-	-	-

Note: These instructions are new with the 80286; they are not available with the 8088 or 8086.

The ENTER and LEAVE instructions are used to reserve and unreserve blocks of bytes on the stack for nested subroutines. ENTER takes two operands; the first specifies how many bytes are to be reserved, the second specifies the nesting level. LEAVE undoes the work of ENTER by restoring the stack pointer to its original, pre-ENTER value.

The BOUND instruction is used to ensure that the user's attempt to access an element in a signed array is valid. Signed arrays begin with two word values that specify the boundaries of the array. The first word contains the offset of the array's first element, the second contains the offset of its last element.

BOUND has the general form

```
BOUND   reg16,source
```

where *reg16* is the user's index register and *source* is the 32-bit address of the low-index indicator. If the value in *reg16* is less than the value of the low-index indicator or greater than the value of the high-index indicator, the 80286 issues a Type 5 interrupt.

As you will learn in Chapter 6, the PC AT's Type 5 interrupt prints the contents of the screen! This is clearly not what Intel, the manufacturer of the 80286 intended. In fact, *it is an outright error on the part of the AT's designers.*

If you want Type 5 to do something meaningful for the BOUND instruction, you must redefine this interrupt. Chapter 6 describes the procedure for redefining interrupts.

3.11 Protected Mode Instructions

Besides the instructions we have described, the 80286 recognizes several more that deal with the protected mode. Apparently, IBM is unwilling to support these instructions, because the Macro Assembler doesn't recognize them. But in case you are interested, Table 3-17 lists these additional instructions. For details on them, refer to the Intel Corporation's *iAPX 286 Programmer's Reference Manual.*

Table 3-17. Protected mode instructions.

Mnemonic	Description
ARPL	Adjust Requested Privilege Level
CLTS	Clear Task Switched Flag
LAR	Load Access Rights
LGDT	Load Global Descriptor Table Register
LIDT	Load Interrupt Descriptor Table Register
LLDT	Load Local Descriptor Table Register
LMSW	Load Machine Status Word
LSL	Load Segment Limit
LTR	Load Task Register
SGDT	Store Global Descriptor Table Register
SIDT	Store Interrupt Descriptor Table
SLDT	Store Local Descriptor Table Register
SMSW	Store Machine Status Word
STR	Store Task Register
VERR	Verify Read Access
VERW	Verify Write Access

3.12 Key Point Summary

Following are the key points you learned in this chapter:

1. The 286 can use any of seven techniques or *modes* to obtain the data that an instruction is to operate on. The assembler tells it which mode to use based on the format of the operand in your source program.
2. The simplest addressing modes are *register* and *immediate,* because the 286 obtains the operand directly from a register or from within the instruction itself. With the other five modes—*direct, register indirect, base relative, direct relative,* and *base indexed*—the 286 must calculate a memory address, then read the operand from the addressed location. Calculating the address may involve simply reading the address from

within the instruction, as in direct addressing; then again, it may involve adding as many as three terms, as in base indexed addressing.

3. The 286's *data transfer instructions* move data and addresses between registers or between a register and a memory location or I/O port. Instructions in this group can be further divided into four subgroups: *general-purpose, input/output, address transfer,* and *flag transfer.*
4. The most common general-purpose instruction, Move (MOV), copies a byte or word between a register and a memory location, or between two registers. It can also copy an immediate value (constant) into a register or memory location.

   Other useful general-purpose instructions are Push Word onto Stack (PUSH) and Pop Word off Stack (POP), which are useful for preserving the contents of a register while a program is using it for some other purpose.
5. The address transfer instructions include Load Effective Address (LEA), which loads the offset of a memory location into a register. LEA is common in string operations, where you are required to supply the offset of each string you want to use.
6. The 286 has instructions that can perform arithmetic operations on signed or unsigned binary numbers and on packed or unpacked decimal numbers.
7. A packed decimal number has two digits per byte, while an unpacked decimal number has only one digit per byte. Each digit consists of four bits that represent a value between 0 and 9; since the digits are decimal values rather than binary, we call them binary-coded decimal or *BCD.*
8. There are two separate add instructions. Add (ADD) can add single-byte or single-word numbers and the low-order terms of multi-precision numbers, while Add with Carry (ADC) can add only the higher-order terms of two multi-precision numbers. If you want to increase, say, a counter without affecting the Carry Flag (CF), use Increment Destination by One (INC) instead.
9. There are also two separate subtract instructions, Subtract (SUB) and Subtract with Borrow (SBB), as well as Decrement Destination by One (DEC).
10. Multiply instructions are Multiply (MUL) for unsigned numbers and Integer Multiply (IMUL) for signed numbers. Both take one operand and obtain the second operand from either AL (for byte operations) or AX (for word operations). They return the product in either AH and AL or DX and AX.

    New with the 80286 is a variation of IMUL that multiplies a 16-bit operand by an immediate value and produces a 16-bit product in a register.
11. Divide instructions are Divide (DIV) for unsigned numbers and Integer Divide (IDIV) for signed numbers. Both take the divisor from the instruction operand. If the divisor is a byte, they obtain the dividend

from AH and AL, and return the quotient in AL and the remainder in AH. If the divisor is a word, they obtain the dividend from DX and AX, and return the quotient in AX and the remainder in DX.

12. The 286 always performs arithmetic operations as if the operands were binary numbers. If you are adding, subtracting, or multiplying decimal (BCD) numbers, you must *adjust* the result. To do this, follow the ADD instruction with an ASCII Adjust for Addition (AAA) if the numbers are unpacked or with Decimal Adjust for Addition (DAA) if they are packed. Similarly, follow SUB with ASCII Adjust for Subtraction (AAS) or Decimal Adjust for Subtraction (DAS), or follow MUL with ASCII Adjust for Multiplication (AAM).

    To divide decimal numbers, you must first convert the unpacked dividend, rather than the result, to binary. To do this, precede the DIV instruction with ASCII Adjust for Division (AAD).
13. The sign-extension instructions let you operate on mixed-size data. Convert Byte to Word (CBW) extends a byte in AL to a word in AX, while Convert Word to Doubleword (CWD) extends a word in AX to a doubleword in DX and AX.
14. The 286's *bit manipulation group* includes logical, shift, and rotate instructions.
15. Logical instructions can take the Logical AND (AND), Inclusive-OR (OR), or Exclusive-OR (XOR) of two operands. A variation of AND, called Test (TEST), affects only the flags, not the operands. Finally, Logical NOT (NOT) takes an operand's one's-complement.
16. Shift instructions displace an operand to left or right. Use Shift Arithmetic Left or Right (SAL or SAR) to shift signed numbers; use Shift Logical Left or Right (SHL or SHR) to shift unsigned numbers. These instructions also make for faster multiply and divide operations.
17. Rotate instructions do the same as shifts, except they preserve displaced bits rather than discard them. Rotate Left (ROL) and Rotate Right (ROR) enter a displaced bit into the opposite end of the operand; Rotate Left through Carry (RCL) and Rotate Right through Carry put a displaced bit into CF and insert the CF bit into the operand.
18. *Control transfer instructions* can make the 286 transfer to a different part of the program, either unconditionally or conditionally, or repeatedly execute a block of instructions—that is, *loop*.
19. There are three unconditional transfer instructions. Call a Procedure (CALL) transfers the 286 to a procedure and Return from Procedure (RET) returns it to the calling program. Jump (JMP) makes it continue at a different part of the program.
20. The conditional transfer instructions make the 286 transfer only if a specified condition is satisfied. They are usually preceded by a Compare (CMP) instruction, which sets up the flags.
21. Loop instructions establish repetitive operations based on a count in CX. Variations called Loop If Equal (LOOPE) and Loop If Not Equal

(LOOPNE) provide for an alternate way out of the loop based on ZF = 1 or ZF = 0, respectively.

22. *String instructions* let you operate on blocks of consecutive byte or words. In them, the 286 always assumes that the destination string is in the extra segment and is addressed by DI, while the source string is the data segment and is addressed by SI. In most cases, you put a prefix in front of the string instruction to operate on a number of consecutive elements.
23. The string instructions include Move (MOVS), Compare (CMPS), Scan (SCAS), Load (LODS), Store (STOS), Input (INS), and Output (OUTS). Each is available in three forms, one in which you specify the operand string(s) and two in which you specify only the size of the operands (bytes or words).
24. There are three *interrupt instructions*. Interrupt (INT) activates one of 256 interrupts based on the number you specify. The 286 obtains the address of the interrupt service routine from a 32-bit *interrupt vector* in low memory. Interrupt Return (IRET) returns the processor to the calling program, just as RET does for a procedure. Interrupt If Overflow (INTO) is a conditional form of INT; it activates the interrupt only if the Overflow Flag (OF) is 1.
25. *Processor control instructions* let you regulate the 286 from within a program. They include instructions that control the Carry, Direction, and Interrupt Enable Flags (CF, DF, and IF), and synchronize the 286 to another processor. Also included is No Operation (NOP), which is useful for "patching" assembled object programs.
26. *High-level instructions* are used to communicate with programs written in a block-oriented language such as Pascal.

Differences Between the 80286 and the 8086/8088

The 808286 includes the entire instruction set of the earlier 8088 and 8086 microprocessors, but it also has a few new instructions and some enhancements. The new instructions are:

- Check Array Index Against Bounds (BOUND)
- Make Stack Frame for High-Level Procedure (ENTER)
- Input String (INS, INSB, and INSW)
- Exit High-Level Procedure (LEAVE)
- Output String (OUTS, OUTSB, and OUTSW)
- Pop All General Registers (POPA)
- Push All General Registers (PUSHA)

The enhancements allow you to specify immediate values for some operands that required registers before. Specifically:

- Integer Multiply, Signed (IMUL) can multiply a signed or unsigned word by an immediate value to produce a word-size product,
- Push Word onto Stack (PUSH) can push an immediate value as well as the contents of a register or memory location.
- Shift and rotate instructions can operate with an immediate count value between 1 and 31. In the 8088 and 8086, you had to load values other than 1 into the CL register.

Study Exercises (answers on page 400)

1. Write an instruction that stores the contents of the AX register into a word location called SAVE_AX in the extra segment.
2. What does this sequence do?

```
MOV  AX,0
MOV  BX,AX
MOV  BP,AX
MOV  [BX],AX
MOV  [BP],AX
```

3. Which of the following instructions or sequences are invalid? (Assume variables are defined in the data segment and instructions are defined in the code segment.)

```
(a) K        EQU   1024
             ..
             ..
             MOV   K,AX
(b) TEMP     DB    ?
             ..
             ..
             MOV   AL,TEMP
(c) TEMP     DB    ?
             ..
             ..
             MOV   TEMP,AX
(d) TEMP     DB    ?
    T3       DB    10
             ..
             ..
             MOV   TEMP,T3
(e)          MOV   [BX][BP],AX
(f)          MOV   AL,F
```

4. What value does each of these instructions load into AL?

```
MOV  AL,10H
MOV  AL,10
```

5. List two instructions that clear the AX register to zero.
6. How do these two instructions differ?

```
MOV  BX,OFFSET TABLE+4
LEA  BX,TABLE+4
```

7. How do the ADD and ADC instructions differ?
8. Write a loop that subtracts a three-word variable called V2 from another three-word variable called V1.
9. When do you use INC AL instead of ADD AL,1?
10. What is the difference between a packed and unpacked BCD number?
11. If AX contains 1234H and BX contains 4321H, list the contents of AX after each of these instructions is executed:
    (a) `AND   AX,BX`
    (b) `OR    AX,BX`
    (c) `XOR   AX,BX`
    (d) `NOT   AX`
    (e) `TEST  AX,BX`

12. Write a sequence to *normalize* AX. That is, shift AX left until the most-significant "1" bit is in bit 15. If AX is initially zero or bit 15 already contains a 1, exit immediately.
13. What does a RET instruction do in a procedure?
14. What is wrong with this sequence?

```
CMP  AL,-3
JA   INVALID
```

15. What does this sequence do?

```
START:  MOV   CX,3
        SUB   AX,10
        LOOP  START
```

16. In the instruction MOVS STRING1,STRING2 where are the segments STRING1 and STRING2 located?

4

High-Precision Mathematics

If you have done any assembly language programming on one of the regular 8-bit microprocessors, you are probably impressed with the arithmetic potential of the 80286. For starters, the very fact that the 80286 has built-in multiply and divide instructions means that the hours (or days) of time you normally spend developing multiplication and division programs are available for more stimulating activities, such as playing racquetball.

In this chapter we use the multiply and divide instructions as a base for developing programs that tackle tougher math problems. We will begin with programs that multiply 32-bit signed and unsigned numbers. From there, we discuss how to handle overflow situations in divide operations, and conclude with a program that calculates square roots.

4.1 Multiplication

In Chapter 3 we studied the 80286's two multiplication instructions, Multiply, Unsigned (MUL) and Integer Multiply, Signed (IMUL). These instructions multiply byte or word operands to produce double-length (16- or 32-bit) products.

Is it difficult to multiply numbers larger than 16 bits? Not at all, as you shall see. Anyone who has written a multiplication program for an 8-bit microprocessor knows that just *having* a multiply instruction of any kind makes up for whatever inconvenience you go through to extend its capabilities.

Unsigned 32-Bit × 32-Bit Multiply

The MUL instruction can handle only 8- or 16-bit operands, but you can use it to multiply multi-precision unsigned numbers. For instance, you can use it to multiply two 32-bit numbers. To do this, you calculate a series of 32-bit *cross products*, then combine them to form the final 64-bit product. You learned this method in elementary school to multiply decimal numbers with pencil and paper.

As you probably recall (in these days of pocket calculators, it may be a little hazy), you write the multiplicand with the multiplier below it, and perform a series of multiplications—one for each digit in the multiplier. Each individual multiplication produces a partial product, which you enter directly below the multiplier digit. Thus, each partial product is offset one digit position to the left of the preceding partial product.

For example, 124 times 103 looks like this:

```
  124  Multiplicand
 ×103  Multiplier
 ----
  372  Partial Product #1
 000   Partial Product #2
124    Partial Product #3
-----
12772  Final Product
```

Offsetting the partial products accounts for the *decimal weights* of the multiplier digits. In this example, the 3 is a "ones" digit, the 0 is a "tens" digit, and the 1 is a "hundreds" digit. Therefore, you could write the example as:

$$103 \times 124 = (3 \times 124) + (0 \times 124) + (100 \times 124)$$

or

$$103 \times 124 = (3 \times 1 \times 124) + (0 \times 10 \times 124) + (1 \times 100 \times 124)$$

In this section we will develop a short procedure that multiplies two 32-bit unsigned numbers and yields a 64-bit unsigned product. If you had no multiply instruction you would have to perform 32 separate multiplications, one for each bit in the multiplier.

Fortunately, the 80286 has an instruction that multiplies 16-bit unsigned numbers directly. This instruction, MUL, lets us treat a 32-bit multiplier and a 32-bit multiplicand as two 2-digit numbers, where each digit is 16 bits long. Thus, we can generate the 64-bit product with just *four* multiplications.

Figure 4-1 shows a symbolic representation of the multiplier (digits A and B) and the multiplicand (digits C and D), and illustrates how the four partial products are derived and how they must be aligned to calculate the 64-bit final product. The circled numbers identify the four 16-bit additions you must make to calculate the final product. (For instance, Addition 1 adds the high 16 bits of Product #1 to the low 16 bits of Product #2.)

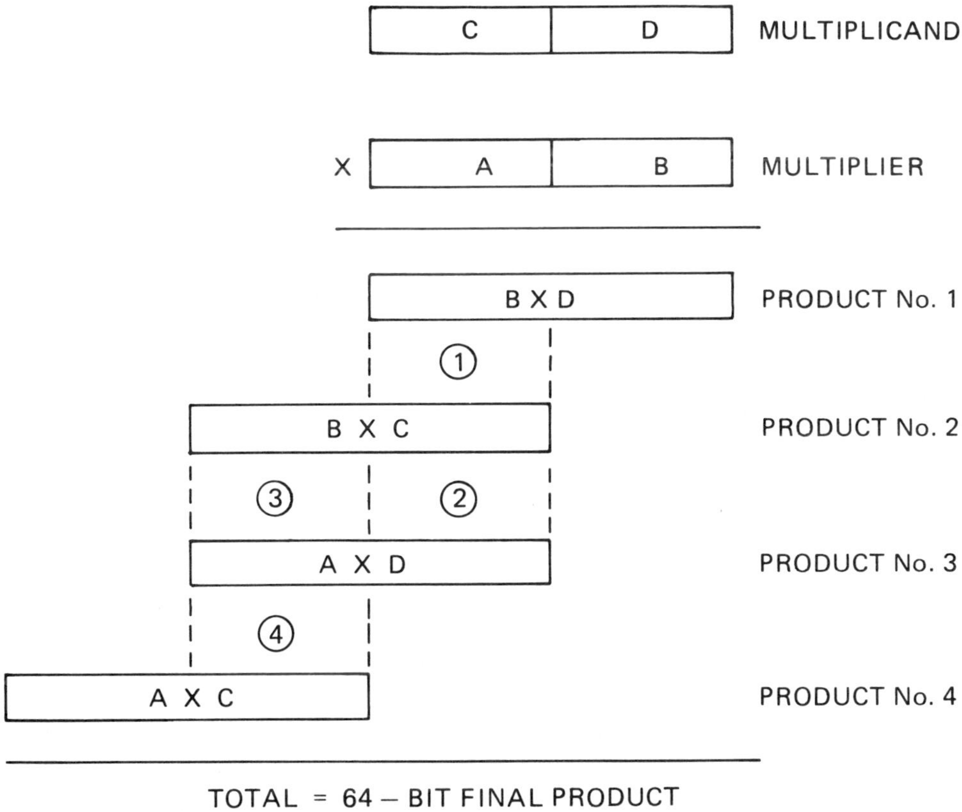

Figure 4-1. Generating a 64-bit product with four 16-bit by 16-bit multiplications.

Using Figure 4-1 as a guide, we can develop a procedure that multiplies two 32-bit numbers. Example 4-1 shows such a procedure called MULU32 that obtains the multiplier and multiplicand from register pairs CX:BX and DX:AX, respectively. It returns the 64-bit unsigned product in these same four registers: DX (high 16 bits), CX (mid-upper 16 bits), BX (mid-lower 16 bits) and AX (low 16 bits). Example 4-1 also shows some scratch locations that you must set up in the data segment.

Example 4-1. 32-bit by 32-bit unsigned multiply procedure.

```
        PAGE   ,132
TITLE   MULU32 - 32-Bit x 32-Bit Unsigned Multiply

;  Multiplies two 32-bit unsigned numbers and generates a
;  64-bit product.
;  Inputs: CX:BX = Multiplier
;          DX:AX = Multiplicand
;  Result: Product in DX, CX, BX, and AX (high to low order).

;  To assemble: MASM MULU32;
;  To link: LINK callprog+MULU32;

        PUBLIC  MULU32
DSEG    SEGMENT PARA 'DATA'
HI_MCND DW      ?
LO_MCND DW      ?
HI_PP1  DW      ?
LO_PP1  DW      ?
HI_PP2  DW      ?
LO_PP2  DW      ?
HI_PP3  DW      ?
LO_PP3  DW      ?
HI_PP4  DW      ?
LO_PP4  DW      ?
DSEG    ENDS

CSEG    SEGMENT PARA 'CODE'
        ASSUME  CS:CSEG,DS:DSEG
MULU32  PROC   FAR
        PUSH   DS               ;Save caller's DS and DI
        PUSH   DI
        MOV    DI,DSEG          ;Initialize DS
        MOV    DS,DI

        MOV    HI_MCND,DX       ;Save multiplicand in memory
        MOV    LO_MCND,AX
        MUL    BX               ;Form partial product #1
        MOV    HI_PP1,DX        ; and save it in memory
        MOV    LO_PP1,AX
        MOV    AX,HI_MCND       ;Form partial product #2
        MUL    BX
        MOV    HI_PP2,DX        ; and save it in memory
        MOV    LO_PP2,AX
        MOV    AX,LO_MCND       ;Form partial product #3
        MUL    CX
        MOV    HI_PP3,DX        ; and save it in memory
        MOV    LO_PP3,AX
        MOV    AX,HI_MCND       ;Form partial product #4
        MUL    CX
        MOV    HI_PP4,DX        ; and save it in memory
        MOV    LO_PP4,AX
```

Example 4-1. (continued).

```
;  Add the partial products to form the final 64-bit product.

         MOV    AX,LO_PP1     ;Low 16 bits
         MOV    BX,HI_PP1     ;Form mid-lower 16 bits
         ADD    BX,LO_PP2     ; with sum #1
         ADC    HI_PP2,0
         ADD    BX,LO_PP3     ; and sum #2
         MOV    CX,HI_PP2     ;Form mid-upper 16 bits
         ADC    CX,HI_PP3     ; with sum #3
         ADC    HI_PP4,0
         ADD    CX,LO_PP4     ; and sum #4
         MOV    DX,HI_PP4     ;Form high 16 bits
         ADC    DX,0          ; including propagated carry
         POP    DI            ;Restore caller's registers
         POP    DS
         RET
MULU32   ENDP
CSEG     ENDS
         END
```

The MULU32 procedure is fairly straightforward if you refer to Figure 4-1 as you look at the instructions and their accompanying comments. To begin, MULU32 saves the multiplicand in memory, then generates the four 32-bit partial products. Once the partial products have been saved in memory, the only remaining step is to add them. Note that the Carry Flag stays intact between additions because MOV does not affect it.

Since a 32-bit operand can represent unsigned values as large as 4.294×10^9, the MULU32 procedure is satisfactory for most applications. (For those that involve larger numbers, you would probably use floating-point math!) However, it is certainly possible to develop a procedure that multiplies 64-bit (or longer) numbers using the cross-products approach.

Signed 32-Bit × 32-Bit Multiply

We described Example 4-1 as a procedure to multiply unsigned numbers, but it can also multiply signed numbers, as long as they are both positive. In other words, Example 4-1 provides a 32-bit × 32-bit "non-negative" multiply procedure.

This procedure cannot properly multiply negative numbers because such numbers are represented in *two's-complement* form. Well, what if we simply replace each MUL instruction in Example 4-1 with an IMUL (Integer Multiply, Signed)? Unfortunately, that won't work, because IMUL assumes that the most-significant bit of each operand is a sign indicator, which is not the case when we generate cross products.

How, then, can we multiply 32-bit signed numbers? One way is to negate the negative operand(s), perform a normal unsigned multiplication, then adjust the product, if necessary. If only one of the operands is negative, you must two's-complement the product. If both are negative, the (positive) product is correct as it stands.

We employ this simple approach in Example 4-2. Here, a byte variable, NEG_IND, holds a "negative indicator." NEG_IND is initially set to zero, and stays that way if both operands are positive. If one of the operands is negative, we take the one's-complement of NEG_IND, which makes it all ones. If both operands are negative, we one's-complement NEG_IND *twice*, which makes it zero again.

Each time we one's-complement NEG_IND, one of the operands is negated (two's-complemented). Because the NEG instruction operates only on byte or word operands, we must two's-complement our 32-bit operands in "brute-force" fashion. This involves one's-complementing the operand, then adding 1.

The MULS32 procedure calls MULU32 to perform the 32-bit by 32-bit multiplication. Since MULU32 is in another assembly module, we must declare it EXTRN at the start of the example. (Remember, the MULU32 module must have a PUBLIC MULU32 statement.) Upon return from MULU32, the state of NEG_IND determines whether the product is correct (NEG_IND zero) or needs negating (NEG_IND nonzero).

The execution time of the MULS32 procedure depends on whether the operands are both positive, both negative, or one of each. Following is a summary of these execution times in both clock cycles and microseconds:

Operands	Maximum Time (Cycles)	Maximum Time (μs)
Both positive	1096	183.03
Opposite signs	1136	189.71
Both negative	1144	191.05

4.2 Division

There are many applications for division, but one of the most common is taking the average of a set of numbers—say, the results of a series of laboratory tests. Example 4-3 shows a typical averaging program.

This procedure, AVERAGE, averages a specified number of unsigned word values pointed to by BX; the word count is contained in CX. It returns

Example 4-2. 32-bit by 32-bit signed multiply procedure.

```
        PAGE   ,132
TITLE   MULS32 - 32-Bit x 32-Bit Signed Multiply

;   Multiplies two 32-bit signed numbers and generates
;   a 64-bit product.
;   Inputs: CX:BX = Multiplier
;           DX:AX = Multiplicand
;   Result: Product in DX, CX, BX, and AX (high to low order).
;   Calls MULU32 (Example 4-1).

;   To assemble: MASM MULS32;
;   To link: LINK callprog+MULS32+MULU32;

        EXTRN    MULU32:FAR
        PUBLIC   MULS32
DSEG    SEGMENT PARA 'DATA'
NEG_IND DB      ?
DSEG    ENDS

CSEG    SEGMENT PARA 'CODE'
MULS32  PROC   FAR
        ASSUME   CS:CSEG,DS:DSEG

;   Initialize the data segment address.

        PUSH   DS              ;Save caller's DS and DI
        PUSH   DI
        MOV    DI,DSEG         ;Initialize DS
        MOV    DS,DI

        MOV    NEG_IND,0       ;Negative indicator = 0
        CMP    DX,0            ;Multiplicand negative?
        JNS    CHKCX           ; No.  Go check multiplier
        NOT    AX              ; Yes. 2s-comp. multiplicand
        NOT    DX
        ADD    AX,1
        ADC    DX,0
        NOT    NEG_IND         ;  and 1s-comp. indicator
CHKCX:  CMP    CX,0            ;Multiplier negative?
        JNS    GOMUL           ; No.  Go multiply
        NOT    BX              ; Yes. 2s-comp. multiplier
        NOT    CX
        ADD    BX,1
        ADC    CX,0
        NOT    NEG_IND         ;  and 1s-comp. indicator
GOMUL:  CALL   MULU32          ;Perform unsigned multiplication
        CMP    NEG_IND,0       ;Does product have right sign?
        JZ     DONE            ; Yes. Exit.
        NOT    AX              ; No.  2s-comp. product
        NOT    BX
        NOT    CX
        NOT    DX
        ADD    AX,1
```

Example 4-2. (continued).

```
        ADC    BX,0
        ADC    CX,0
        ADC    DX,0
DONE:   POP    DI             ;Restore caller's registers
        POP    DS
        RET
MULS32  ENDP
CSEG    ENDS
        END
```

Example 4-3. Word-averaging procedure.

```
        PAGE   ,132
TITLE   AVERAGE - Word-Averaging Procedure

;   Takes the average of a specified number of unsigned
;   word values in the data segment.
;   Inputs: BX = Offset of first word
;           CX = Word count
;   Results: AX = Integer portion of the average
;            DX = Fractional remainder

;   To assemble: MASM AVERAGE;
;   To link: LINK callprog+AVERAGE;

        PUBLIC  AVERAGE
CSEG    SEGMENT PARA 'CODE'
        ASSUME  CS:CSEG
AVERAGE PROC   FAR
        SUB    AX,AX          ;Clear dividend to start
        SUB    DX,DX
        PUSH   CX             ;Save word count on stack
ADD_W:  ADD    AX,[BX]        ;Add next word to total
        ADC    DX,0
        ADD    BX,2           ;  and update the total
        LOOP   ADD_W          ;All words now totaled?
        POP    CX             ; Yes. Retrieve word count
        DIV    CX             ;  and take the average
        RET
AVERAGE ENDP
CSEG    ENDS
        END
```

the integer portion of the average in AX and the fractional remainder in DX. For example, you can use the following sequence to average a 100-word table called TABLE:

```
LEA   BX,TABLE  ;Fetch offset of TABLE
MOV   CX,100    ; and its word count
CALL  AVERAGE   ;Calculate the average
```

In describing the DIV and IDIV instructions (Section 3.5), we mentioned that a divide operation automatically aborts if the divisor is zero or if *overflow* occurs. Overflow occurs when the dividend is so much larger than the divisor that the result register can't hold the quotient. An unsigned division overflows if the dividend is more than 65,535 times greater than the divisor.

Both divide-by-zero and overflow make the 80286 activate a Type 0 (Divide by Zero) interrupt. This interrupt saves the register contents, displays the message

```
Divide Overflow
```

then terminates the program.

The divide operation in Example 4-3 aborts if CX holds zero upon entry. Can an overflow also cause it to abort? No, overflow cannot occur here because the ratio of the dividend (word total) to the divisor (word count) can never exceed 65,536! However, some divide operations (e.g., dividing 200,000 by 2) may produce an overflow. Let's look at a procedure that always gives a valid quotient, irrespective of overflow.

Dealing with Overflow

In some applications, overflow signifies an error. In others, overflow is acceptable, but it means that the program must be able to accommodate a quotient longer than 16 bits. Since the division aborts when the 80286 encounters an overflow condition, how can you obtain a longer quotient? One easy way is to split the 32-bit dividend into two 16-bit numbers, then perform two 16-bit by 16-bit divide operations (which *cannot* produce an overflow).

If the divisor is a 16-bit number called X and the dividend is a 32-bit number represented by Y_1Y_0, you can represent the divide operation as

$$X\overline{)Y_1Y_0}$$

or, more properly, as

$$X\overline{)(Y_1 \times 2^{16}) + Y_0}$$

This division produces two 16-bit quotient digits (Q_1 and Q_0) and two 16-bit remainder digits (R_1 and R_0), as follows:

$$\begin{array}{l} \quad Q_1 \times 2^{16} \\ X\overline{)Y_1 \times 2^{16}} \text{ and } R_1 \times 2^{16} \end{array}$$

$$\begin{array}{l} \quad Q_0 \\ X\overline{)(R_1 \times 2^{16}) + Y_0} \text{ and } R_0 \end{array}$$

As you see, the combination of these two operations produces a 32-bit quotient, Q_1Q_0, and a 16-bit remainder, R_0. (The interim remainder R_1, if there is one, disappears during the second divide operation.) If no overflow occurs, Q_1 is zero, and the result is returned as $0Q_0$ and R_0.

We can use this approach to develop a divide procedure that *always* returns a valid quotient and remainder, regardless of overflow. Example 4-4 gives a procedure called DIVUO that does the job. It divides a 32-bit dividend in DX (high word) and AX (low word) by a 16-bit divisor in BX, and produces a 32-bit quotient in BX:AX and a 16-bit remainder in DX.

The DIVUO procedure is comprised of four steps:

1. Check whether the divisor in BX is zero. If so, activate the Type 0 interrupt to abort the operation.
2. Change the Type 0 interrupt vector in absolute locations 0 (offset) and 2 (segment) so that it points to a new interrupt service routine—the one labeled OVR_INT in Example 4-4.
3. Perform the division. In the absence of overflow, the 80286 continues to the next consecutive instruction (SUB BX,BX). If overflow occurs, it activates the Type 0 interrupt service routine, which is now OVR_INT.
4. Restore the original Type 0 interrupt vector from values placed on the stack.

With or without overflow, the DIVUO procedure returns a 32-bit quotient (BX:AX) and a 16-bit remainder (DX). If no overflow occurs, BX is zero.

4.3 Square Root

In this final section we develop a program to calculate the integer square root of a 32-bit unsigned number, using the classical method of successive approximations known as Newton's method. This method says that *if A is an approximation for the square root of a number N, then*

Example 4-4. Division procedure that accounts for overflow.

```
        PAGE    ,132
TITLE   DIVUO - Division With Overflow

;   This divide procedure determines the correct quotient
;   and remainder, regardless of overflow.
;   Inputs: BX = Divisor
;           DX:AX = Dividend
;   Results: BX:AX = Quotient
;            DX = Remainder

;   To assemble: MASM DIVUO;
;   To link: LINK callprog+DIVUO;

        PUBLIC  DIVUO
CSEG    SEGMENT PARA 'CODE'
        ASSUME  CS:CSEG
DIVUO   PROC    FAR
        CMP     BX,0            ;Divisor = 0?
        JNZ     DVROK
        INT     0               ; Yes. Abort the divide
DVROK:  PUSH    ES              ;Save working registers
        PUSH    DI
        PUSH    CX
        MOV     DI,0            ;Fetch current INT 0 vector
        MOV     ES,DI
        PUSH    ES:[DI]         ; and save it on the stack
        PUSH    ES:[DI+2]
        LEA     CX,OVR_INT      ;Make INT 0 vector
        MOV     ES:[DI],CX      ; point to OVR_INT
        MOV     CX,SEG OVR_INT
        MOV     ES:[DI+2],CX
        DIV     BX              ;Perform the division
        SUB     BX,BX           ;If no overflow, BX = 0
RESTORE: POP    ES:[DI+2]       ;Restore INT 0 vector
        POP     ES:[DI]
        POP     CX              ;Restore registers
        POP     DI
        POP     ES
        RET

;   This interrupt service routine executes if the divide
;   operation produces overflow.

OVR_INT: POP    CX              ;Modify ret. addr. offset
        LEA     CX,RESTORE      ; to skip SUB BX,BX
        PUSH    CX
        PUSH    AX
        MOV     AX,DX           ;Set up 1st dividend, 0-Y1
        SUB     DX,DX
        DIV     BX              ;Q1 is in AX, R1 is in DX
        POP     CX              ;Pop orig. AX into CX
        PUSH    AX              ;Save Q1 on stack
```

Example 4-4. (continued).

```
          MOV     AX,CX            ;Set up 2nd dividend, R1-Y0
          DIV     BX               ;Q0 is in AX, R0 is in DX
          POP     BX               ;Final quotient is in BX:AX
          IRET
DIVUO     ENDP
CSEG      ENDS
          END
```

A1 = (N/A + A)/2

is a better approximation.

To illustrate, suppose you want the square root of a number that has the value N. To get the first approximation, use the formula (N/200) + 2. To get the second approximation, divide N by the first approximation, then average the two results. To get the third approximation, divide N by the second approximation and average, and so on. For example, to find the square root of 10,000:

N = 10,000; first approximation is (10,000/200) + 2, or 52
10,000/52 = 192, (192 + 52)/2 = 122
10,000/122 = 81, (122 + 81)/2 = 101
10,000/101 = 99, (101 + 99)/2 = 100
10,000/100 = 100

So the square root of 10,000 is 100. We know that 100 *is* the square root, rather than just another intermediate approximation, because 100 times 100 is 10,000.

This particular number, 10,000, happens to have an integer square root, but not many numbers do. For example, the square root of 9999 is not an integer. Thus, if we try to computerize the successive approximation method and use

root x root = number

as the "all done" criteria, the processor repeats the approximation instructions indefinitely, because the square of the *integer* approximation will never be 9999. Surely there must be a better way to stop the processor once it has found the closest, or "best," square root for a number.

You can use several different methods to end the approximation procedure. The one that best suits your needs depends on how accurate your answer must be and how much execution time you are willing to invest to get that answer.

For instance, you can let the 80286 execute the loop 10 times, and assume that that answer is accurate enough. Although it satisfies many applications, this method is rather arbitrary. For a more precise solution, you can let the 80286 continue looping until it finds two successive approximations that are identical or differ by only one. We take the latter approach in our example.

Example 4-5 gives a procedure (SQRT32) that uses successive approximations to calculate the integer square root of a 32-bit number. It obtains the source number from DX (high word) and AX (low word), and returns the 16-bit square root in BX.

To begin, the procedure saves BP, DX, and AX on the stack, then copies the Stack Pointer (SP) into BP; now BP points to AX on the stack. It then derives the first approximation using the formula (N/200) + 2.

The instruction at NXT_APP starts a loop that extends to the label DONE. With each pass through the loop, the 286 calculates a new approximation by dividing the 32-bit source number (read from the stack) by the preceding approximation, then averaging the two results. It averages results by right-shifting AX, which effectively divides it by 2. Using SHR instead of DIV here saves quite a bit of execution time—2 cycles for SHR versus 14 for DIV.

The procedure checks each new approximation against the preceding one, looking for approximations that are identical or differ by only 1 (+1 or -1). If either of these conditions occur, the processor transfers to DONE; otherwise, it goes back to NXT_APP to calculate a new approximation. At DONE, the 286 puts the final square root value in BX, then pops the source number (AX and DX) and the original value of BP off the stack.

Study Exercise (answer on page 402)

1. An interesting observation made a few years ago gives us a simple way to calculate square roots. It is: *The square root of an integer is equal to the number of successively higher odd numbers that can be subtracted from it.*

   Figure 4-2 shows how you can extract the square root of 25 using this method. (Skeptics will want to try a few additional cases.) In this example, a total of five odd numbers—1, 3, 5, 7, and 9—can be subtracted from 25, so the square root is 5.

   Develop a procedure that employs this algorithm to take the square root of the 32-bit unsigned number in DX (high word) and AX (low word), and returns the 16-bit square root in BX. As with Example 4-5, AX and DX should be returned intact.

Example 4-5. Square root of a 32-bit number.

```
        PAGE   ,132
TITLE   SQRT32 - Square Root

;   Calculates the square root of a 32-bit integer.
;   Input: DX:AX = Integer
;   Result: BX = Square root
;   The original number in DX:AX is unaffected.

;   To assemble: MASM SQRT32;
;   To link: LINK callprog+SQRT32;

        PUBLIC  SQRT32
CSEG    SEGMENT PARA 'CODE'
        ASSUME  CS:CSEG
SQRT32  PROC   FAR
        PUSH   BP              ;Save contents of BP
        PUSH   DX              ; and source number DX:AX
        PUSH   AX
        MOV    BP,SP           ;BP points to AX on the stack
        MOV    BX,200          ;As a first approx,
        DIV    BX              ; divide source number by 200,
        ADD    AX,2            ; then add 2
NXT_APP: MOV   BX,AX           ;Save this approx. in BX
        MOV    AX,[BP]         ;Read source number again
        MOV    DX,[BP+2]
        DIV    BX              ;Divide by last approx.
        ADD    AX,BX           ;Average last two approxs.
        SHR    AX,1
        CMP    AX,BX           ;Last two approxs. identical?
        JE     DONE
        SUB    BX,AX           ; No. Check for diff. of 1
        CMP    BX,1
        JE     DONE
        CMP    BX,-1
        JNE    NXT_APP
DONE:   MOV    BX,AX           ;Put result in BX
        POP    AX              ;Restore source number
        POP    DX
        POP    BP              ; and scratch register BP
        RET
SQRT32  ENDP
CSEG    ENDS
        END
```

```
 25
- 1  Partial square root = 1
 24
- 3  Partial square root = 2
 21
- 5  Partial square root = 3
 16
- 7  Partial square root = 4
  9
- 9  Square root         = 5
  0
```

Figure 4-2. Obtaining a square root with odd-number subtractions.

5

Operating on Data Structures

There are almost as many ways to organize information in memory as there are kinds of information to be organized. These organizational techniques vary with the application, and have such names as lists, arrays, strings, and look-up tables. These are all different kinds of *data structures.*

The subject of data structures can (and does) fill many volumes, so we can't hope to give it an exhaustive treatment in a book like this. Instead, we will concentrate on just three basic structures: *lists, look-up tables,* and *text files.*

Lists hold units of data (bytes or words), called *elements,* arranged sequentially in memory. The sequence can be *consecutive,* where elements occupy adjacent memory locations, or *linked,* where each element contains a "pointer" to the next one in the list. Moreover, the elements may be arranged randomly or in ascending or descending order.

Look-up tables are data structures that hold information (either data or addresses) that has a defined relationship to a known value. A telephone directory is a look-up table; knowing a name, you can look up an associated telephone number.

Text files consist of non-numeric information such as letters, reports, and telephone lists.

5.1 Unordered Lists

In our ordered society, where telephone book listings are arranged alphabetically and house numbers increase or decrease as you go up or down a street, unordered *anythings* somehow seem bothersome. Still, not everything can be neatly ordered, so unordered lists remain a fact of life in many applications, particularly those that involve random data or data that change with time. For example, computerized weather stations may store hourly temperature readings in unordered lists and manufacturers may log monthly shipping statistics in them.

Most lists are comprised of an element count byte (or word) and one or more data elements. When you work with a list, you generally want to add or delete elements, or search for one of a certain value. These operations are fairly easy to do.

1. To add an element, store it at the end of the list and add 1 to the element count.
2. To delete an element, move the rest of the elements upward in memory, then subtract 1 from the element count.
3. To search for a value, compare each element to the search value, starting with the first element in the list.

Adding an Element to an Unordered List

Procedure ADD_TO_UL, shown in Example 5-1, is the kind of program you would use to create an unordered list or add an element to an existing one. In this case, the list contains word values (either signed or unsigned).

ADD_TO_UL reads the element count into CX, then scans the data elements for the value in AX. If this value is already in the list (the final value of ZF is 0), the 286 pops the starting address back into DI and returns. Otherwise, it adds the value to the end of this list and increases the element count by one.

How long does this procedure take to execute? That depends on the number of elements and whether the search value is already in the list. The primary factor is how many times the Scan String (SCASW) instruction gets repeated. SCASW executes in (5 + 8N) cycles, where *N* is the number of repetitions. Let's examine the timing for both cases—value is not in the list and value is in the list—for a list that has N data elements.

If the search value is not in the list, the SCASW instruction executes N times. The remaining instructions in the procedure execute only once, and take 44 cycles. Therefore,

$$\begin{aligned}\text{Execution Time} &= 5 + 8N + 44 \\ &= 8N + 49 \text{ cycles}\end{aligned}$$

Thus, adding an element to a 100-element list takes 849 cycles, or 141.78 μs.

Example 5-1. Add an element to an unordered list.

```
        PAGE    ,132
TITLE   ADD_2_UL - Add to Unordered List

;    Adds the value in AX to an unoredered list in the
;    extra segment, if that value is not already in the list.
;    Inputs: DI = Starting address of the list
;            First location = List length (words)
;    Results: None
;    DI and AX are returned unaltered.

;    Assemble with: MASM ADD_2_UL;
;    Link with: LINK callprog+ADD_2_UL;

        PUBLIC  ADD_TO_UL
CSEG    SEGMENT PARA 'CODE'
        ASSUME  CS:CSEG
ADD_TO_UL PROC  FAR
        CLD                     ;Make DF=0, to scan forward
        PUSH    DI              ;Save starting address
        PUSH    CX
        MOV     CX,ES:[DI]      ;Fetch word count
        ADD     DI,2            ;Make DI point to 1st data el.
REPNE   SCASW                   ;Value already in list?
        POP     CX
        JNE     ADD_IT
        POP     DI              ; Yes. Restore starting addr.
        RET                     ;  and exit.
ADD_IT: MOV     ES:[DI],AX      ; No.  Add it to end of list,
        POP     DI              ;  then update element count
        INC     WORD PTR ES:[DI]
        RET                     ;  and exit.
ADD_TO_UL ENDP
CSEG    ENDS
        END
```

If the search value is in the list, the 286 should take an average of N/2 comparisons to locate it, because 50 percent of the time a search value will be in the lower half of the list and 50 percent of the time it will be in the upper half. This means scanning should take (5 + 4N) cycles, theoretically. The remaining instructions in the procedure take an additional 29 cycles. Therefore, on the average,

$$\begin{aligned}\text{Execution Time} &= 5 + 4N + 29 \\ &= 4N + 34 \text{ cycles}\end{aligned}$$

Thus, finding an element in an unordered 100-element list takes an average of 434 cycles, or 72.48 μs.

Deleting an Element from an Unordered List

To delete an element from an unordered list, you must find it, then move the rest of the elements up one position. In doing this, you write over the deletion "victim." Since an element has been removed, you decrease the element count (the first location in the list) by one.

To illustrate, Figure 5-1A shows a list of bytes in memory. Since the list has six data elements, the first location (LIST) holds the value 6. Figure 5-1B shows what the list looks like after the fourth element (14) has been deleted. The list then has only five data elements and the values 97 and 8 have moved up in memory, eradicating the deleted value.

The DEL_UL procedure in Example 5-2 performs just such an operation, using AX to specify the value to be deleted. As in Example 5-1, DI points to the start of the list.

The instructions that precede REPNE load the element count into CX and the address of the first data element into DI, then scan the list for the search value. These instructions are identical to the ones at the beginning of Example 5-1. If the search value is in the list (ZF = 1), the 286 jumps to DELETE.

At DELETE, the processor takes one of two paths. If the element to be deleted is at the end of the list (CX contains zero), the 286 jumps to DEC_CNT, where it simply decreases the list's element count. If the deletion victim is anywhere else in the list, the loop at NEXT_EL moves all remaining elements up one position, overwriting the victim. The element count is then decreased by one to reflect the deletion.

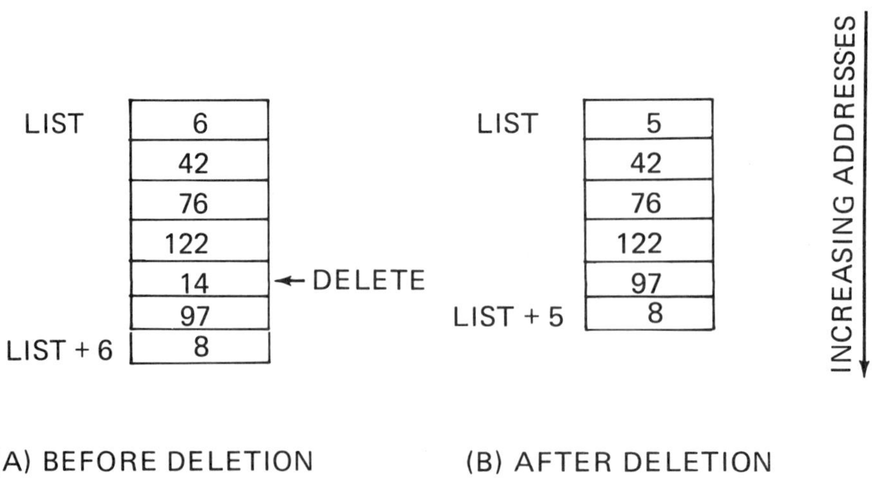

Figure 5-1. How a deletion affects a list.

Example 5-2. Delete an element from an unordered list.

```
        PAGE ,132
TITLE   DEL_UL - Delete from Unordered List

;  Deletes the value in AX from an unordered list in the
;  extra segment, if that value is in the list.
;  Inputs: DI = Starting address of the list
;          First location = Length of list (words)
;  Results: None
;  DI and AX are unaltered.

;  Assemble with: MASM DEL_UL;
;  Link with: LINK callprog+DEL_UL;

        PUBLIC  DEL_UL
CSEG    SEGMENT PARA 'CODE'
        ASSUME  CS:CSEG
DEL_UL  PROC    FAR
        CLD                     ;Make DF=0, to scan forward
        PUSH    BX              ;Save scratch register BX
        PUSH    DI              ; and starting address
        MOV     CX,ES:[DI]      ;Fetch element count
        ADD     DI,2            ;Make DI point to 1st data el.
REPNE   SCASW                   ;Value in the list?
        JE      DELETE          ; If so, go delete it.
        POP     DI              ; Otherwise, restore registers
        POP     BX
        RET                     ;  and exit.

;  The following instructions delete an element from the list,
;  as follows:
;    (1)  If the element lies at the end of the list,
;         delete it by decreasing the element count by 1.
;    (2)  Otherwise, delete the element by moving all
;         subsequent elements up by one position.

DELETE: JCXZ    DEC_CNT         ;If (CX) = 0, delete last el.
NEXT_EL: MOV    BX,ES:[DI]      ;Move one element up in list
        MOV     ES:[DI-2],BX
        ADD     DI,2            ;Point to next element
        LOOP    NEXT_EL         ;Repeat until all els. moved
DEC_CNT: POP    DI              ;Decrease el. count by 1
        DEC     WORD PTR ES:[DI]
        POP     BX              ;Restore contents of BX
        RET                     ; and exit
DEL_UL  ENDP
CSEG    ENDS
        END
```

Maximum and Minimum Values in an Unordered List

You may sometimes want to find the largest and smallest values in an unordered list. A reasonable approach is to initially declare the first element as both the maximum and the minimum value, then compare each of the remaining elements in the list to those values. If your program finds an element that is less than the minimum, it makes that value the new minimum. Similarly, if it finds an element that is greater than the maximum, it makes that value the new maximum.

The procedure MINMAX in Example 5-3 applies this method to an unordered list of unsigned word values whose starting address is in DI. MINMAX returns the maximum and minimum values in AX and BX, respectively.

This procedure has two parts. The first part calculates the number of comparisons to make (element count - 1) and sets up the first data element as both the maximum and minimum norm. The second part loops through the list searching for a new minimum or maximum. It records new minimums in BX and new maximums in AX.

Although MINMAX processes lists of unsigned word values, you can easily modify it to search for the maximum and minimum in lists of signed words: simply replace JAE CHKMAX with JGE CHKMAX and JBE NEXTEL with JLE NEXTEL. For the reason behind this, see Table 3-11 in Section 3.6.

5.2 Sorting Unordered Data

If you are plotting information versus time or processing text, you can accept the information in unordered form. However, in many applications it is better to have the information arranged in increasing or decreasing order, because it is easier to analyze that way.

How can you rearrange a list of unordered data? There is a considerable amount of literature on this subject, but we'll concentrate on one common sorting technique called the *bubble sort.* If you want to investigate other sorting techniques, D. E. Knuth's classic *The Art of Computer Programming. Volume 3: Sorting and Searching* (Addison-Wesley) is an excellent starting point.

Bubble Sort

The bubble sort technique is so named because it makes list elements "rise" upward in memory (to higher-numbered addresses) like soap bubbles

Example 5-3. Maximum and minimum values in an unordered list.

```
        PAGE    ,132
TITLE   MINMAX - Maximum & Minimum in an Unordered List

;   Finds the maximum and minimum words in an unordered
;   list in the extra segment.
;   Inputs: ES:DI = Starting address of the list
;           First location = Length of list (words)
;   Results: AX = Maximum
;            BX = Minimum
;   DI is unaltered.

;   Assemble with: MASM MINMAX;
;   Link with: LINK callprog+MINMAX;

        PUBLIC  MINMAX
CSEG    SEGMENT PARA 'CODE'
        ASSUME  CS:CSEG
MINMAX  PROC    FAR
        PUSH    CX
        PUSH    DI              ;Save starting address
        MOV     CX,ES:[DI]      ;Fetch element count
        DEC     CX              ;Get ready for count-1 compares
        ADD     DI,2            ;Point to first element
        MOV     BX,ES:[DI]      ;Declare it both minimum
        MOV     AX,BX           ; and maximum
CHKMIN: ADD     DI,2            ;Point to next element
        CMP     ES:[DI],BX      ;Compare element to minimum
        JAE     CHKMAX          ;New minimum found?
        MOV     BX,ES:[DI]      ; Yes. Put it in BX
        JMP     SHORT NEXTEL
CHKMAX: CMP     ES:[DI],AX      ;Compare element to maximum
        JBE     NEXTEL          ;New maximum found?
        MOV     AX,ES:[DI]      ; Yes. Put it in AX
NEXTEL: LOOP    CHKMIN          ;Check entire list
        POP     DI              ;Restore starting address
        POP     CX
        RET                     ; and exit
MINMAX  ENDP
CSEG    ENDS
        END
```

rise in the air. A bubble sort works its way through a list sequentially; it starts with the first element, and compares each element to the next one in the list.

If the bubble sort program finds an element that is greater than its higher-addressed neighbor, it exchanges these elements. It then compares the next two elements, exchanges them if required, and so on. By the time the 286 gets to the last element, the highest-valued element will have "bubbled-up" to that final list position.

In sorting with this algorithm, the processor usually makes several passes through the list, as you can see from the simple example in Figure 5-2. Here, the first pass "bubbles" 50 to the end of the list and the next two passes bubble 40 and 30 to the next highest positions. Therefore, this particular list gets sorted in three passes.

Seeing pass-by-pass "snapshots" of the list, as in Figure 5-2, makes it easy for *you* to know when a list is entirely sorted, but how can a *computer* know this? Unless you give it a specific pass count or tell it when to stop in some other way, the computer goes merrily along, executing pass after pass, ad infinitum. Since the number of sorting passes depends on the initial arrangement of the list, we have no way of providing an exact pass count in a program. As an alternative, we set up a special *exchange flag* that the computer can use to find out when to stop sorting.

The exchange flag is set to 1 before each sorting pass. Any sorting pass that includes an element exchange operation changes it to 0. Therefore, after each pass, the value of the exchange flag tells the computer whether to continue sorting. A 0 tells it to make another pass through the list; a 1 indicates the list is sorted, and tells it to stop sorting. Figure 5-3 shows a flowchart of the bubble sort algorithm.

As you can see, even if a list is already in order at the outset, it takes the processor one pass to deduce this fact. If one pass is the minimum, what *maximum* number of passes may you anticipate? Since the five-number list in Figure 5-2 was already partially sorted, we made only three sorting passes to put it in ascending order. One more pass is needed to detect that this list is indeed sorted, making four passes altogether.

If that list was initially arranged in descending order (the worst case), the processor would make five passes through it—four passes to sort the data and one more to determine that no further sorting was needed. From this observation, we can state with *an N-element list takes from one to N passes to sort, with (N + 1)/2 passes being the average.*

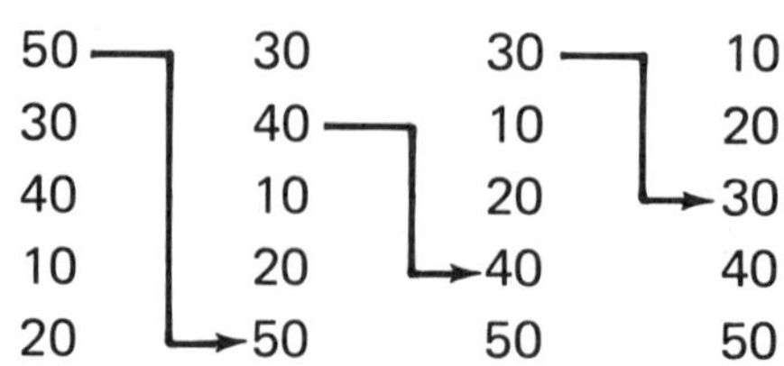

Figure 5-2. A bubble sort "bubbles" the largest numbers to the end.

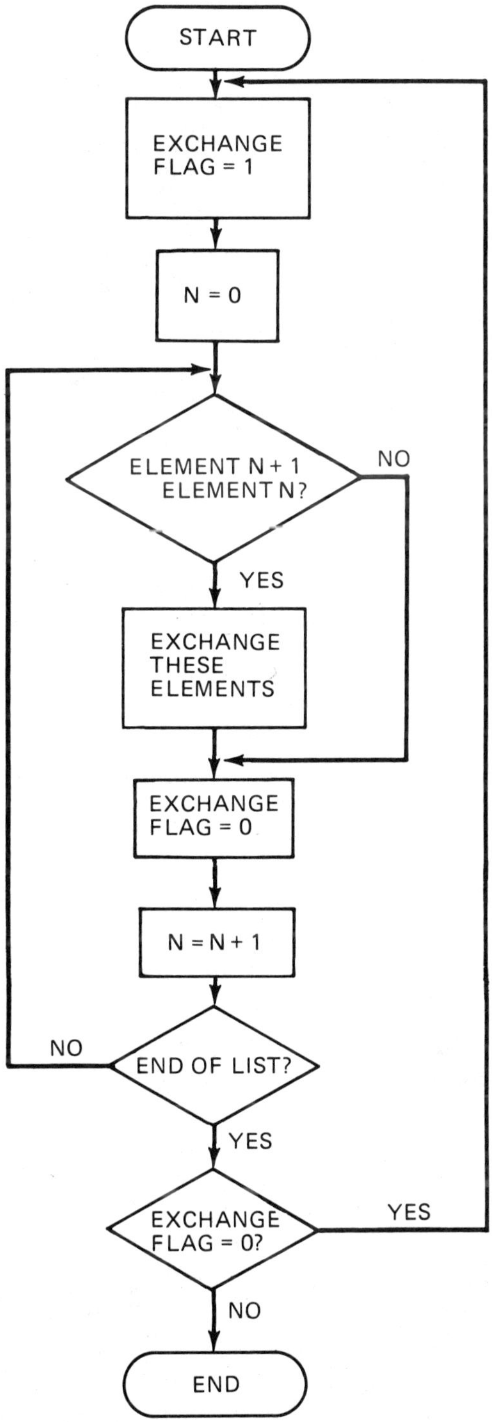

Figure 5-3. The bubble sort algorithm.

Bubble Sort Program

With the preceding background in bubble sort theory and a flowchart showing what needs to be done, we are prepared to write a sorting program. Example 5-4 shows a procedure (B_SORT) that sorts a list of word values. (You can easily modify it to sort a list of bytes.)

As usual, the list is in the extra segment and its starting address is in DI. B_SORT uses BX to hold the exchange flag (which always contains either 1 or 0) and AX to hold the element value that is being compared to the next element in the list.

The B_SORT procedure also uses two word variables in the data segment: *SAVE_CNT* holds the comparison count (element count - 1) and *START_ADDR* holds the starting address of the list. B_SORT uses these variables to reinitialize CX and DI at the beginning of each new sort operation.

Although the B_SORT procedure has a lot of instructions, it is quite simple. After calculating the values for SAVE_CNT and START_ADDR, the procedure initializes the exchange flag (BX = 1), the comparison counter (CX), and the element pointer (DI). At the label NEXT, the 286 loads an element into AX, then compares it with the next element in memory.

If the second element is less than the first, the 286 loads it into AX and stores the two elements back into memory, in reverse order. Because an exchange took place, the processor clears BX to zero. The LOOP instruction at CONT transfers control back to NEXT until the entire list has been processed.

When all elements have been compared, a CMP instruction checks whether the exchange flag (BX) is zero. If it is, at least one exchange took place during the preceding sorting pass, so the 286 jumps back to INIT to begin a new pass. Otherwise, if BX is still 1 after a sorting pass, the list is finally sorted, so the 286 restores DI from START_ADDR and BX and AX from the stack, then returns.

Streamlining the Bubble Sort Program

The bubble sort procedure in Example 5-4 has one subtle, but noteworthy, deficiency: it sorts some elements needlessly. To be specific, during each sorting pass B_SORT compares every pair of elements in the list. Note, however, that each pass "bubbles" one element to its final position in the list. That is, the first pass bubbles the highest-valued element to the end of the list, the second pass bubbles the next highest-valued element to the next-to-last position, and so on. Thus, since the elements at the end of the list have

Example 5-4. Bubble sort procedure.

```
        PAGE    ,132
TITLE   B_SORT - Bubble Sort

;   Arranges the 16-bit elements of a list in the extra
;   segment in ascending order, using bubble sort.
;   Inputs: ES:DI = Starting address of the list
;           First location = Length of list (words)
;   DI is unaltered.

;   Assemble with: MASM B_SORT;
;   Link with: LINK callprog+B_SORT;

DSEG    SEGMENT PARA 'DATA'
SAVE_CNT DW   ?
START_ADDR DW ?
DSEG    ENDS

        PUBLIC  B_SORT
CSEG    SEGMENT PARA 'CODE'
        ASSUME  CS:CSEG,DS:DSEG
B_SORT  PROC   FAR
        PUSH   DS             ;Save caller's registers
        PUSH   CX
        PUSH   AX
        PUSH   BX
        MOV    AX,DSEG        ;Initialize DS
        MOV    DS,AX
        MOV    START_ADDR,DI   ;Save starting address
        MOV    CX,ES:[DI]     ;Fetch element count
        DEC    CX             ;Get ready for count-1 compares
        MOV    SAVE_CNT,CX    ;Save this value in memory
INIT:   MOV    BX,1           ;Exchange flag (BX) = 1
        MOV    CX,SAVE_CNT    ; and load this count into CX
        MOV    DI,START_ADDR   ;Load start address into DI
NEXT:   ADD    DI,2           ;Address a data element
        MOV    AX,ES:[DI]     ; and load it into AX
        CMP    ES:[DI+2],AX    ;Is next el. < this el.?
        JAE    CONT           ; No.  Go check next pair
        XCHG   ES:[DI+2],AX    ; Yes. Exchange these elmts.
        MOV    ES:[DI],AX
        SUB    BX,BX          ; and make exchange flag 0
CONT:   LOOP   NEXT           ;Process entire list
        CMP    BX,0           ;Any exchanges made?
        JE     INIT           ; If so, process list again
        MOV    DI,START_ADDR   ; If not, restore registers
        POP    BX
        POP    AX
        POP    CX
        POP    DS
        RET                   ;  and exit.
B_SORT  ENDP
CSEG    ENDS
        END
```

reached their final (sorted) positions, you may exclude them from subsequent sorting passes!

To exclude sorted elements, *each pass through the list should involve one less comparison than its predecessor.* We can make this happen by modifying our procedure so that the value in SAVE_CNT decrements before each new pass.

To do this, simply change the sixth, seventh, and eighth instructions in the procedure to bring the decrement-count operation under the label INIT. You must also add one more instruction after the decrement, to make the processor exit if SAVE_CNT is 0. Here is a summary of the changes:

Original

```
        DEX   CX
        MOV   SAVE_CNT,CX
INIT:   MOV   BX,1
```

Revised

```
        MOV   SAVE_CNT,CX
INIT:   MOV   BX,1
        DEC   SAVE_CNT
        JZ    SORTED
```

Here, SORTED is the label on the MOV instruction that restores the contents of DI from START_ADDR. Example 5-5 shows a new bubble sort procedure (BUBBLE) that has these changes.

For any given list, BUBBLE makes the same number of sorting passes as the B_SORT procedure in Example 5-4. But because BUBBLE makes about half as many *comparisons*, it executes much faster than B_SORT.

For example, to sort 100 elements arranged in decreasing order, B_SORT makes 100 passes, with 99 comparisons in each pass—a total of 9,900 comparisons. By contrast, BUBBLE makes 100 passes, with 99 comparisons in the first pass and one in the last pass, for an average of 50 comparisons—a total of 5,500 comparisons.

To compare B_SORT and BUBBLE, I sorted two lists of 16-bit elements using both procedures. Both lists were initially arranged in decreasing order. The first list, which had 500 elements, was sorted in 2.5 seconds by B_SORT and in 1.5 seconds by BUBBLE. Sorting the second list, which had 1000 elements, took B_SORT 10.0 seconds and BUBBLE 5.0 seconds. Based on these tests, we can conclude that *BUBBLE sorts a list 40 to 50 percent faster than B_SORT.* (If you're curious, sorting the 1000-word list on a regular IBM PC takes B_SORT 28.0 seconds and BUBBLE 16.5 seconds. Hence, the AT does the job about three times faster than the PC!)

Note that the sorting time rises dramatically as you take on longer lists. Our bubble sort procedures can sort up to 32K words, but you'd better be prepared to wait if your list is anywhere near that long. In fact, a "worst-case" list of even 2,000 words takes BUBBLE 20 seconds to sort—four times longer than a 1,000-word list.

Example 5-5. A better bubble sort procedure.

```
        PAGE   ,132
TITLE   BUBBLE - Better Bubble Sort

;   Arranges the 16-bit elements os a list in the extra
;   segment in ascending order, using bubble sort.
;   Inputs: ES:DI = Starting address of the list
;           First location = Length of the list (words)
;   DI Is unaltered.

;   Assemble with: MASM BUBBLE;
;   Link with: LINK callprog+BUBBLE;

DSEG     SEGMENT PARA 'DATA'
SAVE_CNT DW    ?
START_ADDR DW ?
DSEG     ENDS

        PUBLIC  BUBBLE
CSEG    SEGMENT PARA 'CODE'
        ASSUME  CS:CSEG,DS:DSEG
BUBBLE  PROC   FAR
        PUSH   DS              ;Save caller's registers
        PUSH   CX
        PUSH   AX
        PUSH   BX
        MOV    AX,DSEG         ;Initialize DS
        MOV    DS,AX
        MOV    START_ADDR,DI    ;Save starting address in memory
        MOV    CX,ES:[DI]      ;Fetch element count
        MOV    SAVE_CNT,CX     ;Save this value in memory
INIT:   MOV    BX,1            ;Exchange flag (BX) = 1
        DEC    SAVE_CNT        ;Get ready for count-1 compares
        JZ     SORTED          ;Exit if SAVE_CNT is 0
        MOV    CX,SAVE_CNT     ; and load this count into CX
        MOV    DI,START_ADDR    ;Load start address into DI
NEXT:   ADD    DI,2            ;Address a data element
        MOV    AX,ES:[DI]      ; and load it into AX
        CMP    ES:[DI+2],AX     ;Is next el. < this el.?
        JAE    CONT             ; No.  Go check next pair
        XCHG   ES:[DI+2],AX     ; Yes. Exchange these elements
        MOV    ES:[DI],AX
        SUB    BX,BX            ; and make exchange flag 0
CONT:   LOOP   NEXT            ;Process entire list
        CMP    BX,0            ;Any exchanges made?
        JE     INIT            ; If so, process list again
SORTED: MOV    DI,START_ADDR    ; If not, restore registers
        POP    BX
        POP    AX
        POP    CX
        POP    DS
        RET                    ;  and exit.
BUBBLE  ENDP
CSEG    ENDS
        END
```

5.3 Ordered Lists

Now that you know how to sort a list, let's discuss how to search for a specific value, and then see how to add and delete elements.

Searching an Ordered List

In Section 5.1 we learned that locating a value in an unordered list requires searching through it element by element. This takes an average of N/2 comparisons for an N-element list. If a list is *ordered*, however, you can use any of several search techniques to find a value. For all but the shortest lists, most of these techniques are faster and more efficient than searching sequentially.

Binary Search

One common technique for searching ordered lists is called the *binary search*. Its name reflects the fact that it divides the list into a series of progressively shorter halves ("bi" is Latin for "two") and eventually closes in on one element. A binary search starts in the middle of the list and determines whether the search value lies above or below that point. It then takes *that* half of the list and divides *it* into halves, and so on.

The flowchart in Figure 5-4 shows how to make a binary search on an ordered list, producing an address as the result. If the search value is in the list, the address is that of the matching element. If the value is not in the list, the address is that of the last location to be compared. Of course, the program that performs this search must also return some kind of indicator that tells you whether the address reflects a successful or unsuccessful search.

Example 5-6 shows a procedure (B_SEARCH) you can use to search an ordered list of unsigned words. The fact that this procedure operates on words instead of bytes requires us to make a few changes to our basic algorithm. For one thing, because words lie two bytes apart in memory, we must include instructions that ensure the index is always a multiple of two; that is, an *even* value. For the same reason, we terminate a search, and declare it unsuccessful, when the index has decreased to 2 (instead of 0).

In this procedure, the search value is in AX and the starting address of the list is in DI. B_SEARCH returns the result address in SI, and CF tells whether the value was found (CF = 0) or not found (CF = 1).

The B_SEARCH procedure begins with a step that is not shown in the basic binary search algorithm (Figure 5-4): it compares the search value with the first and last elements in the list. If the search value is less than the first

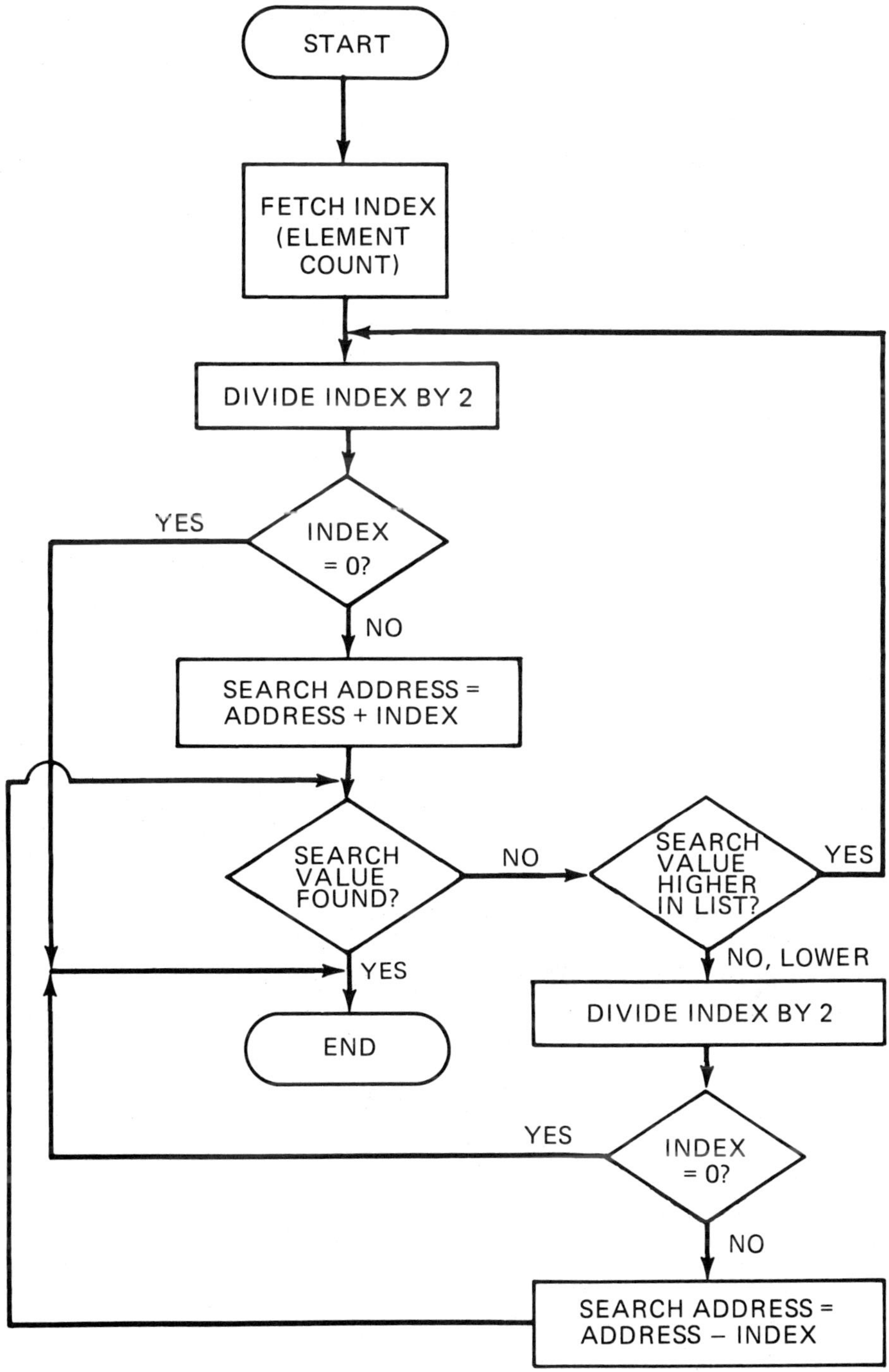

Figure 5-4. Binary search algorithm.

Example 5-6. 16-bit binary search procedure.

```
         PAGE   ,132
TITLE    B_SEARCH - Binary Search Procedure

;   Searches an ordered list in the extra segment for the
;   word value contained in AX.
;   Inputs: ES:DI = Starting address of the list
;           First location = Length of list (words)
;   Results: If the value is in the list,
;              CF = 0
;              SI = Offset of matching element
;            If the value is not in the list,
;              CF = 1
;              SI = Offset of last element compared
;   AX and DI are unaffected.

;   Assemble with: MASM B_SEARCH;
;   Link with: LINK callprog+B_SEARCH;

DSEG     SEGMENT PARA 'DATA'
START_ADDR DW ?
DSEG     ENDS

         PUBLIC  B_SEARCH
CSEG     SEGMENT PARA 'CODE'
         ASSUME  CS:CSEG,DS:DSEG
B_SEARCH PROC FAR
         PUSH   DS              ;Save caller's DS register
         PUSH   AX
         MOV    AX,DSEG         ;Initialize DS
         MOV    DS,AX
         POP    AX

;   Find out if AX lies beyond the boundaries of the list.

         CMP    AX,ES:[DI+2]    ;Search value < or = first el.?
         JA     CHK_LAST        ; No.  Go check last element
         LEA    SI,ES:[DI+2]    ; Yes. Fetch addr. of first el.
         JE     EXIT            ;If value = 1st element, exit
         STC                    ;If value < 1st element, set CF
         JMP    EXIT            ;and then exit
CHK_LAST: MOV   SI,ES:[DI]      ;Point to last element
         SHL    SI,1
         ADD    SI,DI
         CMP    AX,ES:[SI]      ;Search value > or = last el.?
         JB     SEARCH          ; No.  Go search list
         JE     EXIT            ; Yes. Exit if value = last el.
         STC                    ;If value > last element, set CF
         JMP    EXIT            ;   and then exit
;   Search for value within the list.

SEARCH:  MOV    START_ADDR,DI   ;Save starting address in memory
         MOV    SI,ES:[DI]      ;Fetch index
```

Example 5-6. (continued).

```
EVEN_IDX: TEST SI,1            ;Force index to an even value
        JZ     ADD_IDX
        INC    SI
ADD_IDX: ADD   DI,SI           ;Calculate next search address
COMPARE: CMP   AX,ES:[DI]      ;Search value found?
        JE     ALL_DONE        ; If so, exit
        JA     HIGHER          ; Otherwise, find correct half

;   These instructions are executed if the search value is lower
;   in the list.

        CMP    SI,2            ;Index = 2?
        JNE    IDX_OK
NO_MATCH: STC                  ; If so, set CF
        JE     ALL_DONE        ;  and exit
IDX_OK: SHR    SI,1            ; If not, divide index by 2
        TEST   SI,1            ;Force index to an even value
        JZ     SUB_IDX
        INC    SI
SUB_IDX: SUB   DI,SI           ;Calculate next address
        JMP    SHORT COMPARE   ;Go check this element

;   These instructions are executed if the search value is higher
;   in the list.

HIGHER: CMP    SI,2            ;Index = 2?
        JE     NO_MATCH        ; If so, go set CF and exit
        SHR    SI,1            ; If not, divide index by 2
        JMP    SHORT EVEN_IDX  ;Go check next element

;   Following are exit instructions.

ALL_DONE: MOV SI,DI            ;Move compare address into SI
        MOV    DI,START_ADDR   ;Restore starting address
EXIT:   POP    DS
        RET                    ; and exit
B_SEARCH ENDP
CSEG    ENDS
        END
```

element or greater than the last element, or if it matches one of those elements, the procedure terminates without further ado. If these initial checks fail, however, the 286 proceeds to the search operation, starting at SEARCH.

After saving DI in memory, the 286 copies the index (word count) from the first location of the list into SI, and forces it to an even value. This index is added to DI to form the address of the middle element in the list, the starting point for the binary search. The 286 then compares the search value to this middle element, and jumps to ALL_DONE if the values match. In the absence of a match, the 286 determines whether to continue its search in the upper half of the list (using the instructions that start at HIGHER) or the lower half.

These paths are similar in that both do the following:

1. Check whether the index is equal to 2. If it is, the 286 sets CF to 1 (to indicate a non-match), then transfers to ALL_DONE to exit.
2. Divide the index by 2 by shifting it right one position.
3. Force the shifted index to an even value.

However, to search lower in the list, the 286 subtracts the index (SI) from the current address (DI); to search higher, it adds the index to the current address.

This process repeats until the index has decreased to 2 or the search value is found. Either way, the procedure ends at ALL_DONE, where DI is moved to SI and the original contents of DI are retrieved from memory.

How much more efficient is a binary search than a straight sequential, element-by-element scan—the kind we used in Examples 5-1 and 5-2? In "An Introduction to Algorithm Design" (*Computer,* February 1979, pp. 66-78), Jon L. Bentley stated that while a sequential search of an N-element list requires an average of N/2 comparisons, a binary search requires an average of $\log_2 N$ comparisons. Therefore, sequentially scanning a 100-element list averages 50 comparisons, but a binary search does the same job with about seven comparisons!

Of course, you normally search a list for a value in order to *do* something to the matching element. Typically, you either want to add the value to the list or delete it from the list. Let's see how to perform those operations.

Adding an Element to an Ordered List

You can add an element to an ordered list in four steps:

1. Find out where the value is to be added.
2. Clear a location for the entry by moving all higher-valued elements down one position.
3. Insert the entry at the newly-vacated element position.
4. Add 1 to the element count, to reflect the insertion.

The B_SEARCH procedure we just developed gives us a good clue as to where the entry should be added: it returns the address of the element where the search stopped. To complete Step 1, we need to determine whether to insert the entry just *before* or just *after* that final search element. You can determine that by comparing the entry value to the final search element.

Example 5-7 shows a procedure (ADD_TO_OL) that performs the four steps we just listed. It begins by calling B_SEARCH, to find out whether the entry value is already in the list. Recall that B_SEARCH returns an address in SI and a found/not-found indicator in the Carry Flag (CF).

Upon return from B_SEARCH, the ADD_TO_OL procedure interrogates CF, and exits if CF is 0 (since that means the entry is already in the list). If CF is 1, however, the procedure saves the last-searched address in BX and calculates the address of the last element (in CX). Subtracting the contents of SI from this address gives the number of bytes that must be moved higher in memory to make room for the insertion. Dividing this result by 2 (right-shifting it) tells you how many *words* to move. If the entry value is less than the last-compared element, that element must also be moved, so we increase the move count (CX) by 1.

At CHECK_CNT, the 286 checks the move count. If it is zero, the entry is simply tacked on to the end of the list. Otherwise, this value must be inserted in the list; this requires moving all subsequent elements down one word position.

The instructions starting at MOVE_ELS move elements down one by one, starting with the last word in the list. When all required elements have been moved, the 286 inserts the entry (AX) in the newly-vacated slot, then increases the element count by 1.

Deleting an Element from an Ordered List

It is much easier to delete an element from an ordered list than it is to add one. All we must do is find the proper element, move all subsequent elements up one location, and decrement the element count.

Example 5-8 shows a typical delete procedure (DEL_OL), which uses B_SEARCH (Example 5-6) to locate the intended deletion "victim." As usual, the list's starting address is in DI and the value to be deleted is in AX.

If B_SEARCH locates the entry value in the list, DEL_OL uses its address, and the address of the end of the list, to determine how many words to move up. The four-instruction loop at MOVEM performs the move operation. When the 286 has moved all words, it decreases the list's element count to reflect the deletion.

Example 5-7. Add an element to an ordered list.

```
        PAGE   ,132
TITLE   ADD_2_OL - Add Entry to an Ordered List

;   Adds the element in AX to an ordered list in the
;   extra segment, if that value is not already in the list.
;   Inputs: DI = Starting address of the list
;           First location = List length (words).
;   Result: None
;   DI and AX are unaltered.
;   The B_SEARCH procedure (Example 5-6) is used to conduct
;   the search.

;   Assemble with: MASM ADD_2_OL;
;   Link with: LINK callprog+ADD_2_OL+B_SEARCH;

        EXTRN B_SEARCH:FAR
        PUBLIC  ADD_TO_OL
CSEG    SEGMENT PARA 'CODE'
        ASSUME  CS:CSEG
ADD_TO_OL PROC  FAR
        PUSH   CX              ;Save caller's registers
        PUSH   SI
        PUSH   BX
        CALL   B_SEARCH        ;Is the value in the list?
        JNC    GOODBYE         ; If so, exit
        MOV    BX,SI           ; If not, copy compare addr. to BX
        MOV    CX,ES:[DI]      ;Find address of last element
        SHL    CX,1
        ADD    CX,DI           ; and put it in CX
        PUSH   CX              ;Save this address on the stack
        SUB    CX,SI           ;Calculate no. of words to be moved
        SHR    CX,1
        CMP    AX,ES:[SI]      ;Should compare el. be moved,too?
        JA     EXCLUDE
        INC    CX              ; Yes. Increase move count by 1
        JNZ    CHECK_CNT
EXCLUDE: ADD   BX,2            ; No.  Adjust insert pointer
CHECK_CNT: CMP CX,0            ;Move count = 0?
        JNE    MOVE_ELS
        POP    SI              ; If so, store value at end of list
        MOV    ES:[SI+2],AX
        JMP    SHORT INC_CNT    ;  then go increase element count
MOVE_ELS: POP  SI              ;Load start address for move
        PUSH   BX              ;Save insert address on stack
MOVE_ONE: MOV  BX,ES:[SI]      ;Move one element down in list
        MOV    ES:[SI+2],BX
        SUB    SI,2            ;Point to next element
        LOOP   MOVE_ONE        ;Repeat until all are moved
        POP    BX              ;Retrieve insert address
        MOV    ES:[BX],AX      ;Insert AX in the list
INC_CNT: INC   WORD PTR ES:[DI] ;Add 1 to element count
```

Example 5-7. (continued).

```
GOODBYE: POP   BX             ;Restore registers
         POP   SI
         POP   CX
         RET                  ; and exit
ADD_TO_OL ENDP
CSEG     ENDS
         END
```

Example 5-8. Delete an element from an ordered list.

```
        PAGE   ,132
TITLE   DEL_OL - Delete Element From Ordered List

;  Deletes the value in AX from the ordered list in the
;  extra segment, if the value is in the list.
;  Inputs: ES:DI = Starting address of the list
;          First location = Length of list (words)
;  AX and DI are unaffected.
;  The B_SEARCH procedure (Example 5-6) is used to conduct
;  the search.

;  Assemble with: MASM DEL_OL;
;  Link with: LINK callprog+DEL_OL+B_SEARCH;

        EXTRN B_SEARCH:FAR
        PUBLIC  DEL_OL
CSEG    SEGMENT PARA 'CODE'
DEL_OL  PROC  FAR
        ASSUME  CS:CSEG
        PUSH  CX             ;Save caller's registers
        PUSH  SI
        PUSH  BX
        CALL  B_SEARCH       ;Is the value in the list?
        JC    ADIOS          ; If not, exit
        MOV   CX,ES:[DI]     ; If so, find addr. of last element
        SHL   CX,1
        ADD   CX,DI          ; and put it in CX
        CMP   CX,SI          ;Is the last el. to be deleted?
        JE    CNT_M1         ; Yes. Go decrement el. count
        SUB   CX,SI          ; No.  Calculate move count
        SHR   CX,1
MOVEM:  MOV   BX,ES:[SI+2]   ;Move one element up in list
        MOV   ES:[SI],BX
        ADD   SI,2           ;Point to next element
        LOOP  MOVEM          ;Repeat until all are moved
```

Example 5-8. (continued).

```
CNT_M1: DEC    WORD PTR ES:[DI] ;Decrease element count by 1
ADIOS:  POP    BX               ;Restore registers
        POP    SI
        POP    CX
        RET                     ; and exit
DEL_OL  ENDP
CSEG    ENDS
        END
```

5.4 Look-Up Tables

Many programs use tables to hold values that they need for processing. Sometimes these tables hold numbers that take too much time to calculate, such as sines of angles. Other times, they hold parameters that have some defined relationship to a program input, but which cannot be calculated. For instance, you can't expect the computer to calculate someone's telephone number based on their name.

Applications like these call for a *look-up table*. As the name implies, a look-up table obtains an item of information (an *argument*) based on a known value (a *function*).

Look-up tables can replace complicated or time-consuming conversion operations, such as extracting the square root or cube root of a number, or deriving a trigonometric function (sine, cosine, etc.) of an angle. Look-up tables are especially efficient when a function covers only a small range of arguments (e.g., the cubes of numbers between 1 and 20). By using a look-up table, the computer doesn't need to perform complex calculations each time it needs a value.

In general, look-up tables save time in all but the simplest cases. (For instance, you wouldn't use a look-up table to store arguments that are always twice the value of a function.) But since look-up tables usually take up large amounts of memory storage space, they are most efficient in applications where you are willing to sacrifice memory space for execution speed.

Because look-up applications are so common, the 286 has a special instruction, *Translate (XLAT)*, for this purpose. XLAT looks up a value in a byte table, using the contents of BX as a base address and the contents of AL as an index into the table, and returns it in AL. This section includes examples of look-up operations on both byte tables and word tables.

Look-Up Tables Can Replace Equations

You can save processing time and program development time by providing the results of complex equations in a look-up table. For example, a look-up table can provide the sine or cosine of an angle.

Sine of an Angle

As you may recall from high school trigonometry, the sines of all angles between 0° and 360° form the curve shown in Figure 5-5A. Mathematically, you can approximate the curve with this formula

$$\text{sine}(X) = X - \frac{X^3}{3!} + \frac{X^5}{5!} - \frac{X^7}{7!} + \frac{X^9}{9!} \ldots$$

It is possible to write a program to make this calculation, but the program would probably require a few milliseconds to execute. If your application requires very precise sines, you may be forced to write such a program, but most applications are better served by an angle-to-sine look-up table.

If an application needs the sine of any angle between 0° and 360°, where the angle is an integer in degrees, how many sine values must the table contain—360? No, we can get by with a table of only *91 sine values*—one for each angle between 0° and 90°.

To understand how this can be so, look at Figure 5-5A again. If we call the leftmost quarter of the graph (angles from 0° to 90°) Quadrant 1, we see that:

1. Sines in Quadrant 2 (91° to 180°) are the "mirror image" of those in Quadrant 1.
2. Sines in Quadrant 3 (181° to 270°) are the "negative inverse" of those in Quadrant 1.
3. Sines in Quadrant 4 (271° to 360°) are the "negative inverse, mirror image" of those in Quadrant 1.

That is, the sines in Quadrants 2, 3, and 4 bear some simple relationship to those in Quadrant 1.

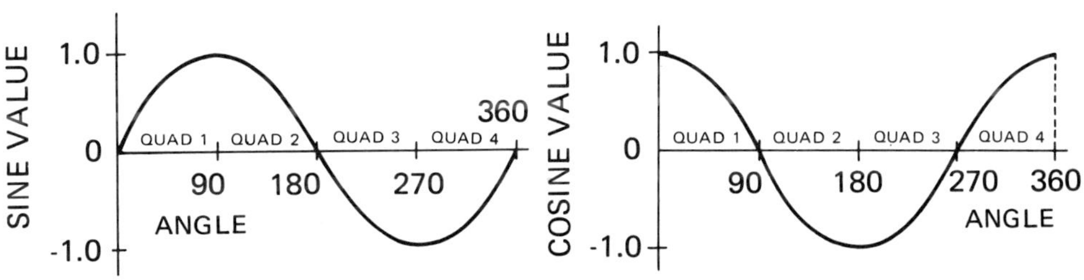

(A) SINES (B) COSINES

Figure 5-5. Sines and cosines of angles between 0 and 360 degrees.

Therefore, if you store the values in Quadrant 1 in a look-up table, your program can find the sine of an angle in any quadrant by making these conversions:

If the angle X is between	Take
0° and 90°	Sine(X)
91° and 180°	Sine(180 - X)
181° and 270°	-Sine(X - 180)
271° and 360°	-Sine(360 - X)

These relationships let us construct a flowchart for an angle-to-sine conversion program. This flowchart, shown in Figure 5-6, derives the sine as a sign-and-magnitude value. That is, the high-order bit of the result gives the sign of the sine (0 = positive, 1 = negative) and the remaining bits give the sine's magnitude, its absolute value.

Example 5-9 gives an angle-to-sine look-up procedure called *FIND_SINE* that accepts angles from 0° to 360° in AX and returns a 16-bit sign-and-magnitude sine value in BX. The sines are stored as integers in the look-up table SINES. You must divide them by 10,000 to use them as operands.

To begin, the 286 checks the size of the angle. If it is less than 181°, the processor jumps to SIN_POS; otherwise, it sets the most-significant bit of a sign register (CX) to 1—because sines above 180° are negative—and subtracts 180 from the angle.

With the correct sign now in Bit 15 of CX, the CMP instruction at SIN_POS compares the input angle to 91°. If the angle is greater than or equal to 91°, it must be subtracted from 180. You might expect to perform this subtraction with the instruction SUB 180,AX, but the 286 does not offer this form. That being the case, we make the subtraction by negating AX, then adding 180 to the result. The four instructions at GET_SIN load the angle into BX, double it to form a word index, look up the sine in SINES, and OR it with the sign in CX.

Cosine of an Angle

As Figure 5-5B shows, the cosine curve is nothing more than the sine curve shifted one quadrant to the left. Therefore, the cosine of any given angle is equal to the sine of an angle that is 90° greater. That is,

cosine(X) = sine(X+90)

Knowing this, we can use the SINES table in Example 5-9 to look up the cosine of an angle as well as its sine. Example 5-10 shows a procedure that

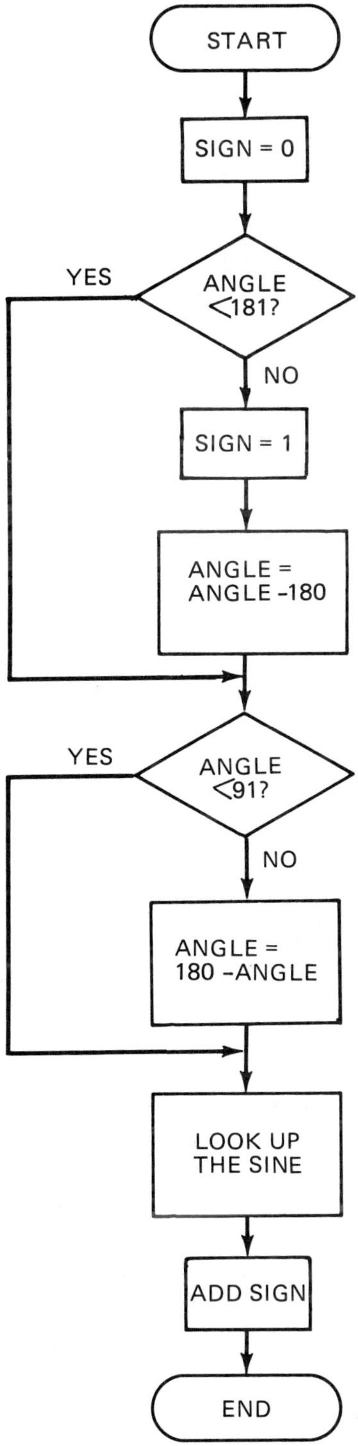

Figure 5-6. Flowchart for angle-to-sine conversion program.

Example 5-9. Look up the sine of an angle.

```
        PAGE    ,132
TITLE   SINE - Sine of an Angle

;   Returns the sine of an angle.
;   Input: AX = Angle (0 to 360)
;   Result: BX = Sine, in sign-and-magnitude form
;   AX is unaffected.

;   Assemble with: MASM SINE;
;   Link with: LINK callprog+SINE;

DSEG    SEGMENT PARA 'DATA'
SINES   DW     0,175,349,523,698,872      ;0-5
        DW     1045,1219,1392,1564,1736 ;6-10
        DW     1908,2079,2250,2419,2588 ;11-15
        DW     2756,2924,3090,3256,3420 ;16-20
        DW     3584,3746,3907,4067,4226 ;21-25
        DW     4384,4540,4695,4848,5000 ;26-30
        DW     5150,5299,5446,5592,5736 ;31-35
        DW     5878,6018,6157,6293,6428 ;36-40
        DW     6561,6691,6820,6947,7071 ;41-45
        DW     7193,7313,7431,7547,7660 ;46-50
        DW     7771,7880,7986,8090,8191 ;51-55
        DW     8290,8387,8480,8572,8660 ;56-60
        DW     8746,8829,8910,8988,9063 ;61-65
        DW     9135,9205,9272,9336,9397 ;66-70
        DW     9455,9511,9563,9613,9659 ;71-75
        DW     9703,9744,9781,9816,9848 ;76-80
        DW     9877,9903,9926,9945,9962 ;81-85
        DW     9976,9986,9994,9998,10000 ;86-90
DSEG    ENDS

        PUBLIC  FIND_SINE
CSEG    SEGMENT PARA 'CODE'
        ASSUME  CS:CSEG,DS:DSEG
FIND_SINE PROC  FAR
        PUSH  DS              ;Save the caller's registers
        PUSH  AX
        PUSH  CX

        MOV   BX,DSEG         ;Initialize DS
        MOV   DS,BX

        SUB   CX,CX           ;Initialize sign to 0
        CMP   AX,181          ;Angle < 181 degrees?
        JB    SIN_POS         ; Yes. Continue with sign = 0
        MOV   CX,8000H        ; No.  Set sign = 1
        SUB   AX,180          ;   and subtract 180 from angle
SIN_POS: CMP  AX,91           ;Angle < 91 degrees?
        JB    GET_SIN         ; Yes. Go look up sine
        NEG   AX              ; No.  Subtract angle from 180
        ADD   AX,180
```

Example 5-9. (continued).

```
GET_SIN: MOV   BX,AX         ;Make angle a word index
         SHL   BX,1
         MOV   BX,SINES[BX]   ; and look up the sine value
         OR    BX,CX         ;Combine sine with sign bit
         POP   CX
         POP   AX
         POP   DS
         RET                 ; and exit
FIND_SINE ENDP
CSEG     ENDS
         END
```

does this. As with FIND_SINE, you must divide the result of FIND_COS by 10,000.

Incidentally, note that the sine and cosine curves are symmetric about the vertical axis; thus, sines and cosines of negative angles have the same magnitudes as their positive counterparts. For example, the sine and cosine of -25° have the same magnitudes as those of +25°. This means you can also use FIND_SINE and FIND_COS for an angle between -1° and -360° if you supply its *absolute value* in AX.

Look-Up Tables Can Perform Code Conversions

Look-up tables can also hold coded data such as display codes, printer codes, and messages. Example 5-11 shows a procedure that performs multiple look-ups. It converts a hexadecimal digit in AL to its ASCII, BCD, and EBCDIC equivalents, and returns them in CH, CL, and AH, respectively.

When you transmit data between the computer and a printer, display, or some other peripheral in the system, it takes a form called *ASCII* (for American Standard Code for Information Interchange). *EBCDIC* (Extended Binary-Coded Decimal Interchange Code) is a transmission protocol for data processing and communications systems.

Jump Tables

Some look-up tables contain *addresses* rather than data values. For example, an error routine may use a look-up table to find the starting address of one particular message in a set of possible messages. Similarly, an interrupt service routine may use a look-up table to call one of several interrupt handler programs, depending on which type of service a particular device re-

Example 5-10. Look up the cosine of an angle.

```
        PAGE   ,132
TITLE   COSINE - Cosine of an Angle

;   Returns the cosine of an angle.
;   Input: AX = Angle (0 to 360)
;   Result: BX = Cosine, in sign-and-magnitude form
;   AX is unaffected.
;   Calls the FIND_SINE procedure (Example 5-9).

;   Assemble with: MASM COSINE;
;   Link with: LINK callprog+COSINE+SINE;

        EXTRN FIND_SINE:FAR
        PUBLIC  FIND_COS
CSEG  SEGMENT PARA 'CODE'
        ASSUME  CS:CSEG
FIND_COS PROC FAR
        PUSH   AX
        ADD    AX,90            ;Add 90 for use by FIND_SINE
        CMP    AX,360           ;Is the result > 360?
        JNA    GET_COS
        SUB    AX,360           ; If so, subtract 360
GET_COS: CALL  FIND_SINE        ;Look up the cosine
        POP    AX
        RET
FIND_COS ENDP
CSEG    ENDS
        END
```

quested. Another routine may use a look-up table to call one of several subprograms, based on which option a user has selected from a menu. In all these applications (and there are many more), the look-up table that holds the addresses is called a *jump table.*

Example 5-12 illustrates a jump table application that might appear in a computer-assisted education program. This procedure, *SEL_OPT,* transfers to an ADDITION, SUBTRACTION, MULTIPLICATION, or DIVISION routine, based on whether a student has selected 0, 1, 2, or 3 from a menu.

SEL_OPT checks whether the entered code is valid, and jumps to an error-reporting routine if it is greater than 3. A valid code becomes an index that SEL_OPT uses to make an indirect jump to the appropriate routine. When the student finishes, the routine's RET instruction returns control to the program that called SEL_OPT; in this case, the one that displays the menu.

Example 5-11. Convert a hex digit to ASCII, BCD, and EBCDIC.

```
        PAGE   ,132
TITLE   CONV_HEX -  Convert Hex to ASCII, BCD and EBCDIC

;  Converts a hexadecimal digit to its ASCII, BCD, and
;  EBCDIC equivalents.
;  Input: AL = Hex digit
;  Results: CH = ASCII character
;           CL = BCD digit
;           AH = EBCDIC character
;  AL is unaffected.

;  Assemble with: MASM CONV_HEX;
;  Link with: LINK callprog+CONV_HEX;

DSEG    SEGMENT PARA 'DATA'
ASCII   DB     '0123456789ABCDEF'
BCD     DB     0,1,2,3,4,5,6,7,8,9,10H,11H,12H,13H,14H,15H
EBCDIC  DB     0F0H,0F1H,0F2H,0F3H,0F4H,0F5H,0F6H,0F7H
        DB     0F8H,0F9H,0C1H,0C2H,0C3H,0C4H,0C5H,0C6H
DSEG    ENDS

        PUBLIC  CONV_HEX
CSEG    SEGMENT PARA 'CODE'
        ASSUME  CS:CSEG,DS:DSEG
CONV_HEX PROC FAR
        PUSH  DS            ;Save the caller's registers
        PUSH  BX
        PUSH  DX

        MOV   BX,DSEG       ;Initialize DS
        MOV   DS,BX

        MOV   DL,AL         ;Save the input value in DL
        LEA   BX,ASCII      ;Look up the ASCII value
        XLAT  ASCII
        MOV   CH,AL         ; and load it into CH
        MOV   AL,DL
        LEA   BX,BCD        ;Look up the BCD value
        XLAT  BCD
        MOV   CL,AL         ; and load it into CL
        MOV   AL,DL
        LEA   BX,EBCDIC     ;Look up the EBCDIC value
        XLAT  EBCDIC
        MOV   AH,AL         ; and load it into AH
        MOV   AL,DL         ;Restore registers
        POP   DX
        POP   BX
        POP   DS
        RET                 ; and exit
CONV_HEX ENDP
CSEG    ENDS
        END
```

Example 5-12. Multiple-choice selection procedure.

```
;   This procedure runs one of four routines based on a
;   user selection code in AL.
;   The contents of AX and DI are affected.
;   Store this address table in the data segment.

CHOICE  DW  ADDITION,SUBTRACTION,MULTIPLICATION,DIVISION

;   Here is the selection procedure.

SEL_OPT   PROC   FAR
          CMP    AL,3          ;Invalid choice?
          JA     ERROR
          CBW                  ; No.  Convert code to a word,
          MOV    DI,AX         ;  then move code into DI
          SHL    DI,1          ;  and convert it to an index
          JMP    CHOICE[DI]    ;Jump to selected routine
ERROR:    ..
          ..
          RET
ADDITION:
          ..
          ..
          RET
SUBTRACTION:
          ..
          ..
          RET
MULTIPLICATION:
          ..
          ..
          RET
DIVISION:
          ..
          ..
          RET
SEL_OPT   ENDP
```

5.5 Text Files

In the preceding sections we have been working with data structures that contain numbers. However, word processing and other applications involve manipulating non-numeric information—primarily text files.

Text files are lists whose elements are strings of ASCII characters. For instance, a text file that holds personnel information for a corporation contain one element, or *record,* for each employee. In turn, each record has several sub-records, or *fields*, that list the employee's name, identification number, shift, pay rate, and so on. The string instructions are particularly convenient for manipulating text files.

You can manipulate text files with the same basic techniques you used for numeric files. But because of their multi-record construction, the programs that operate on text files must be somewhat different that those that operate on simple byte or word lists.

For instance, searching a text file usually requires you to compare a *part* of each entry (perhaps just the name field) to the search value, rather than comparing the entire entry. Similarly, bubble-sorting a text file requires you to compare single fields of adjacent entries, but move *entire* entries whenever an exchange is required.

As a simple example of a text file operation, let's look at a program that sorts a list of names and telephone numbers. The first location in the list holds a two-byte count of the entries.

Each entry in the list is 42 bytes long, divided into three fields: a 15-byte surname, a 15-byte first name/initial, and a 12-byte phone number. Any unused bytes in a field are assumed to contain ASCII "blank" characters. Hence, a typical entry in the list looks like this:

```
DB   'CORNELL',8 DUP (' ')
DB   'RAY',12 DUP (' ')
DB   '728-732-8437'
```

(Of course, you normally build text files by typing them in from the keyboard. For now, let's just assume the files are already in memory.)

Example 5-13 shows a procedure (PHONE_NOS) that bubble-sorts a telephone list stored in the extra segment. Its construction is similar to that of the BUBBLE procedure in Example 5-5. (Note the use of PUSHA and POPA to preserve the general registers. Since these instructions are unique to the 80286, you will have to convert them to PUSHes and POPs to run this procedure on an IBM PC or XT.)

To begin, the procedure reads the entry count and the address of the first entry into two variables, SAVE_CNT and FIRST_ENT. The instructions between NEXT and SWAPEM set up and execute a CMPS operation. Here, DI points to an entry's surname field and SI points to the next entry's surname field, where these fields lie 42 bytes apart in memory.

The loop at SWAPEM exchanges two entries when needed. Since the entries are 42 bytes long, loop counter CX is initialized to 42. The remainder of the procedure is similar to Example 5-5.

Example 5-13. Sort a telephone list.

```
        PAGE   ,132
TITLE   PHONE_# - Sort a Telephone List

;  This procedure sorts a telephone list alphabetically.
;  The list consists of an entry count word, followed by
;  the individual entries.
;  Each entry is 42 bytes long, and divided into three
;  fields: surname (15 bytes), first name/initial (15
;  bytes, and telephone number (12 bytes).
;  Input: ES:DI = Address of entry count word

;  Assemble with: MASM PHONE_#;
;  Link with: LINK callprog+PHONE_#;

.286c
DSEG    SEGMENT PARA 'DATA'
SAVE_CNT DW   ?
FIRST_ENT DW  ?
DSEG    ENDS

        PUBLIC  PHONE_NOS
CSEG    SEGMENT PARA 'CODE'
        ASSUME  CS:CSEG,DS:DSEG
PHONE_NOS PROC  FAR
        PUSHA                   ;Save general registers
        MOV    AX,DSEG          ;Initialize DS
        MOV    DS,AX
        CLD                     ;Set DF = 0, to move forward
        MOV    CX,ES:[DI]       ;Fetch entry count
        MOV    SAVE_CNT,CX      ;Save this value in memory
        ADD    DI,2             ;Get address of first entry
        MOV    FIRST_ENT,DI     ; and save this address
INIT:   MOV    BX,1             ;Exchange flag (BX) = 1
        DEC    SAVE_CNT         ;Get ready for count-1 compares
        JZ     SORTED           ;Exit if SAVE_CNT is 0
        MOV    CX,SAVE_CNT      ;Load compare count into CX
        MOV    BP,FIRST_ENT     ; and first entry addr. into BP
NEXT:   MOV    DI,BP            ;Address one entry with DI
        MOV    SI,BP            ; and the next entry with SI
        ADD    SI,42
        PUSH   CX               ;Save current compare count
        MOV    CX,15            ;Compare 15-byte surnames
REPE    CMPS   ES:BYTE PTR[SI],ES:[DI]
                                ;Is next surname < this surname?
        JAE    CONT             ; No.  Go check next pair
        MOV    CX,42            ; Yes. Exchange these entries
SWAPEM: MOV    AL,ES:[BP]
        XCHG   ES:[BP+42],AL
        MOV    ES:[BP],AL
        INC    BP
        LOOP   SWAPEM
        SUB    BX,BX            ;Set exchange flag = 0
```

Example 5-13. (continued).

```
CONT:    POP    CX            ;Reload compare count
         LOOP   NEXT          ;Go compare next two names
         CMP    BX,0          ;Were any exchanges made?
         JE     INIT          ; If so, make another pass
SORTED:  POPA                 ; If not, restore registers
         RET                  ;  and exit.
PHONE_NOS ENDP
CSEG     ENDS
         END
```

Note that PHONE_NOS does not account for duplicate surnames. Upon finding one, it *should* look at the first name fields of those entries and perform a second, alphabetical sort to put them in order. You might like to modify Example 5-13 to do this.

Study Exercises (answers on page 403)

1. The list-processing procedures in this chapter don't check whether the list is empty (it has a count—which contains 0—but no data elements) before conducting an add, delete, or search operation. To remedy this, modify Example 5-1 so that AX becomes the first data element in a list if the list is empty. You can then use the modified procedure to build *new* lists as well as to add elements to existing lists.
2. Write a procedure that searches an ordered list for the value in AX and, if the value is found, *replaces* the contents of the matching element with the value in BX.

6

Using the System Resources

The preceding chapters of this book deal mostly with the 80286 microprocessor. Therefore, what we have said so far applies to any 286-based microcomputer. In this chapter you will learn how to use the built-in resources of your IBM PC AT.

By "resources" we mean the routines that form the computer's main operating program; its Basic I/O System or *BIOS*. The BIOS stores keyboard characters, displays information on the screen, and transfers data to or from the disk drives, printer, and whatever else is attached to your computer.

In short, without BIOS, the PC AT would be just a collection of metal, plastic, and electrical circuits. BIOS is the AT's native intelligence that makes it a computer.

We will begin by taking a brief look at how memory is organized in the PC AT, then we will describe usable programs that are stored in the BIOS chips and other programs that DOS puts into memory. Most of these are *interrupt service routines,* which means your programs can call them by executing INT instructions.

6.1 System Memory

As we mentioned earlier, when the 80286 is operating in the real address mode, it can address one megabyte of memory. Figure 6-1 shows how the PC AT uses this space.

The base model AT comes with 256K bytes of RAM (Random Access Memory), which responds to addresses 0 through 3FFFF. These RAM chips are mounted on the AT's main circuit board, its *System Board*. The lowest 1.5K bytes of this area are used by the system; we discuss how under *Interrupt Assignments* in this section.

Address	Contents
00000	256K BASE MODEL RAM
40000	256K ENHANCED MODEL RAM
80000	128K ADD-ON MEMORY AREA
A0000	128K VIDEO RAM AREA
C0000	128K I/O ADAPTER ROM AREA
E0000	64K USER ROM AREA
F0000	24K POWER-ON SELF-TEST (POST) ROM
F6000	32K RESIDENT BASIC ROM
FE000	8K BIOS ROM

Figure 6-1. System memory map.

The enhanced model AT comes with 256K additional bytes of RAM (locations 40000 through 7FFFF) on the System Board, bringing the total to 512K bytes. The 128K bytes starting at location 80000 accept add-on memory boards, which can expand the computer to 640K bytes.

The remaining 360K in the one-megabyte address space is reserved for system use. Locations A0000 through BFFFF form a 128K block of RAM where the AT stores graphics and display data.

Memory space from location C0000 onward is dedicated to ROM (Read-Only Memory) usage. The first 128K bytes are reserved for ROMs on plug-in adapter cards. The 64K bytes starting at location E0000 are available for user-provided ROM; the System Board has two spare sockets that accept 32K ROM chips. Finally, the highest-numbered 40K locations, F6000 through FFFFF, hold the ROM chips that contain the Power-On Self Test (POST), Resident BASIC, and BIOS programs.

If you have the IBM Macro Assembler or some other relocating assembler, you needn't worry about where the computer will store your programs and data in memory. However, you *should* understand the interrupt assignments in the system, so you can use the built-in interrupts and add others of your own.

Interrupt Assignments

As we just mentioned, the lowest 1.5K (1536) bytes of memory—locations 0 through 5FF—are reserved for system use. BIOS, BASIC, and DOS use the last 512 bytes for working ("scratchpad") storage. The first 1024 bytes hold what is called an *interrupt vector table.* This is a table of 32-bit addresses, or *vectors,* that point to the computer's interrupt service routines.

The 80286 provides for up to 256 different interrupts, numbered 0 through 255 in decimal or 0 through FF in hexadecimal. When the 286 receives an interrupt (either from your program, as an INT instruction, or from an external device), it multiplies the interrupt number by 4 to form the address of an interrupt vector in the table. It then reads the contents of the vector into its Instruction Pointer (IP) and Code Segment (CS) register, and starts executing the instructions at that address.

Figure 6-2 shows how this process works for interrupt Type 4AH; note that each step is numbered. Type 4AH is an alarm interrupt, described later in this chapter.

When the 80286 executes INT 4AH, it saves the return address and flags on the stack (not shown), then takes the operand (step 1) and multiplies it by 4 to calculate the offset into the vector table. This produces 128H (step 2). Location 0:128 contains the address of Type 4AH's interrupt service routine—F000:1805, in this case. Note that the address is stored in the 286's backward scheme, with low bytes preceding high bytes. These address components, 1805 and F000, are loaded into the IP and CS registers, respectively (step 3).

Now, having received a new execution address, the 286 transfers there (step 4) and begins executing instructions. We show location F000:1805 as containing MOV AH,5, but it can contain any other valid instruction. Finally, when the 286 encounters the IRET instruction at the end of the interrupt routine, it retrieves the return address from the stack and continues execution there (step 5).

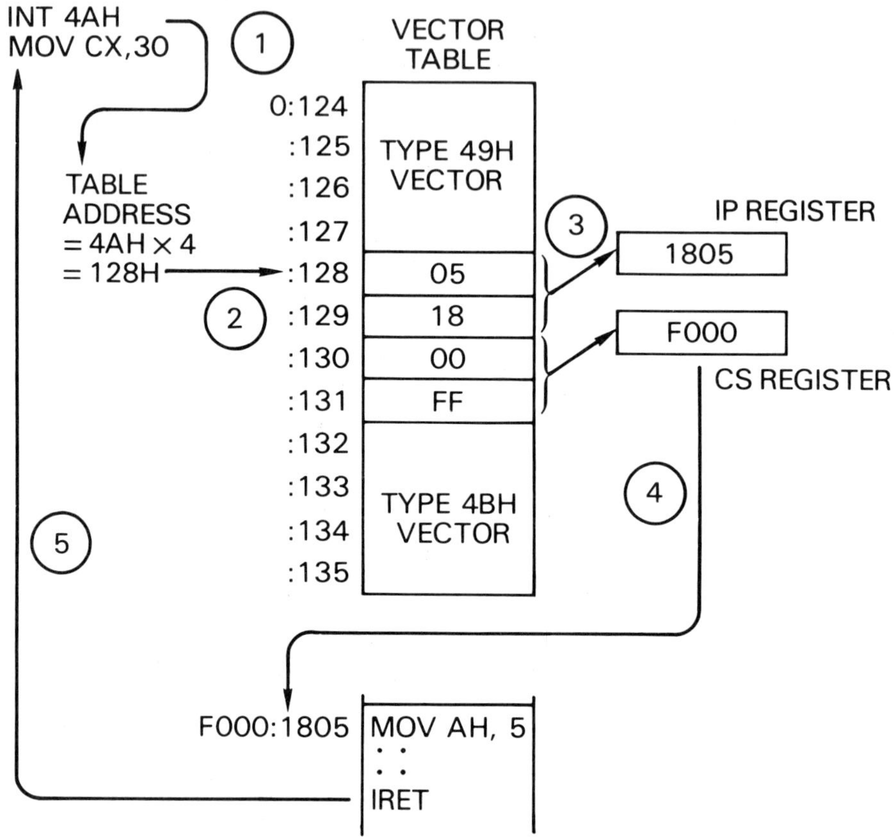

Figure 6-2. Steps performed by an interrupt.

Table 6-1 gives a general summary of the PC AT's interrupts, including the addresses where the interrupt vectors are stored and which interrupt types they respond to. The following sections describe each of these groups in detail.

Table 6-1. Interrupt assignments.

Addresses	Interrupts	Description
0-7F	0-1F	BIOS interrupt vectors
80-FF	20-3F	DOS interrupt vectors
100-17F	40-5F	More BIOS interrupt vectors
180-19F	60-67	User interrupt vectors
1A0-1BF	68-6F	Reserved
1C0-1DF	70-77	I/O interrupt vectors
1E0-1FF	78-7F	Reserved
200-3C3	80-F0	BASIC interrupt vectors
3C4-3FF	F1-FF	Reserved

6.2 BIOS Interrupts

The BIOS interrupts give you a way to access the AT's powerful built-in features. Table 6-2 summarizes the BIOS interrupt vector assignments, and shows what segment number and offset each vector receives when you switch the power on and boot DOS.

Table 6-2. BIOS interrupt vectors.

Interrupt	Name	Initial Value Points to:
80286 Interrupt Vectors		
0	Divide Error	DOS error message routine
1	Single-Step	IRET instruction
2	Nonmaskable	NMI_INT (F000:E2C3)
3	Breakpoint	IRET instruction
4	Overflow	IRET instruction
5	Print Screen	PRINT_SCREEN (F000:FF54)
6	Reserved	D11 (F000:1805)
7	Reserved	D11 (F000:1805)
8259 Interrupt Vectors		
8	8254 System Timer	TIMER_INT (F000:FEA5)
9	Keyboard	KB_INT (F000:E987)
A	Reserved	D11 (F000:1805)
B	Reserved (Communications)	D11 (F000:1805)
C	Reserved (Communications)	D11 (F000:1805)
D	Reserved (Alt. Printer)	D11 (F000:1805)
E	Floppy Disk	DISK_INT (F000:EF57)
F	Reserved (Printer)	IRET instruction
BIOS Entry Points		
10	Video	VIDEO_IO (F000:F065)
11	Equipment Check	EQUIPMENT (F000:F84D)
12	Memory Size	MEMORY_SIZE_DETERMINE (F000:F841)
13	Disk	DOS routine (0070:0CB9) *See text.*
14	Communications	RS232_IO (F000:E739)
15	I/O System Extensions	CASSETTE_IO (F000:F859)
16	Keyboard	KEYBOARD_IO (F000:E82E)
17	Printer	PRINTER_IO (F000:EFD2)
18	Resident BASIC	– (F600:0000)
19	Reboot	BOOT_STRAP (F000:E6F2)
1A	Time of Day	TIME_OF_DAY (F000:FE6E)
40	Floppy Disk	DISKETTE_IO (F000:EC59)

Table 6-2. BIOS interrupt vectors (continued).

Interrupt	Name	Initial Value Points to:
User-Supplied Routines		
1B	Keyboard Break	DOS routine (0070:01E7)
1C	Timer Tick	IRET instruction
4A	Alarm	D11 (F000:1805)
Data Table Pointers		
1D	Video Parameters	VIDEO_PARMS (F000:F0A4)
1E	Floppy Disk Parameters	DISK_BASE (F000:EFC7)
1F	Graphics Character Extensions	— (F000:0000)
41	Fixed Disk #1 Parameters	— (F000:E411)
46	Fixed Disk #2 Parameters	FD_TBL (F000:E401)

Note that the addresses are shown using a shorthand notation of the form *segment:offset*. I didn't pull this idea out of thin air; it's the standard form you need whenever you use DEBUG to display the contents of memory.

However, *do not* use these addresses in your programs, because IBM may change them when it updates the AT or DOS. We give them only to help you find listings of interrupt service routines in the IBM Technical Reference manual. Section 5 of the Technical Reference contains a complete listing of the BIOS. However, IBM developed the BIOS is a modular fashion that can make it difficult to find things. To help you get your bearings, we will spend a few minutes examining the general arrangement of the listing.

Overview of the BIOS Listing

Within Chapter 5 of the *Technical Reference,* IBM has divided the BIOS listing into 21 parts. In the order of appearance, they are:

- *ROS Map*—Alphabetic and numeric lists that show the address of every symbol that is declared PUBLIC. ("ROS" is a mainframe term for "Read-Only Storage"; it means the same as ROM.)

  The ROS Map shows the segment number as 0000, but it should actually be F000. For example, the address for label A1 is listed as 0000:E729; it should actually read F000:E729. Hence, if you run the DEBUG U (Unassemble) command **u f000:e729,** the screen should show the same instructions that start at label A1 in the *Technical Reference's* BIOS listing.

- *Test 1* through *Test 7*—The tests the AT performs when you switch the power on. These tests make preliminary checks to ensure that your computer can at least run programs.
- *Sys Init*, *GDT_BLD*, and *SIDT_BLD*—Initialization routines for the 80286's protected mode.
- *Diskette*—Floppy disk interrupt service routines.
- *Disk*—Fixed (hard) disk interrupt service routines.
- *Keyboard*—Keyboard interrupt service routines.
- *Printer*—Printer interrupt service routines.
- *RS232*—Communications interrupt service routines.
- *Video*—Display interrupt service routines.
- *BIOS*, *BIOS 1*, and *BIOS 2*—Interrupt service routines that perform miscellaneous "housekeeping" jobs, regulate memory and the system timer, and communicate with joysticks and other peripherals that may be attached to the computer.
- *ORGS*—This module includes system messages, parameter tables, and initialization routines for the disk drives, printer, and display.

  More importantly to programmers, it also includes the instructions that the 80286 executes when it receives an interrupt. Invariably, these are not the actual interrupt service routines, but simply a JMP *to* the service routine, which is in another module. In the descriptions that follow, besides describing what each interrupt does, we will tell you which interrupt service routine it executes and where you can find that routine in the BIOS listing—assuming, of course, that IBM doesn't change the Technical Reference.

80286 Interrupt Vectors

Type 0, Divide Error

This interrupt activates if a divide instruction (DIV or IDIV) produces a quotient that is too large to be contained in the result register, or if you attempt to divide by zero. When either happens, Type 0 stops the program and displays *Divide Overflow*, then returns control to DOS.

Type 1, Single-Step

This interrupt is designed to let you run programs one instruction at a time, so you can debug them. DOS makes this vector point to an Interrupt Return (IRET) instruction. Thus, executing an INT 1 instruction makes the 80286 jump to the IRET instruction, then return to the instruction that follows INT 1. DEBUG's Trace (T) command uses this interrupt to single-step through programs.

Type 2, Nonmaskable Interrupt

For every interrupt but this one, you can force the processor to ignore interrupt requests from external devices. To do this, set the Interrupt Enable Flag (IF) to 0 with a CLI instruction. Type 2 is a *nonmaskable* interrupt; it cannot be "locked out" or disabled.

The AT's memory expansion options use the Nonmaskable Interrupt (NMI, for short) to report storage errors. The location to which this interrupt transfers, NMI_INT, contains a JMP to interrupt service routine NMI_INT_1 at location F000:3E76; see the *BIOS* portion of the BIOS listing. NMI_INT_1 displays the error message *Parity Check 1* (for errors on the System Board) or *Parity Check 2* (for errors on add-on boards). Then it locks out external interrupts with a CLI instruction and halts the processor with HLT.

The optional 80287 Math Coprocessor also uses the NMI interrupt to report errors. In this case, of course, you need additional software to determine whether the interrupt was caused by a memory error or an 80287 error.

Type 3, Breakpoint

This interrupt lets you execute a program until the 80286 reaches a specified "stop" address, or *breakpoint*. DOS makes the Type 3 interrupt vector point to an IRET instruction, but DEBUG temporarily changes it if you use the breakpoint option of the Go (G) command.

Type 4, Overflow

This interrupt activates if the Overflow Flag (OF) is 1 when the 80286 executes an Interrupt If Overflow (INTO) instruction. DOS makes the Type 4 interrupt vector point to an IRET instruction, because IBM can't anticipate what you want to do in case of overflow. They leave this decision up to you.

Type 5, Print Screen

The final interrupt in this group, Type 5, is a BIOS feature. The location to which this interrupt transfers, PRINT_SCREEN, contains a JMP to interrupt service routine PRINT_SCREEN_1 at location F000:46CC; see the *BIOS 2* portion of the BIOS listing. PRINT_SCREEN_1 saves the current cursor position, transmits the information on the screen to the printer, then restores the cursor. Hence, the Type 5 interrupt does the same thing as pressing Shift-PrtSc, but under program control instead of from the keyboard.

Memory location 50:0 holds the print status, as follows:

- During printing, 50:0 contains 1.
- If the print operation is successful, 50:0 contains 0.
- If an error occurs during printing, 50:0 contains 0FFH.

8259 Interrupt Vectors

The 8259, an "interrupt controller" chip on the System Board, can accept interrupt request signals (that is, maskable interrupts) from up to eight different devices in the system. Acting like an electronic traffic officer, it passes the request signal and a device identifier code to the 80286. In the PC AT, only the 8254 system timer, keyboard, and disk controller are attached to the 8259.

Type 8, 8254 System Timer

The 8254 is a chip on the System Board chip that maintains a count of the system clock. You can use it to calculate the elapsed time between two events or to generate time delays. The 8254 issues a Type 8 interrupt every 0.0549254 seconds; that is, it interrupts the 80286 about 18.2 times a second.

The Type 8 interrupt vector points to TIMER_INT, which contains a JMP to interrupt service routine TIMER_INT_1 at location F000:4684; see the *BIOS 2* portion of the BIOS listing. TIMER_INT_1 keeps track of the 8254's interrupts while interrupts are enabled (that is, while IF = 1), so you can use this count to keep track of the time of day. The time count is a 32-bit value in two 16-bit memory locations, TIMER_LOW (0040:006C) and TIMER_HIGH (0040:006E).

The TIMER_INT routine also issues a Type 1C interrupt at every "timer tick." BIOS makes the Type 1C interrupt vector point to an IRET instruction, so you must change the vector if you want the interrupt to do something useful. We will suggest some possible uses for the Type 1C interrupt under *User-Supplied Routines* in this section. We'll also show you how to set and read the time count when we discuss the Type 1A (Time of Day) interrupt under *BIOS Entry Points*.

Type 9, Keyboard

This interrupt activates when you press or release a key. The Type 9 interrupt vector points to KB_INT, which contains a JMP to interrupt service routine KB_INT_1 at location F000:3054; see the *Keyboard* portion of the BIOS listing.

For all practical purposes, consider Type 9 a system interrupt. We discuss a more useful keyboard interrupt, Type 16, under *BIOS Entry Points*.

Type E, Floppy Disk

The disk controller issues this interrupt when a floppy disk drive must read or write data. The Type E interrupt vector points to DISK_INT, which contains a JMP to interrupt service routine DISK_INT_1 at location F000:260E; see the *Diskette* portion of the BIOS listing.

As with Type 9, consider Type E a system interrupt. We discuss a more useful floppy disk interrupt, Type 13, under *BIOS Entry Points.*

BIOS Entry Points

Most of these interrupts perform input and output functions; they let you transfer information to or from the peripherals in the system. Other interrupts in this group let you determine the system configuration and the amount of memory installed, and initialize and read the time of day.

Type 10, Video

This interrupt provides a variety of routines that you can use to display graphics or text material on the screen. We will cover it in detail when we describe graphics operations in Chapter 7.

Type 11, Equipment Check

The Type 11 interrupt determines what options are attached to the computer (based on the switch settings), and returns a summary in AX, as shown in Figure 6-3. For example, on a PC AT that has a monochrome display, two floppy disk drives, and a printer, Type 11 returns (AX) = 4271H. The Type 11 vector points to EQUIPMENT, which contains a JMP to interrupt service routine EQUIPMENT_1 at location F000:3E6C; see the *BIOS* portion of the BIOS listing.

Of course, this information is irrelevant if you are writing software for your own computer, because you already know what equipment it has. However, it is valuable for developing commercial software, because you can customize a program to run on different systems. To do this, you can use the contents of AX to call one of several system-specific procedures.

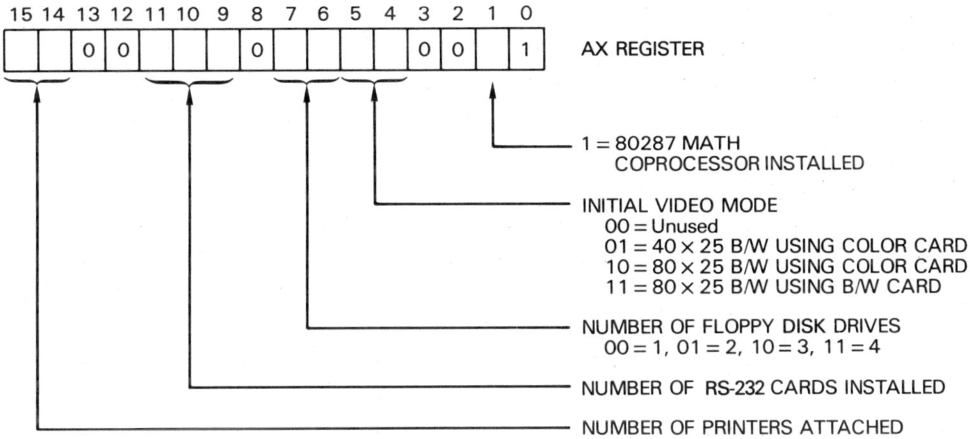

Figure 6-3. Equipment status returned by interrupt 11.

Note especially that bit 1 of AX tells whether the computer has an 80287 Math Coprocessor. If you have written a program that can take advantage of the 80287, use Type 11 to tell it to either execute or skip 80287 instructions.

Type 12, Memory Size

The Type 12 interrupt loads AX with a count of the number of 1K blocks of RAM installed in the first megabyte, based on the switch settings. For a report of installed memory above one megabyte, you must use the Type 15 interrupt's "Extended Memory Size Determine" option.

The Type 12 vector points to MEMORY_SIZE_DETERMINE, which contains a JMP to interrupt service routine MEMORY_SIZE_DETERMINE_1 at location F000:3E62; see the *BIOS* portion of the BIOS listing.

Type 13, Disk

The DOS commands let you operate on *files* in the system. The Type 13 interrupt gives you a greater degree of control over disk information in that it lets you operate on individual *tracks* or *sectors*. Before you activate the Type 13 interrupt, you must load a drive number into the DL register: 0 or 1 selects a floppy disk drive, while 80H or 81H selects a hard disk drive. Then, when you execute INT 13H, the Type 13 transfers to a DOS routine that calls a procedure named DISK_IO at location F000:2A71. DISK_IO determines from DL whether you want to perform an operation on a floppy disk or hard disk. A floppy disk operation makes DISK_IO activate the Type 40 interrupt (a description is upcoming).

Type 13 provides many functions that are valuable for developing disk utilities or copy-protection schemes. But be warned: These operations are *not* for the faint-hearted. They are either a treasure chest or Pandora's box, depending on how skilled (and perhaps lucky) you are. Before attempting a disk operation, carefully read the description of the Fixed Disk and Diskette Adapter that comes with the *Technical Reference* as well as the "INT 13" description in either the *Diskette* or *Disk* portion of the BIOS listing.

Type 14, Communications

This interrupt lets you transmit and receive information through the AT's serial communications port. The Type 14 interrupt vector points to RS323_IO, which contains a JMP to interrupt service routine RS232_IO_1 at location F000:34F5; see the *RS232* portion of the BIOS listing.

Type 15, I/O System Extensions

In the IBM PC, this interrupt supports the cassette interface, and it is also included in PC XT's BIOS, even though the XT has no cassette port. However, for the PC AT, IBM has enhanced Type 15 to provide a variety of additional functions.

The Type 15 interrupt vector points to CASSETTE_IO, which contains a JMP to interrupt service routine CASSETTE_IO_1 at location F000:3FE2; see the *BIOS 1* portion of the BIOS listing. CASSETTE_IO_1 provides 16 options, as selected by the contents of the AH register. Most of these involve the protected mode, so they are beyond the scope of this book. Still, three of the options can be useful for real address mode applications:

- AH = 84H reads the settings of a *joystick.* See the BIOS listing for details.
- AH = 86H generates a *delay,* based on the number of microseconds (i.e., millionths of a second) in CX:DX. It affects only AX; all other registers are preserved. We present a delay program later in this chapter, but this option can be quite handy as well.
- AH = 88H is an *extended memory size determine* option. It loads AX with a count of the number of 1K blocks above the first megabyte.

The computer also activates the Type 15 interrupt automatically when you press the *Sys Req* (System Request) key on the keyboard. However, Type 15 doesn't do anything with the key other than put a number in AL. To make Sys Req do something useful, you must *replace* the Type 15 interrupt service routine with one of your own. More about this later.

Type 16, Keyboard

This is the most commonly used BIOS interrupt for communicating with the keyboard. However, because of the wide range of possibilities it offers, and the versatility that IBM built into it, we will postpone discussing Type 16 until Chapter 8, where we give it the detailed treatment it deserves.

Type 17, Printer

This interrupt lets you communicate with up to three printers (should you be so lucky). It lets you print a character, initialize the printer port, or read the printer status; see Table 6-3. These operations return a status byte in AH (see Figure 6-4), but affect no other registers.

Table 6-3. Printer operations with Type 17 interrupt.

AH	Operation	Input Values	Results*
0	Print a character	AL = Character DX = Printer (0-2)	AH = Status of operation (see Figure 6-4).
1	Initialize printer	DX = Printer (0-2)	Same as above.
2	Read printer status	DX = Printer (0-2)	Same as above.

*AH is changed, other registers are unaffected.

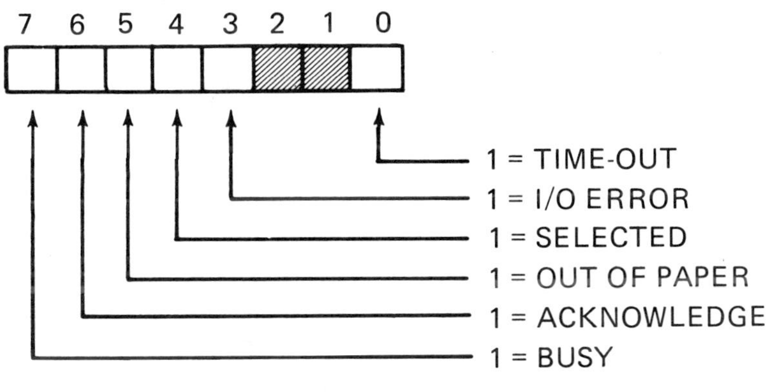

Figure 6-4. Printer I/O status byte.

The Type 17 interrupt vector points to PRINTER_IO, which contains a JMP to interrupt service routine PRINTER_IO_1 at location F000:346F; see the *Printer* portion of the BIOS listing.

Type 18, Resident BASIC

This interrupt calls up Resident BASIC, which is contained in ROM.

Type 19, Reboot

This interrupt forces the computer to reinitialize or "reboot" from disk, as it does when you press Ctrl-Alt-Del. However, in this case the AT skips the internal test routines and loads DOS directly. As usual, if the AT can't find DOS on either a floppy disk or hard disk drive, or if the drive or disk controller card is malfunctioning, it enters Resident BASIC via the Type 18 interrupt.

The Type 19 interrupt vector points to BOOT_STRAP, which contains a JMP to interrupt service routine BOOT_STRAP_1 at location F000:1B66.

Type 1A, Time of Day

This interrupt can be tremendously convenient if you are doing anything that involves time. With it, you can set or read the time and date, or you can turn the computer into an alarm clock by giving it an alarm time up to 24 hours from now. Because Type 1A is so versatile, it is worth discussing in detail. This comes in Section 6.4.

User-Supplied Routines

BIOS activates these interrupts automatically during the course of its normal operation. However, in each case, IBM has simply reserved a vector for the interrupt. That is, each vector points to an interrupt service routine, but the routines don't actually do anything. They just return to the BIOS routine that called them.

To use one of these interrupts, you must prepare an interrupt service routine that does what you want and then put the address of this routine into the vector, so BIOS knows where to find it. DOS contains interrupt service routines that let you change vectors; we will discuss them in Section 6.3

Type 1B, Keyboard Break

The Type 9 (Keyboard) interrupt service routine activates this interrupt when it realizes that you have pressed the Ctrl-Break keys. BIOS makes the Type 1B interrupt vector point to an IRET instruction, but DOS changes it to point to the service routine for the Type 23 (Ctrl-Break Exit Address) interrupt. We describe Type 23, along with other DOS interrupts, in Section 6.3.

Type 1C, Timer Tick

This interrupt is invoked by TIMER_INT_1, the routine that services the Type 8 (8253 System Timer) interrupt. Thus, like the Type 8 interrupt, Type 1C executes about 18.2 times per second.

The Type 1C interrupt lets you assign the 80286 some task with each "tick" of the 8254. BIOS makes the Type 1C interrupt vector point to an IRET instruction, so Type 1C does nothing unless you change this pointer.

You can use the Type 1C interrupt to display the time count in decimal to create an on-screen clock. Or you can make Type 1C's service routine increment a counter to measure how long it takes a program to execute. You can probably think of other applications for this useful interrupt.

Type 4A, Alarm

As we mentioned earlier, the Type 1A (Time of Day) interrupt provides an option that lets you specify a time at which the AT is to activate an "alarm"—that is, run an alarm interrupt service routine that you supply. The alarm routine can sound a tone over the speaker, display a message (say, "You have a one o'clock appointment.") on the screen, or do anything else you want. The Type 4A vector is where you put the address of your alarm routine. We will suggest some possibilities in Section 6.4 when we discuss time operations with the Type 1A interrupt.

Data Table Pointers

Types 1D, 1E, 1F, 41, and 46 are not interrupt vectors at all; they are addresses of data tables. The 1D address points to a table used by the Type 10 interrupt. The 1E address points to a floppy disk table used by the Type 40 interrupt. The 41 and 46 addresses point to fixed disk tables used by the Type 13 interrupt.

Type 1F's location is reserved for a pointer to a graphics table for special characters. But since this table is not in memory, BIOS sets the vector to F000:0000, the beginning of the Power-On Self Test. The DOS 3.0 GRAFTABL command provides an extended character set. When executed, it makes the 1F vector point to a 1K table (at 099A:0060 on my AT) that provides 128 additional characters for the graphics mode. Each character is defined in an 8 × 8 bit (or 8-byte) array, where the first byte defines the top row of the character.

6.3 DOS Interrupts

IBM reserves interrupt types 20 through 3F for DOS use, but only the types listed in Table 6-4 are currently implemented. Most of these interrupts are useful only to DOS, so we won't discuss them here. (See the separate *DOS Technical Reference* manual.) However, the Type 21 (Function Calls) interrupt has a variety of convenient options for interacting with the keyboard, display, printer, disk, and asynchronous communications device.

Table 6-4. DOS interrupts.

Interrupt Number	Name
20	Terminate Program
21	Function Calls
22	Terminate Address
23	Ctrl-Break Exit Address
24	Critical Error Handler
25	Absolute Disk Read
26	Absolute Disk Write
27	Terminate, But Stay Resident
28-2E	Reserved for DOS
2F	Printer
30-3F	Reserved for DOS

Type 21 Function Calls

Table 6-5 is a partial list of the Type 21 function calls. As noted, others for data and time, keyboard, and display are described elsewhere in the book.

Table 6-5. Function calls with the Type 21 interrupt.

AH	Operation	Input Values	Results*
Asynchronous Communications Functions			
3	Wait for asynchronous input character	None	AL = Character
4	Output a character to asynchronous device	DL = Character	None
File Management Functions			
D	Reset default disk drive	None	None

Table 6-5. Function calls with the Type 21 interrupt (continued).

AH	Operation	Input Values	Results*
File Management Functions (continued)			
E	Select default disk drive	DL = Drive number (0 = A, 1 = B, 2 = C)	AL = Number of disk drives (2 for single drive)
19	Get default drive code	None	AL = Default drive code (0 = A, 1 = B, 2 = C)
2E	Set verify state (See also function 54)	DL = 0 AL = 0 to turn verify off = 1 to turn verify on	None
30	Get DOS version number	None	AL = Version number (3 or 2) (Version 1.x returns 0) AH = Revision number BX,CX = 0
Interrupt Vector Functions			
25	Set interrupt vector	DS:DX = Vector address AL = Interrupt number	None
35	Read interrupt vector address	AL = Interrupt number	ES:BX = Vector address
Directory Functions			
39	Create a directory (MKDIR)	DS:DX = Address of ASCIIZ string for directory	None**
3A	Remove a directory (RMDIR)	DS:DX = Address of ASCIIZ string for directory	None**
3B	Change the directory (CHDIR)	DS:DX = Address of ASCIIZ string for new directory	None**

Table 6-5. Function calls with the Type 21 interrupt (continued).

AH	Operation	Input Values	Results*
Directory Functions (continued)			
47	Get current directory	DL = Drive number (0 = default, 1 = A, etc.) DS:SI = Address of 64-byte buffer	DS:SI = Address of ASCIIZ string**
Extended File Management Functions			
36	Get free disk space	DL = Drive number (0 = default, 1 = A, etc.)	AX = 0FFFFH if invalid = Sectors per cluster BX = No. of free clusters DX = Total no. of clusters CX = Bytes per sector
3C	Create a file	DS:DX = Address of ASCIIZ string CX = Attribute of file	AX = File handle**
3D	Open a file	DS:DX = Address of ASCIIZ string AL = 0 to open for reading = 1 to open for writing = 2 to open for reading and writing	AX = File handle**
3E	Close a file handle	BX = File handle	None**
3F	Read from file or device	BX = File handle CX = No. of bytes to read DS:DX = Buffer address	AX = No. of bytes read** = 0 if read from end of file
40	Write to a file or device	BX = File handle CX = No. of bytes to write DS:DX = Buffer address	AX = No. of bytes written**

Table 6-5. Function calls with the Type 21 interrupt (continued).

AH	Operation	Input Values	Results*
File Management Functions (continued)			
41	Delete a file	DS:DX = Address of ASCIIZ string	None**
43	Get file attribute	AL = 0 DS:DX = Address of ASCIIZ string for file	CX = Attribute**
43	Set file attribute	AL = 1 DS:DX = Address of ASCIIZ string for file CX = Attribute	None**
54	Get verify state (See also function 2E)	None	AL = 0 if verify is off = 1 if verify is on
56	Rename a file	DS:DX = Address of ASCIIZ string for old name ES:DI = Address of ASCIIZ string for new name	None**
Get Extended Error Function			
59	Get extended error	BX = 0	AX = Extended code BH = Error class BL = Suggested action CH = Locus

*Besides the registers listed in this column, only AX and the flags are affected.

**If an error occurs, these function calls return CF = 1 and an error code in AX. See Table 6-6 for the meanings of the error codes.

Note: This is a partial list of functions.
For *Time and Date Functions*, see Section 6.4.
For *Keyboard Functions*, see Chapter 8.

Function Call Error Reports

Most of the Directory and Extended File Management functions return CF = 0 if the operation is successful and CF = 1 if an error occurred. Along with CF = 1, they return an error code in AX; Table 6-6 tells what these codes mean.

Table 6-6. Error codes for DOS function calls.

Code	Meaning
1	Invalid function number
2	File not found
3	Path not found
4	Too many open files (no handles left)
5	Access denied
6	Invalid handle
7	Memory control blocks destroyed
8	Insufficient memory
9	Invalid memory block address
10	Invalid environment
11	Invalid format
12	Invalid access code
13	Invalid data
15	Invalid drive was specified
16	Attempted to remove the current directory
17	Not same device
18	No more files
32	Sharing violation
33	Lock violation
34	Invalid disk change
35	FCB unavailable
80	File exists
81	Reserved
82	Cannot make

With DOS 3.00, IBM has also included a Get Extended Error function call (AH = 59H) that provides more comprehensive error information in terms of an *error class*, a *suggested action*, and a *locus*. See the *DOS Technical Reference* manual for details.

File Management Functions

The File Management Functions listed in Table 6-5 are a small portion of the ones available. There are other functions that open and close files, delete files, rename files, etc. However, these operations involve File Control Blocks

(FCBs), and can get quite complicated. When IBM introduced DOS 2.0, they provided us with much easier functions that do the same job—the so-called *Extended* File Management Functions. We'll discuss them shortly.

Interrupt Vector Functions

Functions 25 and 35 let you operate on the interrupt vector addresses. For example, to add an interrupt service routine called NEW_INT to the system and have it respond to *INT 60H*, use this sequence:

```
MOV  AL,60H             ;Put interrupt type in AL
MOV  DX,SEG NEW_INT     ;Put segment number in DS
MOV  DS,DX
LEA  DX,NEW_INT         ; and offset in DX.
MOV  AH,25H             ;Select function call 25.
INT  21H                ;Change the interrupt vector.
```

Remember, an interrupt service routine is simply a procedure with an IRET (rather than a RET) at the end. Hence, NEW_INT has the form

```
NEW_INT  PROC  FAR
     ..   (Instructions in the interrupt service procedure)
     ..
     IRET
NEW_INT  ENDP
```

Directory Functions

These functions let you read the directory name and perform the DOS *MKDIR*, *RMDIR*, and *CHDIR* operations from within a program. Each reports the outcome by setting CF to either 0 (success) or 1 (error). If CF is 1, then AX contains an error code.

In each case, you must provide an ASCII text string that describes the directory. It contains an optional drive specifier (e.g., *C:*), the path, and a byte containing the value zero (not the ASCII code for 0). Because of the zero byte, IBM calls this an "ASCIIZ" string. For example, to switch to a subdirectory called *SALES* off the root directory, put the following statement in the data segment:

```
SALES_DIR  DB  '\SALES',0
```

The code segment would contain

```
        LEA  DX,SALES_DIR    ;Point to subdirectory name.
        MOV  AH,3BH          ;Change the subdirectory.
        INT  21H
        JNC  OKAY            ;Successful?
        ..                   ;No.  Read error code from AX.
        ..
OKAY:
```

Extended File Management Functions

Like the Directory Functions, most Extended File Management Functions require an ASCIIZ string—in this case, one that identifies the file. The ASCIIZ string for a file contains the drive name and path (if required), followed by the filename, extension (if any), and a zero byte. For example, the data segment statement for the file SALESQ4.NE in the SALES directory may have this form:

```
SALESQ4$  DB   '\SALES\SALESQ4.NE',0
```

The Extended File Management Functions involve two terms we haven't encountered: *attribute* and *handle*. An attribute is DOS 2's way of classifying entries on a disk. Each entry has an *attribute byte* whose bits tell whether the entry is a read-only file (bit 0 = 1), a hidden file (bit 1 = 1), a system file (bit 2 = 1), a volume label (bit 3 = 1), a subdirectory name (bit 4 = 1), or an ordinary file (bit 5). Bit 5 is the "archive" bit for fixed disk files; DOS sets it to 1 when you change the file and clears it to 0 when you use the BACKUP command to copy the file to a floppy disk. For floppy disk files, bit 5 is always 1.

Function 43 lets you read or change a file's attribute. Generally you won't want to change the attribute of a volume label or a subdirectory, but you can, say, make a system file hidden. (By hidden, we mean that the file doesn't appear in DIR listings. Therefore, more importantly, it can't be erased!) Function 43 can also make a file *read-only*. Read-only files are "write-protected"; they cannot be changed or erased by normal DOS operations. However, DOS 3 already has an ATTRIB command that can write-protect files, so we would probably use ATTRIB instead.

A handle is a number that identifies an open file or an I/O device. It is similar to the number you assign with a BASIC statement such as *OPEN "DATA" FOR OUTPUT AS #1.* When you start DOS, it assigns the following handles:

- *0* is the standard input device. DOS assigns handle 0 to the keyboard, but you can reassign or "redirect" it to some other device (see "Redirection of Standard Input and Output Devices" in the *DOS* manual). You may, for example, want to redirect 0 to a remote terminal.

- *1* is the standard output device. DOS assigns handle 1 to the display screen, but you can redirect it (see the preceding reference).
- *2* is the standard error output device. It cannot be redirected.
- *3* is the standard auxiliary device.
- *4* is the standard printer.

DOS is set up to accept four additional, user-defined handles (for a total of eight), but you may increase this number.

For example, you can use function 40 to display a message on the screen, the standard output device. Your data segment will contain the message itself, say:

```
MSG     DB    "Please try again."   ;Message
        DB    13,10                 ;Carriage return and line feed
MSGL    EQU   $-MSG                 ;Length of message
```

(Note the little trick here of using MSGL EQU $-MSG to calculate the length.) Your code segment should contain these message-writing instructions:

```
LEA   DX,MSG       ;Put message offset in DX
MOV   CX,MSGL      ;CX tells how many characters to display
MOV   BX,1         ;Use file handle for screen
MOV   AH,40H       ;Display the message
INT   21H
```

DOS Error Message Program

As we mentioned earlier, many of the DOS function calls report errors by setting the Carry Flag (CF) to 1 and loading an error code into AX. We summarized these errors in Table 6-6. To save you from having to look up the error each time, Example 6-1 shows a procedure called SHOW_ERR that uses an error code in AX to display a message telling which error occurred.

To display the message, we cheat a little bit and use INT 21's AH = 9 option, a function we have not yet discussed. This option displays a string ending with a $ character (thus the need for the EOM) whose address is in DS:DX; we discuss it in Chapter 7.

If your calling program has a data segment with a different name than SHOW_ERR's, be sure to save the calling program's DS value. That is, put the following kinds of instructions at the beginning of SHOW_ERR's code segment:

Example 6-1. DOS error message program.

```
        PAGE   ,132
TITLE   SHOW_ERR - Display DOS function call error messages

;   Displays a message based on an error code in AX.
;   All registers are preserved.

;   To assemble: MASM SHOW_ERR;
;   To link: LINK callprog+SHOW_ERR;

        PUBLIC  SHOW_ERR

DSEG    SEGMENT PARA PUBLIC 'DATA'
CR      EQU   13
LF      EQU   10
EOM     EQU   '$'

OUT_OF_RANGE DB 'Error code is not in valid range (1-83)',CR,LF,EOM
RESERVED DB   'Error code is reserved (36-79)',CR,LF,EOM

ER1     DB    'Invalid function number',CR,LF,EOM
ER2     DB    'File not found',CR,LF,EOM
ER3     DB    'Path not found',CR,LF,EOM
ER4     DB    'Too many open files (No handles left)',CR,LF,EOM
ER5     DB    'Access denied',CR,LF,EOM
ER6     DB    'Invalid handle',CR,LF,EOM
ER7     DB    'Memory control blocks destroyed',CR,LF,EOM
ER8     DB    'Insufficient memory',CR,LF,EOM
ER9     DB    'Invalid memory block address',CR,LF,EOM
ER10    DB    'Invalid environment',CR,LF,EOM
ER11    DB    'Invalid format',CR,LF,EOM
ER12    DB    'Invalid access code',CR,LF,EOM
ER13    DB    'Invalid data',CR,LF,EOM
ER14    DB    'No such message',CR,LF,EOM
ER15    DB    'Invalid drive was specified',CR,LF,EOM
ER16    DB    'Attempted to remove the current directory',CR,LF,EOM
ER17    DB    'Not same device',CR,LF,EOM
ER18    DB    'No more files',CR,LF,EOM
ER19    DB    'Disk is write-protected',CR,LF,EOM
ER20    DB    'Unknown unit',CR,LF,EOM
ER21    DB    'Drive not ready',CR,LF,EOM
ER22    DB    'Unknown command',CR,LF,EOM
ER23    DB    'Data error (CRC)',CR,LF,EOM
ER24    DB    'Bad request structure length',CR,LF,EOM
ER25    DB    'Seek error',CR,LF,EOM
ER26    DB    'Unknown media type',CR,LF,EOM
ER27    DB    'Sector not found',CR,LF,EOM
ER28    DB    'Printer out of paper',CR,LF,EOM
ER29    DB    'Write fault',CR,LF,EOM
ER30    DB    'Read fault',CR,LF,EOM
ER31    DB    'General failure',CR,LF,EOM
ER32    DB    'Sharing violation',CR,LF,EOM
ER33    DB    'Lock violation',CR,LF,EOM
ER34    DB    'Invalid disk change',CR,LF,EOM
ER35    DB    'FCB unavailable',CR,LF,EOM
```

Example 6-1. (continued).

```
ER80      DB      'File exists',CR,LF,EOM
ER81      DB      'Reserved',CR,LF,EOM
ER82      DB      'Cannot make',CR,LF,EOM
ER83      DB      'Fail on INT 24',CR,LF,EOM

ERTAB1    DW      ER1,ER2,ER3,ER4,ER5,ER6,ER7,ER8,ER9
          DW      ER10,ER11,ER12,ER13,ER14,ER15,ER16,ER17,ER18
          DW      ER19,ER20,ER21,ER22,ER23,ER24,ER25,ER26,ER27
          DW      ER28,ER29,ER30,ER31,ER32,ER33,ER34,ER35
ERTAB2    DW      ER80,ER81,ER82,ER83
DSEG      ENDS

CSEG      SEGMENT PARA PUBLIC 'CODE'
          ASSUME  CS:CSEG,DS:DSEG

SHOW_ERR PROC FAR

          MOV     SI,DSEG            ;Initialize DS
          MOV     DS,SI

          PUSH    AX                 ;Save input error number
          PUSH    BX                 ;Save other working registers
          PUSH    DX
          CMP     AX,83              ;Check for error code in range
          JG      O_O_R
          CMP     AX,0
          JG      IN_RANGE
O_O_R:    LEA     DX,OUT_OF_RANGE
          JMP     SHORT DISP_MSG

;  Error code is valid.  Determine which table to use.

IN_RANGE: CMP AX,35                  ;Error code 1-35?
          JG      TRY79
          LEA     BX,ERTAB1-2        ; Yes. Point to ERTAB1
          JMP     FORM_ADDR
TRY79:    CMP     AX,79              ;Error code 36-79?
          JG      LAST_4
          LEA     DX,RESERVED        ; Yes. Display "reserved" message
          JMP     DISP_MSG
LAST_4:   LEA     BX,ERTAB2          ;Error code 80-83
          AND     AX,3
FORM_ADDR: SHL    AX,1               ;Point to correct offset
          ADD     BX,AX
          MOV     DX,[BX]            ;Put message address into DX
DISP_MSG: MOV AH,9                   ;Display message string
          INT     21H
          POP     DX                 ;Restore registers
          POP     BX
          POP     AX
          RET                        ;Return to calling program
SHOW_ERR ENDP
CSEG      ENDS
          END
```

```
PUSH  DS        ;Save caller's DS value
MOV   SI,DSEG   ; Initialize DS
MOV   DS,SI
```

and put a POP DS at the end of the code segment.

6.4 Time and Date Operations

The original models of the IBM Personal Computer—the PC, XT, and the Portable Computer—had a facility for you to specify the current time and date. They then based all time-related operations on the values you specified (or used built-in default values if you didn't specify new ones.) However, the time and date were only used as long as you kept the power on; as soon as you turned it off, the computer reverted back to its defaults.

The PC AT also keeps track of the time and date in temporary, or *volatile* memory (to be compatible with the earlier models), but in addition it has a battery-powered circuit that retains these values while the power is off. Then, when you turn the power on, the AT loads the stored values into the temporary locations.

The PC AT has two interrupts that allow you to read and change the time and date settings of both its temporary clock and its battery-powered *real-time clock*. One of these interrupts is built into the BIOS, DOS adds the other.

BIOS Type 1A (Time of Day) Interrupt

The BIOS time and date interrupt is Type 1A (Time of Day). The Type 1A vector points to TIME_OF_DAY, which contains a JMP to interrupt service routine TIME_OF_DAY_1 at location F000:445C; see the *BIOS 2* portion of the BIOS listing. TIME_OF_DAY_1 provides eight different options, as selected by the contents of the AH register (see Table 6-7).

Since you probably won't want to change the time or date from within an assembly language program, options 1, 3, 4, and 5 are of limited value. However, the other options can be quite convenient for a variety of applications. For example, option 0 can be used to generate random numbers, while options 6 and 7 can be used to make the computer do something—whatever you want—at a specified time. Option 2 is handy if you want to make the alarm go off at some specified interval (say, 30 minutes) from the current time.

Table 6-7. Time operations with Type 1A interrupt.

AH	Operation	Input Values	Results*
0	Read the current clock setting	None	CX = High portion of count DX = Low portion of count AL = 0 if timer has not passed 24 hours since last read
1	Set the clock	CX = High portion of count DX = Low portion of count	None
	Note: For the above two functions, the count is in "timer ticks."		
2	Read the real-time clock	None	CH = Hours in BCD CL = Minutes in BCD DH = Seconds in BCD Carry Flag (CF) = 1 if clock is not operating
3	Set the real-time clock	CH = Hours in BCD CL = Minutes in BCD DH = Seconds in BCD DL = 1 if Daylight Savings Time, else 0	None
4	Read the date from the real-time clock	None	CX = Year in BCD (1980 through 2099) DH = Month in BCD DL = Day in BCD Carry Flag (CF) = 1 if clock is not operating
5	Set the date into the real-time clock	CH = Year in BCD (1980 through 2099) DH = Month in BCD DL = Day in BCD	None
6	Set the alarm	CH = Hours in BCD CL = Minutes in BCD DH = Seconds in BCD	Carry Flag (CF) = 1 if clock is not operating or alarm is already enabled
7	Reset (clear) the alarm	None	None

*Besides the registers listed in this column, these routines save all registers except AX and the flags.

Generating Random Numbers

As we mentioned earlier, the Type 8 interrupt maintains a count of the system clock (via interrupts from an internal 8254 System Timer) in two 16-bit memory locations called Timer_LOW and TIMER_HIGH. The AH = 0 option of the Type 1A interrupt reads the current contents of these locations into DX and CX, respectively.

Because TIMER_LOW and TIMER_HIGH continually change, their contents—particularly those of TIMER_LOW—can be interpreted as a *pseudo-random number*! Since the count locations always increase rather than change randomly, they don't provide a true random number. Still, because the time value increases 18.2 times every second, it is "random" enough for most applications.

Being 16 bits long, TIMER_LOW can hold values between 0 and 65,535. To generate a random number between 0 and 51, as you might want to do in a card game program, read TIMER_LOW and divide it by 52. This produces a *remainder* between 0 and 51.

Example 6-2 shows a procedure called RAND_51 that returns a value between 0 and 51 in AH. Note that we strip off the three high bits of TIMER_LOW to prevent the division from overflowing. If we didn't do this, the division would overflow whenever TIMER_LOW exceeds decimal 13260 (i.e., 52 x 255).

Using the Alarm Feature

Options 6 and 7 of the Type 1A interrupt let you make the AT into a versatile (but expensive!) alarm clock. We say "versatile" because unlike ordinary alarm clocks, you can set up the computer to do anything you want when it reaches the alarm time.

To use the alarm feature, you must do the following:

1. Prepare an interrupt service routine that will perform the alarm operation.
2. Store the address of the service routine into the Type 4A interrupt vector.
3. Load the alarm time into CH (hours), CL (minutes), and DH (seconds).
4. Set (enable) the alarm by executing INT 1AH with AH = 6.

To illustrate, Example 6-3 shows the general form of a program that sets up an alarm.

Once you have enabled the alarm, the AT will perform the interrupt service routine each time the real-time clock reaches the time value you loaded

Example 6-2. Generate a random number between 0 and 51.

```
        PAGE   ,132
TITLE   RAND_51 - Random Number Between 0 and 51

;  Generates a pseudo-random number between 0 and 51
;  in the AH register.
;  All registers are preserved.

;  Assemble with: MASM RAND_51;
;  Link with: callprog+RAND_51;

        PUBLIC  RAND_51
CSEG    SEGMENT PARA PUBLIC 'CODE'
        ASSUME  CS:CSEG
RAND_51 PROC    FAR
        PUSH    CX              ;Save INT 1AH registers
        PUSH    DX
        PUSH    AX
        MOV     AH,0            ;Read the timer
        INT     1AH
        MOV     AX,DX           ;Move low count into AX
        AND     AX,1FFFH        ; and strip off high 3 bits
        MOV     DL,52           ;Divide low count by 52
        DIV     DL
        POP     DX              ;Restore AL
        MOV     AL,DL
        POP     DX              ;Restore DX and CX,
        POP     CX
        RET                     ; then exit
RAND_51 ENDP
CSEG    ENDS
        END
```

into CH, CL, and DH. To disable the alarm, you may either restart the computer or execute INT 1AH with AH = 7. Restarting the computer makes it load the Type 4A vector with its original, do-nothing default pointer. Executing INT 1AH keeps your pointer value in the vector, but tells BIOS to stop checking for an alarm.

In Chapter 9 we present a program that makes the speaker emit a beep when the alarm goes off.

Example 6-3. General form of an alarm program.

```
;  This program makes the PC AT execute an interrupt service
;  routine called ALARM at a specified time.

      MOV  AL,4AH          ;Make alarm vector point to ALARM
      MOV  DX,SEG ALARM
      MOV  DS,DX
```

Example 6-3. (continued).

```
        LEA   DX,ALARM
        MOV   AH,25H
        INT   21H
        MOV   CH,hours       ;Specify the alarm time
        MOV   CL,minutes
        MOV   DL,seconds
        MOV   AH,6           ;Set the alarm
        INT   1AH
        ..
        ..
ALARM   PROC
        ..       ;Instructions in alarm routine
        ..
        IRET
ALARM   ENDP
```

DOS Function Calls for Time and Date

Table 6-8 summarizes the DOS Type 21 function calls that relate to the time and date. Note that they are similar to the options that BIOS offers (see Table 6-7), except

- The time and date values are in binary rather than BCD.
- The time and date here are the *temporary* values the AT maintains in memory; changing them does not affect the real-time clock.
- The time is accurate to the nearest one-hundredth of a second, not just to the nearest second.

Timing Programs

Having the time in hundredths of a second is convenient for measuring how long a program (or a portion of one) takes to execute. To do this, read the time, then execute the program and read the time again. Subtracting the starting time from the ending time produces the execution time.

To illustrate, Example 6-4 shows a sequence that measures how long a procedure called SORT takes to execute. The extra instructions after each subtraction convert the result to a positive number.

Generating Delays

The time functions are also useful for generating delays. You will want to generate a delay when you produce sounds through the speaker or display graphics shapes on the screen. For sound, the delay determines how long the

Table 6-8. Time operations with Type 21 interrupt.

AH	Operation	Input Values	Results*
		Note: All time and date values are in binary.	
2A	Get date	None	CX = Year DH = Month DL = Day
2B	Set date	CX = Year (1980-2099) DH = Month DL = Day	AL = 0 if date is valid = FF if date is invalid
2C	Get time	None	CH = Hours CL = Minutes DH = Seconds DL = 1/100 Seconds
2D	Set time	CH = Hours (0-23) CL = Minutes DH = Seconds DL = 1/100 Seconds	AL = 0 if time is valid = FF if time is invalid

*Besides the registers listed in this column, only AX and the flags are affected.

note is sustained. For graphics, it determines how long a shape appears or how long the computer waits before displaying the next shape.

Programs that generate delays usually do the following:

1. Read the current time.
2. Add the current time to the specified time increments to produce a "target" time.
3. Adjust the target time so that hours do not exceed 23, minutes and seconds do not exceed 59, and hundredths of a second do not exceed 99. This involves carrying any excess to the next higher unit.
4. Read the time repeatedly until the current time matches or exceeds the target time.

Figure 6-5 shows a flowchart for producing a time delay based on input values for minutes, seconds, and hundredths of a second. (We assume you won't want to delay for hours at a time, although you could.) Example 6-5 shows a general-purpose delay procedure (DELAY) that uses this approach.

As a final comment about delays, remember that there is also a delay-generator built into the BIOS. This is the AH = 86H option of the Type 15 (I/O System Extensions) interrupt; see *BIOS Entry Points* in Section 6.2.

Example 6-4. Calculate execution time.

```
;   This sequence calculates the execution time of a program
;   called SORT.
;   Results: CH = Hours
;            CL = Minutes
;            DH = Seconds
;            DL = 1/100 Seconds

;   Put these temporary locations in the data segment:

HRS      DB  ?
MINS     DB  ?
SECS     DB  ?
HSECS    DB  ?

;   Here is the timing sequence:

            MOV    AH,2CH       ;Read the start time
            INT    21H
            MOV    HRS,CH       ; and save it
            MOV    MINS,CL
            MOV    SECS,DH
            MOV    HSECS,DL
            CALL   SORT         ;Execute the procedure
            MOV    AH,2CH       ;Read the end time
            INT    21H
            SUB    DL,HSECS     ;Calculate the difference
            JNC    SUB_SECS
            ADD    DL,100
            DEC    DH
SUB_SECS:   SUB    DH,SECS              JNC    SUB_MINS
            ADD    DH,60
            DEC    CL
SUB_MINS:   SUB    CL,MINS
            JNC    SUB_HRS
            ADD    CL,60
            DEC    CH
SUB_HRS:    SUB    CH,HRS
            JNC    DONE
            ADD    CH,24
DONE:       RET
```

Study Exercises (answers on page 404)

1. What is an interrupt vector? What does it contain?
2. Where in memory is the PC AT's interrupt vector table located?
3. Which memory location contains the starting address of the interrupt vector for the Type 4 interrupt?
4. Suppose an interrupt vector contains F000:FEA5. How can you find out what instruction is stored at that location?

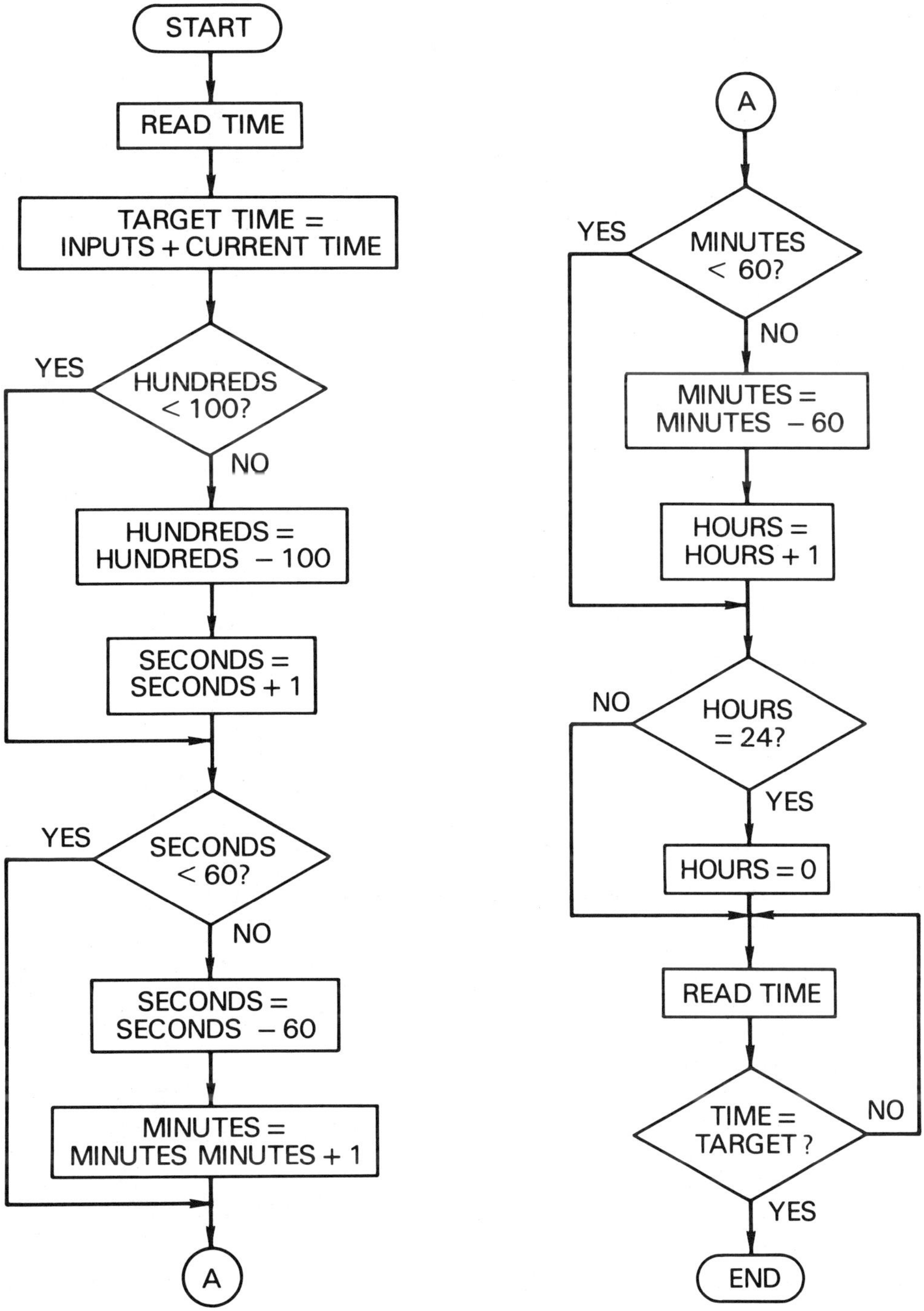

Figure 6-5. Delay flowchart.

Example 6-5. Generate a delay.

```
        PAGE   ,132
TITLE   DELAY - Delay for a specified interval

; Make the processor wait for a specified period.
;  Inputs: AL = Minutes
;          BH = Seconds
;          BL = 1/100 Seconds
;  All registers are preserved.

;  Assemble with: MASM DELAY;
;  Link with: LINK callprog+DELAY;

        PUBLIC  DELAY
CSEG    SEGMENT PARA PUBLIC 'CODE'
        ASSUME  CS:CSEG
DELAY   PROC  FAR
        PUSH  AX                  ;Save affected registers
        PUSH  BX
        PUSH  CX
        PUSH  DX
        MOV   AH,2CH              ;Read current time
        INT   21H

; Add the current time to the input values.

        MOV   AH,CH               ;Hours
        ADD   AL,CL               ;Minutes
        ADD   BH,DH               ;Seconds
        ADD   BL,DL               ;Hundredths

; Propagate any carryover.

        CMP   BL,100              ;Hundredths must be < 100
        JB    SECS
        SUB   BL,100
        INC   BH
SECS:   CMP   BH,60               ;Seconds must be < 60
        JB    MINS
        SUB   BH,60
        INC   AL
MINS:   CMP   AL,60               ;Minutes must be < 60
        JB    HRS
        SUB   AL,60
        INC   AH
HRS:    CMP   AH,24               ;Hours must be < 24
        JNE   CHECK
        SUB   AH,AH
; Wait for interval to elapse.

CHECK:  PUSH  AX                  ;Read the time again
        MOV   AH,2CH
        INT   21H
```

Example 6-5. (continued).

```
        POP   AX
        CMP   CX,AX         ;Compare hours and minutes
        JA    QUIT
        JB    CHECK
        CMP   DX,BX         ;Compare seconds and hunds
        JB    CHECK
QUIT:   POP   DX            ;Restore registers
        POP   CX
        POP   BX
        POP   AX
        RET                 ;Return to calling program
DELAY   ENDP
CSEG    ENDS
        END
```

5. If you want to add your own interrupts to the system, which interrupt numbers may you use?
6. Suppose you have written an interrupt service routine called SHOW_CLOCK that displays the current values for hours and seconds on the screen. Which interrupt's vector should point to SHOW_CLOCK?
7. List the instructions that make the interrupt vector in Exercise 6 point to SHOW_CLOCK.
8. Which instructions would you use to read the real-time clock's current time settings?
9. To use the alarm feature, which interrupt vector should point to your alarm interrupt service routine?
10. Assuming you have loaded the address of an alarm routine into memory, list the instructions you would use to make the AT execute it one hour from now.

7

Video Operations

7.1 Display Modes

If you have standard IBM products, your display connects to the AT through either of two adapter cards. The *Monochrome Display and Parallel Printer Adapter* connects to an IBM Monochrome Display and a parallel printer. The *Color/Graphics Monitor Adapter* connects to a monitor or standard TV set (color or black and white).

Monochrome Adapter

The Monochrome Adapter can display only characters, and only in black and white (or green, or amber, depending on your display). The characters consist of standard letters, numbers, and symbols, plus some simple shapes such as diamonds, squares, smiling faces, and musical note symbols.

The adapter displays characters on an 80-column by 25-line grid on the screen, and obtains these characters from a 4K-byte memory on the card. Hence, we say that the screen is "memory-mapped." Later in this chapter, we describe how the adapter converts the data in its memory into display characters.

Color/Graphics Adapter

The Color/Graphics Monitor Adapter is more versatile than the Monochrome Adapter. Besides text, it can display dot graphics in either black and white or color (up to 16 colors).

In the text mode, the adapter can generate an 80×25 character high-resolution display or a 40×25 character low-resolution display. Further, it has a 16K-byte on-card memory that can store up to four 80×25 character grids or eight 40×25 grids; IBM calls the grids "pages."

In the graphics mode, the adapter divides the screen into a grid of dot-like picture elements, or *pels*, rather like a scoreboard or a time/temperature display. The grids can have a resolution of 320×200 pels or 640×200 pels. With 320×200 resolution, each pel may have any of four colors and the background may have any of 16 colors. The 640×200 mode displays only black and white, because the adapter needs the full 16K bytes of on-card storage to define the on or off states of the pels.

Due to the large number of pels and a palette of 16 colors, programming displays in the graphics mode can be a somewhat complex task. (For more on this topic, refer to the IBM *Technical Reference* manual.) For this reason, we limit our discussion to programming in the text mode, using the block graphics characters in the character set. Further, all procedures in this chapter display in black and white on an 80×25 screen grid. You can easily modify them for color and/or the 40×25 grid, however.

7.2 How the PC AT Displays Characters

Character Codes

As we mentioned in Section 7.1, when the display adapter is operating in the text mode (as it will be unless you have explicitly switched to graphics mode), it forms characters by converting numeric codes in its on-card memory into any of 256 display characters. Table 7-1 shows the relationship between the numeric codes and the display characters.

Note that besides regular letters, numbers, and symbols, the character set includes foreign language letters, Greek and math symbols, arrows, and a variety of other block graphics characters. The graphics characters do not let you create complex graphic displays that compete with Disney or George Lucas, but they are convenient for making sales demonstration programs, games, and flashy business programs.

Attributes

Every character position on the screen actually has two bytes associated with it. The *character code byte*, which we just mentioned, contains the numeric code for the character. The *attribute byte* specifies how the character is to be

Table 7-1. Numeric codes for display characters.

HIGH PART

LOW PART

DECIMAL VALUE	➡	0	16	32	48	64	80	96	112	128	144	160	176	192	208	224	240
⬇	HEXA-DECIMAL VALUE	0	1	2	3	4	5	6	7	8	9	A	B	C	D	E	F
0	0	BLANK (NULL)	►	BLANK (SPACE)	0	@	P	‘	p	Ç	É	á	1/4 Dots On	└	╨	α	≡
1	1	☺	◄	!	1	A	Q	a	q	ü	Æ	í	1/2 Dots On	┴	╤	β	±
2	2	☻	↕	"	2	B	R	b	r	é	FE	ó	3/4 Dots On	┬	╥	γ	≥
3	3	♥	‼	#	3	C	S	c	s	â	ô	ú	│	├	╙	π	≤
4	4	♦	¶	$	4	D	T	d	t	ä	ö	ñ	┤	─	╘	Σ	⌠
5	5	♣	§	%	5	E	U	e	u	à	ò	Ñ	╡	┼	╒	σ	⌡
6	6	♠	▬	&	6	F	V	f	v	å	û	ª	╢	╞	╓	μ	÷
7	7	BEEP •	↨	'	7	G	W	g	w	ç	ù	º	╖	╟	╫	τ	≈
8	8	◘	↑	(	8	H	X	h	x	ê	ÿ	¿	╕	╚	╪	Φ	°
9	9	○	↓	)	9	I	Y	i	y	ë	Ö	⌐	╣	╔	┘	Θ	•
10	A	◙	→	*	:	J	Z	j	z	è	Ü	¬	║	╩	┌	Ω	·
11	B	♂	ESC ←	+	;	K	[	k	{	ï	¢	½	╗	╦	█	δ	√
12	C	♀	∟	,	<	L	\	l	¦	î	£	¼	╝	╠	▄	∞	η
13	D	♪	↔	—	=	M	]	m	}	ì	¥	¡	╜	═	▌	∅	2
14	E	♫	▲	.	>	N	∧	n	∼	Ä	Pts	«	╛	╬	▐	∈	■
15	F	☼	▼	/	?	O	_	o	△	Å	ƒ	»	┐	╧	▀	∩	BLANK 'FF'

shown. That is, it specifies the color of the character and its background, plus the character's intensity (normal or highlighted) and whether it shows steadily or blinks.

Table 7-2 shows the general form of the attribute byte for black and white text. Note that there are five basic display modes: normal (07), normal with underlining (01), reverse video (70H), and a non-display in either black (00) or white (77H). You can also turn on the blinking or intensity bit to get other effects. For example, 87H makes a character blink, while 0FH highlights it and 8FH makes it both highlighted and blinking.

Table 7-3 shows the attribute byte for color text. Here, you can select from 16 character colors and eight background colors, in any combination. You can also make the character blink.

When you turn the computer on, the adapter card sets the entire screen to a normal intensity, non-blinking display, with white characters on a black background—that is, to an attribute value of 07. However, by specifying new attribute values you can change these settings for any position on the screen.

Table 7-2. Attribute byte for black and white text.

7	6	5	4	3	2	1	0		
FG	**Background**			**Foreground**				**Background Color**	**Character Color**
B	0	0	0	I	1	1	1	Black	White
B	0	0	0	I	0	0	1	Black	White*
B	1	1	1	I	0	0	0	White	Black
B	0	0	0	I	0	0	0	Black	Black
B	1	1	1	I	1	1	1	White	White

Notes: *This combination produces underlining.
B = 0 produces non-blinking character
= 1 produces blinking character
I = 0 displays character with normal intensity
= 1 displays character with high intensity (highlighted)

Table 7-3. Attribute byte for color text.

7	6	5	4	3	2	1	0	
FG	**Background**			**Foreground**				
B	**R**	**G**	**B**	**I**	**R**	**G**	**B**	**Color**
	0	0	0	0	0	0	0	Black
	0	0	1	0	0	0	1	Blue
	0	1	0	0	0	1	0	Green
	0	1	1	0	0	1	1	Cyan
	1	0	0	0	1	0	0	Red
	1	0	1	0	1	0	1	Magenta
				0	1	1	0	Brown
	1	1	1	0	1	1	1	White
				1	0	0	0	Dark gray
				1	0	0	1	Light blue
				1	0	1	0	Light green
				1	0	1	1	Light cyan
				1	1	0	0	Light red
				1	1	0	1	Light magenta
	1	1	0	1	1	1	0	Yellow
				1	1	1	1	Bright white

Note: B = 0 produces non-blinking character
= 1 produces blinking character

Memory-Mapping

As we have mentioned, both display adapters include memory in which they store a character code and attribute byte for each character on the screen. The Monochrome Adapter's memory is 4K bytes long, because it must hold a pair of bytes for each position on an 80-column by 25-line screen (2 times 80 times 25 equals 4000). Similarly, the Color/Graphic Adapter's memory is 16K bytes long, to support four 80×25 pages or eight 40×25 pages.

In Section 7.3, we will discuss BIOS and DOS interrupts that write characters to the screen, but it is quite possible to store bytes directly into the adapter's memory. This makes the corresponding characters appear on the screen. Writing directly to the memory is not recommended, however, because IBM may change its location—then you would be overwriting data (perhaps important data). Still, you should know something about how the adapters "map" data in their memories as characters on the screen.

Data in Adapter Memory

The on-card memory in each display adapter is contained in a dedicated area of the PC AT's memory map. *The Monochrome Adapter's 4K memory starts at location B0000, while the Color/Graphic Adapter's 16K memory starts at location B8000.*

In each case, the memory holds a character code byte and attribute byte for each character on the screen. That is, the first two bytes hold the data for line 0, column 0 (the upper left-hand corner of the screen); the next two bytes hold the data for line 0, column 1; and so on, down to the bottom right-hand corner of the screen.

Displaying Adapter Memory

You can easily display the contents of the adapter's memory using DEBUG's D (Dump) command. To do this, start DEBUG, then type **d b000:0** (assuming you have a monochrome display). If you have just started the computer, the first line of the display begins with

```
B000:0000  43 07 75 07 72 07 72 07
```

and the right-hand side of the screen shows

```
C.u.r.r.
```

Here, DEBUG is displaying the start of the DOS "Current date" prompt. Note that it shows a period for each attribute byte because *07* (the attribute value for a normal character) does not represent a displayable character.

Changing the Adapter Memory

To make the screen show something different, you only have to change the contents of the display adapter's memory. There are BIOS and DOS routines to do this (we discuss them in Section 7.3), but let's get cute and use DEBUG's E (Enter) command instead. This involves specifying the address where the changes start, followed by pairs of character code bytes and attribute bytes. For example, to change *Current date* to *Today's date,* enter

```
e b000:0 "T" 07 "o" 07 "d" 07 "a" 07 "y" 07 "'" 07 "s"
```

The moment you press Return at the end of the line, the AT changes the prompt to what you gave it.

You can also display characters in reverse video (black characters on a white background) by entering *70* for the attribute values. Similarly, to show blinking, reverse characters, use *F0* for the attribute. While all of this foolishness probably has little or no practical value, it does demonstrate the kinds of things that are possible if you know how to control the computer's internal operation.

7.3 Video Interrupts

In Chapter 6 we mentioned two different kinds of interrupts you can use to communicate with the display: the Type 10 (Video) interrupt that is built into BIOS and the video options that DOS contributes with its Type 21 function calls.

BIOS Type 10 (Video) Interrupt

This interrupt performs any of 17 different display operations based on a value in AH. The Type 10 interrupt vector points to VIDEO_IO, which contains a JMP to interrupt service routine VIDEO_IO_1 at location F000:3605; see the *Video* portion of the BIOS listing.

VIDEO_IO_1 begins by loading the segment number of the display adapter's memory into the Extra Segment (ES) register. This is B000 for a Monochrome Adapter or B800 for a Color/Graphics Adapter. With ES properly initialized, VIDEO_IO_1 performs the specified I/O operation. Table 7-4 summarizes these operations and shows which registers they use.

Table 7-4. Video operations with Type 10 interrupt.

AH	Operation	Input Values	Results*
CRT Interface Routines			
0	Set video mode (Color/Graphics)	*Text modes* AL = 0 40×25 B/W (default) = 1 40×25 Color = 2 80×25 B/W = 3 80×25 Color *Graphics modes* AL = 4 320×200 Color = 5 320×200 B/W = 6 640×200 B/W	Screen is blank
1	Set cursor mode	CH = Start line for cursor CL = End line for cursor	None
2	Move cursor	DH,DL = Row,column BH = Page number (0 for Graphics)	None
3	Read cursor position	BH = Page number (0 for Graphics)	DH,DL = Row,column of cursor CH,CL = Cursor mode (see AH = 1)
4	Read light pen position	None	AH = 0 Light pen switch not down or not triggered AH = 1 Valid light pen values in registers

Table 7-4. Video operations with Type 10 interrupt (continued).

AH	Operation	Input Values	Results*
CRT Interface Routines (continued)			
			DH,DL = Row,column CH = Raster line (0-199) BX = Pixel column (0-319,639)
5	Select active display page (Text modes)	AL = New page value (0-7 for modes 0 and 1; 0-3 for modes 2 and 3)	None
6	Scroll active page up	AL = Number of lines Blanks lines at bottom of window. AL = 0 clears entire screen. CH,CL = Row,column of top left corner of scroll DH,DL = Row,column of bottom right corner of scroll BH = Attribute to be used on blank line	None
7	Scroll active page down	Same as AH = 6, but blanks line at top of window.	None
Character-Handling Routines			
8	Read character and attribute at cursor position	BH = Display page (Text modes)	AL = Character AH = Attribute (Text modes) Cursor is at original position

Table 7-4. *Video operations with Type 10 interrupt (continued).*

AH	Operation	Input Values	Results*
Character-Handling Routines (continued)			
9	Display character and attribute at cursor position	BH = Display page (Text modes) BL = Attribute (Text) = Color (Graphics) CX = Number of times to repeat character AL = Character	Cursor is at original position
A	Display character (only) at cursor postion	BH = Display page (Text modes) CX = Number of times to repeat character AL = Character	Cursor is at original position
Graphics Routines			
B	Set color palette (320 × 200) graphics)	BH = Palette color ID (0-127) BL = Color to be used with color ID	None
C	Display dot	DX = Row (0-199) CX = Column (0-639) AL = Color value If bit 7 of AL = 1, the color value is exclusive-ORed with the current contents of the dot.	None
D	Read dot	DX = Row (0-199) CX = Column (0-639)	AL = Dot value
Teletype Routines			
E	Display character, then advance cursor	AL = Character BL = Foreground color (Graphics)	Cursor follows character

Table 7-4. Video operations with Type 10 interrupt (continued).

AH	Operation	Input Values	Results*
Teletype Routines (continued)			
13	Display string	ES:BP = String address CX = String length DH,DL = Starting row,column BH = Page number	
		AL = 0	Cursor returns to original position
		BL = Attribute String is *char,char,...char*	
		AL = 1	Cursor follows string
		BL = Attribute String is *char,char,...char*	
		AL = 2	Cursor returns to original position
		String is *char,attr,char,attr...*	
		AL = 3	Cursor follows string
		String is *char,attr,char,attr...*	
Read Video State Routine			
F	Read current video state	None	AL = Current mode (See AH = 0) AH = Number of character columns on screen BH = Active display page

*Besides the registers listed in this column, these routines save all registers except AX and the flags.

CRT Interface Routines

These routines let you set the video mode and the line limits for the cursor, set and read the cursor position, read the light pen position, and control the active display page.

Many of these routines refer to rows and columns on the screen, so you should understand the numbering convention. On IBM Personal Computers, row (line) numbers start with 0 at the top and increase going down the screen. Similarly, column numbers start with 0 at the left and increase to the right.

On the 80×25 grid, for example, rows range from 0 to 24 and columns range from 0 to 79. Therefore, a character at the tenth position on the fourth line is at row 3 and column 9—or (3,9) for short. Figure 7-1 shows this position on the grid.

Of the eight CRT interface options, you will probably use 0, 2, and 3 most often. Option 0 lets you switch video modes on the Color/Graphics Adapter; the Monochrome Adapter only operates in the 80×25 black and white text

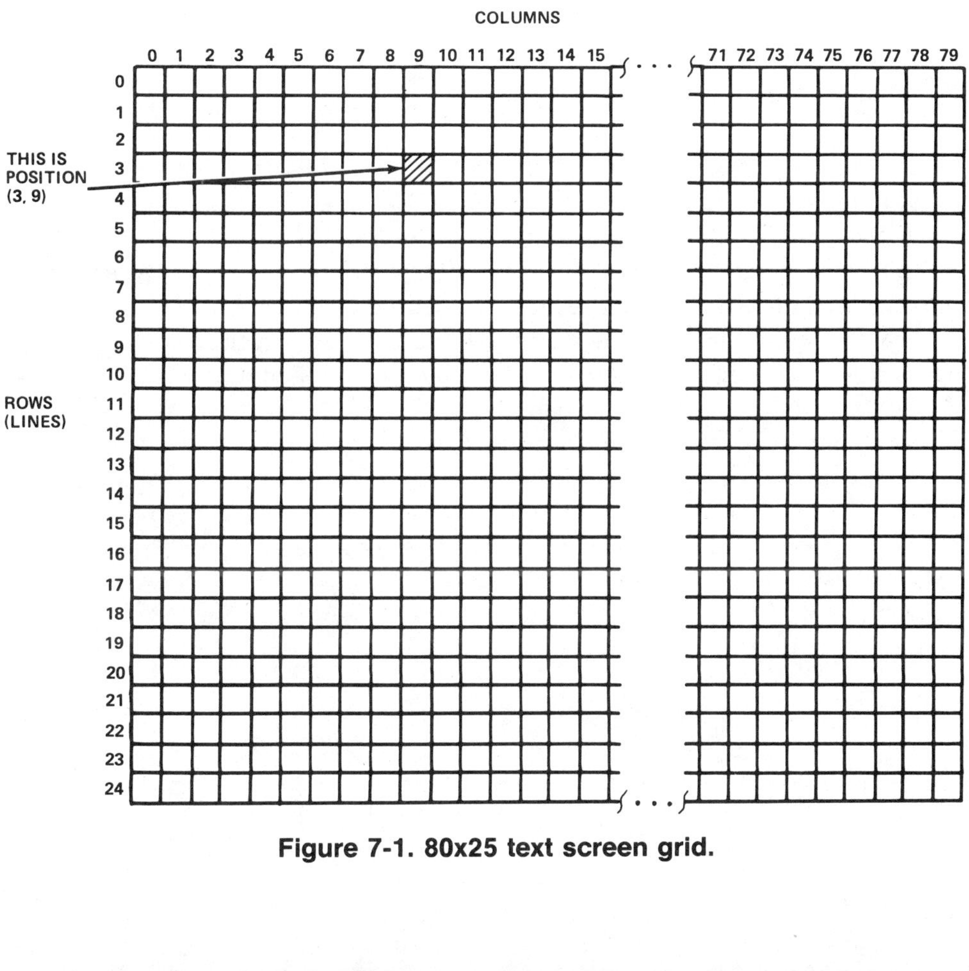

Figure 7-1. 80x25 text screen grid.

mode. This also blanks the screen, even if you choose the mode that's already active. (We use this fact later to create a screen-clearing routine.)

Option 2 lets you move the cursor anywhere on the screen, as determined by a row number in DH and a column number in DL. For example, the following moves it to the top left-hand corner (the *home* position):

```
MOV   DX,0     ;Select the home position
MOV   AH,2     ;Move the cursor there
INT   10H
```

Option 3 is convenient for moving the cursor relative to its current position. For example, to move it two rows down and three columns to the right, use

```
MOV   AH,3  ;Get the current cursor position
INT   10H
ADD   DH,2  ;Increase row by 2
ADD   DL,3  ; and column by 3
MOV   AH,2  ;Move the cursor
INT   10H
```

Character-Handling Routines

These routines transfer characters to or from the screen, then return the cursor to its original position. For the display options, you specify the character by putting its numeric code (per Table 7-1) in AL.

Note the difference between the two display options: AH = 9 outputs a character and an attribute to the cursor location, while AH = A outputs just a character, and uses whatever attribute value that location currently has. The AH = A option is especially convenient with black and white displays, where you rarely change the attribute.

The character-handling routines are useful for doing text mode graphics (or, rather, pseudo-graphics). But because these routines don't automatically advance the cursor, they aren't very efficient for displaying messages or prompts. There, you will want routines that advance the cursor as they go along. We give examples under "Teletype Routines."

Graphics Routines

These routines display and read dots, and set the color palette for 320×200 graphics. Graphics programming can get more complicated than we want for this book. For more details, refer to the *Technical Reference* or one of the graphics books on the market.

Teletype Routines

These two options can display single characters or sequences of characters (strings). For the most part, they use the definitions in Table 7-1 just as the character-handling routines do. However, these routines treat four of the numeric codes as *control characters* rather than graphics characters, as follows:

Numeric Code Hex	Numeric Code Dec	Character Name	Function
07	07	Bell	Emits a one-second "beep"
08	08	Backspace	Moves the cursor one column to the left
0A	10	Line Feed	Moves the cursor down one row
0D	13	Carriage Return	Moves the cursor to the beginning of the line

For this reason IBM calls them "Teletype" routines—they treat the computer's screen like an old-fashioned Teletype machine, even down to the bell.

The Line Feed and Carriage Return characters are convenient for displaying messages. Here, you put the message string on the screen and then issue a Line Feed and Carriage Return to move the cursor to the next line.

The Bell character can be useful, too, because it provides an easy way to beep the speaker. The instructions are:

```
MOV   AL,7      ;Beep the speaker
MOV   AH,0EH
INT   10H
```

You might want to sound a beep to alert the operator that there is a new prompt or error message on the screen, or that a long procedure (say, a sort) has finally finished.

The string-displaying option (AH = 13H) has four modes. For the first two, you specify an attribute value that is to be used for the entire string. For the other two, you must specify an attribute for each character. In each case, the first option puts the cursor back where it started, while the second leaves it at the end of the string.

For example, to display *1986 Profits* on the top line of the screen, put the following in the extra segment:

```
TITL       DB   '1986 Profits'
LEN_TITL   EQU  $-TITLE
```

(the LEN_TITL statement calculates the length of the string) and these instructions in the code segment:

```
MOV   AL,3           ;Select 80x25 color text
MOV   AH,0           ;Change the mode
INT   10H
LEA   BP,TITL        ;Offset of string
MOV   CX,LEN_TITL    ;Character count
MOV   DX,0           ;Start at top left-hand corner
MOV   BL,41H         ;Use blue-on-red lettering
MOV   AL,0           ;Make cursor return
MOV   AH,13H         ;Select the string option
INT   10H            ;Display the string
```

Note that this example produces blue letters on a red background—a masterpiece if there ever was one. However, suppose a committee at your company (there always is one) decides they want *1986* in blue, but *Profits* in alternating green and blue. To do this, you can display the title as two successive strings, with the first using the previous character-only form and the second using the character-and-attribute form. Now your extra segment looks like this:

```
TITLE1    DB   '1986 '
TITLE2    DB   'P',42H,'r',41H,'o',42H,'f',41H,'i',42H
          DB   't',41H,'s',42H
LEN_TITLE2  EQU  $-TITLE2
```

and your code segment contains

```
MOV   AL,3           ;Select 80x25 color text
MOV   AH,0           ;Change the mode
INT   10H
LEA   BP,TITLE1      ;Offset of first string
MOV   CX,TITLE2-TITLE1
MOV   DX,0
MOV   BL,41H         ;Color is blue-on-red
MOV   AL,1           ;Character string
MOV   AH,13H         ;Display the first string
INT   10H
MOV   AH,3           ;Read the cursor position
INT   10H
LEA   BP,TITLE2      ;Offset of second string
MOV   CX,LEN_TITLE2
MOV   AL,3           ;Character-and-attribute string
MOV   AH,13H         ;Display the second string
INT   10H
```

Read Video State Routine

This routine reports the current video mode, screen width, and active display page. Of course, these details only vary for the Color/Graphics Adapter. For a Monochrome system (or one with a compatible adapter such as a Hercules Graphics card), the routine always returns AL = 7, AH = 50H (that is, 80 columns), and BH = 0.

Generally, you need just one of the routine's result values rather than all three. As an illustration, Example 7-1 uses just the mode; it doesn't care about the screen width or page. This short procedure, CLEAR_SCREEN, clears the screen and homes the cursor just like the DOS *CLS* command.

Example 7-1. Clear the screen.

```
        PAGE   ,132
TITLE   CLR_S - Clear the screen

;   Clears the screen and homes the cursor.
;   All registers are preserved.

;   Assemble with: MASM CLR_S;
;   Link with: LINK callprog+CLR_S;

        PUBLIC  CLEAR_SCREEN
CSEG    SEGMENT PARA PUBLIC 'CODE'
        ASSUME  CS:CSEG
CLEAR_SCREEN PROC FAR
        PUSH   AX
        PUSH   BX
        MOV    AH,15             ;Read the video mode
        INT    10H
        MOV    AH,0              ;Set the video mode
        INT    10H
        POP    BX
        POP    AX
        RET                      ;Return to caller
CLEAR_SCREEN ENDP
CSEG    ENDS
        END
```

DOS Function Calls for Video

Table 7-5 summarizes the DOS Type 21 function calls that relate to video operations. As you can see, there are only four options here, three that display or print a character and one that displays a string. This is one of the few areas in which DOS actually provides less flexibility than the BIOS.

Table 7-5. Video operations with Type 21 interrupt.

AH	Operation	Input Values	Results*
2	Display a character (with Ctrl-Break check)	DL = Character	Cursor follows character
5	Print a character	DL = Character	None
6	Display a character (no Ctrl-Break check)	DL = Character	Cursor follows character
9	Display a string	DS:DX = String address. String must end with $.	Cursor follows string

These DOS options use the character set in the same way as the BIOS Teletype routines. That is, they display block graphics characters for all but four numeric codes—the ones for the Bell, Backspace, Line Feed, and Carriage Return functions. They also advance the cursor.

Note that the string display function (9) requires the string to end with a dollar sign ($). It uses the $ to calculate the length of the string. Contrast this with the BIOS Type 10 string option (13H), which requires you to supply the string length in CX.

Moving to the Next Line

For message strings, you may want the cursor to advance to the next line automatically. To make it do this, precede the $ with Carriage Return and Line Feed characters, as in

```
MESSAGE  DB  'The sort operation is finished.',13,10,'$'
```

7.4 Simple Text Mode Graphics

So far we have been discussing only standard text operations, ones we can use to display messages. However, the block graphics characters in the AT's repertoire (see Table 7-1), allow us to produce some rather primitive, but effective, graphics.

Diagonal Line

As an example of text mode graphics, let's display a diagonal "line" on the screen. We'll start the line at the top left-hand corner and advance down the screen one row and one column at a time. We will use the "smile face" character (code 02 in Table 7-1) to form it. Thus, the first face is at screen position (0,0), the next is at (1,1), and so on.

Example 7-2 shows a procedure (DIAG_LINE) that plots the line. It uses four of the Type 10 interrupt options: AH = 15 reads the display page number into BH, AH = 0 selects the 80x25 black-and-white text mode, AH = 2 moves the cursor, and AH = 10 sends the character to the screen.

7.5 Basics of Animation

The diagonal line-drawing procedure in Example 7-2 produces a display that does not move. The faces just sit there and smile at you (probably saying, "Have a nice day.") In many applications, however, you want to move the shape on the screen. That is, you want to *animate* it.

Producing animated affects is not as difficult as you might expect. In fact, it takes only five steps:

1. Plot the shape on the screen.
2. Wait a period of time, so the shape is visible.
3. Erase the shape.
4. Change the shape's row and column coordinates.
5. Repeat the process, starting at Step 1.

You can generate a time delay (step 2) by calling the DELAY procedure we developed in Example 6-5. DELAY obtains minutes, seconds, and 1/100 seconds from AL, BH, and BL, respectively.

To erase a shape from the screen you can either *clear* that portion of the screen, by writing blank (code 0) characters, or *replot* the shape in black. To replot in black, you can either write a blank character with the Type 10 interrupt's AH = 9 option or give the character the black-on-black attribute (BL = 0) with the AH = A option.

The Old Moving Face Trick

Example 7-3 shows a new line-plotting procedure that "moves" the smile face down the diagonal in half-second spurts. The main procedure (MOVE_FACE) has only four more instructions than the DIAG_LINE pro-

Example 7-2. Display a diagonal line.

```
        PAGE   ,132
TITLE   DIAGLINE - Display a Diagonal Line

;   Draws a diagonal line of "smile faces," starting
;   at the top left corner of the screen.

;   Assemble with: MASM DIAGLINE;
;   Link with: LINK DIAGLINE;

STACK   SEGMENT PARA STACK 'STACK'
        DB     64 DUP('STACK   ')
STACK   ENDS

CSEG    SEGMENT PARA 'CODE'
        ASSUME  CS:CSEG,SS:STACK
DIAG_LINE PROC  FAR

;   Set up the stack to contain the proper values so this
;   program can return to DEBUG.

        PUSH   DS               ;Put return seg. addr. on stack
        MOV    DI,0             ;Clear a register
        PUSH   DI               ;Put zero return addr. on stack

        MOV    AH,15            ;Set BH to active display page
        INT    10H
        MOV    AH,0             ;Select 80x25 B/W text mode
        MOV    AL,2
        INT    10H
        MOV    CX,1             ;Character count = 1
        MOV    DX,0             ;Start at row 0, column 0
SET_CRSR: MOV  AH,2             ;Set new cursor position
        INT    10H
        MOV    AL,2             ;Display char. is smile face
        MOV    AH,10            ;Write char. to the screen
        INT    10H
        INC    DH               ;Point to next row
        INC    DL               ; and column position
        CMP    DH,25            ;Bottom of screen?
        JNE    SET_CRSR
        RET                     ; Yes. Exit.
DIAG_LINE ENDP
CSEG    ENDS
        END    DIAG_LINE
```

cedure of Example 7-2. These call a half-second delay procedure (DLY_HALF) and erase the face by sending a blank (0) code to the screen.

You might like to experiment with longer or shorter delays. To see (or *not see*) the face travel at maximum speed, omit the delay altogether.

Example 7-3. Animate a diagonal line display.

```
        PAGE    ,132
TITLE   MOVEFACE - Animate a Diagonal Line Display

;   This procedure moves a "smile face" diagonally down
;   the screen, starting at the top left corner, with
;   a 1/2-second delay between moves.

;   Assemble with: MASM MOVEFACE;
;   Link with: LINK MOVEFACE+DELAY;

        EXTRN DELAY:FAR
STACK   SEGMENT PARA STACK 'STACK'
        DB      64 DUP('STACK   ')
STACK   ENDS

CSEG    SEGMENT PARA 'CODE'
        ASSUME  CS:CSEG,SS:STACK
MOVE_FACE PROC  FAR

;   Set up the stack to contain the proper values so this
;   program can return to DEBUG.

        PUSH    DS              ;Put return seg. addr. on stack
        MOV     DI,0            ;Clear a register
        PUSH    DI              ;Put zero return addr. on stack

        MOV     AH,15           ;Set BH to active display page
        INT     10H
        MOV     AH,0            ;Select 80x25 B/W text mode
        MOV     AL,2
        INT     10H
        MOV     CX,1            ;Character count = 1
        MOV     DX,0            ;Start at row 0, column 0
SET_CRSR: MOV   AH,2            ;Set new cursor position
        INT     10H
        MOV     AL,2            ;Display char. is smile face
        MOV     AH,10           ;Write char. to the screen
        INT     10H
        CALL    DLY_HALF        ;Wait a half-second
        SUB     AL,AL           ; then erase the face
        MOV     AH,10
        INT     10H
        INC     DH              ;Point to next row
        INC     DL              ; and column position
        CMP     DH,25           ;Bottom of screen?
        JNE     SET_CRSR
        RET                     ; Yes. Exit.
MOVE_FACE ENDP
;   This procedure generates a one-half second delay.
```

Example 7-3. (continued).

```
DLY_HALF PROC
         SUB    AL,AL             ;Set minutes to zero
         SUB    BH,BH             ;Set seconds to zero
         MOV    BL,50             ;Set hundredths to 50
         CALL   DELAY
         RET
DLY_HALF ENDP
CSEG     ENDS
         END    MOVE_FACE
```

7.6 Shape Tables

Shapes that are formed from several characters are almost as easy to manipulate as single characters, like our smile face. But multi-character shapes require multiple write operations, one for each character in the shape.

If a shape consists of just two or three characters, you can probably display it with a few successive output operations. However, if it contains many characters, or you want to display two or more shapes simultaneously, you should consider defining it in a *shape table.*

A shape table contains the character code, attribute, and row and column offset for each character in a display shape. You already know what the character code and attribute are. The row and column offsets are the vertical and horizontal distances between the previous character and the current character; they tell the computer how to draw the shape.

To illustrate, Figure 7-2 shows a "car" constructed with seven text characters. Moving left to right, the body consists of the letter R (code 52H), a 1/2-dots-on character (B1), and two solid boxes (DB); the first two characters are in reverse video, the second two are in normal video. The wheels, which are letter Os (4F), and the smile face (02) are in normal video. My son Ryan designed this shape.

Figure 7-2 shows the row and column offsets in parentheses. The first character we plot is the letter R, so its offsets are (0,0). Next we plot the 1/2-dots-on character. It is on the same row as the R, but one column to the right, so its offsets are (0,1). Similarly, the front characters of the body also have offsets of (0,1).

Next we draw the front wheel, which has offsets of (1,0) from the rightmost character of the body, and then the back wheel, with offsets of (0,-3) from the front wheel. Finally, the smiling driver has offsets of (-2,1) from the back wheel.

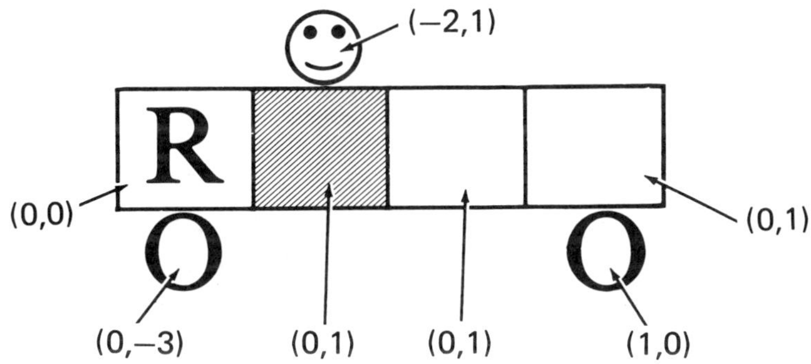

Figure 7-2. Row and column offsets for a text mode "car."

Each shape parameter is a byte value, so the shape table must contain four bytes for each character. If you are operating on more that one shape table, each shape table should also include a character count byte. Figure 7-3 shows the shape table for the "car" we just described.

```
CAR  DB  7                ;Shape contains seven characters
     DB  52H,70H,0,0      ;Rear character of body
     DB  0B1H,70H,0,1     ;Driver's compartment
     DB  0DBH,7,0,1       ;Next character of body
     DB  0DBH,7,0,1       ;Front character of body
     DB  4FH,7,1,0        ;Front wheel
     DB  4FH,7,0,-3       ;Rear wheel
     DB  2,7,-2,1         ;Smile face
```

Figure 7-3. Shape table for text mode "car".

Generalized Display Procedure

After erasing the screen (use CLEAR_SCREEN in Example 7-1), your display program should execute a routine that loads shape table parameters into the appropriate registers, then issues the output command. Put this routine in a loop, where it repeats until every character in the shape table has been output.

With the screen erased, you can call the procedure in Example 7-4 to plot a shape on the screen. For instance, this instruction sequence plots our text mode "car" with the body on line 20:

```
CALL  CLEAR_SCREEN   ;Clear the screen
LEA   DI,CAR         ;DI points to car shape table
MOV   DH,20          ;Body is on line 20,
MOV   DL,0           ; starting in column 0
CALL  DSPLY_SHAPE    ;Draw the car
```

Example 7-4. Construct a shape from a shape table.

```
        PAGE    ,132
TITLE   D_SHAPE - Construct a Shape From a Shape Table

;   Constructs a shape on the screen using a shape table.
;   Inputs: DS:DI = Address of shape table
;           DH,DL = Row,column of first character
;   The shape table consists of a character count byte
;   followed by a code, attribute, row offset, and
;   column offset for each character in the shape.
;   No registers are affected.

;   Assemble with: MASM D_SHAPE;
;   Link with: LINK callprog+D_SHAPE;

        PUBLIC  DSPLY_SHAPE
CSEG    SEGMENT PARA 'CODE'
        ASSUME  CS:CSEG
DSPLY_SHAPE PROC FAR
        PUSH    AX              ;Save registers
        PUSH    BX
        PUSH    CX
        PUSH    DX
        PUSH    DI
        MOV     AH,15           ;Set BH to active page
        INT     10H
        SUB     CH,CH           ;Clear high byte of count
        MOV     CL,[DI]         ;CL holds char. count
        INC     DI              ;DI points to first char.
NEXT_CHAR: ADD DH,[DI+2]        ;Update row pointer
        ADD     DL,[DI+3]       ; and column pointer
        MOV     AH,2            ;Move cursor
        INT     10H
        MOV     AL,[DI]         ;Fetch char. value
        MOV     BL,[DI+1]       ; and attribute
        PUSH    CX              ;Preserve character count
        MOV     CX,1            ;Write char. to screen
        MOV     AH,9
        INT     10H
        POP     CX              ;Restore char. count
        ADD     DI,4            ;DI points to next char. bloack
        LOOP    NEXT_CHAR       ;When all characters are displayed
        POP     DI              ; restore registers
        POP     DX
        POP     CX
        POP     BX
        POP     AX
        RET                     ; and exit
DSPLY_SHAPE ENDP
CSEG    ENDS
        END
```

A Mover and Shaper

You can animate a complex shape such as our "car" the same way you animate a single-character shape. To make a multi-character shape move on the screen, plot it, wait for some time to elapse, erase it, then redraw it in a new location.

As we mentioned earlier, to erase a shape, you can either clear the part of the screen where the shape is displayed or redraw the shape in black. But be aware that if there are several shapes on the screen, you must somehow keep track of where the shape to be erased is located at any given time. This may be a problem if the shape is moving.

Example 7-5 shows a procedure that moves a shape from left to right across the screen. The main procedure, MOVE_SHAPE, plots the shape on the screen using the same general approach as DSPLY_SHAPE. Two additional procedures, DLY_QRTR and ERASE, provide the delay period (1/4 second, in this case) and the screen erase function.

Here, ERASE erases the shape by replotting it with an attribute of zero. This produces a black-on-black display (that is, a *non-display*). ERASE also increments the column number—the variable COL_NO in the data segment—at the end of the erase operation. Since the rightmost column on the screen is Column 79, MOVE_SHAPE stops when any character in the shape has a column number equal to or greater than 80.

We can use MOVE_SHAPE to move our text mode "car" across the screen on line 20 with this sequence:

```
CALL  CLEAR_SCREEN  ;Clear the screen
LEA   DI,CAR        ;DI points to car shape table
MOV   DH,20         ;Body is on line 20,
MOV   DL,0          ; starting in column 0
CALL  MOVE_SHAPE    ;Move the car
```

Note that although MOVE_SHAPE only moves horizontally, you can easily modify it to move vertically or diagonally. Simply change the row coordinate (rather than the column coordinate) or both the row and the column coordinates after each display-delay-erase sequence.

Example 7-5. Animate a multi-character shape.

```
        PAGE    ,132
TITLE   M_SHAPE - Animate a Multi-Character Shape

;   Moves a shape horizontally across the screen, with
;   a 1/4-second delay between moves.
;   Inputs: DS:DI = Address of shape table
;           DH,DL = Row,column of first character
;   All registers are preserved.

;   Assemble with: MASM M_SHAPE;
;   Link with: LINK callprog+M_SHAPE+DELAY;

DSEG      SEGMENT PARA PUBLIC 'DATA'
CHAR_CNT DW      ?
POINTER DW       ?
LINE_NO DB       ?
COL_NO   DB      ?
DSEG      ENDS

        PUBLIC  MOVE_SHAPE
        EXTRN   DELAY:FAR
CSEG    SEGMENT PARA PUBLIC 'CODE'
        ASSUME  CS:CSEG,DS:DSEG
MOVE_SHAPE PROC FAR
        PUSH    DS              ;Save caller's registers
        PUSH    AX
        PUSH    BX
        PUSH    CX
        PUSH    DX
        PUSH    DI

        MOV     BX,DSEG         ;Initialize DS
        MOV     DS,BX

        MOV     AH,15           ;Set BH to active page
        INT     10H
        SUB     CH,CH           ;Clear high byte of count
        MOV     CL,[DI]         ;CL holds char. count
        INC     DI              ;DI points to first char.
        MOV     CHAR_CNT,CX     ;Save character count,
        MOV     POINTER,DI      ; shape table pointer,
        MOV     LINE_NO,DH      ; and coordinates
        MOV     COL_NO,DL

;   These instructions plot the shape on the screen.

PLOT_NEXT: ADD DH,[DI+2]        ;Update row pointer
        ADD     DL,[DI+3]       ; and column pointer
        CMP     DL,80           ;Is this char. off the screen?
        JB      MOV_CRSR
        CALL    ERASE           ; If so, erase shape and exit
```

Example 7-5. (continued).

```
        POP   DI
        POP   DX
        POP   CX
        POP   BX
        POP   AX
        POP   DS
        RET
MOV_CRSR: MOV AH,2            ; Otherwise, move the cursor
        INT   10H
        MOV   AL,[DI]         ;Fetch char. value
        MOV   BL,[DI+1]       ; and attribute
        PUSH  CX              ;Preserve character count
        MOV   CX,1            ;Write char. to screen
        MOV   AH,9
        INT   10H
        POP   CX              ;Restore char. count
        ADD   DI,4            ;DI points to next char. block
        LOOP  PLOT_NEXT       ;When all characters are displayed
        CALL  DLY_QRTR        ; wait a quarter-second
        CALL  ERASE           ; then erase the shape
        JMP   SHORT PLOT_NEXT
MOVE_SHAPE ENDP

;  This procedure erases a shape by replotting it with
;  attribute = 0.

ERASE   PROC
        MOV   CX,CHAR_CNT     ;Reload character count,
        MOV   DI,POINTER      ; shape table pointer,
        MOV   DH,LINE_NO      ; line number
        MOV   DL,COL_NO       ; and column number
ERASE_NEXT: ADD DH,[DI+2]
        ADD   DL,[DI+3]
        MOV   AH,2
        INT   10H
        MOV   AL,[DI]         ;To erase a character, use an
        MOV   BL,0            ; attribute of 0
        PUSH  CX
        MOV   CX,1
        MOV   AH,9
        INT   10H
        POP   CX
        ADD   DI,4
        LOOP  ERASE_NEXT
        MOV   CX,CHAR_CNT     ;Reload character count,
        MOV   DI,POINTER      ; shape table pointer
        MOV   DH,LINE_NO      ; and line number
        INC   COL_NO          ;Point to next column
        MOV   DL,COL_NO
        RET                   ; and return to caller
ERASE   ENDP
```

Example 7-5. (continued).

```
;  This procedure generate a one-quarter second delay.

DLY_QRTR PROC
         SUB   AL,AL          ;Set minutes to zero
         SUB   BH,BH          ;Set seconds to zero
         MOV   BL,25          ;Set hundredths to 25
         CALL  DELAY
         RET
DLY_QRTR ENDP
CSEG     ENDS
         END
```

Study Exercises (answers on page 405)

1. When you switch on a computer that has a Color/Graphics Adapter, which video mode does the screen use? Which mode does it use for a Monochrome Adapter?
2. In text mode, what attribute value produces each of the following kinds of characters?
   (a) White on black
   (b) White on black, underlined
   (c) Black on white
   (d) Red on blue
   (e) Red on blue, blinking
3. List instructions that do the following:
   (a) Read the current cursor position
   (b) Determine the active display page
   (c) Determine whether the computer has a Monochrome or Color/Graphics Adapter
   (d) Move the cursor to the beginning of the bottom line
   (e) Display a white-on-black letter M at the top left-hand corner of the screen
4. Suppose you have written a program that is to display the messages *Sort Program* and *Press any key to begin* on separate lines. But instead it produces

   ```
   Sort ProgramPress any key to begin
   ```

   Why does it do this?
5. Write a program to display a message of the form

   Try again. You have *n* starfighters left.

where *n* is a number between 1 and 6 in CX.

6. In addition to moving a shape on the screen, you can introduce another element of animation by having the shape *change* as it moves. To discover how to do this, develop a procedure that moves a "bird" across the screen, and changes the bird's shape from a lowercase "v" character (code 76H in Table 7-1) to a "dash" character (code 0C4H), or vice versa, with each new column. Start the bird at row 20, column 0, and display it for one-tenth of a second each time it moves.
7. Game programs often use random numbers to move shapes around on the screen. To get acquainted with this topic, develop a program that displays a "smile face" (character code 2) at column 0 of a randomly-derived line number, then moves the face across the screen.

   The face should always advance one column at a time, but may move one line lower or higher, depending on whether a random number generator produces 0 (down one line), 1 (up one line), or 2 (same line).

   The display operation should end when the face crosses line 0, line 24, or column 79. Use the Type 1A (Time of Day) interrupt to derive both the initial line number and the up/down/same indicator; see Example 6-2 in Section 6.4.

8

Keyboard Operations

This chapter gives a brief (and simplified) explanation of how the keyboard works and suggests ways you may communicate with it.

8.1 ASCII

If you have used different kinds of microcomputers, you know that they are generally incompatible (unfortunately). For example, an IBM PC's floppy disk drive cannot read disks that have been produced by an Apple II. Similarly, one cannot run TRS-80 programs on a Macintosh. Even the operating systems differ; the PC-DOS *DIR* command, for instance, may be *CATALOG* on other computers.

However, there is one area in which microcomputer companies are fairly consistent: nearly all use a numeric coding scheme called *ASCII* (for American Standard Code for Information Interchange) to transmit information within their computers. For example, when you type a *T*, the keyboard circuitry sends the ASCII number for T into the computer. And when your program displays or prints a T, the computer sends the same numeric code to the screen or printer circuits. The same applies to disks; a T in a text file (such as an assembly language source program) is stored in its ASCII form. In short, *anything to do with text usually involves ASCII.*

Since the computer translates characters to ASCII automatically, you may wonder why I bother to mention it. The reason is, at some time or other you will probably have to deal directly with ASCII codes. We'll be delving into ASCII from time to time throughout the rest of this book.

Inside ASCII

ASCII (pronounced "as-key") characters are eight bits long. The high-order bit is either 0 or 1—depending on which computer you are using—and the remaining seven bits contain the numeric code for the character. IBM Personal Computers require a 0 in the high bit.

Within seven bits, ASCII codes can represent 128 different number combinations, from 00H to 7FH. Table 8-1 shows what character each ASCII code represents.

Table 8-1. Standard ASCII character set.

LSD \ MSD		0 000	1 001	2 010	3 011	4 100	5 101	6 110	7 111
0	0000	NUL	DLE	SP	0	@	P		p
1	0001	SOH	DC1	!	1	A	Q	a	q
2	0010	STX	DC2	"	2	B	R	b	r
3	0011	ETX	DC3	#	3	C	S	c	s
4	0100	EOT	DC4	$	4	D	T	d	t
5	0101	ENQ	NAK	%	5	E	U	e	u
6	0110	ACK	SYN	&	6	F	V	f	v
7	0111	BEL	ETB	'	7	G	W	g	w
8	1000	BS	CAN	(	8	H	X	h	x
9	1001	HT	EM	)	9	I	Y	i	y
A	1010	LF	SUB	*	:	J	Z	j	z
B	1011	VT	ESC	+	;	K	[	k	{
C	1100	FF	FS	,	<	L	\	l	|
D	1101	CR	GS	–	=	M	]	m	}
E	1110	SO	RS	•	>	N	↑	n	~
F	1111	SI	US	/	?	O	←	o	DEL

NUL — Null
SOH — Start of Heading
STX — Start of Text
ETX — End of Text
EOT — End of Transmission
ENQ — Enquiry
ACK — Acknowledge
BEL — Bell
BS — Backspace
HT — Horizontal Tabulation
LF — Line Feed
VT — Vertical Tabulation
FF — Form Feed
CR — Carriage Return
SO — Shift Out
SI — Shift In

DLE — Data Link Escape
DC — Device Control
NAK — Negative Acknowledge
SYN — Synchronous Idle
ETB — End of Transmission Block
CAN — Cancel
EM — End of Medium
SUB — Substitute
ESC — Escape
FS — File Separator
GS — Group Separator
RS — Record Separator
US — Unit Separator
SP — Space (Blank)
DEL — Delete

To find the ASCII code for a character, combine the most-significant digit (MSD) from the top row with the least-significant digit (LSD) from the left-hand column. For example, the letter "A" has an MSD of 4 and an LSD of 1, so its code is 41H.

Note that besides the usual letters, numbers, and symbols that appear on a keyboard, the ASCII character set includes control characters such as CR (Carriage Return), FF (Form Feed), and LF (Line Feed). It also includes some characters that are used in communications, such as ACK (Acknowledge), STX (Start of Text), and EOT (End of Transmission).

However, if you study Table 8-1 for any amount of time (granted, it doesn't make very interesting reading) you realize that it does not include the AT's special keys. For example, the function keys are missing, as are the keys on the numeric keypad. This presented a special problem to IBM's keyboard designers, and they came up with a rather interesting solution.

Extended ASCII

To add codes for the extra keys, IBM's designers could have used a second character set in which bit 7 is 1 rather than 0. Doing that would have provided 256 codes, the standard set that ranges from 00H to 7FH and another that ranges from 80H to FFH. The designers didn't use the high bit, however, although doing so would have been convenient. Instead, they chose a technique in which non-ASCII characters cause the computer to obtain a code from a second set of 128 characters, a set whose codes have meanings that IBM has defined.

This technique furnishes IBM Personal Computers with a character set of 256 codes, which IBM calls *Extended ASCII*. We discuss how the AT uses the second group of codes (the so-called "Extended Codes") later in this chapter.

8.2 How the Keyboard Works

Here is how the PC AT's keyboard works. Whenever you press or release a key, the keyboard unit saves a byte in its internal memory. This byte consists of a "pressed" or "released" code (1 or 0, respectively) in bit 7 and a key identifier or *scan code* in the remaining bits. There are 84 scan codes, one for each key on the keyboard. Once the keyboard unit has stored a byte in its memory, it sends the BIOS a Type 9 interrupt, saying "I have something for you."

The keyboard unit's memory can store up to 16 bytes, or 8 press-and-release operations (i.e., keystrokes). This allows you to type even while the computer's microprocessor is busy, as it is while dumping the screen to the printer, for example.

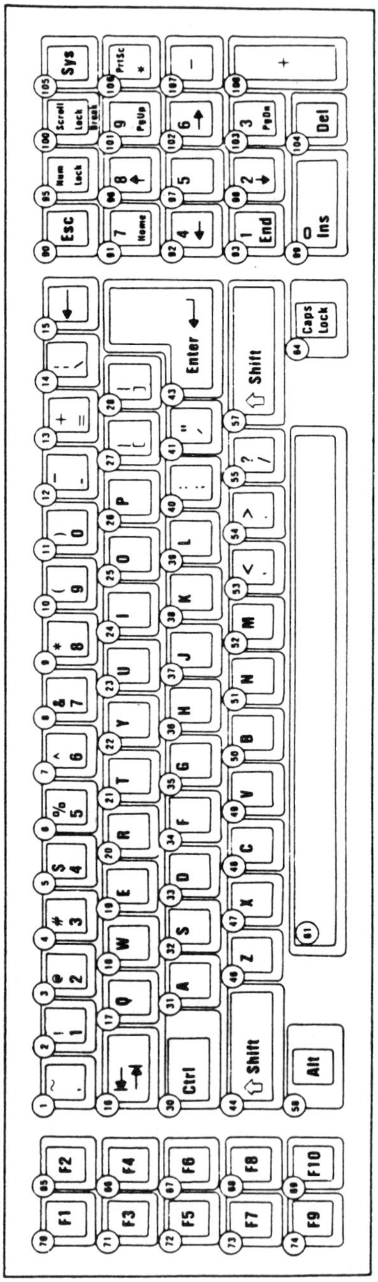

Figure 8-1. Keyboard layout with key numbers. (Courtesy of IBM Corp.)

If interrupts are enabled, BIOS' Type 9 interrupt routine (KB_INT_1) reads bytes from the keyboard unit's memory and translates them into character codes. KB_INT_1 also checks whether there have been several "presses" without a "release"; this lets it produce character codes that reflect Shift, Ctrl, or Alt being held down while you press a second key. Upon completion, the Type 9 routine stores the scan code and the character code in a special portion of memory called the "keyboard buffer."

With space for 15 keystrokes, the buffer is big enough, and the software fast enough, to keep up with the fastest typists. But if you somehow manage to press a key when the buffer is full, BIOS ignores the key and beeps the speaker.

Character Codes and Scan Codes

Figure 8-1 shows a drawing of the AT's keyboard with each key numbered. These are just reference numbers; you won't use them in your programs.

Tables 8-2 and 8-3 list the scan code and character that each key produces. We need two separate tables because keys in the numeric keypad are affected by Num Lock.

Table 8-2. Scan codes and characters, except numeric keypad.

Key No. (Dec)	Scan Code (Hex)	Base Case	Upper Case	Ctrl	Alt
1	29	(grave)	˜ (tilde)	N.A.	N.A.
2	2	1	!	N.A.	-1
3	3	2	@	-1	-1
4	4	3	#	N.A.	-1
5	5	4	$	N.A.	-1
6	6	5	%	N.A.	-1
7	7	6	^	RS	-1
8	8	7	&	N.A.	-1
9	9	8	*	N.A.	-1
10	A	9	(	N.A.	-1
11	B	0	)	N.A.	-1
12	C	- (hypen)	_	US	-1
13	D	=	+	N.A.	-1
14	2B	\	¦	FS	N.A.
15	E	Backspace	Backspace	DEL	N.A.
16 Tab	F	Tab	-1	N.A.	N.A.
17	10	q	Q	DC1	-1
18	11	w	W	ETB	-1
19	12	e	E	ENQ	-1

Table 8-2. Scan codes and characters, except numeric keypad (continued).

Key No. (Dec)	Scan Code (Hex)	Base Case	Upper Case	Ctrl	Alt
20	13	r	R	DC2	-1
21	14	t	T	DC4	-1
22	15	y	Y	EM	-1
23	16	u	U	NAK	-1
24	17	i	I	HT	-1
25	18	o	O	SI	-1
26	19	p	P	DLE	-1
27	1A	[	{	ESC	-1
28	1B	]	}	GS	N.A.
30 Ctrl	1D	N.A.	N.A.	N.A.	N.A.
31	1E	a	A	SOH	-1
32	1F	s	S	DC3	-1
33	20	d	D	EOT	-1
34	21	f	F	ACK	-1
35	22	g	G	BEL	-1
36	23	h	H	BS	-1
37	24	j	J	LF	-1
38	25	k	K	VT	-1
39	26	l	L	FF	-1
40	27	;	:	N.A.	N.A.
41	28	'	"	N.A.	N.A.
43 Enter	1C	CR	CR	LF	N.A.
44 Shift	2A	N.A.	N.A.	N.A.	N.A.
46	2C	z	Z	SUB	-1
47	2D	x	X	CAN	-1
48	2E	c	C	ETX	-1
49	2F	v	V	SYN	-1
50	30	b	B	STX	-1
51	31	n	N	SO	-1
52	32	m	M	CR	-1
53	33	, (comma)	<	N.A.	N.A.
54	34	. (period)	>	N.A.	N.A.
55	35	/	?	N.A.	N.A.
57 Shift	36	N.A.	N.A.	N.A.	N.A.
58 Alt	38	N.A.	N.A.	N.A.	N.A.
61 Space	39	SP	SP	SP	SP
64 Caps Lock	3A	N.A.	N.A.	N.A.	N.A.
65 F2	3C	-1	-1	-1	-1
66 F4	3E	-1	-1	-1	-1
67 F6	40	-1	-1	-1	-1
68 F8	42	-1	-1	-1	-1
69 F10	44	-1	-1	-1	-1
70 F1	3B	-1	-1	-1	-1
71 F3	3D	-1	-1	-1	-1

Table 8-2. Scan codes and characters, except numeric keypad (continued).

Key No. (Dec)	Scan Code (Hex)	Base Case	Upper Case	Ctrl	Alt
72 F5	3F	-1	-1	-1	-1
73 F7	41	-1	-1	-1	-1
74 F9	43	-1	-1	-1	-1
90 Esc	1	ESC	ESC	ESC	N.A.
95 Num Lock	45	N.A.	N.A.	-2	N.A.
100 Scroll	46	N.A.	N.A.	-2	N.A.
105 Sys Req	54	-2	N.A.	N.A.	N.A.
106	37	*	-2	-1	N.A.

Notes: -1 See *Extended Codes* in this section.
-2 See *Special Key Combinations* in this section.

Table 8-3. Scan codes and characters for numeric keypad.

Key No. (Dec)	Scan Code (Hex)	Base Case	Num Lock	Ctrl	Alt
91	47	Home (-1)	7	Clear Screen	N.A.
92	4B	← (-1)	4	Reverse Word (-1)	N.A.
93	4F	End (-1)	1	Erase to EOL (-1)	N.A.
96	48	↑ (-1)	8	N.A.	N.A.
97	4C	N.A.	5	N.A.	N.A.
98	50	↓ (-1)	2	N.A.	N.A.
99	52	Ins (-1,-2)	0	N.A.	N.A.
101	49	PgUp (-1)	9	Top of Text and Home	N.A.
102	4D	→ (-1)	6	Advance Word (-1)	N.A.
103	51	PgDn (-1)	3	Erase to EOS (-1)	N.A.
104	53	Del (-1,-2)	.	-2	-2
107	4A	- (minus)	-	N.A.	N.A.
108	4E	+	+	N.A.	N.A.

Notes: -1 See *Extended Codes* in this section.
-2 See *Special Key Combinations* in this section.

Most individual keys and combinations generate a standard ASCII code. Keys that have no ASCII equivalent, such as Alt and the function keys, return zero for the character code. The zero indicates that your program must examine a second code to find out which key or keys was pressed. We discuss these so-called *Extended Codes* shortly. Other non-ASCII keys produce special operations, such as printing the screen contents. We summarize combinations that BIOS simply ignores; Tables 8-2 and 8-3 show them as *N.A.* (Not Available).

Extended Codes

When you read a key in from the keyboard, BIOS returns its character code and scan code in AL and AH, respectively. Non-ASCII keys return zero in AL and an "extended code" in AH. Table 8-4 lists the extended codes and shows which key combinations they represent.

Table 8-4. Extended codes for the keyboard.

Extended Code	Key(s)
3	Ctrl-2
F	Shift-Tab (back Tab)
10-19	Alt-Q through Alt-P (top row of letters)
1E-26	Alt-A through Alt-L (middle row of letters)
2C-32	Alt-Z through Alt-M (bottom row of letters)
3B-44	F1 through F10 (function keys, unshifted)
47	Home
48	↑
49	PgUp
4B	←
4D	→
4F	End
50	↓
51	PgDn
52	Ins
53	Del
54-5D	Shift-F1 through Shift-F10
5E-67	Ctrl-F1 through Ctrl-F10
68-71	Alt-F1 through Alt-F10
72	Ctrl-PrtSc (start or stop echo to printer)
73	Ctrl ← (previous word)
74	Ctrl → (next word)
75	Ctrl-End (erase to end of line)
76	Ctrl-PgDn (erase to end of screen)
77	Ctrl-Home (clear screen and home cursor)
78-83	Alt-1 through Alt-= (top row of keyboard)
84	Ctrl-PgUp (top 25 lines of text and home cursor)

Special Key Combinations

The following keys produce special effects:

- *Alt-Ctrl-Del* restarts or "reboots" the computer.
- *Ctrl-Break* invokes the Type 1B (Keyboard Break) interrupt. Ctrl-Break returns AL = 0 and AH = 0.

- *Ctrl-Num Lock* makes the computer wait for you to press any key but Num Lock. This gives you a way to suspend an operation (generally, listing a program), then resume.
- *Shift-PrtSc* invokes the Type 5 (Print Screen) interrupt.
- *Sys Req* invokes the Type 15 (System I/O Extensions) interrupt.
- Ctrl, Shift, Num Lock, Scroll Lock, and Ins are control keys. The service routine for the Type 16 (Keyboard) interrupt returns a "shift status" byte that tells you when one of these keys is pressed.

8.3 Keyboard Interrupts

In Chapter 6 we mentioned two different kinds of interrupts you can use to communicate with the keyboard: the Type 16 interrupt that is built into the BIOS and the keyboard options that DOS contributes within its Type 21 function calls.

BIOS Type 16 (Keyboard) Interrupt

The Type 16 (Keyboard) interrupt provides rudimentary keyboard operations that can be useful if you want a program to run independent of DOS. The Type 16 vector points to KEYBOARD_IO, which contains a JMP to interrupt service routine KEYBOARD_IO_1 at location F000:2FC8; see the *Keyboard* portion of the BIOS listing. KEYBOARD_IO_1 provides three different options, as selected by the contents of the AH register (see Table 8-5).

Table 8-5. Keyboard operations with Type 16 interrupt.

AH	Operation	Input Values	Results
0	Wait for keyboard character, then read it	None	AL = Character AH = Scan Code
1	Read the next keyboard buffer character	None	If Zero Flag (ZF) = 0, AX = Next buffer character If ZF = 1, buffer is empty
2	Get keyboard status byte	None	AL = Status byte (See Figure 8-2.)

The upper half of Figure 8-2 shows the arrangement of the status byte returned by the AH = 2 option. The upper four bits of this byte (KB_FLAG in the BIOS listing) tell whether various keyboard modes are on (1) or off (0), while the lower four bits tell whether the Alt, Ctrl, or Shift key is being pressed.

The lower half of Figure 8-2 shows KB_FLAG_1, a companion byte to KB_FLAG that gives additional keyboard status information. BIOS uses KB_FLAG_1 internally, but doesn't provide a way to read it into a register. However, KB_FLAG_1 follows KB_FLAG in memory, so you can obtain it by reading the contents of location 418H (KB_FLAG is at 417H).

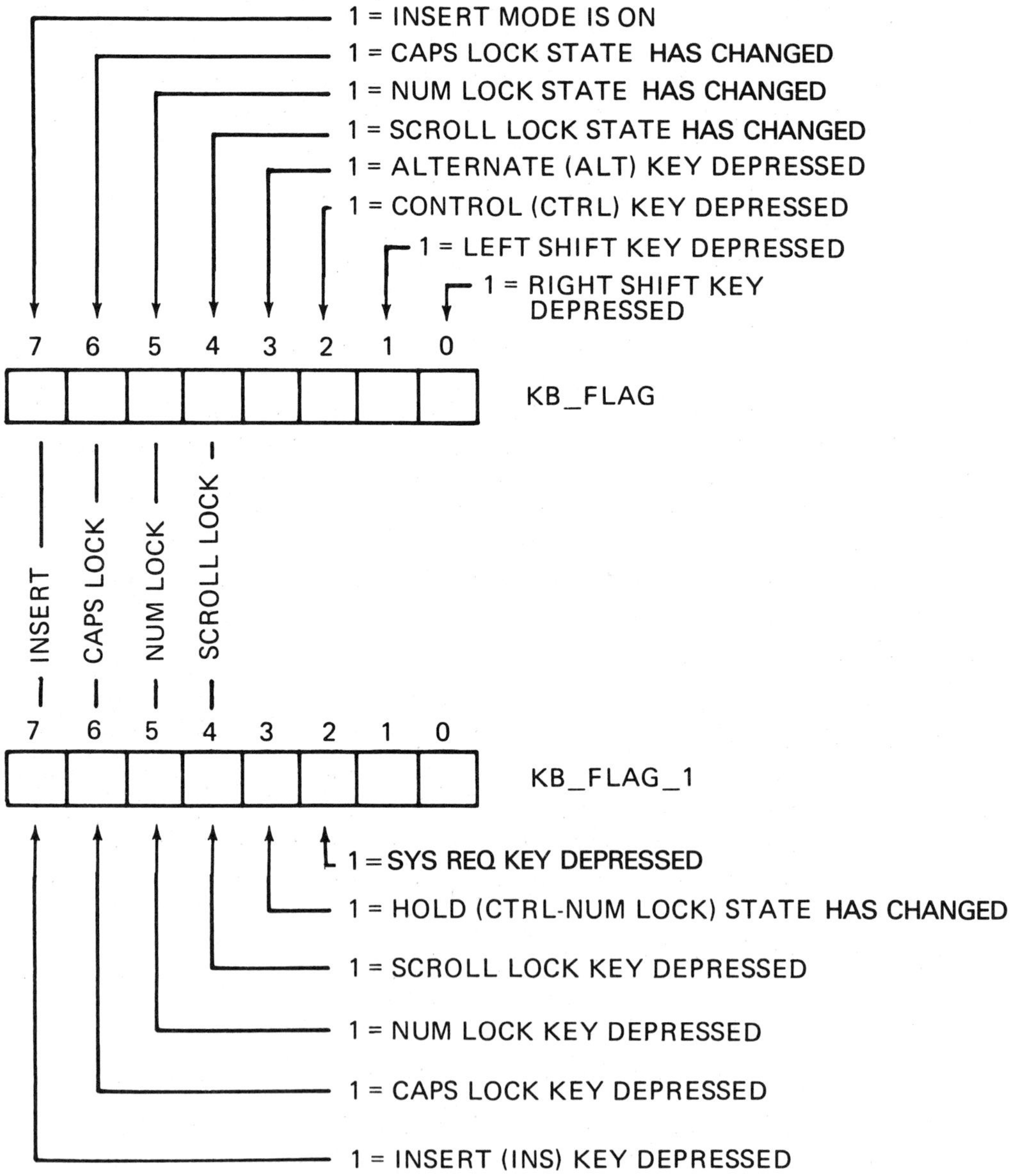

Figure 8-2. Keyboard status bytes.

As we just mentioned, the Type 16 interrupt allows one to create programs that are independent of DOS. If that's of no concern, you are better off using the more flexible capabilities of the keyboard function calls provided by the DOS Type 21 interrupt.

DOS Function Calls for Keyboard

Table 8-6 summarizes the DOS Type 21 function calls that relate to the keyboard. As you can see, they are straightforward; they read individual key characters into AL or a sequence of characters (a *string*) into memory. Unless you're looking for some unusual key combinations, you should find these functions convenient to use.

Reading Individual Keys

Interactive programs often require the user to respond to a prompt or select from a menu by typing a single letter or number. For example, suppose your program displays a message that tells the user to press either *Y* or *N* (perhaps to continue or stop). A Y response makes the program jump to a set of instructions labeled YES, while an N makes it jump to instructions labeled NO. Any other key makes it wait for either Y or N. This sequence does the job:

```
GET_KEY:  MOV   AH,1        ;Read a key (and display it)
          INT   21H
          CMP   AL,'Y'      ;Is it Y?
          JE    YES         ; If so, jump to YES
          CMP   AL,'N'      ;Is it N?
          JE    NO          ; If so, jump to NO
          JNE   GET_KEY     ; Otherwise, wait for Y or N
```

Here, we accept only an uppercase Y or N, but some users may simply press a key and not Shift. To accept lowercase responses as well, insert additional tests using *CMP AL,'y'* and *CMP AL,'n'*.

Checking for Y, N, or any other letter, number, or symbol is easy, because your CMP operand is the character itself enclosed in quotation marks. But what if you want to check for, say, the Enter (Return) key? The form *CMP AL,'Enter'* won't work; the assembler thinks you're trying to compare a byte in AL with a five-character string, and produces an error message. Instead, you must specify the Enter key's ASCII code as the second operand. Table 8-2 shows that Enter (key 30) produces a "CR" character. Referring to Table 8-1, you discover that the ASCII code for CR is hexadecimal 0D or decimal 13. This is the number you use in the CMP instruction. For example, sup-

Table 8-6. Keyboard operations with Type 21 interrupt.

AH	Operation	Input Values	Results
1	Wait for keyboard character, then display it (with Ctrl-Break check)*	None	AL = Character
6	Read keyboard character (no Ctrl-Break check)*	DL = 0FFH	AL = Character, if available = 0, if no character is available
7	Wait for keyboard character, but do not display it (no Ctrl-Break check)*	None	AL = Character
8	Same as function 7, but with Ctrl-Break check*	None	AL = Character
A	Read keyboard string into buffer	DS:DX = Buffer address First buffer byte = Buffer size	Second buffer byte = Number of chars. read
B	Read keyboard status	None	AL = 0FFH if no character is available = 0 if character is available
C	Clear keyboard buffer and call a keyboard function	AL = Keyboard function number (1, 6, 7, 8, or A)	Per keyboard function

*Some key combinations generate "extended codes," and may require two function calls. See Section 8.2 for details.

pose you are writing a program that displays some instructions and tells the user "Press Enter to continue." To wait for the Enter key, use the sequence

```
WAIT_HERE:  MOV  AH,7    ;Wait for Enter
            INT  21H
            CMP  AL,13
            JNE  WAIT_HERE
```

Note that we use the AH = 7 option instead of AH = 1 because we don't want to display the key (since Enter doesn't produce a displayable character).

Accepting Extended Codes

As we discussed in Section 8.2, when you read a non-ASCII key, the AT returns zero for the character code. The zero indicates that you must do another key operation to obtain the key's extended code.

For our purposes, this means that if your program can accept a function key or numeric keypad key, it must do the following things:

1. Read a character from the keyboard.
2. Compare the character byte to zero.
3. If the byte contains zero, read another character. This character will contain the extended code of the key.

For example, suppose your program displays a menu and asks the user to choose option 1, 2, or 3 by pressing F1, F2, or F3; any other key produces an error message. The response-checking part should look something like this:

```
        MOV  AH,7      ;Wait for a key
        INT  21H
        CMP  AL,0      ;Is it an extended code?
        JE   GET_EC    ; Yes.  Read the extended code
        JMP  ERROR     ; No.  Display error message
GET_EC: MOV  AH,7
        INT  21H
        CMP  AL,3BH    ;F1?
        JE   OPTION1
        CMP  AL,3CH    ;F2?
        JE   OPTION2
        CMP  AL,3DH    ;F3?
        JE   OPTION3
        JMP  ERROR     ;Invalid key.  Display error message
```

Reading Strings

Many applications require the user to enter a name or address or some other string. The Type 21 interrupt's function A does this for you. To use function A, you must reserve space in the data segment equal to the maximum number of keystrokes plus two. This consists of:

- A byte value equal to the maximum number of keystrokes plus one.
- An uninitialized byte into which function A will put the number of keystrokes the user actually enters.
- A block of uninitialized bytes that will hold the keystrokes themselves.

Hence, the general form of the string is

```
stringname  DB  keys-plus-one, keys-plus-one DUP(?)
```

For example, to reserve space for a string of up to 50 keystrokes, put this statement in the data segment:

```
USER_STRING  DB  51,51 DUP(?)
```

The string-reading instructions are:

```
LEA  DX,USER_STRING  ;Make DX point to buffer
MOV  AH,0AH          ;Read the string
INT  21H
```

Function A puts the count of the keystrokes received (excluding Return) in the second byte of the string and leaves DS:DX pointing to the first byte. In many cases, you want the character count in the CX register and want DS:DX to point to the first string character. READ_KEYS, the procedure in Example 8-1, does that job.

Responding to Prompts

In many cases, display strings are prompts, in which case the user must supply data from the keyboard. Suppose, for example, you want the user to enter his or her name. To do this, we can combine the AH = 9 (string display) option of the Type 21 interrupt with the READ_KEYS procedure from Example 8-1.

Here, the data segment might contain

```
GET_NAME  DB  'Please enter your name: $'
```

and the code segment contains

```
LEA   DX,GET_NAME   ;Display the prompt
MOV   AH,9
INT   21H
CALL  READ_KEYS     ;Read the response
```

After this sequence, DS:DX points to the string containing the name and CX holds the character count.

8.4 ASCII/Binary Code Conversions

As you now know, the BIOS always converts keyboard characters to ASCII. If these characters represent *numbers*, you must convert them to binary or BCD before the processor can operate on them. Likewise, before you can print a number or display it on the screen, you must put it in ASCII form.

Example 8-1. Read a string from the keyboard.

```
        PAGE   ,132
TITLE   READKEYS - Read up to 50 keystrokes

; This procedure reads up to 50 keys.
;  Inputs: None
;  Results: DS:DX = String address
;              CX = Character count

;  Assemble with: MASM READKEYS;
;  Link with: LINK callprog+READKEYS;

        PUBLIC  READ_KEYS
DSEG    SEGMENT PARA PUBLIC 'DATA'
USER_STRING DB  51,51 DUP(?)
DSEG    ENDS

CSEG    SEGMENT PARA PUBLIC 'CODE'
        ASSUME  CS:CSEG,DS:DSEG

READ_KEYS PROC  FAR
        PUSH    AX
        MOV     AX,DSEG         ;Initialize DS
        MOV     DS,AX
        LEA     DX,USER_STRING  ;Read the string
        MOV     AH,0AH
        INT     21H
        SUB     CH,CH           ;Read character count into CX
        MOV     CL,USER_STRING+1
        ADD     DX,2            ;Make DX point to text
        POP     AX              ;Restore AX
        RET                     ;Return to calling program
READ_KEYS ENDP
CSEG    ENDS
        END
```

We address both problems in this section: how to convert an ASCII number to binary and how to convert a binary number to ASCII. (Converting between ASCII and BCD involves similar procedures, but as the textbooks say, "That exercise is left to the reader.")

Converting ASCII Strings to Binary

Table 8-7 shows the ASCII codes for the decimal digits 0 through 9. As you can see, they range in value from 30H to 39H. Also note that the binary equivalent of a decimal digit is simply the low four bits of the ASCII code.

Table 8-7. ASCII codes for decimal digits.

ASCII Value (Hex)	Decimal Digit
30	0
31	1
32	2
33	3
34	4
35	5
36	6
37	7
38	8
39	9

As we said before, decimal numbers can be expressed as a series of digits multiplied by powers of 10. For example:

$$237 = (7 \times 1) + (3 \times 10) + (2 \times 100)$$

or

$$237 = (7 \times 10^0) + (3 \times 10^1) + (2 \times 10^2)$$

Since we enter numbers one digit at a time, an ASCII-based decimal to binary conversion routine must account for their decimal weights. This means the routine must include one or more multiply-by-10 operations. For example, if the operator types 93, you must multiply the 9 by 10 before adding the 3. In general, the conversion process proceeds in this order:

- The conversion routine must convert the first (most-significant) digit to binary by stripping off the four high-order bits of the ASCII code, then store the binary value as a partial result.
- The routine must convert any subsequent digits to binary, multiply the previous partial result by 10, then add the new digit to the product (this produces a new partial result).

ASCII-to-Binary Conversion Algorithm

You generally need to convert negative as well as positive numbers, and numbers that include a decimal point, so our conversion program must account for minus (-) and point (.) characters, too. Figure 8-3 is a flowchart for an algorithm to convert an ASCII string in memory into a two's-complement

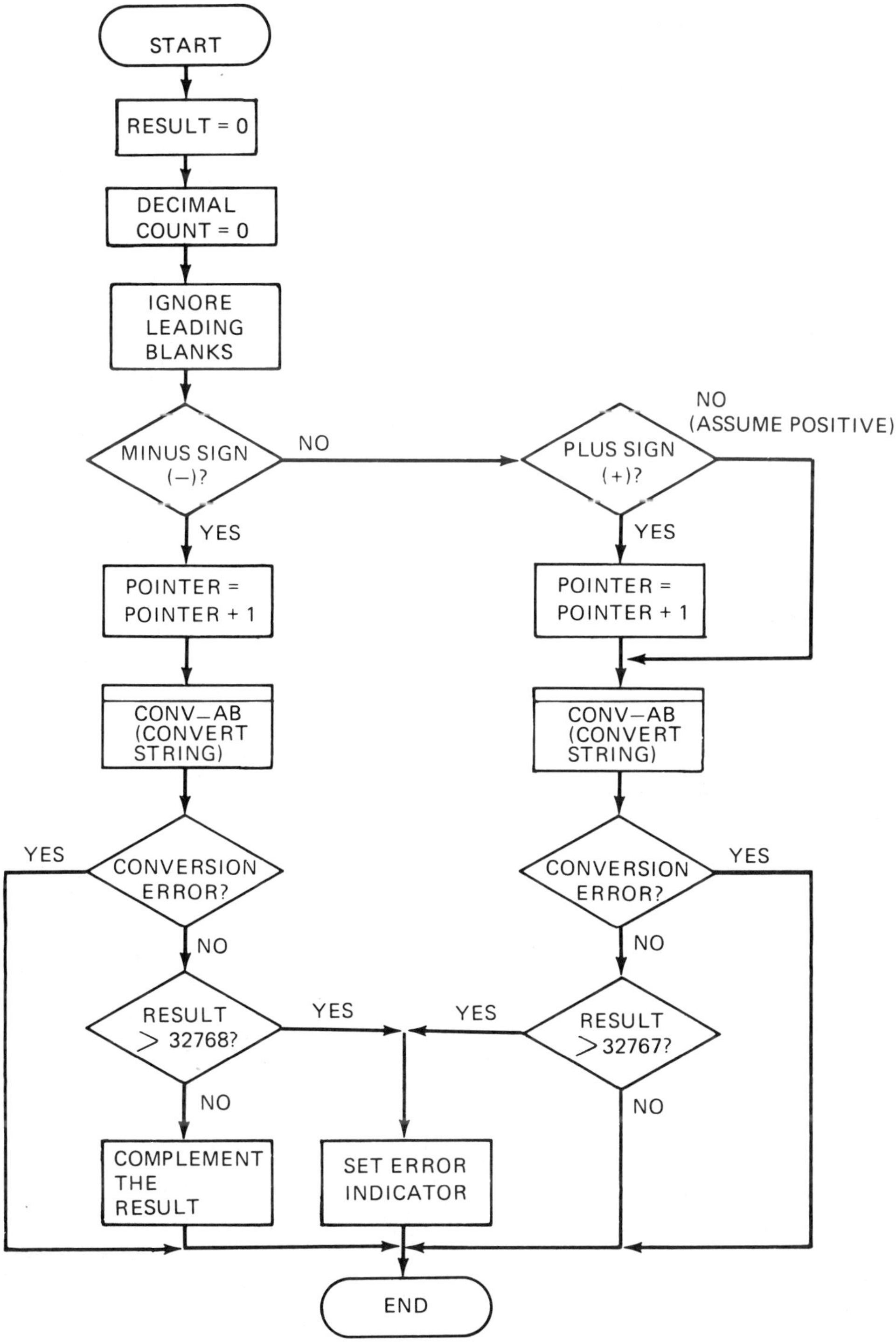

Figure 8-3. Algorithm to convert an ASCII string to binary.

(signed) binary number. We assume that the number fits into 16 bits, so its limits are -32768 and +32767.

To begin, the result and decimal count (the number of digits to the right of the decimal point) are set to zero, and the program scans past any leading blanks. At this point, the program takes one of two paths, depending on whether the number is negative or positive. These paths are similar, except that a converted negative number is checked against -32,768 and must be complemented, while a positive number is checked against 32,767. A procedure called CONV_AB, which is flowcharted in Figure 8-3A, makes the actual conversion.

The CONV_AB procedure begins by checking whether the next string character is a decimal point. If it is, CONV_AB records the remaining character count as the *decimal count*, then advances the string pointer. If the next character is not a decimal point, CONV_AB checks whether it is a decimal digit. If this character is not a digit, CONV_AB declares it "invalid" and sets an error indicator, then returns to the calling program.

Upon finding a valid digit character, CONV_AB multiplies the current partial result by 10, then converts the ASCII character to a digit and adds it to the result. If the addition produces a carry, CONV_AB sets the error indicator and returns. Otherwise it increments the pointer and returns to the decimal point-checking instructions. When the entire string has been converted, CONV_AB returns to the calling program.

ASCII-to-Binary Conversion Program

Example 8-2 shows a procedure that implements the preceding algorithm. This procedure (ASCII_BIN) converts an ASCII string in the data segment—perhaps one entered with the READ_KEYS procedure, Example 8-1—into a 16-bit signed number.

ASCII_BIN obtains the starting address of the string from DS:DX and the character count (7 maximum) from CX. By no coincidence, these are the parameters that READ_KEYS produces. ASCII_BIN returns the 16-bit value in AX, the number of digits after the decimal point (if any) in DX, and the address of the first non-convertible character in DI.

The value in DX indicates the magnitude of the result. This tells you what *scale factor* to apply if you are operating on converted numbers of mixed sizes. The contents of DX can range from 0 (the result is an integer) to 5 (the result is a pure fraction). For example, if AX contains 1000H (decimal 4096) and DX contains 2, your result represents the decimal value 40.96.

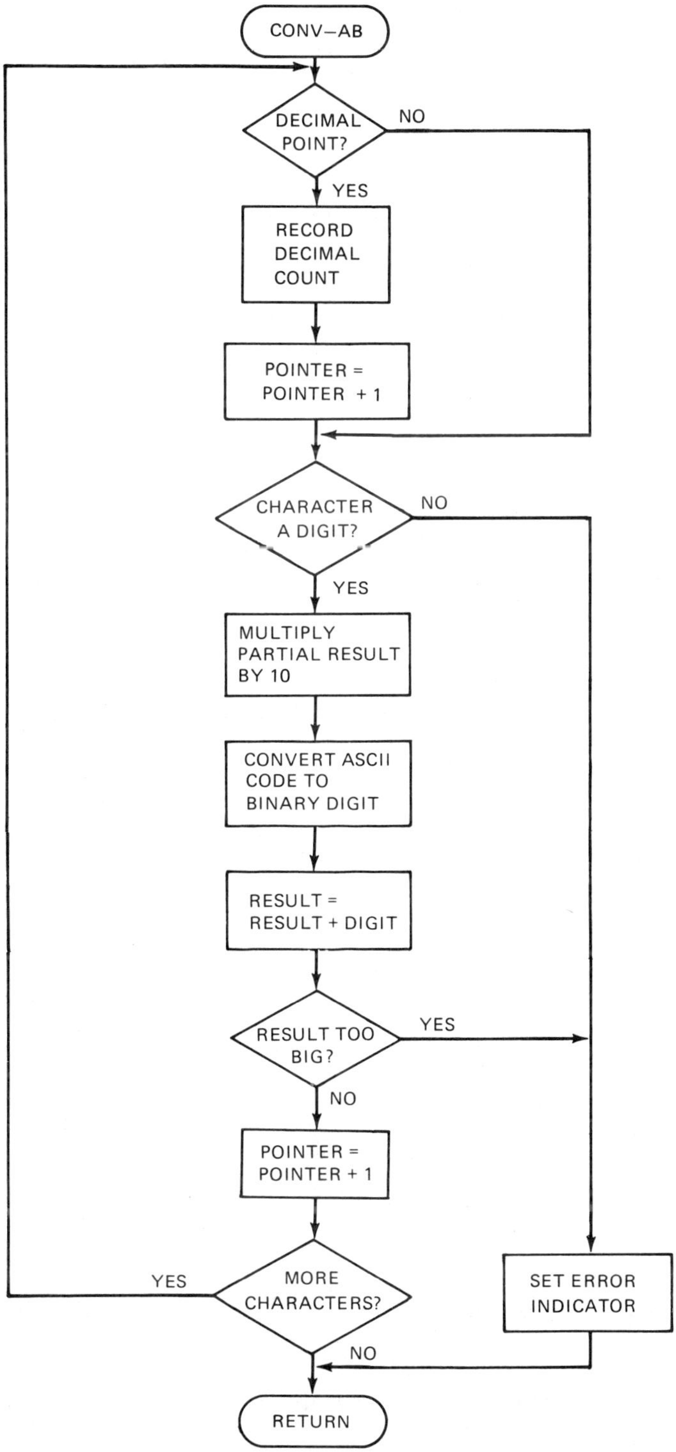

Figure 8-3A. Procedure called by ASCII conversion algorithm.

Example 8-2. Convert an ASCII string to binary.

```
        PAGE   ,132
TITLE   ASC_BIN - Convert ASCII to Binary

;   Converts an ASCII string to its 16-bit, two's-complement
;   binary equivalent.
;   Inputs: DS:DX = Starting address of string
;              CX = Character count
;   Results: CF = 0 indicates no error
;                  AX = Binary value
;                  DX = Count of digits after decimal point
;                  DI = 0FFH
;             CF = 1 indicates error
;                  DS:DI = Address of non-convertible character
;   DX and CX are unaffected.

;   Assemble with: MASM ASC_BIN;
;   Link with: LINK callprog+ASC_BIN;

        PUBLIC  ASCII_BIN
.286c
CSEG    SEGMENT PARA 'CODE'
        ASSUME  CS:CSEG
ASCII_BIN PROC  FAR
        PUSH    BX              ;Save BX and CX
        PUSH    CX
        MOV     BX,DX           ;Put offset in BX
        SUB     AX,AX           ;To start, result = 0
        SUB     DX,DX           ; decimal count = 0
        MOV     DI,0FFH         ; assume no bad characters
        CMP     CX,7            ;String too long?
        JA      NO_GOOD         ; If so, go set CF and exit
BLANKS: CMP     BYTE PTR [BX],' ' ;Scan past leading blanks
        JNE     CHK_NEG
        INC     BX
        LOOP    BLANKS
CHK_NEG: CMP    BYTE PTR [BX],'-' ;Negative number?
        JNE     CHK_POS
        INC     BX              ; If so, increment pointer
        DEC     CX              ;  decrement the count,
        CALL    CONV_AB         ;  convert the string
        JC      THRU
        CMP     AX,32768        ;Is the number too small?
        JA      NO_GOOD
        NEG     AX              ; No.  Complement the result
        JS      GOOD
CHK_POS: CMP    BYTE PTR [BX],'+' ;Positive number?
        JNE     GO_CONV
        INC     BX              ; If so, increment pointer
        DEC     CX              ;  decrement the count,
```

Example 8-2. (continued).

```
GO_CONV: CALL CONV_AB       ;Convert the string
         JC   THRU
         CMP  AX,32767      ;Is the number too big?
         JA   NO_GOOD
GOOD:    CLC
         JNC  THRU
NO_GOOD: STC                ; If so, set Carry Flag
THRU:    POP  CX            ;Restore registers
         POP  BX
         RET                ; and exit
ASCII_BIN ENDP

;  This procedure performs the actual conversion.

CONV_AB PROC
        PUSH  BP            ;Save scratch registers
        PUSH  BX
        MOV   BP,BX         ;Put pointer in BP
        SUB   BX,BX         ; and clear BX
CHK_PT: CMP   DX,0          ;Was a decimal point found?
        JNZ   RANGE         ; If so, skip following check
        CMP   BYTE PTR DS:[BP],'.' ;Decimal point?
        JNE   RANGE
        DEC   CX            ; If so, decrement count,
        MOV   DX,CX         ;  and record it in DX
        JZ    END_CONV      ;  Exit if CX = 0
        INC   BP            ;  Increment pointer
RANGE:  CMP   BYTE PTR DS:[BP],'0' ;If the character is not a
        JB    NON_DIG       ; digit...
        CMP   BYTE PTR DS:[BP],'9'
        JBE   DIGIT
NON_DIG: MOV  DI,BP         ; put its address in DI,
        STC                 ; set the Carry Flag,
        JC    END_CONV      ; and exit
DIGIT:  IMUL  AX,10         ;Multiply the digit in AX by 10
        MOV   BL,DS:[BP]    ; Fetch ASCII code
        AND   BX,0FH        ; save only high bits,
        ADD   AX,BX         ; and update partial result
        JC    END_CONV      ; Exit if result is too big
        INC   BP            ; Otherwise, increment BP
        LOOP  CHK_PT        ; and continue
        CLC                 ;When done, clear Carry Flag
END_CONV: POP BX            ;Restore registers
        POP   BP
        RET                 ; and return to caller
CONV_AB ENDP
CSEG    ENDS
        END
```

If you want to add this value to a previous result that returned 3 in DX, you must first divide the previous result by 10. Similarly, to add 40.96 to a previous result that returned 0 in DX, you must first divide the new result by 100.

The Carry Flag (CF) indicates if an error occurred during the conversion. If CF is 0, the results are valid, but if CF is 1, ASCII_BIN detected one of the following errors:

- If the string was longer than seven characters (CX > 7), AX and DX hold 0 and DI holds 00FFH.
- If ASCII_BIN found an invalid character, DI holds its offset value.
- If a number was out-of-range (more negative than -32768 or more positive than 32767), AX is nonzero and DI holds 00FFH.

To check the validity of the answer, call ASCII_BIN in this context:

```
           CALL  ASCII_BIN   ;Call the conversion procedure
           JNC   VALID       ;Is the answer valid?
           OR    DI,DI       ; No.  Find the error condition
           JNZ   INV_CHAR
           OR    AX,AX
           JNZ   RANGE_ER
           ..                ;  String was too long.
           ..
RANGE_ER:  ..                ;  Number out-of-range.
           ..
INV_CHAR:  ..                ;  Invalid character.
           ..
VALID:     ..                ;The answer is valid.
           ..
```

Converting Binary Numbers to Strings

To print a result or display it on the screen, you must convert it to ASCII. Fortunately, this is easy to do. To convert a 16-bit binary number to ASCII, you need a program that determines how many 1s, 10s, 100s, 1000s, and 10000s the number contains, and that converts each of those counts into an ASCII character. You can either output the ASCII characters as they are calculated or store them in memory as a string and output them later with another program.

Example 8-3 is a procedure called BIN_ASCII that converts a 16-bit binary number in AX to an ASCII string in memory. To derive the various counts, BIN_ASCII successively divides the contents of AX by 10, and uses the remainder of each divide operation to build the string. BIN_ASCII returns the address of the converted string in DS:DX and the character count in CX.

Example 8-3. Convert a binary number to a string.

```
        PAGE    ,132
TITLE   BIN_ASC - Convert Binary to ASCII

;   Converts a signed binary number to a six-byte ASCII
;   string (sign plus five digits) in the data segment.
;   Inputs: AX = Number to be converted
;           DS:DX = Starting address of string buffer
;   Results: DS:DX = Starting address of string
;            CX = Character count
;   Other registers are preserved.

;   Assemble with: MASM BIN_ASC;
;   Link with: LINK callprog+BIN_ASC;

        PUBLIC  BIN_ASCII
CSEG    SEGMENT PARA PUBLIC 'CODE'
        ASSUME  CS:CSEG
BIN_ASCII PROC  FAR
        PUSH    DX              ;Save the caller's registers
        PUSH    BX
        PUSH    SI
        PUSH    AX
        MOV     BX,DX           ;Put offset in BX
        MOV     CX,6            ;Fill buffer with spaces
FILL_BUFF: MOV  BYTE PTR [BX],' '
        INC     BX
        LOOP    FILL_BUFF
        MOV     SI,10           ;Get ready to divide by 10
        OR      AX,AX           ;If value is negative,
        JNS     CLR_DVD
        NEG     AX              ; make it positive
CLR_DVD: SUB    DX,DX           ;Clear upper half of dividend
        DIV     SI              ;Divide AX by 10
        ADD     DX,'0'          ;Convert remainder to ASCII digit
        DEC     BX              ;Back up through buffer
        MOV     [BX],DL         ;Store char. in the string
        INC     CX              ;Count converted character
        OR      AX,AX           ;All done?
        JNZ     CLR_DVD         ; If not, get next digit
        POP     AX              ; Yes. Get original value
        OR      AX,AX           ;Was it negative?
        JNS     NO_MORE
        DEC     BX              ; Yes. Store sign
        MOV     BYTE PTR [BX],'-'
        INC     CX              ;  and increase character count
NO_MORE: POP    SI              ;Restore registers
        POP     BX
        POP     DX
        RET                     ; and exit
BIN_ASCII ENDP
CSEG    ENDS
        END
```

Study Exercises (answers on page 410)

1. Why does IBM call the set of keyboard codes "Extended ASCII?"
2. When you read a key, what does a character code value of zero indicate?
3. What is the extended code for function key F2?
4. What is the difference between the Type 21 interrupt's AH = 1 and AH = 8 options?
5. Develop a procedure to calculate the elapsed time between two key depressions. Assume the user presses only regular keys, not ones that have extended codes.
6. To find out the *minimum* time between keystrokes, execute the procedure in Exercise 5 and, when you see the cursor, press the space bar twice, quickly.

9

Let There Be Sound!

In earlier chapters we discussed interrupts that let you control the screen, keyboard, disks, time and date, and other things within the computer. Unfortunately, there are no built-in DOS or BIOS tools for generating sound through the speaker, so we have to derive some methods of our own. A good point of reference is the SOUND statement included in BASIC.

SOUND produces a tone of a specified frequency and duration. The frequency can range from 37 to 32767 Hertz (cycles per second); the duration from 0 to 65535 "clock ticks." (Clock ticks are the 8254 Timer interrupts we discussed in Chapter 6. Recall that they occur about 18.2 times a second. Hence, SOUND can produce durations of more than one hour.) In this chapter we develop an assembly language counterpart of SOUND, and use it to play music through the speaker.

9.1 How the Speaker Works

Most input and output (I/O) operations in the AT are regulated by an *8255 Programmable Peripheral Interface (PPI)* chip on the System Board. The PPI contains three 8-bit registers; two for input functions and one for output functions. The input registers are assigned I/O port numbers 60H and 62H; the output register is assigned I/O port number 61H.

As Figure 9-1 shows, either or both of two sources can drive the speaker, as selected by two bits in the PPI's output register. When bit 0 is 1, the 8254 Timer chip drives the speaker. When bit 1 is 1, the speaker goes on, and stays on until bit 1 becomes 0. The programs in this chapter use the Timer technique.

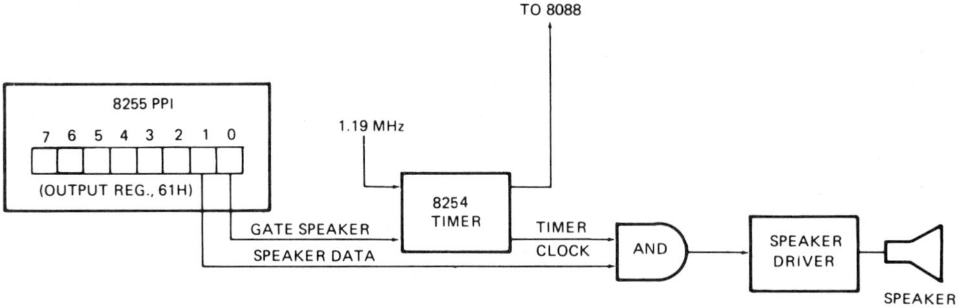

Figure 9-1. Speaker drive system.

9.2 Programming the Speaker

To avoid reinventing the wheel, we have modeled our sound procedure after one that the BIOS uses to beep the speaker if its Power-On Self Test finds a hardware error. This procedure, called BEEP, starts at F000:17AA; see the *Test 4* portion of the *Technical Reference*'s BIOS listing.

The BIOS "BEEP" Procedure

BEEP generates an 896-Hz tone for one or more half-second intervals, based on an interval count in BL. The interval count (1 for a half-second "short beep", 6 for a three-second "long beep") is set by the calling procedure, ERROR_BEEP.

BEEP configures the 8254 Timer to generate a frequency output, then sends a "divisor" value of 533H to the 8254's Timer 2. This selects a frequency of 896 Hz. After that, BEEP forces Bits 0 and 1 of AL to be 1 and outputs AL to the 8255's output register (I/O port 61H), which turns on the speaker. A subsequent loop keeps the speaker on for one or more half-second intervals, based on the value in BL.

A Generalized Sound Generator

BEEP is a fairly good model for a general sound-generating procedure, but we need to change two aspects of its design. First, BEEP can only produce 896-Hz tones; we want to be able to produce tones of any frequency. Second, BEEP's durations are multiples of 1/2 seconds; we want multiples of 1/100 of a second, or 10 *milliseconds*. (A millisecond is one thousandths of a second.)

The BEEP procedure shows us that sending a value of 533H to Timer 2 makes it generate an 896-Hz tone. Therefore, to generate a tone of any other frequency we must multiply 533H by 896/Frequency. If our sound procedure accepts a frequency in DI, the following instructions produce the correct value for Timer 2 in AX:

```
MOV  DX,14H          ;Timer divisor =
MOV  AX,533H*896     ; 533H*896/Frequency
DIV  DI
```

You can generate a 10-millisecond delay by calling the DELAY procedure in Example 6-5 as follows:

```
SUB    AL,AL   ;Make minutes and seconds zero
MOV    BH,AL
MOV    BL,1    ;Set 1/100 seconds to 1
CALL   DELAY
```

By making these changes to BEEP, we can write a general-purpose procedure that produces sounds of any frequency (as specified by DI) and any duration, in increments of 0.01 seconds (as specified by CL, BH, and BL). Example 9-1 shows this assembly language SOUND procedure.

As we note in the prelude to this procedure, SOUND can generate tones between 19 and 65535 Hz. (The lower limit, 19 Hz, is the smallest value of DI that can be divided into our numerator without producing an overflow. Here, the numerator is 533H*896, or 1,192,576. The upper limit is, of course, superfluous, because humans can only hear up to about 20,000 Hz. Still, these limits better the BASIC SOUND statement's range of 37 to 32767 Hz.

9.3 Music, Music, Music

We can now build on our general-purpose sound procedure to play tunes through the speaker. To do this, however, we must know how frequencies relate to musical notes.

Figure 9-2 shows a portion of a piano keyboard spanning two *octaves* (an octave is eight notes) and the frequency of each note in Hertz. The lower octave runs from low C to middle C, while the upper octave runs from middle C to high C.

In this drawing each key is marked with its standard note name. The white keys (A through G) play the *natural* notes. The black keys play the *accidentals*, the sharped and flatted notes. Black keys produce tones one-half note higher (sharp) or one-half note lower (flat) than the white keys beside them.

We now have all the necessary data to develop a music-playing program. What should this program do? It should look up a series of frequencies and

Example 9-1. Speaker-beeper procedure.

```
        PAGE   ,132
TITLE   SOUND  - The Speaker-Beeper
;   Produces a tone of a specified frequency and duration.
;   Inputs: DI = Frequency in Hertz (19 to 65535)
;           CL = Duration in minutes (0 to 255)
;           BH = Duration in seconds (0 to 255)
;           BL = Duration in 1/100 seconds (0 to 99)
;   All registers are preserved.

;   Assemble with: MASM SOUND;
;   Link with: LINK callprog+SOUND+DELAY;

        EXTRN DELAY:FAR
        PUBLIC  SOUND
CSEG    SEGMENT PARA 'CODE'
        ASSUME  CS:CSEG
SOUND   PROC   FAR
        PUSH   AX               ;Save registers
        PUSH   CX
        PUSH   DX
        PUSH   DI
        MOV    AL,0B6H          ;Write timer mode register
        OUT    43H,AL
        MOV    DX,14H           ;Timer divisor =
        MOV    AX,533H*896      ;533H*896/Frequency
        DIV    DI
        OUT    42H,AL           ;Write Timer 2 count low byte
        MOV    AL,AH
        OUT    42H,AL           ;Write Timer 2 count high byte
        IN     AL,61H           ;Get current Port B setting
        MOV    AH,AL            ; and save it in AH
        OR     AL,3             ;Turn speaker on
        OUT    61H,AL
        MOV    AL,CL            ;Wait for the specified interval
        CALL   DELAY
        MOV    AL,AH            ;Recover value of port
        OUT    61H,AL
        POP    DI               ;Restore registers
        POP    DX
        POP    CX
        POP    AX
        RET                     ; and exit
SOUND   ENDP
CSEG    ENDS
        END
```

durations in two tables and make repeated calls to SOUND to play the notes through the speaker.

The frequencies are, of course, obtained from Figure 9-2. The durations depend on what tempo you want and how many beats the note should be

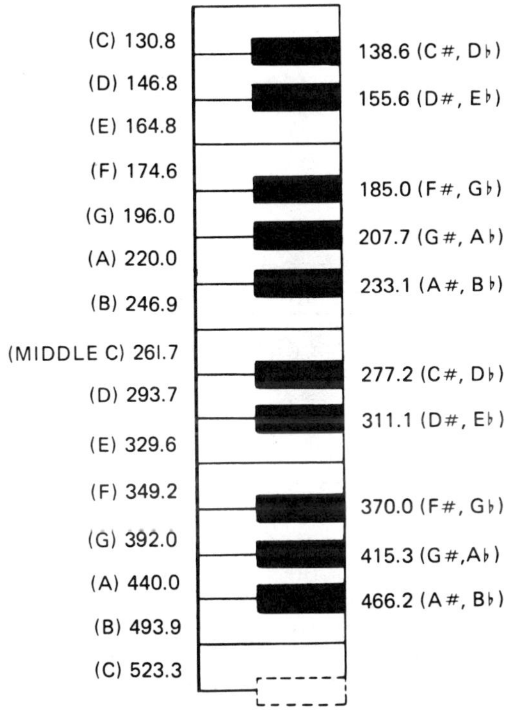

Figure 9-2. Two octaves on a piano.

sustained. In 4/4 time, which has four beats to a measure, a *whole note* is sustained for four beats, a *half note* for two beats, a *quarter note* for one beat, an *eighth note* for one-half beat, and so on.

As a simple illustration, Figure 9-3 shows the music for "Mary Had a Little Lamb," along with its frequency and duration tables. Most are quarter notes, but the second and fourth bars end with half notes (E and G, respectively) and the final bar consists of a whole note (C).

To build the duration table, we arbitrarily give a whole note a duration of one second. Therefore, a half note lasts a half-second and a quarter note lasts a quarter-second. The final value in the frequency table (0FFFFH) is not a note at all; it is a code that tells the note-playing procedure when to stop.

Music-Playing Procedure

Now that we have the SOUND procedure and the frequency and duration tables, we must develop a procedure that accesses the tables and calls SOUND to "play" the tune. Example 9-2 lists a procedure called PLAY that does this. PLAY assumes that the data segment addresses of the frequency and duration tables are in SI and BP, respectively.

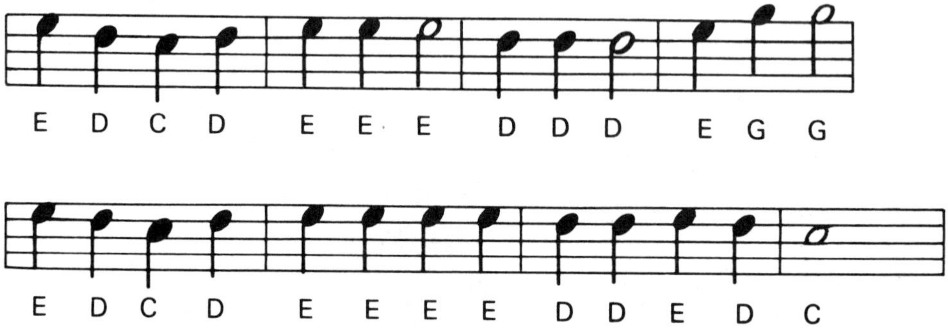


```
MARY FREQ  DW 330, 294, 262, 294, 3 DUP (330)  ; BARS 1 & 2
           DW 294, 294, 294, 330, 392, 392     ; BARS 3 & 4
           DW 330, 294, 262, 294, 4 DUP (330)  ; BARS 5 & 6
           DW 294, 294, 330, 294, 262, 0FFFFH; BARS 7 & 8
MARY TIME  DW 6 DUP (25), 50                   ; BARS 1 & 2
           DW 2 DUP (25, 25, 50)               ; BARS 3 & 4
           DW 12 DUP (25), 100                 ; BARS 5 - 8
```

Figure 9-3. Mary Had a Little Lamb.

Tune Module

We need another module that does three things:

1. Defines the frequency and duration tables for the tune we want to play.
2. Puts the table offsets in SI and DI, respectively.
3. Calls PLAY.

Example 9-3 shows this tune module for "Mary Had a Little Lamb." Just for fun, we have also included the lively old standard "Turkey In the Straw" (Example 9-4).

Example 9-2. Music-playing procedure.

```
        PAGE  ,132
TITLE   PLAY  - Music-Playing Procedure

;  This procedure plays a tune through the speaker,
;  based on two tables in the data segment.
;  Inputs: DS:SI = Address of frequency table
;          DS:BP = Address of duration table
;  The frequency table must end with 0FFFFH.
;  Calls SOUND (Example 9-1).
;  All registers are preserved.

;  Assemble with: MASM PLAY;
;  Link with: LINK callprog+PLAY+SOUND+DELAY:

        EXTRN   SOUND:FAR
        PUBLIC  PLAY
CSEG    SEGMENT PARA 'CODE'
        ASSUME  CS:CSEG
PLAY    PROC  FAR
        PUSH  BX              ;Save the caller's registers
        PUSH  CX
        PUSH  DI
        PUSH  SI
        PUSH  BP
FREQ:   MOV   DI,[SI]         ;Read next frequency
        CMP   DI,0FFFFH       ;End of tune?
        JE    END_PLAY        ; If so, exit
        MOV   BL,DS:[BP]      ; Otherwise, fetch the duration
        SUB   CL,CL
        SUB   BH,BH
        CALL  SOUND           ;Play the note
        ADD   SI,2            ;Update the table pointers
        INC   BP
        JNZ   FREQ            ;Go process next note
END_PLAY: POP BP              ;Restore registers
        POP   SI
        POP   DI
        POP   CX
        POP   BX
        RET                    ; and exit
PLAY    ENDP
CSEG    ENDS
        END
```

Example 9-3. Play "Mary Had a Little Lamb."

```
      PAGE    ,132
TITLE MARY    - Mary Had a Little Lamb

;  This program plays "Mary Had a Little Lamb" using
;  the PLAY procedure (Example 9-1).

;  Assemble with: MASM MARY;
;  Link with: LINK MARY+PLAY+SOUND+DELAY;

EXTRN PLAY:FAR
STACK SEGMENT PARA STACK 'STACK'
      DB      64 DUP('STACK   ')
STACK ENDS

DSEG  SEGMENT PARA 'DATA'
MARY_FREQ DW  330,294,262,294,3 DUP(330) ;Bars 1 & 2
      DW      294,294,294,330,392,392    ;Bars 3 & 4
      DW      330,294,262,294,4 DUP(330) ;Bars 5 & 6
      DW      294,294,330,294,262,0FFFFH ;Bars 7 & 8
MARY_TIME DB  6 DUP(25),50               ;Bars 1 & 2
      DB      2 DUP(25,25,50)            ;Bars 3 & 4
      DB      12 DUP(25),100             ;Bars 5-8
DSEG  ENDS

CSEG  SEGMENT PARA 'CODE'
      ASSUME  CS:CSEG,DS:DSEG,SS:STACK
MARY_PROC PROC  FAR

;  Set up the stack to contain the proper values so this
;  program can return to DOS.

      PUSH    DS      ;Put return seg. addr. on stack
      MOV     CX,0    ;Clear a register
      PUSH    CX

      MOV     AX,DSEG   ;Initialize DS
      MOV     DS,AX

;  Initialize SI and BP, then call PLAY.

      LEA     SI,MARY_FREQ
      LEA     BP,DS:MARY_TIME
      CALL    PLAY
      RET
MARY_PROC ENDP
CSEG  ENDS
      END     MARY_PROC
```

Example 9-4. Play "Turkey In the Straw."

```
        PAGE     ,132
TITLE TURKEY   - Turkey in the Straw

;   Plays "Turkey in the Straw."

;   Assemble with: MASM TURKEY;
;   Link with: LINK TURKEY+PLAY+SOUND+DELAY;

EXTRN PLAY:FAR
STACK SEGMENT PARA STACK 'STACK'
        DB       64 DUP('STACK   ')
STACK ENDS

DSEG   SEGMENT PARA 'DATA'
TRKY_FREQ DW   294,262,233,233,262,233,175,147,156 ;Line 1
        DW       175,196,175,147,175,233,262,294,294 ;Line 2
        DW       294,262,233,262
        DW       294,262,262,294,262,233,233,262     ;Line 3
        DW       233,175,147,156
        DW       175,196,175,147,175,233,262,294,349 ;Line 4
        DW       349,294,233,262
        DW       294,262,233,294,349,294,349,349     ;Line 5
        DW       294,349,294,349,311,392,311,392,392 ;Line 6
        DW       311,392,311,392,466,466,349,349     ;Line 7
        DW       294,294,262,233,262,294,349,392     ;Line 8
        DW       349,294,233,262,294,262,233,0FFFFH
TRKY_TIME DB   2 DUP(12),25,6 DUP(12)              ;Line 1
        DB       4 DUP(12),25,2 DUP(12),2 DUP(25)    ;Line 2
        DB       4 DUP(12)
        DB       3 DUP(25),2 DUP(12),25,6 DUP(12)    ;Line 3
        DB       4 DUP(12),25,2 DUP(12),2 DUP(25)    ;Line 4
        DB       4 DUP(12)
        DB       2 DUP(25),50,12,25,12,2 DUP(25)     ;Line 5
        DB       12,25,12,50,2 DUP(12,25),25         ;Line 6
        DB       12,25,12,50,4 DUP(25)               ;Line 7
        DB       3 DUP(25),3 DUP(12),25,5 DUP(12)    ;Line 8
        DB       3 DUP(25)
DSEG   ENDS

CSEG   SEGMENT PARA 'CODE'
        ASSUME   CS:CSEG,DS:DSEG,SS:STACK
TRKY_PROC PROC   FAR
        PUSH     DS        ;Put return seg. addr. on stack
        MOV      CX,0      ;Clear a register
        PUSH     CX
        MOV      AX,DSEG   ;Initialize DS
        MOV      DS,AX
        LEA      SI,TRKY_FREQ
        LEA      BP,DS:TRKY_TIME
        CALL     PLAY
        RET
TRKY_PROC ENDP
CSEG   ENDS
        END      TRKY_PROC
```

Music from the Keyboard

Since we already know which frequencies produce piano notes, we can go a step further and develop a procedure that makes the speaker sound a note when you press the corresponding letter key on the computer's keyboard. Although we probably cannot arrive at a reasonable approach that lets you produce all 88 notes on a piano, we can easily provide notes for the two octaves shown in Figure 9-2. To do this, we design the program so that you get lower-octave notes by pressing just a letter key (A through G) and upper-octave notes by pressing Shift and a letter key.

What about sharps and flats? The computer has no flat symbol, but it does have the sharp symbol (#) as the uppercase character on the 3 key. Therefore, we let you press 3 to select a sharp and (arbitrarily) 2 to select a flat.

When musicians compose, they put sharp or flat symbols immediately after the note name (e.g., they write "A sharp" as *A#*). Thus, the ideal computer procedure is probably one in which the player produces a sharped note by pressing a letter key, then 3 (for example, A3). However, that requires the computer to wait after a letter key to see whether the next key is 2 (sharp), 3 (flat), or another letter key. To avoid this, we ask the player to indicate sharp or flat *before* pressing the letter key.

Example 9-5 shows a procedure called KBD_MUSIC that lets you "play" piano notes from the keyboard. Note that is has the frequencies for two octaves in a data segment table and calls SOUND (Example 9-1) to play each note for 1/10 second.

While KBD_MUSIC is running, press a letter key to play a lower-octave note or Shift-letter key to play an upper-octave note. To produce a flatted or sharped note, press 2 or 3 (with Shift, if appropriate) before selecting the note. Press the Return key to exit to DOS.

Example 9-5. Music from the keyboard.

```
        PAGE    ,132
TITLE KEYMUSIC - Keyboard Music
;   This procedure makes the computer keyboard function like a
;   two-octave piano keyboard (Figure 9-2).
;   Instructions:
;      o  To play a lower-octave natural note, press a letter
;         key (A-G).
;      o  To play an upper-octave natural note, hold Shift
;         down and press a letter key.
;      o  To play a flat or sharp, press the 2 or 3 key
;         and then the letter key.
;      o  To exit, press Return.
;   This procedure calls SOUND (Example 9-1).

;   Assemble with: MASM KEYMUSIC;
;   Link with: LINK KEYMUSIC+SOUND+DELAY;

        EXTRN    SOUND:FAR
STACK SEGMENT PARA STACK 'STACK'
        DB       64 DUP('STACK   ')
STACK ENDS

DSEG  SEGMENT PARA 'DATA'
FREQS DW       220,247,131,147,165,175,196 ;Naturals, lower oct.
      DW       440,494,262,294,330,349,392 ;Naturals, upper oct.
      DW       233,262,139,156,175,185,208 ;Sharps, lower oct.
      DW       466,523,277,311,349,370,415 ;Sharps, upper oct.
      DW       208,233,123,136,156,165,185 ;Flats, lower oct.
      DW       415,466,247,277,311,330,370 ;Flats, upper oct.
 DSEG ENDS

CSEG  SEGMENT PARA 'CODE'
KBD_MUSIC PROC   FAR
        ASSUME  CS:CSEG,DS:DSEG,SS:STACK

;   Set up the stack to contain the proper values so this
;   program can return to DOS.

        PUSH     DS     ;Put return seg. addr. on stack
        MOV      CX,0   ;Clear a register
        PUSH     CX

;   Initialize the data segment address.

        MOV      AX,DSEG
        MOV      DS,AX

NEW_NOTE: MOV AH,0             ;Read the next key
        INT      16H
        CMP      AL,0DH        ;Is it Return?
        JNE      LWR_FLT
        RET                    ;  If so, exit
```

Example 9-5. (continued).

```
LWR_FLT: SUB   SI,SI
      CMP      AL,'2'
      JNE      UPR_FLT
      MOV      BX,56   ;Possible lower octave flat
GET_LC: MOV   AH,0
      INT      16H
      JMP      SHORT CHK_LO
UPR_FLT: CMP   AL,'@'
      JNE      LWR_SHP
      MOV      BX,70   ;Possible upper octave flat
GET_UC: MOV   AH,0
      INT      16H
      JMP      SHORT CHK_UO
LWR_SHP: CMP   AL,'3'
      JNE      UPR_SHP
      MOV      BX,28   ;Possible lower octave sharp
      JMP      SHORT GET_LC
UPR_SHP: CMP   AL,'#'
      JNE      LWR_NAT
      MOV      BX,42   ;Possible upper octave sharp
      JMP      SHORT GET_UC
LWR_NAT: MOV   BX,0    ;Possible lower octave natural
      CMP      AL,'a'
      JB       UPR_NAT
      CMP      AL,'g'
      JA       NEW_NOTE
      JNA      NEW_FREQ
UPR_NAT: MOV   BX,14   ;Possible upper octave natural
      JMP      SHORT CHK_UO

;  Check whether the key selects lower octave (a - g).

CHK_LO: CMP    AL,'a'
      JB       NEW_NOTE
      CMP      AL,'g'
      JA       NEW_NOTE
      JNA      NEW_FREQ

;  Check whether the key selects upper octave (A - G).

CHK_UO: CMP    AL,'A'
      JB       NEW_NOTE
      CMP      AL,'G'
      JA       NEW_NOTE

;  Convert the ASCII key code to an index in SI, then use
;  that index to look-up a frequency and call SOUND to play
;  the note for 0.01 second.

NEW_FREQ: AND  AL,0FH
      SHL      AL,1
      SUB      AH,AH
      ADD      SI,AX
      MOV      DI,FREQS-2[BX][SI]
      MOV      BL,10   ;Duration is 1/10 second
```

Example 9-5. (continued).

```
        SUB     CL,CL
        MOV     BH,CL
        CALL    SOUND
        JMP     SHORT NEW_NOTE
KBD_MUSIC ENDP
CSEG    ENDS
        END     KBD_MUSIC
```

9.4 Sound the Alarm!

We are now about to present the final programming example in this book—one that sets the alarm. This program (Example 9-6) is quite long, but it does the following:

1. Reads the alarm vector (4A) and saves it on the stack.
2. Resets the alarm, because if you try to set the alarm after it has been previously set, DOS sets the Carry Flag and does nothing (see Table 6-7 in Section 6.4).
3. Makes the alarm vector point to a procedure called ALARM that beeps the speaker three times.
4. Asks the user to enter the alarm time—hour, minute, and second—using a procedure called GET_TIME, and converts these values to packed BCD. In each case, the alarm program checks to make sure that the user has entered a valid time. GET_TIME also does some error-checking; it calls a CHECK procedure that ensures that the user's digits are in the range 0 to 9.
5. Sets the alarm using the AH = 6 of the Type 1A interrupt.
6. Restores the Type 4A interrupt vector from the values on the stack.

The supplementary disk for this book also includes a program called CLRALARM that resets the alarm.

Example 9-6. Set the alarm.

```
        PAGE   ,132
TITLE SETALARM - Set the alarm
;  Sets the alarm based on user values.

.286c
        EXTRN SOUND:FAR,DELAY:FAR
STACK   SEGMENT PARA STACK 'STACK'
        DB     64 DUP('STACK   ')
STACK   ENDS

DSEG    SEGMENT PARA PUBLIC 'DATA'
BAD_DATA DB    'Digits must be between 0 and 9',13,10,'$'
BAD_HRS  DB    'Hours must be between 0 and 23',13,10,'$'
BAD_MINS DB    'Minutes must be between 0 and 59',13,10,'$'
BAD_SECS DB    'Seconds must be between 0 and 59',13,10,'$'

CRLF    DB     13,10,'$'

PROMPT  DB     'Set the alarm time.',13,10
        DB     'Enter values or press Enter for zero'
        DB     13,10,'$'
ASK_HRS DB     'HOUR (0-23): $'
ASK_MINS DB    'MINUTE (0-59): $'
ASK_SECS DB    'SECOND (0-59): $'
USER$   DB     3,3 DUP(?)      ;User's response
DSEG    ENDS

CSEG    SEGMENT PARA PUBLIC 'CODE'
        ASSUME  CS:CSEG,SS:STACK,DS:DSEG
ENTRY   PROC   FAR             ;Entry point

        PUSH   DS              ;Set up return address
        SUB    AX,AX
        PUSH   AX

        MOV    AL,4AH          ;Read the Type 4A vector
        MOV    AH,35H
        INT    21H
        PUSH   ES              ; and save it on the stack
        PUSH   BX

        MOV    AH,7            ;Reset the alarm
        INT    1AH

        MOV    AL,4AH          ;Make the 4A vector point to ALARM
        MOV    DX,SEG ALARM
        MOV    DS,DX
        LEA    DX,ALARM
        MOV    AH,25H
        INT    21H
```

Example 9-6. (continued).

```
        MOV     AX,DSEG         ;Point to DSEG
        MOV     DS,AX

        LEA     DX,PROMPT       ;Ask for alarm hour
        MOV     AH,9
        INT     21H
HOUR:   LEA     DX,ASK_HRS
        MOV     AH,9
        INT     21H
        CALL    GET_TIME        ;Convert it to BCD
        JC      HOUR
        CMP     BL,23H          ;Make sure it's < 24
        JNA     HRS2CH
        LEA     DX,BAD_HRS
        MOV     AH,9
        INT     21H
        JMP     HOUR
HRS2CH: MOV     CH,BL           ; and put it in CH

MIN:    LEA     DX,ASK_MINS     ;Ask for alarm minutes
        MOV     AH,9
        INT     21H
        CALL    GET_TIME        ;Convert it to BCD
        JC      MIN
        CMP     BL,59H          ;Make sure it's < 60
        JNA     MIN2CL
        LEA     DX,BAD_MINS
        MOV     AH,9
        INT     21H
        JMP     MIN
MIN2CL: MOV     CL,BL           ; and put it in CL

SEC:    LEA     DX,ASK_SECS     ;Ask for alarm seconds
        MOV     AH,9
        INT     21H
        CALL    GET_TIME        ;Convert it to BCD
        JC      SEC
        CMP     BL,59H          ;Make sure it's < 60
        JNA     SEC2DH
        LEA     DX,BAD_SECS
        MOV     AH,9
        INT     21H
        JMP     SEC
SEC2DH: MOV     DH,BL           ; and put it in DH

        MOV     AH,6           ;Set the alarm
        INT     1AH

RES:    POP     DX              ;Restore the 4A vector
        POP     DS
        MOV     AL,4AH
        MOV     AH,35H
        INT     21H
        RET                     ; and exit
ENTRY   ENDP
```

Example 9-6. (continued).

```
; Following is the alarm routine.

ALARM   PROC
        PUSHA                   ;Save the caller's registers
        MOV     CH,3            ;Beep three times
        MOV     DI,1000         ;Beep for one second
        SUB     CL,CL
        MOV     BH,1
        SUB     BL,BL
BEEP:   CALL    SOUND
        SUB     AL,AL           ;Wait for one second
        MOV     BH,1
        SUB     BL,BL
        CALL    DELAY
        DEC     CH
        JNZ     BEEP
        POPA                    ;Restore the registers
        IRET
ALARM   ENDP

; This procedure reads up to two keys into string
; buffer USER$, then converts them into a packed
; BCD number in BL.
; If either key is invalid, it prints an error
; message and sets CF to 1.

GET_TIME PROC
        LEA     DX,USER$        ;Read user's response
        MOV     AH,0AH
        INT     21H
        LEA     DX,CRLF         ;Advance to next line
        MOV     AH,9
        INT     21H
        CMP     USER$+1,1       ;Check key count
        JAE     CONVERT
        SUB     BL,BL           ;User pressed Enter
        RET
CONVERT: MOV    AL,USER$+2      ;Get first key
        CALL    CHECK           ;Check this character
        JC      LEAVE           ;If it is valid,
        AND     AL,0FH          ; convert it to BCD
        MOV     BL,AL
        CMP     USER$+1,2       ;Is there another key?
        JB      CLR_CF
        SHL     BL,4            ;Yes.  Put first digit in high bits
        MOV     AL,USER$+3      ;Get second key
        CALL    CHECK           ;Check this character
        JC      LEAVE           ;If it is valid,
        AND     AL,0FH          ; convert it to BCD
        OR      BL,AL
CLR_CF: CLC
LEAVE:  RET
GET_TIME ENDP
```

Example 9-6. (continued).

```
; This procedure checks whether an entry value is
; between 0 and 9.  If not, it displays an error
; message and sets CF to 1.

CHECK   PROC
        CMP   AL,'0'       ;If entry is < 0
        JB    ERROR
        CMP   AL,'9'       ; or > 9,
        JA    ERROR        ; print message
        CLC                ;Otherwise, clear CF and return
        RET
ERROR:  LEA   DX,BAD_DATA  ;Display error message
        MOV   AH,9
        INT   21H
        STC                ;Set CF and return
        RET
CHECK   ENDP
CSEG    ENDS
        END   ENTRY
```

10

Macros

Macros are subroutine-like "miniprograms" you can insert in source programs by mentioning their names. In this chapter we describe how to create macros and use them in programs. Then we present a set of useful macros and show you how to put them into a "macro library."

10.1 Introduction to Macros

As we just mentioned, a macro is a sequence of assembler statements (instructions and pseudo-ops) that may appear several times in a program. Like procedures, macros have names. Once a macro has been defined, you can enter its name in your source program wherever you normally type the instruction sequence.

Macros vs Procedures

Although macros and procedures both provide a shorthand reference to a frequently-used instruction sequence, they are not the same. The code for a procedure occurs once in a program, and the processor transfers to it (i.e., *CALLs* it) as needed. By contrast, the code for a macro may occur many times within a program; the assembler replaces each occurrence of a macro name with the instructions that name represents. (We say the assembler "expands" the macro.) Therefore, when you execute the program, the processor executes the macro instructions "in-line," without transferring elsewhere in memory, as it does with a procedure. Hence, *a macro name is a user-defined assembler directive;* it provides commands to the assembler, rather than to the microprocessor.

Macros have three advantages over procedures:

1. Macros are *dynamic*. You can easily change how the macro operates (not merely what it operates on) each time, by changing its input parameters. By contrast, you can only vary the data that gets passed to a procedure, making procedures much more inflexible.
2. Macros make faster-executing programs, because the processor is not delayed by call and return instructions, as it is with procedures.
3. Macros can be entered into a *macro library* that programmers can draw from to create other programs.

Nothing comes for free, however. Macros have a major drawback that procedures do not have: since a macro gets expanded every time it is used, it tends to make machine language programs longer by filling memory with repeated instruction sequences.

Macros Speed Up Programming

Macros can speed up your programming and debugging work, as well as any program updating you might do in the future. They speed up programming because you create a macro just once, then use it wherever you want it in a program. Rather than entering along sequence of instructions, you enter only the macro name that represents them. (Macros have this in common with subroutines.)

Macros can speed up debugging because you create and debug each macro individually. Once a macro is working properly, you should never have to worry about whether *that* portion of your program is correct. You can concentrate on finding errors elsewhere.

Programs that include macros are generally easier to read and understand. That means they are also easier to update.

Let's see how macros can ease your workload. For example, suppose you want to clear the screen. To do this, you could enter the following instructions in your program:

```
MOV  AH,15  ;Read the video state
INT  10H
MOV  AH,0   ;Set the video state
INT  10H
```

Similarly, to home the cursor (move it to the top left-hand corner), enter

```
MOV  DH,0   ;Select row 0
MOV  DL,0   ; and column 0
MOV  AH,2   ;Select cursor-moving option
INT  10H    ;Move the cursor
```

These instruction sequences are short, but it's still bothersome to re-enter them every time you need them. However, if you have defined these sequences as macros, you can enter the following instead:

```
CLS   ;Clear the screen
HOME  ;Move cursor to home position
```

Which program would you expect someone to understand more readily? For that matter, which would *you* want to tackle, say, six months later?

Finally, macros also make a program easier to change. Change the macro definition and the assembler automatically uses the new version everywhere it used the old one previously.

Contents of Macros

Every macro definition has three parts:

1. *Header*—The MACRO pseudo-op, with the *name* of the macro in the label field and, optionally, a *dummy-list* in the operand field. The *dummy-list* identifies variables—input parameters you can change each time you call the macro.
2. *Body*—The sequence of assembler statements (instructions and pseudo-ops) that define what the macro does.
3. *Terminator*—The ENDM pseudo-op, which marks the end of the macro definition. If you omit ENDM, the assembler displays the error message "End of file encountered on input file."

For example, the following is a simple macro you can use to add word-size values:

```
ADD_WORDS  MACRO  TERM1,TERM2,SUM
     MOV  AX,TERM1
     ADD  AX,TERM2
     MOV  SUM,AX
           ENDM
```

The assembler doesn't care whether you specify register names, memory locations, or immediate values for the operands (you can't use an immediate for SUM, of course). As long as the final form is legal, the assembler makes the substitutions without complaining. For example, at one place in a program, you could add two memory locations by entering

```
ADD_WORDS  PRICE,TAX,COST
```

This makes the assembler insert the following instructions in the program:

```
MOV   AX,PRICE
ADD   AX,TAX
MOV   COST,AX
```

Somewhere else you can add two registers by entering

```
ADD_WORDS  BX,CX,DX
```

This time the assembler inserts

```
MOV   AX,BX
ADD   AX,CX
MOV   DX,AX
```

Note how much easier it is to pass parameters to macros than to procedures. With a macro, you just enter the parameter; with a procedure, you must put it in a register or memory location.

10.2 Macro Pseudo-Ops

Table 10-1 summarizes the macro pseudo-ops provided by the IBM Macro Assembler. We have divided them into four groups: general-purpose, repeat, conditional, and listing.

Table 10-1. Macro pseudo-ops.

Pseudo-Op	Function
General-Purpose	
MACRO	Format: name MACRO [dummy-list] .. .. ENDM Assigns a *name* to a sequence of assembler statements. Every MACRO definition must end with an ENDM pseudo-op.
LOCAL	Format: LOCAL dummy-list Makes the assembler create a unique symbol for each entry in *dummy-list*, and substitute that symbol for each occurrence of the entry in the expansion.
Repeat	
IRP	Format: IRP dummy,<argument-list> .. .. ENDM Makes the assembler repeat the statements between IRP and

Table 10-1. Macro pseudo-ops (continued).

Pseudo-Op	Function
Repeat (continued)	
	ENDM once for each argument in <*argument-list*>. Each repetition substitutes the next item in <*argument-list*> for each occurrence of *dummy* in the block.
IRPC	Format: `IRPC dummy,string` `..` `..` `ENDM` Makes the assembler repeat the statements between IRPC and ENDM once for each character in character in *string* for every occurrence of *dummy* in the block.
REPT	Format: `REPT expression` `..` `..` `ENDM` Makes the assembler repeat the statements between REPT and ENDM *expression* times.
Conditional	
EXITM	Format: `EXITM` Terminates a macro expansion based on the result of a conditional pseudo-op.
IF1	Format: `IF1 expression` `..` `..` `ENDIF` True if assembler is executing pass 1. Generally used to INCLUDE a macro library file in a source program.
IFB	Format: `IFB <argument>` `..` `..` `ENDIF` True if *argument* is blank. The angle brackets are required.
IFNB	Format: `IFNB <argument>` `..` `..` `ENDIF` True if *argument* is not blank. The angle brackets are required.

Table 10-1. Macro pseudo-ops (continued).

Pseudo-Op	Function
Listing	
.LALL	Format: `.LALL` Lists the complete macro text (including comments) for all expansions.
.SALL	Format: `.SALL` Excludes macro text from listings.
.XALL	Format: `.XALL` Lists only macro lines that generate object code. This is the default setting.

General-Purpose Pseudo-Ops

We have already discussed the MACRO pseudo-op; it gives the macro's name and lists the names of the operands the macro uses, if any.

LOCAL Pseudo-Op

If your macro contains labeled instructions or pseudo-ops, you must tell the assembler to change the labels every time it expands the macro. Otherwise, you end up with "Symbol is Multi-Defined" errors. The LOCAL pseudo-op tells the assembler which labels to change each time.

For example, the following macro (WAIT) makes the processor wait until the value COUNT has been decremented to zero. Declaring the label *NEXT* LOCAL allows us to use this macro more than once in a program.

```
WAIT   MACRO   COUNT
         LOCAL  NEXT
         PUSH   CX          ;Save current CX
         MOV    CX,COUNT    ;Move count to CX
NEXT:    LOOP   NEXT        ;Loop until count is 0
         POP    CX          ;Restore CX
       ENDM
```

Note that LOCAL immediately follows the MACRO statement. If used, *LOCALs must be the first statements in a macro.* They must precede everything else, even comments.

Declaring a label LOCAL also lets you reuse it in other macros. The assembler gives the label a new internal name each time it expands the macro; hence, no duplication.

Repeat Pseudo-Ops

The REPT, IRP, and IRPC pseudo-ops make the assembler repeat sequences of assembler statements in a macro.

REPT obtains its repetition count from an *expression* in the operand field. For example, the following macro allocates *LNGTH* bytes in memory, and initializes them with the values 1 through *LNGTH*, respectively:

```
ALLOCATE  MACRO  TLABEL,LNGTH
TLABEL   EQU   THIS BYTE
VALUE  =  0
  REPT  LNGTH
  VALUE  =    VALUE+1
         DB  VALUE
  ENDM
          ENDM
```

Note that we need two ENDMs here; the first marks the end of the REPT, the second marks the end of the MACRO definition.

After defining ALLOCATE, we can use it to set up a 40-byte table, called TABLE1, with this sequence:

```
DATA     SEGMENT  PARA 'DATA'
ALLOCATE  TABLE1,40
DATA     ENDS
```

The second repeating pseudo-op, IRP, lets you list the arguments that are to be substituted for a *dummy* symbol with each repetition. For example, the sequence

```
IRP  VALUE,<1,2,3,5,7,11,13,17,19,23>
   DW  VALUE*VALUE*VALUE
ENDM
```

sets up a 10-word table that contains the cubes for the first ten prime numbers.

IRPC is the same as IRP, but its arguments are string variables rather than numbers. IRPC takes two operands, a *dummy* symbol and a *string*, and repeats the statements in the block once for each character in the string. Each repetition substitutes the next character in the string for every occurrence of *dummy* in the block.

For example, the sequence

```
IRPC  CHAR,0123456789
    DB  CHAR
ENDM
```

sets up a 10-byte text string that contains the ASCII codes for the digits 0 through 9.

Conditional Pseudo-Ops

These pseudo-ops are similar to the conditionals we discussed in Section 2.10. That is, the assembler tests whether the condition is satisfied. If so, it assembles the statements between IF and ENDIF; if not, it skips them.

IF1 Pseudo-Op

The IF1 (If Pass 1) pseudo-op is used to read a macro library file into a source program. We will discuss it in Section 10.4.

IFB Pseudo-Op

If you enter fewer parameters than a macro expects, the assembler normally sets the omitted or *blank* parameters to zero. However, IFB (If Blank) lets you specify some alternate course of action for blank parameters. IFB is commonly used to make a macro terminate early if some needed parameter is missing. We talk more about terminating early when we discuss EXITM later in this section.

IFNB Pseudo-Op

When the assembler encounters IFNB (If Not Blank), it assembles the enclosed instructions only if the user has supplied a value for the parameter; otherwise, it skips them.

For example, a macro that reads a name may expect you to call it using the form

```
GET_NAME  FIRST-NAME,MIDDLE-INITIAL,LAST-NAME
```

The macro definition for GET_NAME would include instructions that obtain the first name, then the middle initial, then the last name. However, you should make some provision for omitting the middle initial, since not everybody has one. You can do this by using IFNB to include the middle-initial instructions only if the user supplies an initial. Hence, GET_NAME's definition would have the following general form:

```
GET_NAME  MACRO  first-name,middle-initial,last-name
          ..     (These instructions read the first name)
```

```
          ..
IFNB <middle-initial>
          ..    (These instructions read the middle initial)
          ..
ENDIF
          ..    (These instructions read the last name)
          ..
          ENDM
```

With this safeguard, you may now use a form like *GET NAME John,,Brown* without wondering how the assembler will react to the missing initial.

IFNB can also help avoid assembly errors caused by missing operands. For example, if your macro includes the statement *PUSH reg_name,* and you omit *reg_name* from the parameter list, the assembler tries to assemble it as *PUSH 0*—which is not what you intended. To protect against this, use

```
IFNB  <reg_name>
  PUSH  reg_name
ENDIF
```

(In this case, you probably need similar protection for the matching *POP reg_name.*)

EXITM Pseudo-Op

The EXITM (Exit Macro) pseudo-op makes the assembler stop expanding a macro early, based on the result of a conditional pseudo-op, as in

```
IFB <name>
  EXITM
ENDIF
```

For example, recall the ALLOCATE macro that we defined with the REPT pseudo-op. The following new definition makes the assembler allocate the table space only if the LNGTH parameter is less than 50:

```
ALL_LT_50  MACRO  LNGTH
     VALUE = 0
     IF LNGTH GE 50
       EXITM
     ENDIF
     REPT LNGTH
       VALUE = VALUE + 1
       DB  VALUE
     ENDM
           ENDM
```

Listing Pseudo-Ops

The .LALL, .SALL, and .XALL pseudo-ops control how much macro text gets included in an assembly listing (LST). If you omit these options, the assembler assumes you want .XALL. That is, it lists only the lines that generate object code, and leaves out stand-alone comments and pseudo-ops that don't reserve memory locations.

The .LALL pseudo-op produces a full listing, including comments, while .SALL omits all macro text from the listing. You might use .LALL to generate a copy of a program for your files, then reassemble using .SALL to generate the listing you use once the macros have been completely debugged.

10.3 Macro Operators

The MACRO Assembler also provides four operators that you can use with macros; see Table 10-2.

Table 10-2. Macro operators.

Operator	Function
&	Format: `text&text` Concatenates (joins) text or symbols.
;;	Format: `;;comment` Omits *comment* from macro expansion and from listing, even one produced with .LALL.
!	Format: `!character` Used in an argument to make the assembler use the *character* as a literal value, rather than as a symbol.
%	Format: `%symbol` Converts *symbol* to a number. When the assembler expands the macro, it substitutes the number for the symbol.

& Operator

The & operator lets you create custom labels and operands. For example, the following macro sets up a byte table that has a specified name and length:

```
DEF_TABLE  MACRO  SUFFIX,LNGTH
     TABLE&SUFFIX  DB  LNGTH DUP(?)
           ENDM
```

Then, if you enter *DEF_TABLE A,5* in a program, the assembler converts it to

```
TABLEA  DB  5 DUP(?)
```

;; Operator

The ;; operator makes the assembler omit comments from the macro expansion. Without comments, your final program takes up less memory and therefore assembles faster. When defining macros, use the regular ; operator only for the comments that are absolutely necessary, use ;; for the rest.

10.4 Defining Macros in Source Programs

There are two ways to use macros: you can enter their definitions at the beginning of the program or read them into the program from a separate macro library file. In this section we describe how to enter macros directly into a program; we will discuss macro libraries in Section 10.5.

If you have a special-purpose macro that you need in only one program, you can define it in the program, then call it as needed. Let's look at an illustration.

Example 7-3 in the graphics chapter is a program that draws a diagonal line of "smile face" characters down the screen. Example 10-1 shows a new version that uses macros to transfer registers to and from the stack (PUSH_REGS and POP_REGS), move the cursor (MOVE_CURSOR), and display the face character (PRINT_AL). Although the total text is longer—because of the macro definitions—the actual procedure text is quite a bit shorter, and more readable.

The disadvantage of entering macros directly into a program is that this limits them to that particular program. To use them in other programs, you can put them in a macro library.

10.5 Macro Library

A macro library is a disk file that contains definitions of macros you may need in several programs. Once you have created this file, you can read it into any source program. This makes all of the macros in the library available to that program. To use any one of them, just mention its name.

Example 10-1. Diagonal line program using macros.

```
TITLE   NEWDIAG - Diagonal Line Program with Macros

;  Assemble with: MASM NEWDIAG;
;  Link with: LINK NEWDIAG;

;**********************************************************
;  Macro definitions.
;**********************************************************
PUSH_REGS MACRO reg_list

;;  Save registers on the stack.

        IRP   reg,<reg_list>
        PUSH  reg
        ENDM
        ENDM
POP_REGS MACRO  reg_list

;;  Retrieve registers from the stack.

        IRP   reg,<reg_list>
        POP   reg
        ENDM
        ENDM
MOVE_CURSOR MACRO

;;  Move the cursor to the row and column positions in
;;  DH and DL, respectively.

        MOV   AH,2          ;;Select cursor-moving option
        INT   10H
        ENDM
PRINT_AL MACRO

;;  Display the character in AL.

        MOV   CX,1          ;;Display just one character
        MOV   AH,14         ;;Select display option
        INT   10H
        ENDM

;**********************************************************
;  Beginning of program.
;**********************************************************
STACK   SEGMENT PARA STACK 'STACK'
        DB    64 DUP('STACK   ')
STACK   ENDS

CSEG    SEGMENT PARA 'CODE'
DIAG_LINE PROC  FAR
        ASSUME  CS:CSEG,SS:STACK
```

Example 10-1. (continued).

```
;   Set up the stack to contain the proper values so this
;   program can return to DEBUG.

        PUSH   DS                ;Put return seg. addr. on stack
        MOV    DI,0              ;Clear a register
        PUSH   DI                ;Put zero return addr. on stack

        PUSH_REGS <AX,BX,CX,DX>  ;Save registers
        MOV    AH,15             ;Set BH to active display page
        INT    10H
        MOV    AH,0              ;Select 80x25, B/W, Alpha
        MOV    AL,2
        INT    10H
        MOV    DX,0              ;Start at row = 0, column = 0
SET_CRSR: MOVE_CURSOR            ;Set new cursor position
        MOV    AL,2              ;Display char. is smile face
        PRINT_AL
        INC    DH                ;Point to next row
        INC    DL                ; and column position
        CMP    DH,25             ;Bottom of screen?
        JNE    SET_CRSR
        POP_REGS <DX,CX,BX,AX>   ; Yes. Restore registers
        RET                      ; and exit
DIAG_LINE ENDP
CSEG    ENDS
        END    DIAG_LINE
```

Creating a Macro Library

You can create a macro library using EDLIN or a word processor, just as you create a standard program.

Guidelines for Defining Macros

Macros in a library should be general-purpose routines that you can use in virtually any program. Therefore, you should design them so they do their intended tasks, but don't conflict with any program that uses them. Here are a few guidelines to help you design efficient macros:

1. Document the macros as thoroughly as possible. Include lots of comments. Remember, your macro definitions should be meaningful to anyone who has to use them, not just to you.
2. Use the ;; operator to enter comments and use the Tab key (rather than the space bar) to separate fields. This helps keep the size of your programs to a minimum, which allows them to assemble faster.

3. Keep macros as general as possible. If you need a special-purpose macro, define it using a more general macro, if possible. For example, the macro library we introduce in this chapter includes a macro called LOCATE that moves the cursor to a specified row and column position. Then we define a separate macro called HOME that moves the cursor to the upper left-hand corner of the screen. HOME's definition is simply LOCATE 0,0.
4. If the macro includes labels, list them in a LOCAL statement.
5. Save every register that the macro uses except output registers. Do this as usual, with PUSHes at the beginning of the macro and POPs at the end.
6. If a macro definition requires a task that is performed by a previously-defined macro, call that macro to do it.

Reading a Macro Library into a Program

To read a macro library into a source program, you must give the assembler its name with an INCLUDE statement. However, if you do this with only, say, INCLUDE MACRO.LIB, the assembler unnecessarily reads the library during both pass 1 and pass 2.

To avoid this repetition, put the INCLUDE in an IF1 *conditional structure*, as follows:

```
IF1
  INCLUDE MACRO.LIB
ENDIF
```

Doing this makes the assembler read the library during pass 1, but not during pass 2. Moreover, since the assembler produces the listing during pass 2, the INCLUDEd text does not appear on it.

Purging Macros

A disadvantage of using a macro library is that when the assembler INCLUDEs it, all of its macros get read in and stored in the assembler's work space in memory. This includes macros that are not going to be used in this assembly, thus wasting work space and possibly creating an "out of memory" error condition. To avoid this problem, you can *purge* unneeded macros to free up the space occupied by their definitions. To do this, simply list the purge victims immediately after your INCLUDE, as in

```
INCLUDE MACRO.LIB
PURGE CLS,HOME,LOCATE
```

Macro Descriptions

In the remainder of this chapter we describe and define more than 30 macros that you might want to put in a macro library. Included are macros that perform common DOS and BASIC functions (e.g., clear the screen, read keyboard data) and others that perform common assembly language tasks (e.g., save registers, convert between strings and numbers).

Table 10-3 lists the names of the macros, divided into seven functional groups: general-purpose, conversion, cursor-related, display, keyboard, sound, and time. The subsections that follow present more detailed information.

Table 10-3. Macros in the macro library.

General-Purpose Macros		
DELAY	PUSH_REGS	SET_DS
DELAY_AL_BX	POP_REGS	SET_ES
MAKE_STACK	RAND	
Conversion Macros		
$2BIN	BIN2$	KEY_$2BIN
Cursor-Related Macros		
CLS	HOME	MOVE_CURSOR
CR	LF	POS
CRLF	LOCATE	TAB
Display Macros		
MESSAGE	PRINT_NUMBER	SHOW_AL
MESSAGE_DX	PRINT$	VIDEO_STATE
PRINT_AL	PRINT_DX	
Keyboard Macros		
INKEY	IN$	
INKEY_I	IN$_DX	
Sound Macros		
BEEP	SOUND	SOUND_REGS
Time Macros		
READ_TIME	SET_TIME	

General-Purpose Macros

DELAY [,minutes][,seconds][,hundredths]

Action: Makes the computer wait for a specified interval.

Inputs: Optional **minutes** (0 to 59), **seconds** (0 to 59), and **hundredths** of a second (0 to 99).

Outputs: None.

Comments: Same as DELAY_AL_BX, but DELAY bases the wait interval on user values rather than register values.

Examples:
```
DELAY ,30,50    ;Wait 30.5 seconds
DELAY 1,30      ;Wait 1.5 minutes
```

DELAY_AL_BX

Action: Makes the computer wait for a specified interval.

Inputs: AL = Minutes
BH = Seconds
BL = Hundredths of seconds

Outputs: None. AL, BH, and BL are unaffected.

Comments: Same as DELAY, but DELAY_AL_BX uses register inputs rather than user values.

Examples:
```
MOV  AL,0  ;Wait 1.5 seconds
MOV  BH,1
MOV  BL,50
DELAY_AL_BX
```

MAKE_STACK stack-name

Action: Creates a standard stack segment (that is, reserves 64 repetitions of 'STACK   ') and gives it the specified name.

Inputs: **stack-name** is name of stack segment.

Outputs: None.

Example:
```
MAKE_STACK MY_STACK    ;Stack seg. is named MY_STACK
```

PUSH_REGS <reg0[,reg1,...]>

Action: Pushes registers on the stack, in the specified order.

Inputs: Register names, separated by commas and enclosed with angle brackets.

Outputs: None.

Example:
```
PUSH_REGS <AX,BX,DX>    ;Save AX, BX, and DX
```

POP_REGS <reg0[,reg1,...]>

Action: Pops registers off the stack, in the specified order.

Inputs: Register names, separated by commas and enclosed with angle brackets.

Outputs: Specified registers change according to stack values.

Comments: List registers in the opposite order of PUSH_REGS.

Example:
```
POP_REGS <DX,BX,AX>    ;Retrieve DX, BX, and AX
```

RAND limit

Action: Produces a random integer between 0 and **limit.**
Inputs: **limit** (4 to 127)
Outputs: (AL) = Random number
Example: `RAND 85   ;Generate random number between 0 and 85`

SET_DS dseg-name

Action: Loads the address of the data segment into DS.
Inputs: **dseg-name** is name of data segment.
Outputs: DS points to data segment.

SET_ES eseg-name

Action: Loads the address of the extra segment into ES.
Inputs: **eseg-name** is name of data segment.
Outputs: ES points to extra segment.

Conversion Macros

$2BIN string-name

Action: Converts a string in the data segment to a signed number in AX.
Inputs: **string-name** refers to starting address of string.
String Format: String may be up to seven bytes long, where the first byte holds the character count. First significant character may be a minus (-) or plus (+) sign, the rest must be numeric digits (0 through 9). For example,

```
MY_STRING  DB  6,'-16540'
```

Outputs: If string is legal, CF = 0 and (AX) = Number
If string is illegal, CF = 1
Comments: To convert a number entered from the keyboard, use KEY_$2BIN.
Example:

```
$2BIN  MY_STRING    ;Convert MY_STRING to number
JC     PRINT_ERROR
```

BIN2$ string-name

Action: Converts the signed contents of AX to a string in the data segment.
Inputs: **string-name** refers to starting address of target string.
String Format: Seven reserved bytes. For example,

```
MY_STRING  DB  7 DUP(?)
```

Output: None. AX is unaffected.
Example: `BIN2$  MY_STRING   ;Convert AX to string`

KEY_$2BIN

Action: Converts a sequence of keyboard characters to a signed number in AX.
Inputs: None.

Outputs: If string is legal, CF = 0 and (AX) = Number
If string is illegal, CF = 1

Comments: To convert a string in the data segment, see $2BIN.

Example:
```
KEY_$2BIN           ;Read number from keyboard
JC   PRINT_ERROR
```

PRINT_NUMBER See *Display Macros.*

Cursor-Related Macros

CLS

Action: Clears the screen.
Inputs: None.
Outputs: None.

CR

Action: Carriage Return. Moves the cursor to the beginning of the current line.
Inputs: None.
Outputs: None.
Comments: See also CRLF.

CRLF

Action: Carriage Return/Line Feed. Moves the cursor to the beginning of the next line.
Inputs: None.
Outputs: None.

HOME

Action: Moves the cursor to the upper left-hand corner of the screen.
Inputs: None.
Outputs: None.
Comments: Same as LOCATE 0,0.

LF

Action: Line Feed. Moves the cursor to the next line.
Inputs: None.
Outputs: None.
Comments: (1) See also CRLF.
(2) If the cursor is already on the bottom line, LF moves it to the top line.

LOCATE row,column

Action: Moves cursor to the specified position.
Inputs: **row** (0 to 24) and **column** (0 to 79).
Outputs: None.
Comments: (1) Same as MOVE_CURSOR, but LOCATE works with user values rather than register values.

(2) If **row** exceeds 24, LOCATE moves cursor to line 0.
(3) If **column** exceeds 79, LOCATE moves cursor to column 0.
(4) See also HOME.

Example: `LOCATE 24,79 ;Move cursor to lower right corner.`

MOVE_CURSOR

Action: Moves cursor to row in DH and column in DL.
Inputs: (DH) = Row number
(DL) = Column number
Outputs: None. DH and DL are unaffected.
Comments: (1) Similar to LOCATE, but MOVE_CURSOR works with register values rather than user values.
(2) If DH exceeds 24, cursor moves to line 0.
(3) If DL exceeds 79, cursor moves to column 0.
(4) Use POS to read current cursor position.

POS

Action: Reads current cursor position.
Inputs: None.
Outputs: (DH,DL) = Row, column numbers
(CH,CL) = Cursor mode

TAB column

Action: Moves the cursor to the specified **column**.
Inputs: **column** (0 to 79)
Outputs: None.
Comments: If the cursor is beyond the specified position, TAB moves it to that column on the next line.
Example: `TAB 40 ;Tab to column 40`

Display Macros

MESSAGE string-name

Action: Displays a message string in the data segment.
Inputs: **string-name**
String Format: String must end with a $ character. For example,

```
ILLEGAL  DB  'Illegal input value.  Try again.$'
```

Outputs: None.
Comments: Same as MESSAGE_DX, but MESSAGE takes its string specifier from a user name rather than from a register.
Example: `MESSAGE ILLEGAL ;Display ILLEGAL message`

MESSAGE_DX

Action: Displays a message string in the data segment whose offset is in DX.

Inputs: DS:DX = Starting address of string
String Format: Same as for MESSAGE.
Outputs: None. DS and DX are unaffected.
Comments: Same as MESSAGE, but MESSAGE_DX takes its string specifier from a register rather than from a user name.
Example:
```
LEA   DX,ILLEGAL    ;Display ILLEGAL message
MESSAGE_DX
```

PRINT_AL

Action: Displays the character in AL, then advances the cursor.
Inputs: AL = Character code.
Outputs: None. AL is unaffected.
Comments: To keep the cursor at the display position, use SHOW_AL instead.
Example:
```
MOV   AL,'P'    ;Display "P", then move the cursor
PRINT_AL
```

PRINT_NUMBER

Action: Displays the signed number in AX.
Inputs: None.
Outputs: None. AX is unaffected.

PRINT$ string-name

Action: Display a string in the data segment.
Inputs: **string-name**
String Format: String beginning with a character count byte.
Outputs: None.
Comments: Same as PRINT$_DX, but PRINT$ obtains its string specifier from a user name rather than from a register.

PRINT$_DX

Action: Displays a string in the data segment whose offset is in DX.
Inputs: DS:DX = Starting address of string
String Format: Same as PRINT$.
Outputs: None. DS and DX are unaffected.
Comments: Same as PRINT$, but PRINT$_DX obtains its string specifier from a register rather than from a user name.

SHOW_AL

Action: Displays the character in AL, but does not move the cursor.
Inputs: AL = Character code
Outputs: None. AL is unaffected.
Comments: To advance the cursor after displaying the character, use PRINT_AL instead.
Example:
```
MOV   AL,'P'    ;Display "P" at the cursor position
SHOW_AL
```

VIDEO_STATE

Action: Reports video state.

Inputs: None.
Outputs: AL = Current mode
AH = Number of columns on screen
BH = Active page

Keyboard Macros

INKEY

Action: Waits for a key, then reads its ASCII code into AL and displays it.
Inputs: None.
Outputs: AL = ASCII code for key
Comments: (1) To read a key without displaying it, use INKEY_I instead.
(2) See Appendix B for ASCII codes.

INKEY_I

Action: Waits for a key, then reads its ASCII code into AL, but does not display it.
Inputs: None.
Outputs: AL = ASCII code for key
Comments: (1) To display the key you read, use INKEY instead.
(2) See Appendix B for ASCII codes.

IN$ string-name

Action: Reads a sequence of keyboard characters into a buffer in the data segment.
Inputs: **string-name** is name of buffer.
Buffer Format: The buffer must be three bytes longer than the string it is to hold. The first byte specifies the maximum string length plus one. For example, the following buffer accepts strings of up to 10 characters:

```
STRING_BUFF  DB  11,12 DUP(?)
```

Outputs: Second byte of the buffer contains the actual length of the input string, in bytes.
Comments: (1) Same as IN$_DX, but IN$ obtains the buffer specifier from the user rather than from a register.
(2) IN$ accepts keys until the user presses Enter. The computer beeps when the buffer is full.
Example: `IN$  STRING_BUFF    ;Read keys into buffer`

IN$_DX

Action: Reads a sequence of keyboard characters into a buffer in the data segment.
Inputs: DS:DX = Starting address of buffer
Buffer Format: Same as IN$.
Outputs: Second byte of the buffer contains the actual length of the input string, in bytes. DS and DX are unaffected.

Comments: (1) Same as IN$, but IN$_DX obtains the buffer specifier from a register rather than from the user.
(2) IN$_DX accepts keys until the user presses Enter. The computer beeps when the buffer is full.

Example:
```
LEA   DX,STRING_BUFF    ;Read keys into buffer
IN$_DX
```

KEY_$2BIN See *Conversion Macros.*

Sound Macros

BEEP

Action: Beeps the speaker for one-half second.
Inputs: None.
Outputs: None.
Comments: Same as SOUND 1000,50.

SOUND freq[,minutes][,seconds][,hundredths]

Action: Produces a tone of a specified frequency and duration.
Inputs: **freq** is in Hertz (19 to 65535).
Outputs: None.
Comments: Same as SOUND_REGS, but SOUND bases the tone on user values rather than register values.

Example:
```
SOUND 262,100    ;Sound Middle C for one second
```

SOUND_DI_BX

Action: Produces a tone of a specified frequency and duration.
Input: DI = Frequency in Hertz (19 to 65535)
CL = Duration in minutes (0 to 255)
BH = Duration in seconds (0 to 255)
BL = Duration in 1/100 seconds (0 to 99)
Outputs: None. Registers are unaffected.
Comments: Same as SOUND, but SOUND_REGS uses register inputs rather than user values.

Example:
```
MOV   DI,262    ;Sound Middle C for one second
MOV   CL,0
MOV   BH,1
MOV   BL,0
SOUND_REGS
```

Time Macros

READ_TIME

Action: Reads the current time.
Inputs: None.
Outputs: (CH) = Hours
(CL) = Minutes

(DH) = Seconds
(DL) = 1/100 seconds

SET_TIME [hours][,minutes][,seconds][,hundredths]

Action: Sets the time.

Inputs: Optional **hours** (0 to 23), **minutes** (0 to 59), **seconds** (0 to 59), and **hundredths** of a second (0 to 99). Omitted operands become 0.

Outputs: None.

Example: `SET_TIME 1,,30    ;Set time to 1:00:30 AM`

Macro Definitions

The remainder of this chapter lists the definitions for each of the macros in the library, in alphabetical order. If you have suggestions about improving any of them, or want to suggest additional definitions, please contact the author through Brady Communications Company.

Cross-References

Many of the macros in the library call other macros. Therefore, if you change or delete a macro, it may affect others. Table 10-4 is a cross-reference table for the library. It lists which macros each macro definition uses and which ones it is used in.

Table 10-4. Cross-reference table for macro library.

Macro	Used in	Uses
$2BIN	KEY_$2BIN	—
BEEP	—	SOUND
BIN2$	PRINT_NUMBER	—
CLS	—	—
CR	CRLF	MOVE_CURSOR, POS
CRLF	—	CR, LF
DELAY	SOUND_REGS	DELAY_AL_BX
DELAY_AL_BX	DELAY	READ_TIME
HOME	—	LOCATE
IN$	KEY_$2BIN	—
IN$_DX	IN$	—
INKEY	—	—
INKEY_I	—	—
KEY_$2BIN	—	$2BIN, IN$
LF	CRLF, TAB	MOVE_CURSOR, POS
LOCATE	HOME	MOVE_CURSOR
MAKE_STACK	—	—

Table 10-4. Cross-reference table for macro library (continued).

Macro	Used in	Uses
MESSAGE	—	MESSAGE_DX
MESSAGE_DX	MESSAGE	—
MOVE_CURSOR	CR, LF, LOCATE	VIDEO_STATE
POP_REGS	—	—
POS	CR, LF, TAB	VIDEO_STATE
PRINT_AL	PRINT$_DX	VIDEO_STATE
PRINT_NUMBER	—	BIN2$, PRINT$
PRINT$	PRINT_NUMBER	PRINT$_DX
PRINT$_DX	PRINT$	—
PUSH_REGS	—	—
RAND	—	—
READ_TIME	DELAY_AL_BX	—
SET_DS	—	—
SET_ES	—	—
SET_TIME	—	—
SHOW_AL	—	VIDEO_STATE
SOUND	BEEP	SOUND_REGS
SOUND_REGS	SOUND	—
TAB	—	LF, POS, VIDEO_STATE
VIDEO_STATE	CR, LF, MOVE_CURSOR, POS, PRINT_AL, SHOW_AL, TAB	—

```
$2BIN   MACRO string_name
        LOCAL BLANKS,CHK_NEG,CHK_POS,GO_CONV,GOOD,NO_GOOD,THRU
        LOCAL CONV_AB,RANGE,NON_DIG,DIGIT,END_CONV,SKIPIT

;;  Convert the specified string to a signed binary number
;;  in AX.  The first byte in the string must hold its
;;  character count.
;;  If the conversion is successful, CF = 0; otherwise, CF = 1.

        PUSH  BX              ;;Save working registers
        PUSH  CX
        SUB   AX,AX           ;;To start, result = 0
        SUB   CX,CX           ;;Read count into CX
        MOV   CL,string_name
        LEA   BX,string_name+1 ;;Put first addr. in BX
BLANKS: CMP   BYTE PTR [BX],' ' ;;Scan past leading blanks
        JNE   CHK_NEG
        INC   BX
        LOOP  BLANKS

;;  Execute these instructions if the first string character
;;  is a minus sign.

CHK_NEG: CMP  BYTE PTR [BX],'-'
        JNE   CHK_POS
        INC   BX              ;;Increment pointer,
        DEC   CX              ;; decrement the count,
        CALL  CONV_AB         ;; and convert the string
        JC    THRU
        CMP   AX,32768        ;;Is the number too small?
        JA    NO_GOOD
        NEG   AX              ;; No. Complement the result
        JS    GOOD

;;  Execute these instructions if the first string character
;;  is not a minus sign.

CHK_POS: CMP  BYTE PTR [BX],'+'
        JNE   GO_CONV
        INC   BX              ;;Increment the pointer,
        DEC   CX              ;; decrement the count,
GO_CONV: CALL CONV_AB         ;; and convert the string
        JC    THRU
        CMP   AX,32767        ;;Is the number too big?
        JA    NO_GOOD
GOOD:   CLC
        JNC   THRU
NO_GOOD: STC                  ;; If so, set Carry flag
THRU:   POP   CX              ;;Restore registers
        POP   BX
        JMP   SKIPIT          ;; and exit
```

```
;;  This subroutine performs the actual conversion.

CONV_AB PROC
        PUSH  BP                ;;Save scratch registers
        PUSH  BX
        PUSH  SI
        MOV   BP,BX             ;;Put pointer in BP
        SUB   BX,BX             ;; and clear BX
RANGE:  CMP   BYTE PTR DS:[BP],'0' ;;If character is not
        JB    NON_DIG           ;; a digit...
        CMP   BYTE PTR DS:[BP],'9'
        JBE   DIGIT
NON_DIG: STC                    ;; set the Carry flag
        JC    END_CONV          ;; and exit.
DIGIT:  MOV   SI,10             ;;The character is a digit,
        PUSH  DX
        MUL   SI                ;; so multiply AX by 10
        POP   DX
        MOV   BL,DS:[BP]        ;;Fetch ASCII code,
        AND   BX,0FH            ;; save only low bits,
        ADD   AX,BX             ;; and update result.
        JC    END_CONV          ;;Exit if result is too big.
        INC   BP                ;;Otherwise, increment BP
        LOOP  RANGE             ;; and continue
        CLC                     ;;When done, clear Carry
END_CONV: POP SI                ;;Restore registers
        POP   BX
        POP   BP
        RET
CONV_AB ENDP
SKIPIT: NOP
        ENDM

BIN2$   MACRO string_name
        LOCAL FILL_BUFF,CLR_DVD,NO_MORE

;;  Convert a signed number in AX to a string in the data
;;  segment.  String must be seven bytes long; the first
;;  byte is used to hold a character count.

        PUSH  DX                ;;Save affected registers
        PUSH  CX
        PUSH  BX
        PUSH  SI
        PUSH  AX
        LEA   BX,string_name+1  ;;BX points to first char.
        MOV   CX,6              ;;Fill buffer with spaces
FILL_BUFF: MOV  BYTE PTR [BX],' '
        INC   BX
        LOOP  FILL_BUFF
        MOV   SI,10             ;;Get ready to divide by 10
        OR    AX,AX             ;;If value is negative,
        JNS   CLR_DVD
        NEG   AX                ;; make it positive
```

```
CLR_DVD: SUB   DX,DX          ;;Clear upper half of dividend
         DIV   SI             ;;Divide AX by 10
         ADD   DX,'0'         ;;Convert remainder to ASCII digit
         DEC   BX             ;;Back up through buffer
         MOV   [BX],DL        ;;Store char. in the string
         OR    AX,AX          ;;All done?
         JNZ   CLR_DVD        ;; If not, get next digit
         POP   AX             ;; Yes.  Get original value
         OR    AX,AX          ;;Was it negative?
         JNS   NO_MORE
         DEC   BX             ;; Yes.  Store sign
         MOV   BYTE PTR [BX],'-'
NO_MORE: MOV   string_name,6  ;;Record char. count
         POP   SI             ;;Restore registers
         POP   BX
         POP   CX
         POP   DX
         ENDM

BEEP     MACRO

;;  Beep the speaker for 1/2 second at frequency of 1000 Hz.
         SOUND 1000,50
         ENDM

CLS      MACRO

;;  Clear the screen and home the cursor.

         PUSH  AX
         PUSH  BX
         MOV   AH,15          ;;Read the video mode
         INT   10H
         MOV   AH,0           ;;Set the video mode
         INT   10H
         POP   BX
         POP   AX
         ENDM

CR       MACRO

;; Move the cursor to beginning of current line.

         PUSH  CX             ;;Save affected registers
         PUSH  DX
         POS                  ;;Read row number into DH
         SUB   DL,DL          ;;Make column 0
         MOVE_CURSOR
         POP   DX
         POP   CX
         ENDM
```

```
CRLF    MACRO

;;  Move cursor to beginning of next line

        CR                      ;;Carriage return
        LF                      ;;Line feed
        ENDM

DELAY   MACRO minutes,seconds,hsecs

;;  Wait for a specified interval.

        PUSH   AX
        PUSH   BX
        MOV    AL,minutes       ;;Move minutes into AL
        MOV    BH,seconds       ;;     seconds into BH
        MOV    BL,hsecs         ;;     hundredths into BL
        DELAY_AL_BX             ;;Generate the delay
        POP    BX
        POP    AX
        ENDM

DELAY_AL_BX MACRO
        LOCAL SECS,MINS,HRS,CHECK,QUIT

;;  Wait for the interval specified in AL (minutes), BH
;;  (seconds), and BL (hundredths).

        PUSH   AX
        PUSH   BX
        PUSH   CX
        PUSH   DX
        READ_TIME               ;;Read current time

;;  Add the current time to the input values.

        MOV    AH,CH            ;;Hours
        ADD    AL,CL            ;;Minutes
        ADD    BH,DH            ;;Seconds
        ADD    BL,DL            ;;Hundredths

;;  Propagate any carryover.

        CMP    BL,100
        JB     SECS
        SUB    BL,100
        INC    BH
SECS:   CMP    BH,60
        JB     MINS
        SUB    BH,60
        INC    AL
MINS:   CMP    AL,60
        JB     HRS
        SUB    AL,60
        INC    AH
```

```
HRS:     CMP   AH,24
         JNE   CHECK
         SUB   AH,AH
CHECK:   READ_TIME              ;;Read the time again
         CMP   CX,AX
         JA    QUIT
         JB    CHECK
         CMP   DX,BX
         JB    CHECK            ;;Repeat for delay time
QUIT:    POP   DX               ;;Restore registers
         POP   CX
         POP   BX
         POP   AX
         ENDM

HOME     MACRO

;;   Move cursor to upper left-hand corner.

         LOCATE  0,0
         ENDM

INKEY    MACRO

;;   Read the next key into AL, and display it.

         PUSH  CX               ;;Save registers
         PUSH  AX
         MOV   AH,1             ;;Select key option
         INT   21H              ;;Read the key
         POP   CX               ;;Restore AH
         MOV   AH,CH
         POP   CX               ;;Restore CX
         ENDM

INKEY_I MACRO

;;   Read the next key into AL, but don't display it.

         PUSH  CX               ;;Save registers
         PUSH  AX
         MOV   AH,8             ;;Select key option
         INT   21H              ;;Read the key
         POP   CX               ;;Restore AH
         MOV   AH,CH
         POP   CX               ;;Restore CX
         ENDM
```

```
IN$_DX  MACRO

;;  Read keyboard characters into a buffer in the data
;;  segment.  DS:DX = Buffer address.

        PUSH   AX
        MOV    AH,0AH          ;;Select keyboard read option
        INT    21H             ;;Read keyboard
        POP    AX
        ENDM

IN$     MACRO string_name

;;  Read keyboard characters into the specified buffer
;;  in the data segment.

        PUSH   DX
        LEA    DX,string_name
        IN$_DX
        POP    DX
        ENDM

KEY_$2BIN MACRO
        LOCAL TEMP,SAVE

;;  Read a sequence of keyboard characters and convert them
;;  to a signed number in AX.

        JMP    SAVE            ;;Skip temporary buffer
TEMP    DB     7,8 DUP(?)
SAVE:   PUSH   DS              ;;Save affected registers
        PUSH   CX
        MOV    CX,CS           ;;Make DS point to code segment
        MOV    DS,CX
        IN$    TEMP            ;;Read string into TEMP
        $2BIN  TEMP+1          ;;Make the conversion
        POP    CX              ;;Restore registers
        POP    DS
        ENDM

LF      MACRO

;; Move the cursor to next line (same column position).
;; If it is on the bottom line, move it to the top line.

        PUSH   CX              ;;Save affected registers
        PUSH   DX
        POS                    ;;Read row number into DH
        INC    DH              ;; and increment it
        MOVE_CURSOR            ;;Move cursor to new position
        POP    DX
        POP    CX
        ENDM
```

```
LOCATE   MACRO row,col

;;  Move the cursor to the specified row and column.

        PUSH  DX
        MOV   DH,row         ;;Move the cursor
        MOV   DL,col
        MOVE_CURSOR
        POP   DX
        ENDM

MAKE_STACK MACRO stack_name

;;  Set up the stack segment

stack_name SEGMENT PARA STACK 'STACK'
        DB    64 DUP('STACK   ')
stack_name ENDS
        ENDM

MESSAGE MACRO string_name

;;  Display the specified data segment string. String must
;;  end with a $ character.

        PUSH  DX
        LEA   DX,DS:string_name
        MESSAGE_DX
        POP   DX
        ENDM

MESSAGE_DX MACRO

;;  Display a message string in the data segment whose
;;  offset is in DX.  String must end with a $ character.

        PUSH  AX
        MOV   AH,9           ;;Select string display option
        INT   21H            ;;Display the string
        POP   AX
        ENDM

MOVE_CURSOR MACRO
        LOCAL OK,VS

;;  Move the cursor to the row and column positions in
;;  DH and DL, respectively.  If the row exceeds 24 or
;;  the column exceeds 79, MOVE_CURSOR makes them 0.

        PUSH  AX             ;;Save affected registers
        PUSH  BX
        CMP   DH,24          ;;Wrap-around inputs if needed
        JNA   OK
        SUB   DH,DH
```

```
OK:     CMP   DL,79
        JNA   VS
        SUB   DL,DL
VS:     VIDEO_STATE          ;;Read display page into BH
        MOV   AH,2           ;;Select cursor-moving option
        INT   10H            ;;Move the cursor
        POP   BX             ;;Restore registers
        POP   AX
        ENDM

POP_REGS MACRO  reg_list

;;  Retrieve registers from stack

        IRP   reg,<reg_list>
        POP   reg
        ENDM
        ENDM

POS     MACRO

;;  Read the current row and column numbers into DH and DL,
;;  and the current cursor mode into CH and CL.

        PUSH  AX             ;;Save affected registers
        PUSH  BX
        VIDEO_STATE          ;;Read display page into BH
        MOV   AH,3           ;;Select cursor-reading option
        INT   10H            ;;Read the cursor
        POP   BX             ;;Restore registers
        POP   AX
        ENDM

PRINT_AL MACRO

;;  Display the character in AL, then advance the cursor.

        PUSH  AX             ;;Save affected registers
        PUSH  BX
        PUSH  CX
        PUSH  AX             ;;Preserve input value
        VIDEO_STATE          ;;Read display page into BH
        POP   AX             ;;Restore input value
        MOV   CX,1           ;;Display just one character
        MOV   AH,14          ;;Select display option
        INT   10H            ;;Display the character
        POP   CX
        POP   BX
        POP   AX
        ENDM
```

```
PRINT_NUMBER MACRO
        LOCAL TEMP,SAVE

;;  Display the signed contents of AX.

        JMP   SAVE              ;;Skip temporary buffer
TEMP    DB    7 DUP(?)
SAVE:   PUSH  DS                ;;Save affected registers
        PUSH  CX
        MOV   CX,CS             ;;Make DS point to code segment
        MOV   DS,CX
        BIN2$ TEMP              ;;Make the conversion
        PRINT$ TEMP             ;;Display it
        POP   CX                ;;Restore registers
        POP   DS
        ENDM

PRINT$  MACRO string_name

;;  Display a specified data segment string.
;;  First byte in the string holds the character count.

        PUSH  DX
        LEA   DX,string_name
        PRINT$_DX
        POP   DX
        ENDM

PRINT$_DX MACRO
        LOCAL STRIP,NEXT_C,NO_BLNK

;;  Display a data segment string whose offset is in DX.
;;  First byte in the string holds the character count.

        PUSH  AX                ;;Save affected registers
        PUSH  CX
        PUSH  SI
        SUB   CX,CX             ;;Clear count register
        MOV   SI,DX             ;;Put string pointer in SI
        MOV   CL,[SI]           ;;Read character count
        INC   SI                ;;Point to first character
STRIP:  LODSB                   ;;Skip leading blanks
        CMP   AL,' '
        JNE   NO_BLNK
        LOOP  STRIP
NEXT_C: LODSB                   ;;Read character
NO_BLNK: PRINT_AL               ;; and display it
        LOOP  NEXT_C
        POP   SI
        POP   CX
        POP   AX
        ENDM
```

```
PUSH_REGS MACRO reg_list

;;   Save registers on stack

          IRP    reg,<reg_list>
          PUSH   reg
          ENDM
          ENDM

RAND      MACRO limit
          LOCAL STRIP

;;   Generate a pseudorandom integer between 0 and "limit,"
;;   inclusive, and return it in AL.

          PUSH   CX              ;;Save affected registers
          PUSH   DX
          PUSH   AX
          MOV    AH,0            ;;Read the timer
          INT    1AH
          MOV    AX,DX           ;;Move low count into AX
          MOV    CL,limit        ;;Move limit into CL

;;   Strip enough high bits off the dividend (AX) to
;;   ensure against divide overflow.

          MOV    DH,3FH          ;;Set up AND mask in DH
          CMP    CL,64
          JAE    STRIP
          SHR    DH,1            ;;If limit < 64, strip off 3 bits
          CMP    CL,32
          JAE    STRIP
          SHR    DH,1            ;;If limit < 32, strip off 4 bits
          CMP    CL,16
          JAE    STRIP
          SHR    DH,1            ;;If limit < 16, strip off 5 bits
          CMP    CL,8
          JAE    STRIP
          SHR    DH,1            ;;If limit < 8, strip off 6 bits
STRIP:    AND    AH,DH           ;;Strip off the bits
          DIV    CL              ;;Divide result in AX by limit in CL
          MOV    AL,AH           ;;Put remainder in AL
          POP    CX              ;;Restore AH
          MOV    AH,CH
          POP    DX              ;;Restore other registers
          POP    CX
          ENDM
```

```
READ_TIME MACRO

;;   Read the time into CH (hours), CL (minutes), DH
;;   (seconds), and DL (1/100 seconds).

        PUSH   AX
        MOV    AH,2CH            ;;Select time-reading option
        INT    21H               ;;Read the time
        POP    AX
        ENDM

SET_DS  MACRO dseg_name

;;   Load the address of the data segment into DS.

        PUSH   AX
        MOV    AX,dseg_name
        MOV    DS,AX
        POP    AX
        ENDM

SET_ES  MACRO eseg_name

;;   Load the address of the extra segment into ES.

        PUSH   AX
        MOV    AX,eseg_name
        MOV    ES,AX
        POP    AX
        ENDM

SET_TIME MACRO hours,minutes,seconds,hsecs

;;   Set the time.  Blank operands become zero.

        PUSH   AX                ;;Save affected registers
        PUSH   CX
        PUSH   DX
        MOV    CH,hours          ;;Read user values
        MOV    CL,minutes
        MOV    DH,seconds
        MOV    DL,hsecs
        MOV    AH,2DH            ;;Select time set option
        INT    21H               ;;Set the time
        POP    DX
        POP    CX
        POP    AX
        ENDM
```

```
SHOW_AL MACRO

;;  Display the character in AL.  (Keep cursor where it is.)

        PUSH   AX              ;;Save affected registers
        PUSH   BX
        PUSH   CX
        PUSH   AX              ;;Preserve input value
        VIDEO_STATE            ;;Read display page into BH
        POP    AX              ;;Restore input value
        MOV    CX,1            ;;Display just one character
        MOV    AH,10           ;;Select display option
        INT    10H             ;;Display the character
        POP    CX
        POP    BX
        POP    AX
        ENDM

SOUND   MACRO freq,minutes,seconds,hsecs

;;  Produce a tone of a specified frequency and duration.
;;  Frequency is in Hertz (19 to 65535).

        PUSH   DI
        PUSH   CX
        PUSH   BX
        MOV    DI,freq
        MOV    CL,minutes
        MOV    BH,seconds
        MOV    BL,hsecs
        SOUND_REGS
        POP    BX
        POP    CX
        POP    DI
        ENDM

SOUND_REGS MACRO

;;  Produce a tone of a specified frequency and duration.
;;  Inputs: DI = Frequency in Hertz (19 to 65535)
;;  CL = Duration in minutes (0 to 255)
;;  BH = Duration in seconds (0 to 255)
;;  BL = Duration in 1/100 seconds (0 to 99)

        PUSH   AX              ;;Save affected registers
        PUSH   CX
        PUSH   DX
        PUSH   DI
        MOV    AL,0B6H         ;;Write timer mode register
        OUT    43H,AL
        MOV    DX,14H          ;;Timer divisor =
        MOV    AX,533H*896     ;; 533H*896/Frequency
        DIV    DI
        OUT    42H,AL          ;;Write Timer 2 count low byte
        MOV    AL,AH
```

```
        OUT    42H,AL          ;;Write Timer 2 count high byte
        IN     AL,61H          ;;Get current Port B setting
        MOV    AH,AL           ;; and save it in AH
        OR     AL,3            ;;Turn speaker on
        OUT    61H,AL
        MOV    AL,CL           ;;Wait for the specified interval
        DELAY_AL_BX
        MOV    AL,AH           ;;Recover value of port
        OUT    61H,AL
        POP    DI              ;;Restore registers
        POP    DX
        POP    CX
        POP    AX
        ENDM

TAB     MACRO column
        LOCAL DO_TAB,GET_BH

;;  Move cursor to specified column (0 to 79).
;;  If cursor is already beyond this position, TAB goes to
;;  the specified column on the next line.

        PUSH   AX              ;;Save affected registers
        PUSH   BX
        PUSH   CX
        PUSH   DX
        POS                    ;;Read column number into DL
        CMP    DL,column       ;;Cursor beyond this column?
        JBE    DO_TAB
        LF                     ;; If so, advance to next line
        POS                    ;;  and read new cursor position
DO_TAB: MOV    DL,column       ;; Enter user's column number
        CMP    DL,79           ;;Is user's entry too large?
        JNA    GET_BH
        MOV    DL,79           ;; If so, use column 79
GET_BH: VIDEO_STATE            ;;Read active page into BH
        MOV    AH,2            ;;Select cursor-moving option
        INT    10H             ;;Move the cursor
        POP    DX
        POP    CX
        POP    BX
        POP    AX
        ENDM

VIDEO_STATE MACRO

;;  Read current mode into AL, no. of columns into AH,
;;  and active page into BH.

        MOV    AH,15           ;;Select video state option
        INT    10H             ;;Read video state
        ENDM
```

```
        PAGE   ,132
TITLE   MATHCHIP - Check for Math Coprocessor
.287

;  This procedures determines whether the computer
;  has an 80287 Math Coprocessor.

STACK   SEGMENT PARA STACK 'STACK'
        DB    64 DUP('STACK    ')
STACK   ENDS

DSEG    SEGMENT PARA PUBLIC 'DATA'
MP      DB    'Computer has an 80287 $'
NO_MP   DB    'Computer does not have an 80287 $'
DSEG    ENDS

CSEG    SEGMENT PARA PUBLIC 'CODE'
        ASSUME  CS:CSEG,DS:DSEG,SS:STACK

ENTRY   PROC   FAR           ;Entry point

;Set up the stack to contain the proper values so this
;program can return to DOS or DEBUG.

        PUSH   DS
        SUB    AX,AX
        PUSH   AX

        MOV    AX,DSEG       ;Initialize DS
        MOV    DS,AX

        FINIT                ;Initialize the coprocessor
        FSTSW AX             ;Retrieve 80287 status word
        OR     AL,AL         ;Is 80287 present?
        JNZ    NO_287
        LEA    DX,MP         ; Yes.
        JMP    TELL_USER
NO_287: LEA    DX,NO_MP      ; No.
TELL_USER: MOV  AH,09H       ;Print the appropriate message
        INT    21H
        RET                  ;Return to DOS
ENTRY   ENDP
CSEG    ENDS
        END    ENTRY
```

11

Object Libraries

In Chapter 10, we described how to create *macro libraries*, disk files that contain macro definitions. To use any macro in a library, simply INCLUDE the entire library in your program, and mention the macro's name. Therefore, macro libraries save you the bother of typing a macro in every program where you need it.

The Macro Assembler provides a similar facility for program modules. Specifically, it lets you create *object libraries*, disk files that contain object modules. To use any procedure in an object library, you CALL the procedure in your program and declare it external (with an EXTRN statement), as usual. Then, when you run the Linker, you link the library to the calling program module. The Linker automatically extracts the procedure you CALLed, just as if it were in a module by itself.

An object library saves having to remember which disk a procedure is on, as well as the inevitable disk-shuffling job that ensues. Now you must keep track of only one disk, the one that contains the object library. An object library is convenient even if you have a hard disk, because it saves you from specifying each individual module in your LINK command. Simply link the calling program to the library and the Linker extracts the modules it needs.

11.1 Building Object Libraries

The program that handles object libraries is the Library Manager (LIB.EXE) on the assembler disk. To create an object library, you must tell the Library Manager its name and specify the first object module you want to put in the library. To do this, put your assembler disk in drive A and the disk that contains the object module in drive B, then start the computer as usual. Get the B> prompt on the screen, then enter a command of the form

a:lib *libname* + *objmod*;

The Manager automatically supplies the extensions LIB and OBJ to the library and object module names.

For example, to create a library named OBJECT.LIB with SORT.OBJ as its first entry, enter

a:lib object + sort;

11.2 Operating on Object Libraries

Once you have created a library, you can add new modules to it by repeating the preceding command. For example, to add MULU32.OBJ to the OBJECT library, enter

a:lib object + mulu32;

The + here means "add to library." To delete a module from the library, use - (minus) instead of +. For example, to remove MULU32.OBJ, enter

a:lib object - mulu32;

You may also want to copy a module from the library, perhaps to add it to a different library. This requires the * operator. For example, to make a copy of SORT.OBJ, enter

a:lib object * sort;

After that, SORT is still in the library, but the disk contains a copy of it named SORT.OBJ.

The Library Manager also lets you combine the basic operations. The operator -+ replaces a library module with the contents of an object file of the same name. In other words, -+ *updates* a library. For example,

a:lib object -+ sort;

removes SORT from the OBJECT library, then replaces it with the contents of SORT.OBJ from the disk.

Similarly, the operator -* removes an object module from a library, but creates a copy of it on the disk. For example,

a:lib object -* sort

moves SORT from the OBJECT library to a new file called SORT.OBJ.

Getting a Directory of a Library

If you forget which object modules are in a library, you can get the Library Manager to generate a directory file. To do this, enter a command of this form:

a: lib *libname,libname.dir*;

To display the directory, enter

type *libname.dir*

Besides the names of the object modules, the directory lists the symbols that are declared PUBLIC in each one. This tells you the names by which your calling program must refer to procedures, variables, and equates in the library.

11.3 Using Object Libraries

As we mentioned at the beginning of this chapter, to use an object library, you must *link* it to the object module (or modules) that contains your program. The Linker can display a special prompt for this purpose. To obtain it, link using the form

a:link module,,NUL

When the screen shows

```
Libraries [.LIB]:
```

enter the name of your library, then press Return. For example, to link the OBJECT library to an object module called MAIN_PROG, enter **a:link main_prog,,NUL**, then

```
Libraries [.LIB]: object
```

If your program needs object modules from several different libraries, list them in response to the *Libraries* prompt. For example,

```
Libraries [.LIB]: lib1+lib2+lib3
```

12

Structured Programming

One of the best features of the Macro Assembler is that it lets you write *structured* assembly language programs. By "structured," we mean programs that contain high-level statements that perform loops, conditional jumps, and other control tasks that would otherwise take several assembly language instructions. In effect, the structure statements provide the same kinds of complex operations as BASIC. For example, one family of structure statements or *logic structure* does the same thing as an IF-THEN-ELSE statement in BASIC, while another provides a function similar to FOR-NEXT.

But structured programming involves more than simply using structure statements instead of instructions. Rather, it is a *philosophy* of software design that involves

- Top-down design. (Remember, this is an approach in which you build programs by starting with comments and add more and more detail in gradual steps.)
- Label-free programs.
- "GOTO"-free programs (no conditional or unconditional jump instructions).
- Indentation to show levels of nesting in logic structures.
- Listings that are more self-documenting.

The purpose for doing all this is to increase the *quality* of assembly language programs. Quality improvement should be apparent in several areas:

- The developer will understand the logic of the program better.
- The listing will be more readable to someone trying to make changes when he or she is not the author.
- Because the program is more readily understandable, there should be fewer "bugs" in it.
- Reliability and serviceability are improved. This means the program is more apt to work correctly as designed, and future modifications can be

made with more assurances that the changes will fit within the present design without introducing new bugs.
- Improved readability will help make the listing its own best documentation.

The feature that allows you to use structure statements is a program called *SALUT* (for Structured Assembly Language Utility) on the Macro Assembler disk. What you do is enter your program, then run SALUT to convert the structure statements into standard assembly language instructions. From there, you assemble and link the program as usual.

This chapter describes SALUT's structure statements and gives examples and guidelines for using them. It also discusses the steps you must use to assemble and format structured programs.

12.1 Structure Statements and Logic Flow Structures

There are more than a dozen different structure statements, but you must use them in prescribed combinations, in what the Macro Assembler manual calls *logic flow structures*. The manual defines eight different logic flow structures, but we can treat them as three groups:

- *IF* is a decision-making structure. It makes the 80286 execute or skip a set of instructions, depending on whether a specified condition is satisfied. The IF structure is similar to IF-THEN in BASIC.
- *DO* is a repetition structure. It makes the 80286 loop through one or more sets of instructions until a specified condition is satisfied. The DO structure is similar to FOR-NEXT in BASIC.
- *SEARCH* is also a repetition structure, but it is used when you care *which* of several conditions caused the looping to stop. SEARCH executes a unique block of instructions for each exit condition.

Conditions for Logic Flow Structures

Table 12-1 lists the conditions you can use to control the IF, DO, and SEARCH structures. Note that except for NCXZ, they are the same conditions as those for the conditional transfer (Jx) instructions we described in Chapter 3.

A word of caution: CXZ and NCXZ are not always legal in structures. More on this in Section 12.5.

Table 12-1. Conditions for logic flow structures.

Condition	Description	True if...
A	Above	CF = 0 and ZF = 0
AE	Above or Equal	CF = 0
B	Below	CF = 1
BE	Below or Equal	CF = 1 or ZF = 1
C	Carry	CF = 1
CXZ	CX Register is Zero	(CX) = 0
E	Equal	ZF = 1
*G	Greater	ZF = 0 and SF = OF
*GE	Greater or Equal	SF = OF
*L	Less	SF ≠ OF
*LE	Less or Equal	ZF = 1 or SF ≠ OF
NA	Not Above	CF = 1 or ZF = 1
NAE	Not Above nor Equal	CF = 1
NB	Not Below	CF = 0
NBE	Not Below nor Equal	CF = 0 and ZF = 0
NC	No Carry	CF = 0
NCXZ	CX Register Not Zero	(CX) ≠ 0
NE	Not Equal	ZF = 0
*NG	Not Greater	ZF =1 or SF ≠ OF
*NGE	Not Greater nor Equal	SF ≠ OF
*NL	Not Less	SF = OF
*NLE	Not Less nor Equal	ZF = 0 and SF = OF
*NO	No Overflow	OF =0
NP	No Parity (Odd)	PF = 0
*NS	No Sign	SF = 0
NZ	Not Zero	ZF = 0
*O	Overflow	OF = 1
P	Parity (Even)	PF = 1
PE	Parity Even	PF = 1
PO	Parity Odd	PF = 0
*S	Sign	SF = 1
Z	Zero	ZF = 1

*Pertinent for signed (two's-complement) arithmetic.

12.2 IF Structure

IF makes the 80286 either execute or skip a set of instructions, depending on whether a specified condition is true or false. Its basic form is

```
$IF   cond
      A
$ENDIF
```

where *cond* is the test condition (one of the conditions in Table 12-1) and *A* is a block of instructions. If *cond* is true, the 80286 executes the instructions; otherwise, it skips to the statement that follows $ENDIF. (Note that this is the opposite of a conditional jump instruction; a conditional jump *skips* the instructions if the condition is true.) Figure 12-1(A) is a flowchart of the IF structure.

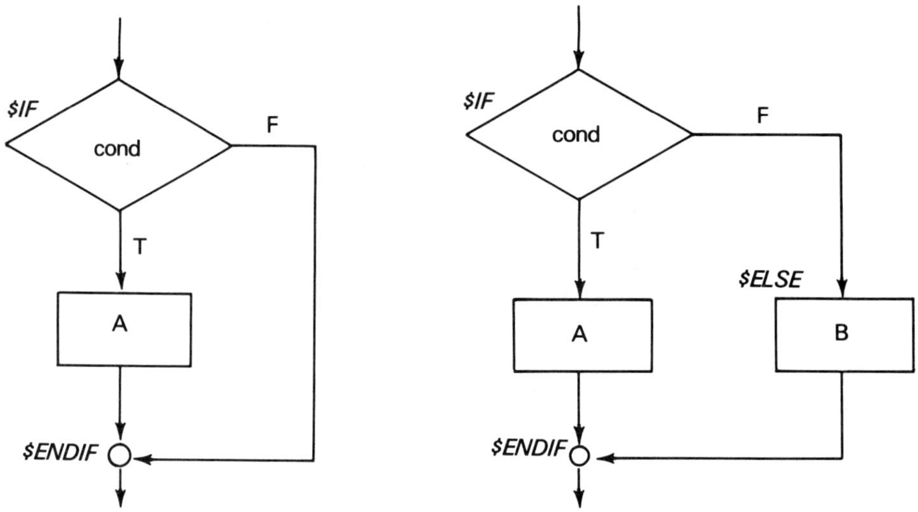

(A) IF (B) IF with ELSE

Figure 12-1. IF structures.

For example, to convert the number in BX to an absolute value, use:

```
CMP   BX,0          ;Value negative?
$IF   L
      NEG   BX      ;If so, make it positive
$ENDIF
```

ELSE Option

As in BASIC, you can also insert an ELSE term to make the 80286 execute an alternate set of instructions if the condition is false. Then IF has the following form:

```
$IF   cond
      A     (Executed if cond is true)
```

```
$ELSE
      B    (Executed if cond is false)
$ENDIF
```

Figure 12-1(B) shows a flowchart of how the $IF-$ELSE-$ENDIF structure operates.

How the IF Structure Operates

The statements $IF, $ELSE, and $ENDIF are actually commands for SALUT. When you run SALUT, it converts these statements to comment lines (so the assembler will ignore them), then generates their assembly language definitions. After that, the assembler can assemble the program as though $IF, $ELSE, and $ENDIF were never there. In the following sections we will describe how SALUT converts an $IF-$ENDIF structure, then how it converts an $IF-$ELSE-$ENDIF structure.

Instructions Generated by $IF-$ENDIF

When SALUT encounters an $IF, it generates a conditional transfer (Jx) instruction that makes the 80286 skip the statements between $IF and the next $ENDIF. Note the word "skip" here. This tells you that the assembler substitutes a Jx instruction that is the *reverse* of what the $IF operand calls for! Hence, it replaces *$IF Z* with *JNZ* and *$IF A* with *JNA*. Of course, since each conditional transfer instruction requires a target, SALUT inserts a label after $ENDIF. For instance, after SALUT has processed $IF and $ENDIF, our preceding example will look like this:

```
      CMP  BX,0          ;Value negative?
;     $IF  L
      JNL  $$IF1
           NEG  BX       ;If so, make it positive
;     $ENDIF
$$IF1:
```

(We just used $$IF1 for illustration; we neither know nor care what label SALUT actually substitutes.)

Instructions Generated by $IF-$ELSE-$ENDIF

For an $IF-$ELSE-$ENDIF structure, SALUT replaces $IF with a Jx to a label following $ELSE, replaces $ENDIF with a second label, and replaces $ELSE with a "short" JMP to the label at $ENDIF. In other words, in the following generalized listings, SALUT translates the statements on the left into those on the right.

```
$IF   cond                            JNcond $$IF1
  A                                   A
$ELSE                                 JMP SHORT $$EN1
                          $$IF1:
  B                                   B
$ENDIF                    $$EN1:
```

Operand Options

The general forms for $IF and $ELSE are:

```
$IF    cond[,AND/OR][,LONG]
$ELSE  [LONG]
```

where *AND* and *OR* let you specify multiple conditions and *LONG* lets you use long blocks of instructions within the structure.

AND and OR Options

So far, we have discussed IF structures that depend only on a single condition. However, as in BASIC, you can make IF consider a combination of conditions with either an AND or an OR.

There are some differences between these assembly language conditionals and those in BASIC, however. For one thing, the processor considers each term in the order it appears; there are no parentheses to tell it how to precede. For another, each AND or OR condition requires a separate $IF statement, so you may put instructions between them.

Here is the general form of $IF with two ANDed terms:

```
      ..    (Test 1)
      ..
$IF   cond1,AND
      ..    (Test 2)
      ..
$IF   cond2
      ..    (Both cond1 and cond2 are true)
      ..
$ENDIF
```

Note that the "Test 2" instructions execute only if *cond1* is true. If it is false, the processor skips to whatever statement follows $ENDIF. (Note also that we use only one $ENDIF, because the AND connects the $IF statements to make one big $IF.)

The instructions that follow the first $IF statement can be used to set up the flag(s) for the second $IF. For example, to print "Weight okay." if WEIGHT is between 31 and 34, you can use:

```
      CMP   WEIGHT,31
$IF   AE,AND
      CMP   WEIGHT,34
$IF   BE
      (Print "Weight okay.")
$ENDIF
```

Of course, you can also include a $ELSE term to do something (say, print "Weight out of range.") if either condition is not satisfied.

Here is the general form of $IF with two ORed terms:

```
      ..    (Test 1)
      ..
$IF   cond1,OR
      ..    (Test 2)
      ..
$IF   cond2
      ..    (cond1 or cond2 is true)
      ..
$ENDIF
```

Here, the processor executes the "Test 2" instructions only if the *cond1* test fails.

LONG Jumps

Because SALUT replaces $IF and $ELSE statements with Jx and JMP SHORT instructions, a block can be no longer than 127 bytes. In 127 bytes, you can put about 50 or 60 instructions, so this is usually no limitation. However, if your IF structure includes a lot of instructions, you must declare $IF or $ELSE *LONG*.

For example, you can use

```
$IF   A,LONG
```

LONG makes SALUT replace *$IF A* with

```
        JA $$XL1
        JMP $$IF1
$$XL1:
```

rather than with *JNA $$IF1*.

12.3 DO Structure

DO makes the 80286 repeat blocks of instructions until a specified condition is satisfied. The DO structure is available in three forms:

- *DO UNTIL* repeats a block of instructions until a condition at the end becomes true.
- *DO WHILE* executes a block of instructions until a condition at the start becomes true. (In other words, it "does" the block while the condition is false.) If the condition is initially true, it skips the block altogether.
- *DO COMPLEX* is a combination of DO UNTIL and DO WHILE that involves two blocks of instructions. It executes the first block, then tests the condition. If the condition is true, it executes the second block and starts again; otherwise, it skips the second block and exits.

Note: The words UNTIL, WHILE, and COMPLEX simply help us distinguish between the three forms of the DO structure. *Don't* enter these words into your programs. (However, IBM *has* provided an alternate form of DO COMPLEX in which you must type the word COMPLEX, but we won't discuss it here.)

DO UNTIL

DO UNTIL structures have the general form

```
$DO
      A
$ENDDO   cond
```

where *cond* is the condition that makes the looping stop. Because the processor tests *cond* at the end of the loop, the instructions always execute at least once. Figure 12-2(A) is a flowchart that shows how DO UNTIL operates.

The DO UNTIL structure is often used to repeat instructions based on a count value in CX. For example:

```
MOV      CX,10
$DO
         ..    (These instructions will be repeated 10 times.)
         ..
$ENDDO   LOOP
```

Here, LOOP decrements CX and loops to $DO if CX is nonzero. The equivalent sequence in BASIC is:

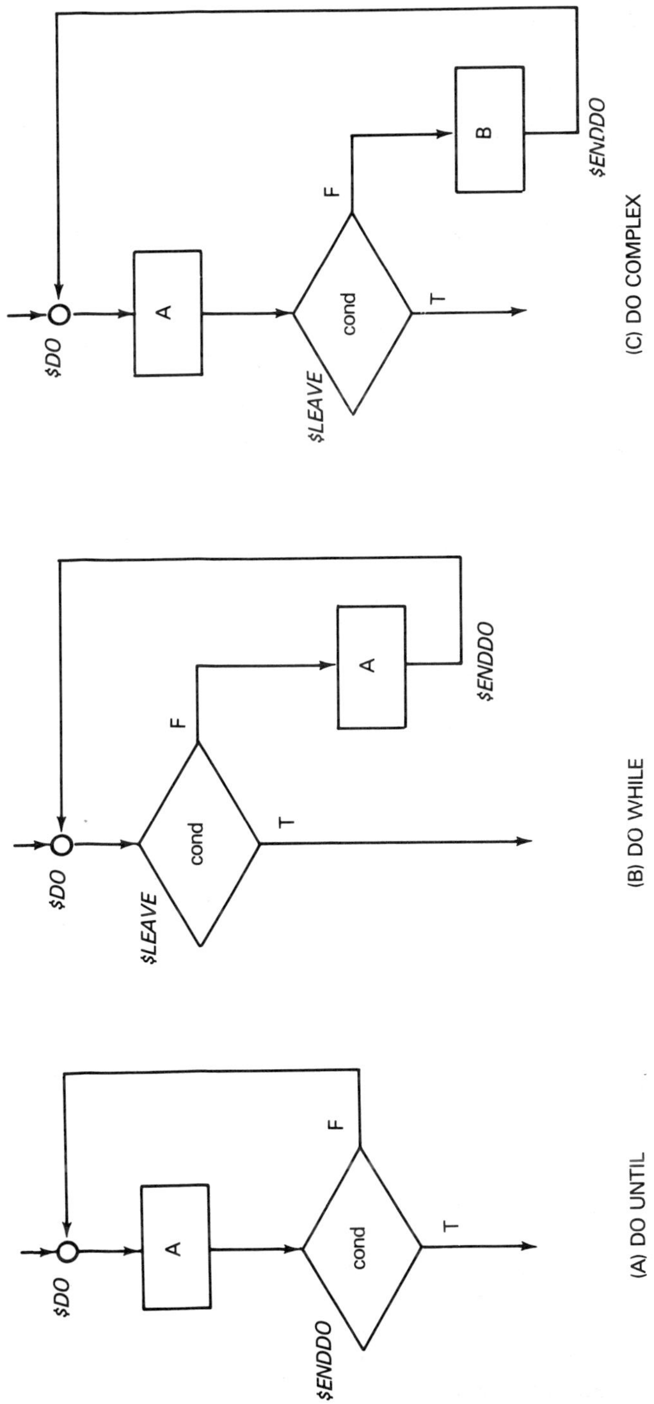

Figure 12-2. DO structures.

```
FOR X=10 TO 1 STEP -1
..
..
NEXT X
```

DO WHILE

The DO WHILE structure has the general form

```
$DO
$LEAVE   cond
      A
$ENDDO
```

where *cond* is the condition that makes the looping stop. Figure 12-2(B) shows a flowchart for DO WHILE.

Note a DO WHILE tests *cond* before the loop instructions are executed, rather than after, as in a DO UNTIL. Hence, if *cond* is initially false, the processor LEAVEs the loop without ever executing it. In effect, DO WHILE says, "Do the following instructions while *cond* has not yet happened."

For example, you can use the DO WHILE form to skip a CX-based loop operation if CX is already zero, as in

```
$DO
$LEAVE   CXZ
      ..
      ..
$ENDDO   LOOP
```

DO COMPLEX

The DO COMPLEX structure is similar to DO WHILE, but it lets you do something both before and after the LEAVE test—thus making the exit in the middle of the loop. The general form is

```
$DO
      A
$LEAVE   cond
      B
$ENDDO
```

As before, *cond* is the condition that makes the looping stop. Figure 12-2(C) shows a flowchart for DO COMPLEX.

Here, the A block instructions establish *cond*, while the B block instructions do whatever a false *cond* implies. For example, to delay a program until the user has entered a correct password, use the following approach:

```
$DO
        (Display "Please enter your password."
        (Check password.  If valid, make CF = 1.)
$LEAVE  C
        (Display "Invalid password.  Please try again.")
$ENDDO
```

Operand Options

Like $IF in Section 12.2, $ENDDO and $LEAVE have *AND* and *OR* options that let you combine conditions and a *LONG* option that lets you use long blocks of instructions. $ENNDO also has *LOOP* options that save you the trouble of decrementing CX. The general forms are:

```
$ENDDO  [cond[,AND/OR]][,LONG]
$ENDDO  [LOOPx][,LONG]
$LEAVE  cond[,AND/OR][,LONG]
```

LOOP Options

For counting loops based on CX, SALUT lets you omit the DEC CX instruction by using the form *$ENDDO LOOP*. That is, instead of

```
$DO
        ..
        ..
        DEC   CX
$ENDDO  CXZ
```

you can use the simpler form

```
$DO
        ..
        ..
$ENDDO  LOOP
```

This makes SALUT replace $DO with a label and $ENDDO with a *LOOP label* instruction. Recall from Section 3.6 that LOOP decrements CX and makes the 80286 transfer to the label if CX is not zero.

To include the state of the Zero Flag (ZF) in the loop decision, you can use one of the following forms:

- *$ENDDO LOOPE* decrements CX, then transfers if CX is not zero and ZF is 1. This locates the first nonzero result in a series of operations.
- *$ENDDO LOOPNE* decrements CX, then transfers if CX is not zero and ZF is 0. This locates the first zero result in a series of operations.

- *$ENDDO LOOPZ* is an alternate form of *$ENDDO LOOPE.*
- *$ENDDO LOOPNZ* is an alternate form of *$ENDDO LOOPNE.*

AND and OR Options

The AND option stops the looping when several conditions are satisfied, while OR stops it when *any* of several conditions is satisfied. For example, here is the general form of a DO structure that stops looping when the user answers "No" to a prompt by pressing either *N* or *n*:

```
$DO
      ..
      ..
      (Display "Continue? (Y/N)")
      (Read user's response into ANSWER)
      CMP   ANSWER,"N"
$ENDDO  E,OR
      CMP   ANSWER,"n"
$ENDDO  E
```

12.4 SEARCH Structure

A SEARCH structure is similar to a DO structure, but SEARCH provides two separate ways to leave a loop: on "success" or "failure." This is handy for applications where you care about *which* condition made the looping stop. For example, you will want to know whether an I/O operation ended successfully or aborted due to an error.

Like DO, the SEARCH structure is available in three forms:

- *SEARCH UNTIL* repeats a block of instructions until either of two conditions at the end becomes true.
- *SEARCH WHILE* repeats a block of instructions while both conditions are false. If either condition is initially true, it does not execute the block at all.
- *SEARCH COMPLEX* is a combination of SEARCH UNTIL and SEARCH WHILE that involves a block of instructions preceding the condition tests and another following them. It executes the first block, then tests the conditions. If either condition is true, it exits; otherwise, it executes the second block and starts again.

Note: As with DO, the words UNTIL, WHILE, and COMPLEX are for description only; *don't* type them into your programs.

SEARCH UNTIL

The SEARCH UNTIL structure has the general form

```
$SEARCH
        A     (Main block)
$EXITIF   cond1
        B     (Executes, then exits, if cond1 is true)
$ORELSE
        C     (Executes if cond1 is false)
$ENDLOOP  cond2
        D     (Executes, then exits, if cond2 is true)
$ENDSRCH
```

where *cond1* and *cond2* are the conditions that can make the looping stop. Here, *cond1* "true" indicates success (you found what you were searching for), while *cond2* "true" indicates failure. Figure 12-3(A) shows the flowchart for SEARCH UNTIL.

Note that the main block, A, always executes at least once. Blocks B and D execute upon the success or failure of the operation, respectively (you might use them to print messages), while block C contains instructions that set up the flags for the $ENDLOOP test.

For example, in an educational program, you can use SEARCH UNTIL to give a student three chances to select the correct answer to a multiple-choice question. The general form might look like this:

```
        MOV   CX,3        ;Set up the count
        (Display the question.)
$SEARCH
        (Read the student's answer.)
        (Make ZF = 1 if answer is correct.)
$EXITIF   Z
        (Display "Congratulations! You are right.")
$ORELSE
        (Display "Sorry, wrong answer.  Try again.")
$ENDLOOP  LOOP
        (Display "No, all three answers were wrong.")
        (Display "The correct answer is " " and give answer.)
$ENDSRCH
```

SEARCH WHILE

The SEARCH WHILE structure has the general form

```
$SEARCH
$LEAVE   cond1
       A    (Executes if cond1 is false)
$EXITIF  cond2
```

```
     B    (Executes, then exits, if cond2 is true)
$ORELSE
     C    (Executes if cond2 is false)
$ENDLOOP
     D    (Executes, then exits, if cond1 is true)
$ENDRCH
```

Figure 12-3(B) shows the flowchart for SEARCH WHILE.

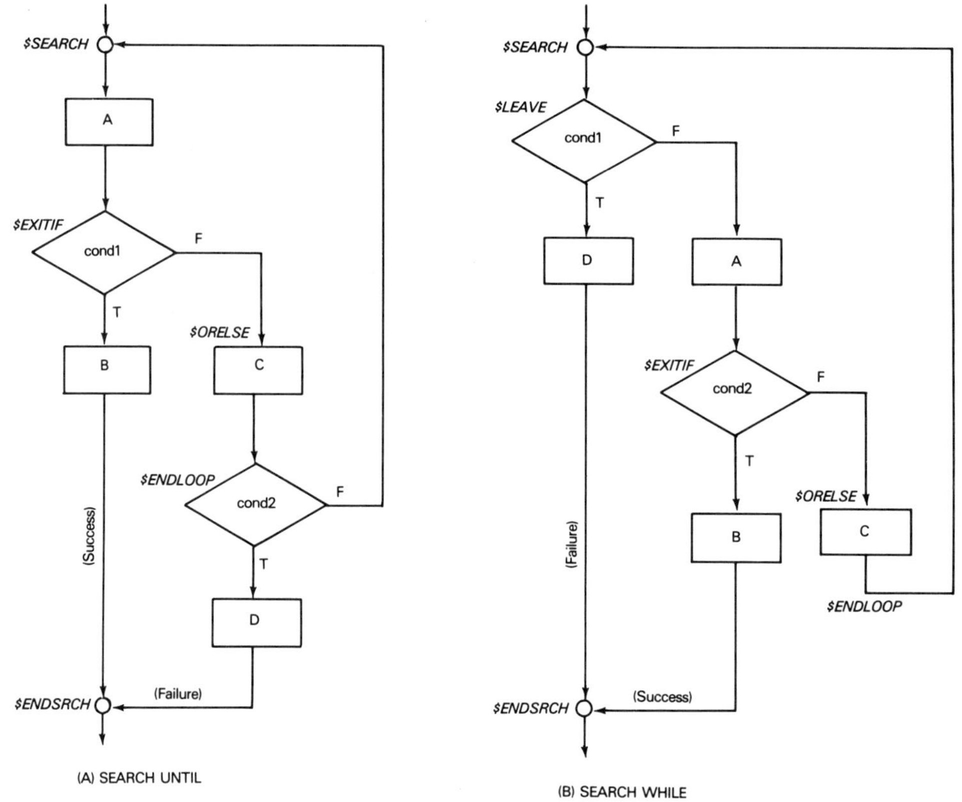

Figure 12-3. SEARCH structures.

Because SEARCH WHILE tests at the very beginning, you can use it to bypass the entire structure if the initial conditions are not satisfied. For example, the following searches for the first zero in a table, and "LEAVEs" immediately if the table is empty:

```
     MOV CX,TABLE_LENGTH      ;Set up the count
     MOV  BX,0                 ;Point to first element
$SEARCH
$LEAVE   CXZ
     CMP  TABLE[BX],0          ;Check for zero
$EXITIF  E
```

```
     (Display "Zero found.")
$ORELSE
     INC   BX                       ;Point to next element
$ENDLOOP  LOOP
     (Display "Zero not found.")
$ENDSRCH
```

SEARCH COMPLEX

The SEARCH COMPLEX structure has the general form

```
$SEARCH
     A
$EXITIF   cond1
     B       (Executes, then exits, if cond1 is true)
$ORELSE
     C       (Executes if cond1 is false)
$LEAVE   cond2
     D       (Executes if cond2 is false)
$ENDLOOP
     E       (Executes, then exits, if cond2 is true)
$ENDSRCH
```

Figure 12-3C shows the flowchart for SEARCH COMPLEX. Note that SEARCH COMPLEX does the same thing as SEARCH UNTIL, but executes Figure 12-3C.

Operand Options

Some SEARCH structure statements have options like those we encountered for IF and DO. Their general forms are:

```
$EXITIF    cond[,AND/OR][,LONG][,NUL]
$ORELSE    [LONG]
$ENDLOOP   [cond[,AND/OR]][,LONG]
$ENDLOOP   [LOOPx][,LONG]
$LEAVE     cond[,AND/OR][,LONG]
```

The only new option is NUL, which you can use with $EXITIF if you omit the B ("success") block from a SEARCH structure. Of course, with B gone, you can also omit $ORELSE. The structure will still work if you omit the B block, but NUL makes it execute faster.

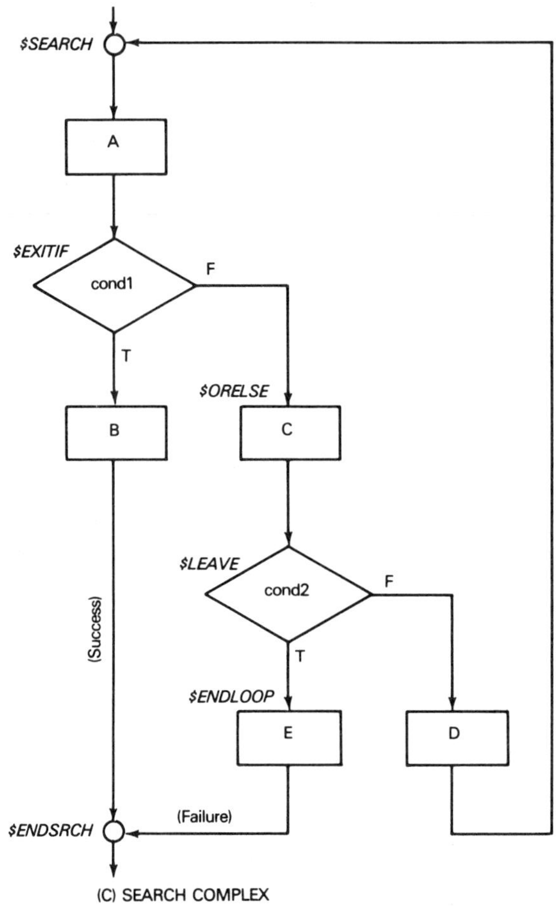

Figure 12-3C. SEARCH COMPLEX structure.

12.5 Restrictions on Using NCXZ and CXZ

As we mentioned earlier, SALUT translates structure statements into their assembly language equivalents. Specifically, it translates conditional statements into Jx or JMP instructions and translates $ENDIF, $DO, $SEARCH, and $ENDSRCH into labels. In doing so, SALUT must often translate a conditional statement into the reverse conditional transfer instruction. For example, it translates *$IF A* into *JNA L1* (where L1 is a label that replaces $ENDIF). However, problems may arise when the CXZ condition is involved, because there is no JNCXZ instruction. Table 12-2 lists the statements that can use NCXZ and CXZ, and shows which is legal in each case.

Table 12-2. Legal uses of NCXZ and CXZ.

Structure Statement	NCXZ	CXZ
$IF cond	Yes	No
$IF cond,OR	No	Yes
$IF cond,AND	Yes	No
$LEAVE cond	No	Yes
$LEAVE cond,OR	No	Yes
$LEAVE cond,AND	Yes	No
$EXITIF cond	Yes	No
$EXITIF cond,AND	Yes	No
$EXITIF cond,OR	No	Yes
$EXITIF cond,AND,NUL	Yes	No
$EXITIF cond,OR,NUL	No	Yes
$EXITIF cond,NUL	No	Yes
$ENDLOOP cond	Yes	No
$ENDLOOP cond,AND	Yes	No
$ENDLOOP cond,OR	No	Yes
$ENDDO cond	Yes	No
$ENDDO cond,AND	Yes	No
$ENDDO cond,OR	No	Yes

12.6 Preparing Structured Programs

Procedure

You can prepare structured programs in about the same way you prepare ordinary programs, except you must pass the source through SALUT, to translate the structures into standard assembly language instructions. SALUT also formats your source program into evenly-spaced columns. The steps are as follows:

1. Prepare the program using your word processor, editor, or EDLIN. Give it a name of the form *filename.SAL,* where SAL stands for Structured Assembly Language.

   Important: When entering the program, start all stand-alone comments and labels in column 1, but start structure statements, unlabeled instructions, and unlabeled pseudo-ops in some column other than col-

umn 1. For example, you might start them in column 2 by pressing the space bar or (using EDLIN) in column 9 by pressing Tab.
2. Run the SAL file through SALUT to generate a formatted source file (*filename.SAL*) and a temporary intermediate file (*filename.ASM*). SALUT renames your original, unformatted source file *filename.BAK*.
3. Assemble the source file using MASM.
4. Delete the temporary .ASM file and, if you wish, the .BAK file.
5. Use the Linker to generate a run module.

Using Top-Down Design With Structured Programs

In Chapter 2 we discussed top-down design, in which you build a program by entering its general outline (often just comment statements), then insert more detail gradually. This approach can also be used to build structured programs. To do this, enter the command statements for a logic structure, then go back and insert the instructions that go between them. To build an IF structure, for example, you might start with

```
$IF       ;If the correct value was specified
$ELSE     ;Since the correct value was not specified
$ENDIF    ;End of correct value test
```

This will not assemble properly yet, since the $IF requires a condition. Adding the condition, we get

```
$IF E     ;If the correct value was specified
$ELSE     ;Since the correct value was not specified
$ENDIF    ;End of correct value test
```

We now have a condition "equal," which must follow a comparison test. Hence, insert the test and get

```
CMP AX,100 ;Check for desired value
$IF E     ;If the correct value was specified
$ELSE     ;Since the correct value was not specified
$ENDIF    ;End of correct value test
```

Note that what we have here will assemble correctly and is actually executable. We can leave this part of the program for awhile and come back later to fill in the "true" and "false" legs of the test. After all, we have enough here to document what must be done; we can add the details later.

The important point in this example is that I have added *comments* along with the instructions. There is no better time to document a program than when writing it, because you will never understand it better than you do then. Don't ever say to yourself, "I will comment it later," because you probably won't. And even if you try, when "later" comes, chances are you won't remember what you were trying to accomplish.

Using SALUT

To use SALUT, get the B> prompt on the screen, then enter a command of the form

```
B>a:salut filename
```

(SALUT assumes the file has the extension SAL unless you specify otherwise.)

When SALUT finishes, the disk in drive B will contain three files: the original source (*filename.BAK*), a formatted version of the source (*filename.SAL*), and a temporary intermediate file (*filename.ASM*). You can now assemble *filename.ASM* as usual, then link *filename.OBJ* to produce the run module, *filename.EXE*.

Batch File for SALUT

Generally, once you have finished with SALUT, you won't want your original source file (now named BAK). And once you have assembled, you won't want the ASM file (because if the program contains errors, you will correct the SAL version rather than the ASM version). Therefore, you will want to erase these two files. To save the bother of erasing them manually, you can create a *batch file* that runs SALUT and the Macro Assembler, then erases the BAK and ASM files. To do this (assuming you want to name the batch file ASMSAL.BAT), enter the following, and press Return after each line:

```
B>copy con: a:asmsal.bat
  a:salut %1
  erase %1.bak
  a:masm %1,,;
  erase %1.asm
  (Press F6)
```

To run this batch file, enter a command of the form

```
B>a:asmsal filename
```

Incidentally, note that the fourth command automatically produces a source listing (LST) file. If you don't want one, create another batch file that has *a:masm %1;* instead.

How SALUT Reformats Programs

Unless you tell it otherwise, SALUT reformats programs as follows:

1. *Labels* and *stand-alone comments* start at column 1.
2. *Structure statements* and *instruction mnemonics* start at column 9.
3. *Operands* start at column 17.
4. *Comments* start at column 41.
5. *Statements inside structures* are indented four spaces.

You can specify other settings if you like. Refer to the *Macro Assembler* manual for details.

To see how this formatting works, suppose you have entered the following sequence in a program:

```
MOV CX,4 ;Perform four operations
MOV BX,0 ;Point to first element
$DO
MOV DEST[BX],0 ;Store zero in next byte
INC BX ;Point to next element
$ENDDO LOOP
```

After SALUT has formatted the sequence, it is arranged as follows:

```
        MOV     CX,4                    ;Perform four operations
        MOV     BX,0                    ;Point to first element
        $DO
            MOV     DEST[BX],0          ;Store zero in next byte
            INC     BX                  ;Point to next element
        $ENDDO  LOOP
```

Indenting Programs Using SALUT

Note that SALUT's reformatting capability is separate from its structure-processing capability. Hence, even if you never use structures (shame on you!), you can still run SALUT to indent your assembly language programs. To do this, enter your program any old way at all (say, put a space or tab between fields), then save the program and give a command of the form

B>a:salut *filename*.asm,*filename*.asm,nul

SALUT indents *filename*.ASM and renames your unformatted version *filename*.BAK.

13

80287 Math Coprocessor

The Intel 80287 Math Coprocessor is a chip that performs complex mathematical calculations. It is designed to extend the arithmetic capability of an 80286 microprocessor. In fact, the IBM PC AT provides an extra socket for an 80287. (The IBM Personal Computer and XT work with a similar chip called the 8087. From a programmer's standpoint, the 8087 and 80287 are nearly identical.)

As you know, the 80286 can already do some arithmetic—but not much. It can operate on only five-digit (two-byte) integers, and provides only the four basic functions: add, subtract, multiply, and divide. On the other hand, the 80287 can perform a wide variety of arithmetic, logarithmic, and trigonometric functions on integer and real numbers up to 18 digits long. And because the 80287's instructions are built into hardware, it can produce a dramatic speed improvement over doing these operations with the 80286.

Intel claims, in fact, that the 80287 can perform numeric operations about 50 to 100 times faster than the 80286 can perform an equivalent software routine. This means, for example, that if an 80286 program takes 2000 microseconds to run a particular arithmetic program, the 80287 may do the same thing in only 20 microseconds!

The 80287 is called a *coprocessor* because it shares programs with the main processor (the 80286). When you run a program that is designed to use the 80287, the 80286 executes the instructions that it recognizes and the 80287 executes those that *it* recognizes. Each intercepts its own instructions. (Think of a construction foreman who has two helpers, an Italian and a Spaniard. The Italian worker performs only orders the foreman gives in Italian, while the Spanish worker performs only those given in Spanish.)

Generally, programs written in a high-level language such as BASIC or Pascal use the 80287 automatically. However, assembly language requires you to either insert 80287 instructions with the 80286's ESC (escape) instruction or buy an assembler that recognizes the 80287 instruction set, such as the IBM Macro Assembler.

This chapter gives a brief overview of the 80287 Math Coprocessor. For full details, refer to the Macro Assembler manual or Intel's *iAPX 286 Programmer's Reference Manual* (this includes a "numeric supplement" dealing with the 80287). As a further aid, the Macro Assembler disk has a file called *FLINS.ASM* that contains examples of most 80287 instructions.

13.1 Internal Registers

The 80287 has eight, 80-bit data registers, plus a status word and a control word, both 16 bits long. The status word is similar to the 80286's flags register. The control word governs the way the 80287 handles rounding, infinity, and precision.

Working with the 80287's data registers is quite different than working with the 80286's registers, in that you generally don't address them individually. Instead, you use them as a *stack*.

The 80287's Stack

Recall that the 80286 uses a stack to hold return addresses during procedure calls and interrupt servicing, and that we can use it to preserve the contents of registers. A stack operates like a plate dispenser in a cafeteria; the last item you put on it is the first one you can remove from it. The 80287's data registers work in the same way. That is, you always put numbers into the top register, and when you do, it pushes the rest of the registers "down" one position in the stack. (Like the 80286, the 80287 does not actually move the registers, it simply changes the contents of a "stack pointer.")

Because the data registers operate as a stack, most of the 80287's instructions use the stack contents implicitly. For example, when you give the 80287 an add instruction, it adds the contents of two numbers on the stack and leaves the result on the stack. If you have worked with a stack-oriented language such as FORTH, you should feel comfortable programming the 80287; otherwise, it will probably take you some time to get used to this concept.

Floating-Point Format

The data registers hold numbers in "floating-point" format, the computer's version of scientific notation. In this notation, you would write -150 as -1.5×10^2.

The 80287's data registers represent floating-point numbers by splitting them into three fields: a 1-bit sign, a 15-bit exponent, and a 64-bit significand (or *mantissa*). Hence, a data register stores -150 with 1 in the sign field, a number representing 2 in the exponent field, and 15 in the significand field.

Fortunately, we can usually forget about how the 80287 stores numbers. But we *do* need to know about what kinds of data it can operate on.

13.2 Data Types

The 80287 can operate on seven types of data: three types of integers (word, short, and long), three types of reals (short, long, and temporary), and packed decimal. Table 13-1 summarizes the data types.

Table 13-1. 80287 data types.

Data Type	Bits	Significant Digits	Range
Word Integer	16	4 or 5	-32,768 to 32,767
Short Integer	32	9	-2×10^{9} to 2×10^{9}
Long Integer	64	18	-9×10^{18} to 9×10^{18}
Short Real	32	6 or 7	10^{-37} to 10^{38}
Long Real	64	15 or 16	10^{-307} to 10^{308}
Temporary Real	80	19	10^{-4932} to 10^{4932}
Packed Decimal	80	18	18 decimal digits + sign

Of the integer types, the two-byte *word integer*, which corresponds to BASIC's integer data type, is useful for indexing arrays and other data structures. Since a word integer can hold values from -32,768 to 32,767, you probably won't find many uses for the short and long integer types.

Short real and *long real* correspond to BASIC's single- and double-precision data types, respectively. Short real numbers are accurate to about seven decimal places. This means that numbers that differ in only the eighth place look the same to the 80287. (For example, it treats 1.23456789 the same as 1.12345681.) Hence, short real numbers are convenient for storing input data, but you should perform calculations using long real numbers to minimize the effect of round-offs. Long real numbers are accurate to about 16 places.

Temporary real is the format the 80287 uses to store numbers in its data registers. Since this format uses a 64-bit significand, every other data type fits into it without loss of precision. With its 80-bit length, the temporary real format shields the user from cumulative rounding errors and from overflow or underflow in intermediate calculations.

Finally, *packed decimal* is used for business and data processing. It can hold up to 18 significant digits, and "packs" them two per byte in memory. You will recall this approach from our discussion of binary-coded decimal (BCD) numbers in Chapter 3.

13.3 Instruction Set

We can divide the 80287's instruction set into six groups: data transfer, arithmetic, comparison, transcendental, constants, and control. Table 13-2 gives their general forms (as usual, square brackets mark optional items) and a short description.

Table 13-2. 80287 instruction set.

Instruction	Description
Data Transfer	
FBLD source	Load packed decimal
FBSTP dest	Store and pop packed decimal
FILD source	Load integer
FIST dest	Store integer
FISTP dest	Store and pop integer
FLD source	Load real
FST dest	Store real
FSTP dest	Store real and pop
FXCH [dest]	Exchange registers
Arithmetic	
FADD [dest,[source]]	Add real
FADDP dest,source	Add real and pop
FIADD source	Add integer
FSUB [dest,[source]]	Subtract real
FSUBP dest,source	Subtract real and pop
FISUB source	Subtract integer
FSUBR [dest,[source]]	Subtract real reversed
FSUBRP dest,source	Subtract real reversed and pop
FISUBR source	Subtract integer reversed
FMUL [dest,[source]]	Multiply real
FMULP dest,source	Multiply real and pop
FIMUL source	Multiply integer
FDIV [dest,[source]]	Divide real
FDIVP dest,source	Divide real and pop
FIDIV source	Divide integer

Table 13-2. 80287 instruction set (continued).

Instruction	Description
Arithmetic (continued)	
FDIVR [dest,[source]]	Divide real reversed
FDIVRP dest,source	Divide real reversed and pop
FIDIVR source	Divide integer reversed
FSQRT	Square root
FSCALE	Scale by a power of two
FPREM	Partial remainder
FRNDINT	Round to integer
FXTRACT	Extract exponent and significand
FABS	Absolute value
FCHS	Change sign
Comparison	
FCOM [source]	Compare real
FCOMP [source]	Compare real and pop
FCOMPP	Compare real and pop twice
FICOM source	Compare integer
FICOMP source	Compare integer and pop
FTST	Test top of stack for zero
FXAM	Examine top of stack
Transcendental	
F2XM1	2 to the X power, minus 1
FYL2X	Y times $\log_2 X$
FYL2XP1	Y times $\log_2(X+1)$
FPTAN	Partial tangent
FPATAN	Partial arctangent
Constants	
FLDZ	Load 0.0
FLD1	Load 1.0
FLDPI	Load pi
FLDL2T	Load $\log_2 10$
FLDL2E	Load $\log_2 e$
FLDLG2	Load common logarithm of 2
FLDLN2	Load natural logarithm of 2
Control	
FLDCW source	Load control word
FSTCW/FNSTCW dest	Store control word

Table 13-2. 80287 instruction set (continued).

Instruction	Description
Control (continued)	
FSTSW/FNSTSW dest	Store status word
FSAVE/FNSAVE dest	Save state
FRSTOR source	Restore state
FLDENV source	Load environment
FSTENV/FNSTENV dest	Store environment
FWAIT	Wait (halt the 80286)
FINIT/FNINIT	Initialize (reset) the 80287
FENI/FNENI	Enable interrupts
FDISI/FNDISI	Disable interrupts
FCLEX/FNCLEX	Clear exceptions
FINCSTP	Increment stack pointer
FDECSTP	Decrement stack pointer
FFREE dest	Free (clear) register
FNOP	No operation

The *data transfer* instructions move numbers to and from the top of the 80287's data register stack.

The *arithmetic* instructions provide the four basic operations (add, subtract, multiply, and divide), plus other convenient functions such as square root and absolute value. The subtract and divide instructions come in two forms. With the standard forms, you subtract a source from a destination or divide a destination by a source. With the "reversed" forms, you subtract a destination from a source or divide a source by a destination. The reversed forms let you leave results in memory, which may only be a source operand.

The *comparison* instructions compare the top number on the stack to another stack number or a memory location. Compares are convenient for finding the largest number in an array or determining whether a number is less than, equal to, or greater than zero.

The *transcendental* instructions compute logarithms and trigonometric functions. Although the 80287 provides only tangent and arctangent instructions, it is fairly easy to derive other trigonometric functions from them.

The *constant* instructions push any of seven constants onto the stack: zero, one, pi, or four logarithmic values. In all cases, the 80287 gives them full temporary real (19-digit) accuracy.

The *control* instructions let you preserve status information, change the way the 80287 rounds results, enable and disable interrupts, and do a variety of other "housekeeping" jobs. One instruction, FWAIT, generates an 80286

WAIT instruction, which prevents it from accessing a memory location that the 80287 is using.

13.4 80287 Programming with the Macro Assembler

You can develop 80287 programs just like 80286 programs, except you must tell the assembler that you are using 80287 instructions. You can do this in either of two ways:

- Enter the command *.287* at the very beginning of the main program module—just after the TITLE statement.
- Assemble the program using the form

  masm *filename*/**R**

Constants

In Section 2.3 we described the four kinds of constants the assembler accepts for regular 80286 programming; these are binary, decimal, hexadecimal, and character. In your work with the 80287, you may use two additional forms:

1. *Decimal real*—A number with a decimal point; for example, 3.14159.
2. *Decimal scientific*—A decimal number followed by E and an exponent value; for example, 2.654E-12.

Data Definition Pseudo-Ops

In Section 13.2, we described the seven types of data the 80287 can accept: three integers (word, short, and long), three reals (short, long, and temporary), and packed decimal. The Macro Assembler provides data definition pseudo-ops that allow us to set up memory variables for each type, as follows:

- For word integers, which are 16 bits long, use *DW* (Define Word).
- For short integers and short reals, which are 32 bits long, use *DD* (Define Doubleword).
- For long integers and long reals, which are 64 bits long, use *DQ* (Define Quadword).

- For temporary reals and packed integers, which are 80 bits long, use *DT* (Define Tenbytes).

Note that DQ and DT are new.

Examples of each form are:

```
WORD_INTEGER    DW   16483
SHORT_INTEGER   DD   145897
LONG_INTEGER    DQ   42765844
SHORT_REAL      DD   3.14159
LONG_REAL       DQ   1.0E-14
TEMP_REAL       DT   1.5E-16
PACKED_DEC      DT   -1457594442553
```

Detecting an 80287

In Chapter 6 we described the Type 11 (Equipment Check) interrupt which lets you determine whether your computer has an 80287, among other things. However, Type 11 does not actually check for the 287 chip—it merely reads the *switch* settings that specify whether the chip is installed. If someone has set the switches incorrectly (and that's not unusual), Type 11 will always report, "Sorry, friend, you don't have a 287 chip." As a more foolproof detection scheme, you can let the 287 itself tell you whether it's there. Example 13-1 shows a program that does this.

Here, we attempt to initialize the 80287 chip with an FINIT instruction, then we read the 287's status word with FSTSW. A zero in the status word's low byte means a 287 is installed; any other value means the socket is empty. Either way, you receive a message on the screen.

13.5 Summary

The 80287 Math Coprocessor is a powerful device that can dramatically improve your computer's ability to perform mathematical calculations. It accepts seven different types of data—three integer, three real, and packed decimal—giving maximum flexibility for any kind of calculation you need. No matter what data type you use, the 80287 performs all internal calculations using an 80-bit floating-point format, which gives accuracy to 19 significant places. This not only means that your answers will be highly precise, but also that you will rarely encounter overflow or underflow errors.

The 80287 provides instructions for adding, subtracting, multiplying, and

Example 13-1. Check for Math Coprocessor.

```
        PAGE   ,132
TITLE   MATHCHIP - Check for Math Coprocessor
.287

;  This procedures determines whether the computer
;  has an 80287 Math Coprocessor.

STACK   SEGMENT PARA STACK 'STACK'
        DB    64 DUP('STACK   ')
STACK   ENDS

DSEG    SEGMENT PARA PUBLIC 'DATA'
MP      DB    'Computer has an 80287 $'
NO_MP   DB    'Computer does not have an 80287 $'
DSEG    ENDS

CSEG    SEGMENT PARA PUBLIC 'CODE'
        ASSUME  CS:CSEG,DS:DSEG,SS:STACK

ENTRY   PROC  FAR              ;Entry point

;Set up the stack to contain the proper values so this
;program can return to DOS or DEBUG.

        PUSH  DS
        SUB   AX,AX
        PUSH  AX

        MOV   AX,DSEG          ;Initialize DS
        MOV   DS,AX

        FINIT                  ;Initialize the coprocessor
        FSTSW AX               ;Retrieve 80287 status word
        OR    AL,AL            ;Is 80287 present?
        JNZ   NO_287
        LEA   DX,MP            ; Yes.
        JMP   TELL_USER
NO_287: LEA   DX,NO_MP         ; No.
TELL_USER: MOV  AH,09H         ;Print the appropriate message
        INT   21H
        RET                    ;Return to DOS
ENTRY   ENDP
CSEG    ENDS
        END   ENTRY
```

dividing both integer and real numbers. It also has a variety of logarithmic and trigonometric instructions, plus special ones that perform tasks you frequently need, such as extracting a square root and finding an absolute value. The slowest instruction takes 1000 clock cycles to execute and the fastest takes just two clocks.

Programming the 80287 in assembly language may take some getting used to, because it has a stack-oriented architecture. However, the short time it takes you to accustom yourself more than makes up for the agony you would have to endure in writing multi-precision arithmetic procedures.

Answers to Study Exercises

Chapter 0. Crash Course in Computer Numbering

1. (a) 1100 (b) 10001 (c) 101101 (d) 1001000
2. (a) 8 (b) 21 (c) 31
3. (a) 8 (b) 15 (c) 1F
4. The hexadecimal value D8 can represent the unsigned number 216 or the signed number -40. To obtain the signed number, convert the hexadecimal value to binary (11011000), then reverse each bit (to make 00100111) and add 1 (to make 00101000, or decimal 40).

Chapter 1. Introduction

1. The 80286 is called a 16-bit microprocessor because it can transfer 16 bits of data at a time. It makes these transfers over a 16-line *data bus* that comes out of the chip.
2. In the real address mode, the 80286 can address one million bytes, or one *megabyte*.
3. When calculating a physical address, the 80286 automatically appends four zeros to the segment number to form the *segment address*. Therefore, it uses 4000H as 40000H and calculates the physical address as

   ```
   Physical address = 2H + 40000H = 40002H
   ```
4. A nanosecond is one billionth of a second, or 10^{-9} seconds. A microsecond is one millionth of a second, or 10^{-6} seconds.
5. The instruction takes 1670 nanoseconds to execute, because on the PC AT, each clock cycle takes 167 nanoseconds.
6. If the AX register contains 1A2BH, AL (its low-order byte) contains 2BH.
7. They are called the code segment, data segment, stack segment, and extra segment. Each can be up to 64K bytes long. They are normally addressed by the CS, DS, SS, and ES register, respectively.
8. Variables are usually stored in the data segment, so the Data Segment (DS) register is used to access them.
9. Bit 7, the Sign Flag (SF), is set to 1 if a subtraction gives a negative result.

Chapter 2. Using an Assembler

1. The assembler allocates one byte for VAR1, ten bytes (each word = two bytes) for VAR2, and ten bytes for VAR3, for a total of *21* bytes.
2. The assembler doesn't put anything into VAR1. The ? operand tells it to simply *reserve* one byte for VAR1. Your program must put a value into VAR1.

   Note that the assembler only puts a value into one location here: it puts 20 into the fifth word of VAR2. It leaves all other locations "undefined."
3. The = statement can be redefined later in the program, the EQU statement cannot.
4. CONST is a *byte* variable, and cannot hold values greater than 255.
5. Every procedure must start with PROC and end with ENDP.
6. You can only call a NEAR procedure from within the segment in which it is defined. You can call a FAR procedure from any segment in the program.
7. This ASSUME tells the assembler to use CS to address any instruction labels in the CSEG segment. In other words, it identifies CSEG as a *code* segment rather than a data, stack, or extra segment.
8. The Linker generates a *relocatable run module* that DOS can store at any convenient place in memory. This frees you from having to decide where to store a program in memory. The Linker also combines two or more object modules.

Chapter 3. 80286 Instruction Set

1. The instruction is MOV ES:SAVE_AX,AX.
2. This sequence stores 0 into the first location of the data segment (addressed by BX) and the stack segment (addressed by BP).
3. a. *Invalid*. A constant cannot be a destination.
   b. *Valid*, but since TEMP has not been initialized, you will get "garbage" in AL.
   c. *Invalid*. You can't move a word value into a byte variable.
   d. *Invalid*. The MOV instruction cannot be used to make a direct memory-to-memory transfer.
   e. *Invalid*. The assembler does not recognize the addressing form [BX][BP]. See Table 3-1 for valid operand formats.
   f. *Invalid*. Hexadecimal operands must be followed with an H suffix. Further, if the operand starts with a letter (A-F), it must be preceded with 0 (zero). The correct form here is MOV AL,0FH.
4. MOV AL,10H puts hexadecimal 10 (decimal 16) into AL, while MOV AL,10 puts decimal 10 (hexadecimal A) into it. Be careful not to confuse hexadecimal and decimal operands; they are entirely different.
5. These instructions clear the AX register:

```
SUB   AX,AX
MOV   AX,0
XOR   AX,AX
```

6. These instructions are identical. Both load the offset of location TABLE+4 into BX. However, LEA is both shorter and more explicit.
7. ADD adds only the operands, while ADC adds the operands plus the Carry Flag (CF).
8. This loop subtracts V2 from V1:

```
        MOV    CX,3          ;Word count = 3
        MOV    BX,0          ;Offset = 0
        CLC                  ;Clear Carry (CF)
NEXT:   MOV    DX,V2[BX]     ;Subtract words
        SBB    V1[BX],DX
        INC    BX            ; and address next word
        INC    BX
        LOOP   NEXT
```

   Note that BX is increased by 2 after each subtraction because words lie two bytes apart in memory. We use two INCs rather than one ADD so as not to disturb the Carry Flag (CF), which the SBB operation uses.
9. Use INC instead of ADD when you don't want to disturb the Carry Flag (CF)?
10. Packed BCD numbers are stored two digits per byte, while unpacked numbers are stored one digit per byte. For example, the BCD value 23 would be stored in AX as 0023H if it is packed and as 0203H if it is unpacked.
11. The results are:
    a. (AX) = 0220H
    b. (AX) = 5335H
    c. (AX) = 5115H
    d. (AX) = 0EDCBH
    e. (AX) = 1234H (because TEST affects only the flags)
12. The sequence to normalize AX is:

```
           TEST   AX,0FFFFH
           JZ     NORM          ;Exit if (AX) = 0
           MOV    CX,15         ;Get set for 15 shifts
NEXT_BIT:  JS     NORM          ;Exit if Bit 15 = 1
           SHL    AX,1          ;Otherwise shift AX left by one
           LOOP   NEXT_BIT
NORM:      ..
           ..
```

13. RET pops a 32-bit return address off the stack. This makes the 286 return to the program that called the procedure.
14. The JA instruction is used with unsigned numbers. You need JG INVALID here.

15. If you think that the sequence subtracts 30 from AX, look again. LOOP decrements CX, then jumps to START if CX is zero. However, the MOV instruction continually reinitializes CX to 3, so CX will *never* reach zero. This kind of endless loop is a common programming error. Watch out for it.
16. STRING1 is in the extra segment, while STRING2 is in the data segment.

Chapter 4. High-Precision Mathematics

1. The Answer 4-1 listing shows a procedure that extracts a square root by subtracting successively higher odd numbers.

Answer 4-1. Calculate square root by subtracting.

```
        PAGE    ,132
TITLE SR32 - Square Root By Odd Numbers

;   Calculate square root by subtracting.
;   Inputs: DX:AX = Integer
;   Result: BX = Square root

;   Assemble with: MASM SR32;
;   Link with: LINK callprog+SR32;

        PUBLIC  SR32
CSEG    SEGMENT PARA 'CODE'
        ASSUME  CS:CSEG
SR32    PROC    FAR
        PUSH    AX              ;Save original number
        PUSH    DX
        PUSH    CX              ; and CX on stack
        MOV     BX,1            ;To start, (BX) = 1
        SUB     CX,CX           ; and (CX) = 0
AGAIN:  SUB     AX,BX           ;Subtract next odd no.from AX
        SBB     DX,0            ; and DX
        JC      DONE            ;Did sub. create a borrow?
        INC     CX              ; No. Increment the square root,
        ADD     BX,2            ;  calculate the next odd no.
        JMP     AGAIN           ;  then go make next subtraction
DONE:   MOV     BX,CX           ; Yes. Transfer result to BX
        POP     CX              ;  and restore the registers
        POP     DX
        POP     AX
        RET
SR32    ENDP
CSEG    ENDS
        END
```

Chapter 5. Operating on Data Structures

1. The Answer 5-1 listing shows the modified version of Example 5-1 that can be used to build a list from scratch, as well as to add a new element to an existing list.

Answer 5-1. Add an element to an unordered list.

```
      PAGE    ,132
TITLE ADD2UL - Add to Unordered List

;  Adds the value in AX to an unordered list in the
;  extra segment, if that value is not already in the list.
;  Inputs: ES:DI = Starting address of the list
;          First location = List length (words)
;  Results: None
;  DI and AX are unaffected.

;  Assemble with: MASM ADD2UL;
;  Link with: LINK callprog+ADD2UL;

      PUBLIC  ADD_TO_UL
CSEG  SEGMENT PARA 'CODE'
      ASSUME  CS:CSEG
ADD_TO_UL PROC  FAR
      CLD                     ;Scan forward
      PUSH    DI              ;Save starting address
      PUSH    CX
      MOV     CX,ES:[DI]      ;Fetch word count
      ADD     DI,2            ;Make DI point to 1st data el.
      CMP     CX,0
      JE      ADD_IT
REPNE SCASW                   ;Value already in list?
      POP     CX
      JNE     ADD_IT
      POP     DI              ; Yes. Restore starting addr.
      RET                     ;  and exit.
ADD_IT: MOV   ES:[DI],AX      ; No.  Add it to end of list,
      POP     DI              ;  then update element count
      INC     WORD PTR ES:[DI]
      RET                     ;  and exit.
ADD_TO_UL ENDP
CSEG  ENDS
      END
```

2. The Answer 5-2 listing shows the find-and-replace procedure.

Answer 5-2. Find and replace procedure.

```
      PAGE     ,132
TITLE REPLACE - Replace an Element in an Ordered List

;   This procedure searches an ordered list in the extra
;   segment for the word value contained in AX.
;   If the matching element is found, its contents are
;   replaced with the value in BX.
;   AX and BX are unaffected.

;   Assemble with: MASM REPLACE;
;   Link with: LINK callprog+REPLACE+B_SEARCH;

DSEG   SEGMENT PARA 'DATA'
START_ADDR DW ?
DSEG   ENDS

      EXTRN    B_SEARCH:FAR
      PUBLIC   REPLACE
CSEG SEGMENT PARA 'CODE'
REPLACE PROC FAR
      ASSUME   CS:CSEG,DS:DSEG
      CALL     B_SEARCH      ;Is the search value in the list?
      JC       QUIT          ; If not, exit
      MOV      ES:[SI],BX    ; If so, replace it with BX
QUIT: RET
REPLACE ENDP
CSEG ENDS
      END
```

Chapter 6. Using the System Resources

1. An interrupt vector is a pointer to an interrupt service routine. That is, it is a pair of words in memory that contain the offset and segment number of a program that the 286 is to execute when it receives an associated INT instruction. For example, the interrupt vector for the Type 4 interrupt points to the interrupt routine to be executed when the 286 receives INT 4.
2. The AT's interrupt vector table is located in the lowest 1K bytes in memory; from location 0 through location 3FF.
3. Since each interrupt vector occupies four bytes (two words) in memory, you obtain the starting address by multiplying the interrupt number by 4. Hence, the starting address of the Type 4 interrupt vector is at location 16 decimal or 10 hexadecimal. In terms of segment and offset, this translates to location 0:10.
4. To find out what instruction a location contains, use DEBUG to "unassemble" starting at that address. In this case,

   u f000:fea5

is the proper DEBUG command.

5. Interrupts 60H through 67H are available for users.
6. The Type 1C (Timer Tick) interrupt should point to SHOW_CLOCK, because it gets executed with every "tick" of the system clock. That is, 18.2 times per second.
7. To make the Type 1C vector point to SHOW_CLOCK:

```
MOV   DX,SEG SHOW_CLOCK  ;Put pointer in DS:DX
MOV   DS,DX
LEA   DX,SHOW_CLOCK
MOV   AL,1CH             ;Put interrupt number in AL
MOV   AH,25H             ;Change the vector
INT   21H
```

8. To read the real-time clock's time settings, use the 2 option of the Type 1A (Time of Day) interrupt. That is,

```
MOV   AH,2
INT   1AH
```

9. The alarm pointer is the Type 4A interrupt vector.
10. To turn on the alarm in one hour, set its time for one hour past the current real-time clock values. The instructions are:

```
            MOV   AH,2     ;Read the time
            INT   1AH
            ADD   CH,1     ;Add 1 to the hours count
            DAA            ; and adjust the result for BCD
            CMP   CH,24H   ;Are hours = 24 (BCD)?
            JNE   SET_ALARM
            SUB   CH,CH    ;If so, make hours = 0
SET_ALARM:  MOV   AH,6     ;Set the alarm
            INT   1AH
```

Chapter 7. Video Operations

1. Both adapters start with black and white text mode. The Color/Graphics uses 40×25, while the Monochrome uses 80×25 (its only mode).
2. (a) White on black—07
   (b) White on black, underlined—01
   (c) Black on white, or reverse video—70H
   (d) Red on blue—14H
   (e) Red on blue, blinking—94H
3. (a) This reads the cursor's row and column into DH and DL:

```
MOV   AH,3
INT   10H
```

(b) This returns the number of the active page in BH:

```
MOV   0FH
INT   10H
```

(c) The instructions in(b) return the current mode in AL. The Monochrome Adapter returns AL = 7; any other number (0-6) indicates a Color/Graphics Adapter.

(d) To move the cursor to the bottom line:

```
MOV   DH,24    ;Select row 24
MOV   DL,0     ; and column 0
MOV   AH,2     ;Move the cursor
INT   10H
```

(e) To display M in the top left corner:

```
MOV   DX,0     ;Select (0,0)
MOV   AH,2     ;Move the cursor
INT   10H
MOV   AL,'M'   ;Character is M
MOV   BL,7     ;White on black attribute
MOV   CX,1     ;Display only one character
MOV   AH,9     ;Put it on the screen
INT   10H
```

4. You probably entered the messages with statements such as

```
MSG1  DB   'Sort Program$'
MSG2  DB   'Press any key to begin.$'
```

To put them on separate lines, include Carriage Return and Line Feed characters in the string, as follows:

```
MSG1  DB   'Sort Program',0DH,0AH,'$'
MSG2  DB   'Press any key to begin.',0DH,0AH,'$'
```

5. To display the number in CX, you must convert it to ASCII by adding 30H. The program you want consists of a data segment with the following statements:

```
MSG_START  DB  'Try again.  You have $'
MSG_END    DB  ' starfighters left.',0DH,0AH,'$'
```

and a code segment that includes

```
LEA  DX,MSG_START  ;Display start of message
MOV  AH,9
INT  21H
MOV  DL,CL         ;Convert number to ASCII
ADD  DL,30H
```

```
MOV   AH,6           ; and display it
LEA   DX,MSG_END     ;Display rest of message
MOV   AH,9
INT   21H
```

6. The Answer 7-6 listing shows the procedure that moves a "bird" across the screen, on line 20.

Answer 7-6. Move a "bird" across the screen.

```
      PAGE     ,132
TITLE MOVEBIRD - Move a Bird Across the Screen

;  Moves a "bird" across the screen, on line 20.

;  Assemble with: MASM MOVEBIRD;
;  Link with: LINK MOVEBIRD+DELAY;

STACK SEGMENT PARA STACK 'STACK'
      DB       64 DUP('STACK   ')
STACK ENDS

      EXTRN    DELAY:FAR
CSEG  SEGMENT PARA 'CODE'
      ASSUME   CS:CSEG,SS:STACK
MOVE_BIRD PROC  FAR

;  Set up the stack to contain the proper values so this
;  program can return to DEBUG.

      PUSH     DS             ;Put return seg. addr. on stack
      MOV      DI,0           ;Clear a register
      PUSH     DI             ;Put zero return addr. on stack

;  This is the main procedure.

      MOV      AH,15          ;Set BH to active display page
      INT      10H
      MOV      AH,0           ;Select 80x25, B/W, Alpha
      INT      10H
      MOV      CX,1           ;Character count = 1
      MOV      DH,20          ;Start at row 20,
      MOV      DL,0           ; column 0
DSPLY_V: MOV   BL,'v'         ;Display a "v"
      CALL     NEXT_BIRD
      CMP      DL,80          ;Done?
      JE       BIRD_DONE
      MOV      BL,0C4H        ; No.  Display a "dash"
      CALL     NEXT_BIRD
      CMP      DL,80          ;Done?
      JNE      DSPLY_V        ; If not, begin again
BIRD_DONE: RET                ; Otherwise, exit.
MOVE_BIRD ENDP
```

```
;   This procedure displays the bird for 1/10-sec., then
;   erases it and advances DL to the next column.

NEXT_BIRD PROC
      MOV     AH,2          ;Move cursor to next position
      INT     10H
      MOV     AH,10         ;Write character to the screen
      MOV     AL,BL
      INT     10H
      CALL    DLY_TENTH     ;Wait 1/10-sec.
      SUB     AL,AL         ; then erase the bird
      MOV     AH,10
      INT     10H
      INC     DL            ;Point to next column
      RET                   ; and return to caller
NEXT_BIRD ENDP

;   This procedure generates a 1/10-second delay

DLY_TENTH PROC
      SUB     AL,AL         ;Set minutes to zero
      SUB     BH,BH         ;Set seconds to zero
      MOV     BL,10         ;Set hundredths to 10
      CALL    DELAY
      RET
DLY_TENTH ENDP
CSEG   ENDS
      END     MOVE_BIRD
```

7. The procedure in the Answer 7-7 listing, which moves a smile face randomly, is a combination of Examples 6-2 and 7-4. The face is displayed for a quarter-second between moves.

Answer 7-7. Move a smile face randomly.

```
TITLE RANDFACE - Move a Smile Face Randomly
      PAGE    ,132

;   Moves a smile face randomly across the screen,
;   in quarter-second spurts.

;   Assemble with: MASM RANDFACE;
;   Link with: LINK RANDFACE+DELAY;

STACK SEGMENT PARA STACK 'STACK'
      DB      64 DUP('STACK   ')
STACK ENDS

      EXTRN   DELAY:FAR
CSEG  SEGMENT PARA 'CODE'
RAND_FACE PROC  FAR
      ASSUME  CS:CSEG,SS:STACK

;   Set up the stack to contain the proper values so this
;   program can return to DEBUG.
```

```
        PUSH     DS             ;Put return seg. addr. on stack
        MOV      DI,0           ;Clear a register
        PUSH     DI             ;Put zero return addr. on stack

;  This is the main procedure.

        MOV      AH,15          ;Set BH to active display page
        INT      10H
        MOV      AH,0           ;Select 80x25, B/W, Alpha
        INT      10H
        MOV      CX,1           ;Character count = 1
INIT_LINE: CALL RAND_8          ;Get a random line number
        AND      DL,1FH
        CMP      DL,24          ; between 0 and 24,
        JA       INIT_LINE
        MOV      DH,DL          ; and put it in DH
        MOV      DL,0           ;Start at column 0
NEXT_FACE: MOV  AH,2            ;Move cursor to next position
        INT      10H
        MOV      AL,2           ;Display smile face
        MOV      AH,10
        INT      10H
        CALL     DLY_QRTR       ;Wait a quarter-second
        SUB      AL,AL          ; then erase the face
        MOV      AH,10
        INT      10H
        MOV      AX,DX          ;Save row,column in AX
LINE_IND: CALL  RAND_8          ;Get a number between 0 and 2
        AND      DL,3
        CMP      DL,2
        JNE      CHK_3

        MOV      DX,AX          ;It's a 2.  Do nothing
        JE       INC_COL
CHK_3: JA        LINE_IND
        CMP      DL,1
        JNE      ITS_0
        MOV      DX,AX          ;It's a 1.  Increment row
        INC      DH
        CMP      DH,25          ; and make sure row < 25
        JE       EXIT_FACE
        JNE      INC_COL
ITS_0: MOV       DX,AX          ;It's a 0.  Decrement row
        DEC      DH
        JS       EXIT_FACE      ; and make sure row is positive
INC_COL: INC     DL             ;Point to next column
        CMP      DL,80
        JNE      NEXT_FACE
EXIT_FACE: RET                  ;Exit.
RAND_FACE ENDP
```

```
;  This procedure generates a quarter-second delay.

DLY_QRTR PROC
        SUB     AL,AL           ;Set minutes to zero
        SUB     BH,BH           ;Set seconds to zero
        MOV     BL,25           ;Set hundredths to 25 (1/4 sec.)
        CALL    DELAY
        RET
DLY_QRTR ENDP

;  This procedure returns a 16-bit random number in DX, but
;  the caller, RAND_FACE, only uses the value in DL.

RAND_8          PROC
        PUSH    AX              ;Save AX and CX
        PUSH    CX
        MOV     AH,0            ;Read the timer
        INT     1AH
        POP     CX              ; and exit
        POP     AX
        RET
RAND_8          ENDP
CSEG    ENDS
        END     RAND_FACE
```

Chapter 8. Keyboard Operations

1. IBM calls its set of keyboard codes "Extended ASCII" because the set contains 256 codes, as opposed to the 128 codes in regular ASCII.
2. A character code of zero means that the key generates an extended code. To obtain it, do another read operation.
3. The extended code for F2 is 3CH (see Table 8-4).
4. The AH = 1 option displays the key; the AH = 8 option does not.
5. The procedure shown in the Answer 8-5 listing measures the elapsed time between two key depressions, and returns the hours in CH (the operator took a coffee break between key depressions), the minutes in CL, the seconds in DH, and 1/100 seconds in DL. Other registers are unaffected.

Answer 8-5. Measure time between key depressions.

```
        PAGE    ,132
TITLE TIMEKEYS - Time between keys

CSEG SEGMENT PARA 'CODE'
        PUBLIC  TIME_KEYS
TIME_KEYS PROC FAR
        ASSUME  CS:CSEG
        PUSH    AX              ;Save AX
        MOV     AH,7            ;When the first key is pressed,
        INT     21H
        SUB     CX,CX           ; set time to zero
```

```
        SUB     DX,DX
        MOV     AH,2DH
        INT     21H
        MOV     AH,7            ;When another key is pressed,
        INT     21H
        MOV     AH,2CH          ; read the time count
        INT     21H
        POP     AX
        RET                     ; and exit
TIME_KEYS ENDP
CSEG ENDS
        END
```

6. I got a minimum of DX = 10H, or 0.16 seconds. However, years of wine, women, song, and computer programming have taken their toll; you may do better. At any rate, this test shows how much faster computers are than humans. The processor can execute *thousands* of instructions in the same time it takes you to press a key twice!

Disk User's Guide

The optional disk holds over 40 programs from this book. Those that are callable procedures are supplied as both *source* (ASM) files and *object* (OBJ) files. Having the source allows you to change a program if you want to. Having the object allows you to link and run the programs without assembling them.

For examples that are complete, executable programs, the disk provides *run* (EXE) files as well as the source and object files. Also included are:

1. EX_PROG.ASM, the source file for the example program in Chapter 2.
2. EX_PROGC.ASM, the COM version of the above program.
3. MAINMOD.ASM and SECMOD.ASM, the program models we presented in Chapter 2.
4. MAINMODC.ASM and SECMODC.ASM, the COM versions of the above models.
5. MACRO.LIB, the macro library, which contains over 30 "miniprograms" or *macros.*

Programs You Can Execute Directly

Table 1 lists the programs for which the disk contains a *run file.* With the DOS prompt (A> or C>) on the screen, you can run any of these programs by simply entering its name. For instance, to play "Turkey In the Straw," enter **turkey** (or **b:turkey,** if the data disk is in drive B).

Files You Must Link

The remaining disk files are general-purpose procedures you can use in your programs. In each case, I have defined the procedure as FAR, so your program must include an EXTRN with a FAR type. For example, to call ADD_TO_OL (Example 5-7 in the book), your program would specify

```
EXTRN   ADD_TO_OL:FAR
```

at the beginning and

```
CALL   ADD_TO_OL
```

Table 1. Programs that have run (EXE) files.

Filename	Example in Book*	Description
CLRALARM	—	Clear (reset) the alarm
DIAGLINE	7-2	Display a diagonal line
HEX2DEC	—	Convert a hex number to decimal
KEYMUSIC	9-5	Play music on the keyboard
MARY	9-3	Play "Mary Had a Little Lamb"
MATHCHIP	13-1	Check for an 80287 Math Coprocessor
MOVEBIRD	(7-6)	Move a "bird" across the screen
MOVEFACE	7-3	Move a "smile face" across the screen
NEWDIAG	10-1	Display a diagonal line using macros
RANDFACE	(7-7)	Move a "smile face" across the screen randomly
SETALARM	9-6	Set the alarm
TURKEY	9-4	Play "Turkey in the Straw"

*Numbers in parentheses indicate answers to Study Exercises. For example, (7-6) means answer #6 for Chapter 7.

where you want to use the procedure. That done, assemble your main program (or "calling program"), then link the specified object (OBJ) files to form a run (EXE) file.

Table 2 summarizes the information you need to use the disk files. Note that for procedures that call other procedures, you must link two or three separate object files. For example, if a program named LISTMAKR calls ADD_TO_OL, the proper link command is

```
link listmakr+add_2_ol+b_search;
```

Table 2. Files you must link.

Link With caller+	Call Procedure With This Name	Example in Book*	Description
ADD_2_OL+ B_SEARCH	ADD_TO_OL	5-7	Add element to ordered list
ADD2UL	ADD_TO_UL	(5-1)	Create an unordered list
ADD_2_UL	ADD_TO_UL	5-1	Add element to unordered list
ASC_BIN	ASCII_BIN	8-2	Convert string to binary number
AVERAGE	AVERAGE	4-3	Average unsigned words

Table 2. Files you must link (continued).

Link With caller+	Call Procedure With This Name	Example in Book*	Description
B_SEARCH	B_SEARCH	5-6	Search ordered list
BIN_ASC	BIN_ASCII	8-3	Convert binary number to string
BUBBLE	BUBBLE	5-5	Bubble-sort an unordered list
CLR_S	CLEAR_SCREEN	7-1	Clear the screen
CONV_HEX	CONV_HEX	5-11	Hex to ASCII, BCD, and EBCDIC
COSINE+SINE	FIND_COS	5-10	Calculate cosine of an angle
D_SHAPE	DSPLY_SHAPE	7-4	Construct shape from shape table
DEL_OL+ B_SEARCH	DEL_OL	5-8	Delete element from ordered list
DEL_UL	DEL_UL	5-2	Delete element from unordered list
DELAY	DELAY	6-5	Delay for a specified interval
DIVUO	DIVUO	4-4	Divide, account for overflow
M_SHAPE+DELAY	MOVE_SHAPE	7-5	Move a shape across the screen
MINMAX	MINMAX	5-3	Find min, max in unordered list
MULS32+MULU32	MULS32	4-2	Multiply 32-bit signed numbers
MULU32	MULU32	4-1	Multiply 32-bit unsigned numbers
PHONE_#	PHONE_NOS	5-13	Sort a telephone list
PLAY+SOUND+ DELAY	PLAY	9-2	Play a tune
RAND_51	RAND_51	6-2	Random number between 0 and 51
READKEYS	READ_KEYS	8-1	Read a string from the keyboard
REPLACE	REPLACE	(5-2)	Replace element in ordered list
SHOW_ERR	SHOW_ERR	6-1	Display error messages for DOS function calls

Table 2. Files you must link (continued).

Link With caller+	Call Procedure With This Name	Example in Book*	Description
SINE	FIND_SINE	5-9	Calculate sine of an angle
SOUND+DELAY	SOUND	9-1	Generate a sound
SQRT32	SQRT32	4-5	Compute square root by Newton
SR32	SR32	(4-1)	Compute square root by subtracting
TIMEKEYS	TIME_KEYS	(8-5)	Find time between keystrokes

*Numbers in parentheses indicate answers to Study Exercises. For example, (5-1) indicates answer #1 for Chapter 5.

A

Hexadecimal/Decimal Conversion

HEXADECIMAL COLUMNS											
6		5		4		3		2		1	
HEX	DEC	HEX	DEC	HEX	DEC	HEX	DEC	HEX	DEC	HEX	DEC
0	0	0	0	0	0	0	0	0	0	0	0
1	1,048,576	1	65,536	1	4,096	1	256	1	16	1	1
2	2,097,152	2	131,072	2	8,192	2	512	2	32	2	2
3	3,145,728	3	196,608	3	12,288	3	768	3	48	3	3
4	4,194,304	4	262,144	4	16,384	4	1,024	4	64	4	4
5	5,242,880	5	327,680	5	20,480	5	1,280	5	80	5	5
6	6,291,456	6	393,216	6	24,576	6	1,536	6	96	6	6
7	7,340,032	7	458,752	7	28,672	7	1,792	7	112	7	7
8	8,388,608	8	524,288	8	32,768	8	2,048	8	128	8	8
9	9,437,184	9	589,824	9	36,864	9	2,304	9	144	9	9
A	10,485,760	A	655,360	A	40,960	A	2,560	A	160	A	10
B	11,534,336	B	720,896	B	45,056	B	2,816	B	176	B	11
C	12,582,912	C	786,432	C	49,152	C	3,072	C	192	C	12
D	13,631,488	D	851,968	D	53,248	D	3,328	D	208	D	13
E	14,680,064	E	917,504	E	57,344	E	3,584	E	224	E	14
F	15,728,640	F	983,040	F	61,440	F	3,840	F	240	F	15
7654		3210		7654		3210		7654		3210	
Byte				Byte				Byte			

POWERS OF 2

2^n	n
256	8
512	9
1 024	10
2 048	11
4 096	12
8 192	13
16 384	14
32 768	15
65 536	16
131 072	17
262 144	18
524 288	19
1 048 576	20
2 097 152	21
4 194 304	22
8 388 608	23
16 777 216	24

$2^0 = 16^0$
$2^4 = 16^1$
$2^8 = 16^2$
$2^{12} = 16^3$
$2^{16} = 16^4$
$2^{20} = 16^5$
$2^{24} = 16^6$
$2^{28} = 16^7$
$2^{32} = 16^8$
$2^{36} = 16^9$
$2^{40} = 16^{10}$
$2^{44} = 16^{11}$
$2^{48} = 16^{12}$
$2^{52} = 16^{13}$
$2^{56} = 16^{14}$
$2^{60} = 16^{15}$

POWERS OF 16

16^n	n
1	0
16	1
256	2
4 096	3
65 536	4
1 048 576	5
16 777 216	6
268 435 456	7
4 294 967 296	8
68 719 476 736	9
1 099 511 627 776	10
17 592 186 044 416	11
281 474 976 710 656	12
4 503 599 627 370 496	13
72 057 594 037 927 936	14
1 152 921 504 606 846 976	15

B

IBM PC Display Characters

HIGH PART

LOW PART

DECIMAL VALUE	➡	0	16	32	48	64	80	96	112	128	144	160	176	192	208	224	240
⬇	HEXA DECIMAL VALUE	0	1	2	3	4	5	6	7	8	9	A	B	C	D	E	F
0	0	BLANK (NULL)	►	BLANK (SPACE)	0	@	P	`	p	Ç	É	á	░	└	╨	∝	≡
1	1	☺	◄	!	1	A	Q	a	q	ü	Æ	í	▒	┴	╤	β	±
2	2	☻	↕	"	2	B	R	b	r	é	FE	ó	▓	┬	╥	γ	≥
3	3	♥	‼	#	3	C	S	c	s	â	ô	ú	│	├	╙	π	≤
4	4	♦	¶	$	4	D	T	d	t	ä	ö	ñ	┤	─	╘	Σ	⌠
5	5	♣	§	%	5	E	U	e	u	à	ò	Ñ	╡	┼	╒	σ	⌡
6	6	♠	▬	&	6	F	V	f	v	å	û	ª	╢	╞	╓	μ	÷
7	7	BEEP •	↨	'	7	G	W	g	w	ç	ù	º	╖	╟	╫	τ	≈
8	8	◘	↑	(	8	H	X	h	x	ê	ÿ	¿	╕	╚	╪	Φ	°
9	9	○	↓	)	9	I	Y	i	y	ë	Ö	⌐	╣	╔	┘	⊖	•
10	A	◙	→	*	:	J	Z	j	z	è	Ü	¬	║	╩	┌	Ω	·
11	B	♂	ESC ←	+	;	K	[	k	{	ï	¢	½	╗	╦	█	δ	√
12	C	♀	∟	,	<	L	\	l	¦	î	£	¼	╝	╠	▄	∞	η
13	D	♪	↔	—	=	M	]	m	}	ì	¥	¡	╜	═	▌	∅	²
14	E	♫	▲	.	>	N	^	n	~	Ä	Pts	«	╛	╬	▐	∈	▮
15	F	☼	▼	/	?	O	_	o	△	Å	f	»	┐	╧	▀	∩	BLANK 'FF'

C

80286 Instruction Times

This appendix contains a table that shows how long each instruction takes to execute and the number of bytes it occupies in memory. Execution times are shown in *clock cycles*. To convert them to nanoseconds, multiply by 167.

The execution times are convenient for comparing the efficiency of one instruction (or a certain form of an instruction) against another. This helps you decide which approach is best, in case you have doubts.

Note the following about the table:

1. An asterisk (*) signifies that the instruction takes one additional clock cycle if you are using *base indexed* addressing (e.g., MOV AX,TABLE[BX][SI]).
2. The abbreviation *m* in Jump, Call, and Return instructions means "the number of bytes in the next instruction." The 80286 needs this additional time to empty its pipeline and read the new instruction from memory. For example, if your program includes JMP THERE, and THERE is the label of a PUSH AX, the JMP instruction takes 8 clock cycles—7 cycles for the JMP itself and one more cycle for the one-byte PUSH instruction.
3. The abbreviation *rep* stands for the number of times the instruction is repeated.
4. The execution time of conditional jump instructions and loop instructions depends on whether the transfer is made. If the transfer *is* made, use the larger number in the Clocks column. Otherwise, if execution "drops through" to the next instruction, use the smaller number. (A similar rule applies to the INTO instruction; use the smaller value if the interrupt does not occur.)

Table C-1. 80286 instruction times.

Instruction	Clocks	Bytes
AAA	3	1
AAD	14	2
AAM	16	1
AAS	3	1
ADC register,register	2	2
ADC register,memory	7*	2-4
ADC memory,register	7*	2-4
ADC register,immediate	3	3-4
ADC memory,immediate	7*	3-6
ADC accumulator,immediate	3	2-3
ADD register,register	2	2
ADD register,memory	7*	2-4
ADD memory,register	7*	2-4
ADD register,immediate	3	3-4
ADD memory,immediate	7*	3-6
ADD accumulator,immediate	3	2-3
AND register,register	2	2
AND register,memory	7*	2-4
AND memory,register	7*	2-4
AND register,immediate	3	3-4
AND memory,immediate	7*	3-6
AND accumulator,immediate	3	2-3
BOUND reg16,source	13*	2
CALL near-proc	7+m	3
CALL far-proc	13+m	5
CALL memptr16	11+m*	2-4
CALL regptr16	7+m	2
CALL memptr32	16+m	2-4
CBW	2	1
CLC	2	1
CLD	2	1
CLI	3	1
CMC	2	1
CMP register,register	2	2
CMP register,memory	6*	2-4
CMP memory,register	7*	2-4
CMP register,immediate	3	3-4
CMP memory,immediate	6*	3-6
CMP accumulator,immediate	3	2-3

Table C-1. 80286 instruction times (continued).

Instruction	Clocks	Bytes
CMPS dest-string, source-string	8	1
CMPS (repeat) dest-string, source-string	5+9(rep)	1
CWD	2	1
DAA/DAS	3	1
DEC register	2	1-2
DEC memory	7*	2-4
DIV reg8	14	2
DIV reg16	22	2
DIV mem8	17*	2-4
DIV mem16	25*	2-4
ENTER immed16,0	11	4
ENTER immed16,1	15	4
ENTER immed16,level	12+4(L)	4
ESC immediate,memory	9-20*	2-4
ESC immediate,register	2	2
HLT	2	1
IDIV reg8	17	2
IDIV reg16	25	2
IDIV mem8	20*	2-4
IDIV mem16	28*	2-4
IMUL reg8	13	2
IMUL reg16	21	2
IMUL mem8	16*	2-4
IMUL mem16	24*	2-4
IMUL dest-reg,reg16,immediate	21	3-4
IMUL dest-reg,memory,immediate	24*	3-4
IN accumulator,immed8	5	2
IN accumulator,DX	5	1
INC register	2	1-2
INC memory	7*	2-4
INS dest-string,DX	5	1
INS (rep) dest-string,DX	5+4(rep)	1
INT immed8	23+m	1-2
INTO	24+m or 3	1
IRET	17+m	1
All conditional jump instructions except JCXZ:		
Jccc short-label	7+m or 3	2
JCXZ short-label	8+m or 4	2

Table C-1. 80286 instruction times (continued).

Instruction	Clocks	Bytes
JMP short-label	7+m	2
JMP near-label	7+m	3
JMP far-label	11+m	5
JMP memptr16	11+m*	2-4
JMP regptr16	7+m	2
JMP memptr32	15+m*	2-4
LAHF	2	1
LDS reg16,mem32	7*	2-4
LEA reg16,mem16	3*	2-4
LEAVE	5	1
LES reg16,mem32	7*	2-4
LOCK	0	1
LODS source-string	5	1
LODS (repeat) source-string	5+4(rep)	1
LOOP short-label	8+m or 4	2
LOOPE/LOOPZ short-label	8+m or 4	2
LOOPNE/LOOPNZ short-label	8+m or 4	2
MOV memory,accumulator	3	3
MOV accumulator,memory	5	3
MOV register,register	2	2
MOV register,memory	5*	2-4
MOV memory,register	3*	2-4
MOV register,immediate	2	2-3
MOV memory,immediate	3*	3-6
MOV seg-reg,reg16	2	2
MOV seg-reg,mem16	5*	2-4
MOV reg16,seg-reg	2	2
MOV memory,seg-reg	3*	2-4
MOVS dest-string, source-string	5	1
MOVS (repeat) dest-string, source-string	5+4(rep)	1
MUL reg8	13	2
MUL reg16	21	2
MUL mem8	16*	2-4
MUL mem16	24*	2-4
NEG register	2	2
NEG memory	7*	2-4
NOP	2	1
NOT register	2	2
NOT memory	7*	2-4

Table C-1. 80286 instruction times (continued).

Instruction	Clocks	Bytes
OR register,register	2	2
OR register,memory	7*	2-4
OR memory,register	7*	2-4
OR register,immediate	3	3-6
OR memory,immediate	7*	3-6
OR accumulator,immediate	3	2-3
OUT immed8,accumulator	3	2
OUT DX,accumulator	3	1
OUTS DX,source-string	5	1
OUTS (rep) DX,source-string	5+4(rep)	1
POP register	5	1
POP memory	5*	2-4
POPA	19	1
POPF	5	1
PUSH register	3	1
PUSH memory	5*	2-4
PUSH immediate	3	2-3
PUSHA	17	1
PUSHF	3	1
RCL/RCR/ROL/ROR register,1	2	2
RCL/RCR/ROL/ROR register,CL	5+1/bit	2
RCL/RCR/ROL/ROR memory,1	7*	2-4
RCL/RCR/ROL/ROR memory,CL	8*+1/bit	2-4
RCL/RCR/ROL/ROR reg,count	5+1/bit	3
RCL/RCR/ROL/ROR memory,count	8*+1/bit	3-5
REP	0	1
REPE/REPZ	0	1
REPNE/REPNZ	0	1
RET (near, no pop)	11+m	1
RET (near, pop)	11+m	3
RET (far, no pop)	15+m	1
RET (far, pop)	15+m	3
SAHF	2	1
SAL/SHL/SAR/SHR register,1	2	2
SAL/SHL/SAR/SHR register,CL	5+1/bit	2
SAL/SHL/SAR/SHR memory,1	7*	2-4
SAL/SHL/SAR/SHR memory,CL	8*+1/bit	2-4
SAL/SHL/SAR/SHR reg,count	5+1/bit	3
SAL/SHL/SAR/SHR memory,count	8*+1/bit	3-5

Table C-1. 80286 instruction times (continued).

Instruction	Clocks	Bytes
SBB register,register	2	2
SBB register,memory	7*	2-4
SBB memory,register	7*	2-4
SBB register,immediate	3	3-4
SBB memory,immediate	7*	3-6
SBB accumulator,immediate	3	2-3
SCAS dest-string	7	1
SCAS (repeat) dest-string	5+8(rep)	1
STC/STD/STI	2	1
STOS dest-string	3	1
STOS (repeat) dest-string	4+3(rep)	1
SUB register,register	2	2
SUB register,memory	7*	2-4
SUB memory,register	7*	2-4
SUB register,immediate	3	3-4
SUB memory,immediate	7*	3-6
SUB accumulator,immediate	3	2-3
TEST register,register	2	2
TEST register,memory	6*	2-4
TEST register,immediate	3	3-4
TEST memory,immediate	6*	3-6
TEST accumulator,immediate	3	2-3
WAIT	3	1
XCHG accumulator,reg16	3	1
XCHG memory,register	5*	2-4
XCHG register,register	3	2
XLAT source-table	5	1
XOR register,register	2	2
XOR register,memory	7*	2-4
XOR memory,register	7*	2-4
XOR register,immediate	3	3-4
XOR memory,immediate	7*	3-6
XOR accumulator,immediate	3	2-3

Note: Shaded instructions are new with the 80286; they are not available on the 8086 or 8088.

D

80286 Instruction Set Summary

Table D-1 summarizes the 80286 instruction set in alphabetical order. For each instruction, it shows the general assembler format and which flags are affected. In the *Flags* column, - means unchanged, * means may have changed, and ? means undefined.

Table D-1. 80286 instruction set.

			Flags								
Mnemonic	**Assembler Format**		**OF**	**DF**	**IF**	**TF**	**SF**	**ZF**	**AF**	**PF**	**CF**
AAA	AAA		?	-	-	-	?	?	*	?	*
AAD	AAD		?	-	-	-	*	*	?	*	?
AAM	AAM		?	-	-	-	*	*	?	*	?
AAS	AAS		?	-	-	-	?	?	*	?	*
ADC	ADC	destination,source	*	-	-	-	*	*	*	*	*
ADD	ADD	destination,source	*	-	-	-	*	*	*	*	*
AND	AND	destination,source	0	-	-	-	*	*	?	*	0
BOUND	BOUND	reg16,source	-	-	-	-	-	-	-	-	-
CALL	CALL	target	-	-	-	-	-	-	-	-	-
CBW	CBW		-	-	-	-	-	-	-	-	-
CLC	CLC		-	-	-	-	-	-	-	-	0
CLD	CLD		-	0	-	-	-	-	-	-	-
CLI	CLI		-	-	0	-	-	-	-	-	-
CMC	CMC		-	-	-	-	-	-	-	-	*
CMP	CMP	destination,source	*	-	-	-	*	*	*	*	*
CMPS	CMPS	dest-string,source-string	*	-	-	-	*	*	*	*	*
CMPSB	CMPSB		*	-	-	-	*	*	*	*	*
CMPSW	CMPSW		*	-	-	-	*	*	*	*	*
CWD	CWD		-	-	-	-	-	-	-	-	-

Table D-1. 80286 instruction set (continued).

Mnemonic	Assembler Format		OF	DF	IF	TF	SF	ZF	AF	PF	CF
			Flags								
DAA	DAA		?	-	-	-	*	*	*	*	*
DAS	DAS		?	-	-	-	*	*	*	*	*
DEC	DEC	destination	*	-	-	-	*	*	*	*	-
DIV	DIV	source	?	-	-	-	?	?	?	?	?
ENTER	ENTER	immed16,level	-	-	-	-	-	-	-	-	-
ESC	ESC	ext-opcode,source	-	-	-	-	-	-	-	-	-
HLT	HLT		-	-	-	-	-	-	-	-	-
IDIV	IDIV	source	?	-	-	-	?	?	?	?	?
IMUL	IMUL	source	*	-	-	-	?	?	?	?	*
IMUL	IMUL	dest[,source],immed	*	-	-	-	?	?	?	?	*
IN	IN	accumulator,port	-	-	-	-	-	-	-	-	-
INC	INC	destination	*	-	-	-	*	*	*	*	-
INS	INS	dest-string,DX	-	-	-	-	-	-	-	-	-
INT	INT	interrupt-type	-	-	0	0	-	-	-	-	-
INTO	INTO		-	-	0	0	-	-	-	-	-
IRET	IRET		*	*	*	*	*	*	*	*	*
JA/JNBE	JA	short-label	-	-	-	-	-	-	-	-	-
JAE/JNB	JAE	short-label	-	-	-	-	-	-	-	-	-
JB/JNAE/JC	JB	short-label	-	-	-	-	-	-	-	-	-
JBE/JNA	JBE	short-label	-	-	-	-	-	-	-	-	-
JCXZ	JCXZ	short-label	-	-	-	-	-	-	-	-	-
JE/JZ	JE	short-label	-	-	-	-	-	-	-	-	-
JG/JNLE	JG	short-label	-	-	-	-	-	-	-	-	-
JGE/JNL	JGE	short-label	-	-	-	-	-	-	-	-	-
JL/JNGE	JL	short-label	-	-	-	-	-	-	-	-	-
JLE/JNG	JLE	short-label	-	-	-	-	-	-	-	-	-
JMP	JMP	target	-	-	-	-	-	-	-	-	-
JNC	JNC	short-label	-	-	-	-	-	-	-	-	-
JNE/JNZ	JNE	short-label	-	-	-	-	-	-	-	-	-
JNO	JNO	short-label	-	-	-	-	-	-	-	-	-
JNP/JPO	JNP	short-label	-	-	-	-	-	-	-	-	-
JNS	JNS	short-label	-	-	-	-	-	-	-	-	-
JO	JO	short-label	-	-	-	-	-	-	-	-	-
JP/JPE	JP	short-label	-	-	-	-	-	-	-	-	-
JS	JS	short-label	-	-	-	-	-	-	-	-	-
LAHF	LAHF		-	-	-	-	-	-	-	-	-
LDS	LDS	reg16,mem32	-	-	-	-	-	-	-	-	-
LEA	LEA	reg16,mem16	-	-	-	-	-	-	-	-	-
LEAVE	LEAVE		-	-	-	-	-	-	-	-	-
LES	LES	reg16,mem32	-	-	-	-	-	-	-	-	-
LOCK	LOCK		-	-	-	-	-	-	-	-	-

Table D-1. 80286 instruction set (continued).

Mnemonic	Assembler Format		OF	DF	IF	TF	SF	ZF	AF	PF	CF
			Flags								
LODS	LODS	source-string	-	-	-	-	-	-	-	-	-
LODSB	LODSB		-	-	-	-	-	-	-	-	-
LODSW	LODSW		-	-	-	-	-	-	-	-	-
LOOP	LOOP	short-label	-	-	-	-	-	-	-	-	-
LOOPE/ LOOPZ	LOOPE	short-label	-	-	-	-	-	-	-	-	-
LOOPNE/ LOOPNZ	LOOPNE	short-label	-	-	-	-	-	-	-	-	-
MOV	MOV	destination,source	-	-	-	-	-	-	-	-	-
MOVS	MOVS	dest-string,source-string	-	-	-	-	-	-	-	-	-
MOVSB	MOVSB		-	-	-	-	-	-	-	-	-
MOVSW	MOVSW		-	-	-	-	-	-	-	-	-
MUL	MUL	source	*	-	-	-	?	?	?	?	*
NEG	NEG	destination	*	-	-	-	*	*	*	*	*
NOP	NOP		-	-	-	-	-	-	-	-	-
NOT	NOT	destination	-	-	-	-	-	-	-	-	-
OR	OR	destination,source	0	-	-	-	*	*	?	*	0
OUT	OUT	port,accumulator	-	-	-	-	-	-	-	-	-
OUTS	OUTS	DX,source-string	-	-	-	-	-	-	-	-	-
POP	POP	destination	-	-	-	-	-	-	-	-	-
POPA	POPA		-	-	-	-	-	-	-	-	-
POPF	POPF		*	*	*	*	*	*	*	*	*
PUSH	PUSH	source	-	-	-	-	-	-	-	-	-
PUSH	PUSH	immediate	-	-	-	-	-	-	-	-	-
PUSHA	PUSHA		-	-	-	-	-	-	-	-	-
PUSHF	PUSHF		-	-	-	-	-	-	-	-	-
RCL/RCR	RCL	destination,1	*	-	-	-	-	-	-	-	*
RCL/RCR	RCL	destination,CL	?	-	-	-	-	-	-	-	*
RCL/RCR	RCL	destination,count	?	-	-	-	-	-	-	-	*
REP	REP		-	-	-	-	-	-	-	-	-
REPE/REPZ	REPE		-	-	-	-	-	-	-	-	-
REPNE/ REPNZ	REPNE		-	-	-	-	-	-	-	-	-
RET	[pop-value]		-	-	-	-	-	-	-	-	-
ROL/ROR	ROL	destination,1	*	-	-	-	-	-	-	-	*
ROL/ROR	ROL	destination,CL	?	-	-	-	-	-	-	-	*
ROL/ROR	ROL	destination,count	?	-	-	-	-	-	-	-	*
SAHF	SAHF		-	-	-	-	*	*	*	*	*
SAL/SHL	SAL	destination,1	*	-	-	-	*	*	?	*	*
SAL/SHL	SAL	destination,CL	?	-	-	-	*	*	?	*	*
SAL/SHL	SAL	destination,count	?	-	-	-	*	*	?	*	*

Table D-1. 80286 instruction set (continued).

Mnemonic	Assembler Format		Flags								
			OF	DF	IF	TF	SF	ZF	AF	PF	CF
SAR	SAR	destination,1	0	-	-	-	*	*	?	*	*
SAR	SAR	destination,CL	?	-	-	-	*	*	?	*	*
SAR	SAR	destination,count	?	-	-	-	*	*	?	*	*
SBB	SBB	destination,source	*	-	-	-	*	*	*	*	*
SCAS	SCAS	dest-string	*	-	-	-	*	*	*	*	*
SCASB	SCASB		*	-	-	-	*	*	*	*	*
SCASW	SCASW		*	-	-	-	*	*	*	*	*
SHR	SHR	destination,1	*	-	-	-	0	*	?	*	*
SHR	SHR	destination,CL	?	-	-	-	0	*	?	*	*
SHR	SHR	destination,count	?	-	-	-	0	*	?	*	*
STC	STC		-	-	-	-	-	-	-	-	1
STD	STD		-	1	-	-	-	-	-	-	-
STI	STI		-	-	1	-	-	-	-	-	-
STOS	STOS	dest-string	-	-	-	-	-	-	-	-	-
STOSB	STOSB		-	-	-	-	-	-	-	-	-
STOSW	STOSW		-	-	-	-	-	-	-	-	-
SUB	SUB	destination,source	*	-	-	-	*	*	*	*	*
TEST	TEST	destination,source	0	-	-	-	*	*	?	*	0
WAIT	WAIT		-	-	-	-	-	-	-	-	-
XCHG	XCHG	destination,source	-	-	-	-	-	-	-	-	-
XLAT	XLAT	source-table	-	-	-	-	-	-	-	-	-
XOR	XOR	destination,source	0	-	-	-	*	*	?	*	0

Note: Shaded instructions are new with the 80286, they are not available with the 8086 or 8088.

E

Some Useful Interrupts

Notes:
1. All numbers are hexadecimal.
2. For results, assume the contents AX have been changed; unless specified, all other registers are unaffected.

Table E-1. Some useful interrupts.

INT	Operation	Input Values	Results*
Keyboard			
21	Wait for keyboard character, then display it (with Ctrl-Break check)*	AH = 1	AL = Character
21	Read keyboard character (no Ctrl-Break check)*	AH = 6 DL = FF	AL = Character, if available = 0 if no character is available
21	Wait for keyboard character, but do not display it (no Ctrl-Break check)*	AH = 7	AL = Character
21	Wait for keyboard character, but do not display it (no Ctrl-Break check)*	AH = 8	AL = Character
21	Read keyboard string into buffer	AH = A DS:DX = Buffer address First buffer byte = Buffer size	Second buffer byte = Number of characters read
21	Read keyboard status	AH = B	AL = FF if no character is available = 0 if character is available
21	Clear keyboard buffer and call a keyboard function	AH = C AL = Keyboard function number (1, 6, 7, 8, or A)	Per keyboard function

Table E-1. Some useful interrupts (continued).

INT	Operation	Input Values	Results*
Video			
10	Set video mode (Color/Graphics)	AH = 0 *Text modes* AL = 0 40×25 B/W (default) = 1 40×25 Color = 2 80×25 B/W = 3 80×25 Color *Graphics modes* AL = 4 320x200 Color = 5 320×200 B/W = 6 640×200 B/W	Screen is blank
10	Move cursor	AH = 2 DH,DL = Row,column BH = Page number (0 for graphics)	None
10	Read cursor position	AH = 3 BH = Page number (0 for graphics)	DH,DL = Row,column of cursor CH,CL = Cursor mode
10	Select active display page (text modes)	AH = 5 AL = New page value (0-7 for modes 0 and 1; 0-3 for modes 2 and 3)	None
10	Read character and attribute at cursor position	AH = 8 BH = Display page (Text modes)	AL = Character AH = Attribute (Text modes) Cursor is at original position.
10	Display character and attribute at cursor position	AH = 9 BH = Display page (Text modes) BL = Attribute (Text) = Color (Graphics) CX = Number of times to repeat character AL = Character	Cursor is at original position
10	Display character (only) at cursor position	AH = A BH = Display page (Text modes) CX = Number of times to repeat character AL = Character	Cursor is at original position
10	Display character, then advance cursor	AH = E AL = Character BL = Foreground color (Graphics)	Cursor follows character
21	Display character (with Ctrl-Break check)	AH = 2 DL = Character	Cursor follows character
21	Display character (no Ctrl-Break check)	AH = 6 DL = Character	Cursor follows character

Table E-1. Some useful interrupts (continued).

INT	Operation	Input Values	Results*
Video (continued)			
10	Display string	AH = 13 ES:BP = String address CX = String length DH,DL = Starting row, column BH = Page number AL = 0 BL = Attribute String is *char,char,...char* AL = 1 BL = Attribute String is *char,char,...char* AL = 2 String is *char,attr,char,attr...* AL = 3 String is *char,attr,char,attr...*	 Cursor returns to original position Cursor follows string Cursor returns to original position Cursor follows string
21	Display string	AH = 9 DS:DX = String address String must end with $.	Cursor follows string
10	Read video state	AH = F	AL = Current mode AH = Number of character columns on screen BH = Active display page
Time			
1A	Read the real-time clock	AH = 2	CH = Hours in BCD CL = Minutes in BCD DH = Seconds in BCD
21	Read the time	AH = 2C	CH = Hours in binary CL = Minutes in binary DH = Seconds in binary DL = 1/100 seconds in binary
21	Set the time	AH = 2D CH = Hours in binary CL = Minutes in binary DH = Seconds in binary DL = 1/100 seconds in binary	AL = 0 if time is valid = FF if time is invalid
Interrupt vector			
21	Set interrupt vector	AH = 25 DS:DX = Vector address AL = Interrupt number	None
21	Read interrupt vector address	AH = 35 AL = Interrupt number	ES:BX = Vector address

Table E-1. Some useful interrupts (continued).

INT	Operation	Input Values	Results*
Miscellaneous			
15	Delay	AH = 86 CX:DX = Delay interval (microseconds)	None
17	Print a character	AH = 0 AL = Character DX = Printer (0-2)	AH = Result status (See Figure 6-4)

*Some key combinations generate extended codes, and may require two function calls.

Index